TEA IN JAPAN

TEA IN JAPAN

ESSAYS
ON THE HISTORY OF
CHANOYU

EDITED BY

PAUL VARLEY

AND

KUMAKURA ISAO

UNIVERSITY OF HAWAII PRESS

HONOLULU

94 93 92 91 90 89 5 4 3 2 1

PUBLISHED WITH THE SUPPORT OF
THE KAMIGATA BUNKA KENKYŪKAI
AT THE UNIVERSITY OF HAWAII
AND BY GRANTS FROM SUMITOMO
METAL INDUSTRIES, LTD.,
SUNTORY LIMITED, MATSUSHITA
ELECTRIC INDUSTRIAL CO., LTD.,
SUMITOMO BANK, LTD., AND
KANSAI ELECTRIC POWER CO., INC.

Library of Congress Cataloging-in-Publication Data

Tea in Japan : essays on the history of chanoyu / edited by Paul
  Varley and Kumakura Isao.
     p.   cm.
  Includes index.
  ISBN 0-8248-1218-2
  1. Japanese tea ceremony—History.   I. Varley, Paul, 1931–
II. Kumakura, Isao.
GT2905.T43   1989
394.1'5—dc19   89–4659
                                                                    CIP

The paper used in this publication meets the minimum require-
ments of American National Standard for Information Sciences—Per-
manence of Paper for Printed Library Materials
                                                    ANSI Z39.48-1984

TO DR. FUJIO MATSUDA

CONTENTS

Plates follow pages 50, 114, and 178

PREFACE

This collection of essays emerged from a conference on the History of *Chanoyu* held in Honolulu in August 1982. The conference was sponsored by the Department of History of the University of Hawaii and was attended by scholars from Japan, the United States, and England: Michael Cooper, Haga Kōshirō, John Whitney Hall, Harada Tomohiko, Kumakura Isao, William R. LaFleur, Theodore M. Ludwig, William H. McNeill, Murai Yasuhiko, Sen Sōshitsu XV, Tanaka Hiromi, Paul Varley, and Glenn T. Webb.

The conference was funded by the Urasenke Foundation, Matsushita Electric, Suntory Limited, the Japan-United States Friendship Commission, and the Japan Studies Endowment Committee and the Kamigata Bunka Kenkyūkai of the University of Hawaii. Special thanks are due to Professor George Akita of the University of Hawaii for initially proposing the conference and for playing the chief role in organizing it, and to Dr. Sen Sōshitsu XV, the Grand Tea Master of Urasenke, who provided so much material and moral support to the conference and to the editors in their task of preparing this collection of essays for publication in English. The editors also wish to thank Martin Collcutt for his skillful translation and adaptation of Professor Haga's essay. This book is dedicated to Dr. Fujio Matsuda, former president of the University of Hawaii, for his unstinting support of the 1982 conference.

As John Whitney Hall discusses in his essay, very little was written in English about *chanoyu* before World War II. In the decades since the war, additional writings on the subject have appeared, most notably in the pages of *Chanoyu Quarterly*, published by the Urasenke Foundation. But the total corpus of English-language material on *cha-*

noyu remains slight, especially in view of the subject's great importance in Japanese cultural history. It was the aim of the conference to provide, through the expertise of scholars from Japan and elsewhere, a comprehensive history of *chanoyu* that would be of interest to all students of Japan.

The collection is divided into two parts. Part One comprises essays that cover the history of *chanoyu* from its origins, beginning with the first records of tea drinking in Japan in the early Heian period, until the commencement of the modern age in the late nineteenth century. Part Two contains commentaries on *chanoyu* and its history by Dr. Sen, John Whitney Hall, and William H. McNeill.

A problem that presented itself to the editors was duplication: the treating of the same topic by different authors. Several authors discussed the historical development of the *wabi* aesthetic, for example, and Haga Kōshirō's essay is devoted entirely to this topic. When the question was one of mere repetition, additional versions after the first were deleted; but when authors had different points to discuss about the same topics, their discussions were left intact.

We decided to use Japanese terminology rather freely in the essays with the hope that it would be helpful in familiarizing readers with the vocabulary they are likely to encounter in other writings on *chanoyu* and its history. An extensive glossary is provided. The known birth and death dates of people mentioned in the essays can be found in the index. In romanizing Japanese names and words, the macrons have been omitted—in accordance with general custom—from such familiar place-names as Kyoto, Tokyo, and Kyushu and from words like Shinto, shogun, and daimyo (which are treated without italicization as part of the vocabulary of English).

Paul Varley

DIVISIONS OF JAPANESE HISTORY

Nara period   (710–784)

Heian period   (794–1185)

Kamakura period   (1185–1333)

Kemmu Restoration   (1333–1336)

Muromachi (Ashikaga) period   (1336–1573)
    Northern and Southern Courts (Nambokuchō) period   (1336–1392)
    Kitayama epoch   (late fourteenth and early fifteenth centuries)
    Higashiyama epoch   (second half of fifteenth century)
    Provincial Wars *(sengoku)* period   (1478–1568)

Age of Unification   (1568–1590)
    Azuchi-Momoyama epoch   (1568–1600 or 1615)

Tokugawa (Edo) period   (1600–1867)
    Kan'ei epoch   (ca. 1600–1670)
    Genroku epoch   (ca. 1675–1725)

Meiji period   (1868–1911)

TEA IN JAPAN

PART ONE

HISTORY OF *CHANOYU*

ONE

THE DEVELOPMENT OF *CHANOYU*:
BEFORE RIKYŪ

Murai Yasuhiko
Translated by Paul Varley

IN the beginning of *The Book of Tea*, Okakura Tenshin states: "Tea-ism is a cult founded on the adoration of the beautiful among the sordid facts of everyday existence."[1] Defining *chanoyu* or the way of tea (*chadō*) is difficult, but I believe Tenshin has succinctly captured its meaning. In a word, *chanoyu* is an art of everyday life.

Yet *chanoyu* is not the same thing as merely drinking tea. Tea drinking is an extremely commonplace act. If one were simply concerned with drinking, one could easily get by with just the minimum number of materials and utensils, such as tea, hot water, and bowls. When we seek to satisfy our thirst by having tea during meals or at work or play, our way of drinking is not likely to be criticized so long as we do not offend others.

In *chanoyu*, on the other hand, there are certain rules or forms of etiquette. These rules (*sarei*) are rationally structured; yet they are also made by people and often differ according to the school of tea. Thus when the practice of *chanoyu* became widespread among the samurai and merchants during the Genroku epoch of the Tokugawa period, a number of guidebooks were published to teach beginners the basic information they would need to attend tea gatherings. A typical example of this kind of book was *Chadō Hayagaten* (A Shortcut to the Way of Tea), published in 1771 and prepared "not for the tea man, but for those unfamiliar with *chanoyu*."[2] Even today, people who do not participate in *chanoyu* wonder why they should purposely suffer in order to drink tea and why it should matter how a person drinks. This, of course, is one theme of criticism of *chanoyu*, and it must be noted. But I believe it is precisely here that the true essence of *chanoyu* as an art of everyday life lies.

What is the difference between plain tea drinking and *chanoyu?* Stated simply, the difference is in the "artificiality" of *chanoyu,* an artificiality it shares with the other arts. It is essential to the arts that they partake of the extraordinary—of artificiality, abstractness, symbolism, and formalism. *Chanoyu* is no exception.

Nevertheless, *chanoyu* seems to be hounded, as just suggested, by doubts and criticisms—even, at times, by cynical charges—that are not directed toward the other arts and apparently will not cease as long as *chanoyu* exists. Why should this be so? Because *chanoyu* has its basis in the everyday act of drinking tea. If the rules of tea drinking are ignored, *chanoyu* is soon reduced to something mundane—and this can happen very easily.

The qualities of the everyday and the artistic stand in a contrasting relationship in *chanoyu,* and the dividing line between the two is extremely obscure. For this very reason, it has always been necessary to distinguish clearly between the everyday and the artistic and to show how they mutually oppose one another. It is also because of such opposition that *chanoyu* has survived.

One is reminded of the following poem by Sen no Rikyū:

> *Chanoyu* is nothing but this:
> Boil water, infuse tea, and drink.
> That is all you need to know.[3]

This assertion of the everyday character of *chanoyu* no doubt contains an admonition against the extravagance that prevailed in tea during Rikyū's time. But for Rikyū there was surely a more fundamental meaning behind the poem. I say this because no one went so far as he, with his liking for black *raku* tea bowls and his creation of a minuscule tea room, in pushing the extraordinary (non-everyday) aspects of *chanoyu* to their polar extremes. It was because Rikyū so well understood the dual character of the everyday and the artistic in *chanoyu* that he felt obliged to explain how "ordinariness" could exist within "artistic artificiality." And the reason why Rikyū is regarded as the perfecter of *chanoyu* is that, from the very beginning and with great vigor, he strove to develop his understanding of tea's duality.

Chanoyu is thus an art form that lies between the everyday and the artistically artificial, and therein is to be found its special nature as an art of life. Yet it is also important, although perhaps obvious, to recognize the historical fact that neither in form nor in content did *chanoyu* simply "exist" or "come into being." Rather, it evolved during the long history of tea drinking and was constantly modified. When Eisai (or Yōsai), for example, introduced the use of *matcha* (powdered tea) to Japan in the early Kamakura period, the concept of *chazen ichimi* ("tea and Zen have the same flavor") was not known, nor was there an aesthetic of *wabi*. The rules of tea that emerged thereafter changed with the times, and it would be wrong to think of them as static.

The use of *matcha* was transmitted from China and developed independently as *chanoyu* in Japan. During this development, what was at first a pursuit of men spread also among women, and today women are in fact predominant in *chanoyu*. As part of the present trend toward internationalization, Europeans and Americans have also become interested in tea. *Chanoyu* is now far more widespread than during the period of its flourishing in medieval times or in the day of Tenshin's *The Book of Tea*. In this sense, then, never before has it been so important to investigate the place of *chanoyu* in Japanese culture. In this essay I shall trace the development of *chanoyu*, in both form and content, during the age before the rise of Sen no Rikyū in the late sixteenth century.

TEA DRINKING IN CHINESE CULTURE

So far as we can judge from the reliable primary sources, the history of tea drinking in Japan began in the early Heian period (that is, at the start of the ninth century). Later accounts, however, state that tea was drunk at court functions during the Nara period. Although we should be careful about hastily accepting such accounts, the cultural theory of the broadleaf evergreen zone that has recently attracted attention suggests there is good reason to think that tea, a plant of this type, grew naturally in the Japanese islands, which are situated at the eastern edge of the zone.[4] In the sixth month of 815, for example, Emperor Saga ordered various provinces, including those of the Kinai and Ōmi and Harima, to grow tea and present it annually as tribute to the court.[5] Since it is hard to believe that the court at this time distributed either tea seeds or seedlings, we may suppose that Saga observed tea growing naturally in the provinces and sought to encourage its use. Yet it does not appear that Saga's order was fully implemented, and in the end the rendering of tea tribute was not established on a permanent basis. Even though tea may for a while have grown naturally in Japan, it is doubtful that the custom of tea drinking became popular among the people in early times.

I believe tea drinking was an aspect of T'ang culture introduced in the early Heian period by Japanese priests who studied in China. The sudden appearance during the Kōnin era (810–823) of a number of records on tea drinking among the courtiers and priests at Emperor Saga's court was largely the work, I believe, of such people as Saichō and Kūkai, who went to China together in 804 and returned respectively in 805 and 806, and in particular Eichū, who made the trip during the Nara period, spent nearly thirty years in the Chinese capital of Ch'ang-an, and returned to Japan about this time. Since we know, even without referring to Lu Yü's *Ch'a Ching*,[6] that the custom of drinking tea was widespread in China during the same age, it is hard to imagine that Eichū did not enjoy the beverage while he was there. In any case, on the occasion in the fourth month of 815 when Eichū received Saga at Sūfukuji and Bonkakuji, the temples of Ōmi that he supervised after his return from China, he personally prepared tea and served it to the emperor.[7] The record of this reception is the earliest account we have of tea drinking in Japan.

About the time he served tea to Saga, Eichū also pointed out the poor quality of the food served during mass at Buddhist temples and recommended to the court that it be improved. No doubt Eichū, who had lived so long in China, made this recommendation because of his enthusiasm for the food in Chinese temples; and we can imagine that he also regarded tea drinking as an exciting new Chinese custom.

Saga himself was a great admirer of the culture of China, as we can observe, for example, from the fact that he commissioned the compilation of anthologies of Chinese poetry and had Chinese-style names inscribed on the tablets of buildings and gates at the palace. It was because of Saga's taste for things Chinese that tea drinking quickly became fashionable at his court and indispensable at poetry sessions and banquets.

In the Chinese poetry written at Saga's court there are references to tea drinking in the early Heian period in terms of Taoist thought and aesthetics. Such Taoist elements in tea later became quite rare, however.

Upon the death of Emperor Saga, the tea drinking that had flourished at the beginning of the ninth century declined in popularity and was kept alive mainly in temples and shrines. We cannot suppose that there was no tea drinking at all among the courtiers, inasmuch as we have, for example, the poems of Sugawara no Michizane on tea that he wrote while on duty in the provinces and at his place of exile after he was banished to Dazaifu. But, judging from the fact that there are virtually no references to it in classical literature, tea seems to have been neglected by the courtiers. One thing is certain: Unlike flower arranging and incense, tea did not evolve at this time into an object of aesthetic taste.

On the other hand, tea continued to be drunk for its medicinal value at temples by members of the Buddhist priesthood. The times of greatest consumption were during the religious ceremonies held at court (at the Shishinden and Gozaisho) during the seasonal readings of the sutras in spring and autumn.[8] Although these ceremonies were not scheduled for fixed times but were held on different dates every year, tea was always served to the priests in attendance on one day during each ceremony. In contrast to the sumptuous meals given to the nobles in attendance, the priests thus received tea, apparently to relieve them of fatigue. Along with tea, the priests got salt, raw ginger, sweet arrowroot, and the like, which were evidently used as flavorings in the preparation of *dancha* (brick tea). From what we can judge, the serving of tea during the seasonal readings of the sutras was part of the *naorai*, a banquet held at the conclusion of a ceremony.

The twenty-six interdicts issued at the end of the tenth century by Ryōgen, the eighteenth head priest of the Tendai sect, are well known for their prohibition against the blustering behavior of unruly priests (*akusō*) on Mount Hiei. But there was also an article in the interdicts prohibiting the recent tendency toward extravagance in serving food and tea during the ceremonies of the sixth and eleventh months.[9] Here we have evidence that the same kind of *naorai* banquets were held on these occasions and that tea was served during them. And indeed, the serving of tea in *naorai* can be regarded as a direct forerunner of such tea gatherings as the *ōchamori*, which appeared during medieval times at Saidaiji Temple.

TRANSMISSION AND SPREAD OF *MATCHA*

Eisai's *Kissa Yōjōki*

The most important event in the history of tea drinking in Japan was the introduction of *matcha* from Sung China by Eisai in the early

Kamakura period at the end of the twelfth century. In the journal *San Tendai Godai Sanki* by the Tendai priest Jōjin, who went to China in the late eleventh century with seven of his disciples, we learn that Jōjin received tea when he had an audience with Emperor Shen-tsung.[10] Thereafter, whenever Jōjin visited government offices or temples, he was either served tea to drink or was given it as a gift. Since *matcha* was then widely used in China, it seems very likely that the tea Jōjin and his disciples drank was of this kind. After a stay in China of ten years, Jōjin died at the capital of K'ai-feng. No doubt Jōjin's disciples, who returned home before he died, introduced *matcha* and its use to Japan. But *matcha* did not at the time become a new fashion among the Japanese.

It is not known whether Eisai, when he brought *matcha* back from China a century later, had in his possession tea seeds or seedlings. Some even question whether Eisai actually brought tea to Japan, inasmuch as his two returns from China were in the ninth and seventh months, the off-season for tea planting.[11] But judging from Eisai's book on the subject, there is no need to strip him of the honor of having reintroduced tea at this time.

Eisai's book is the two-volume *Kissa Yōjōki*, which, because its second volume deals with mulberries, has the alternate name of "The Book of Tea and Mulberries." Volume one, devoted primarily to tea, is a discussion, based on Chinese sources, of tea from a botanical standpoint. The greater part of this discussion clearly is taken from the "tea" section (number 25) under food and drink in volume 867 of the encyclopedia *T'ai-p'ing yü-lan* published in Sung China. Yet the most important part of *Kissa Yōjōki*, dealing with the preparation and drinking of tea, has no citations from Chinese sources. Eisai wrote this part on the basis of practices he personally observed in China, and herein lies the historical significance of his book. Concerning the preparation of tea, Eisai says:

> Tea leaves picked in the morning should be immediately steamed. Dry them during the day and roast them carefully on a roasting shelf through the night until dawn the next day. If you place the leaves in a jar of good quality and cover them carefully with bamboo leaves, they will last for many years.[12]

And about the drinking of tea:

Tea should be made with very hot, clear water. The amount used should be two or three spoonfuls measured with a spoon about the size of a large one-*mon* coin. Adjust how much to use according to taste.[13]

We find no mention of grinding the tea leaves in a mortar or using a whisk, but there is little doubt that the tea in question was *matcha* or powdered tea.

In keeping with its title, *Kissa Yōjōki* recommends tea with its bitter taste as beneficial to the heart and as an elixir of long life. In other words, Eisai propagated tea for its medicinal value and not for the spiritual qualities attributed to it in *Ch'a Ching* and in the Chinese poetry by Japanese of the early Heian period.

In the history of Buddhism, Eisai is remembered as the man who introduced Rinzai Zen to Japan. But in his time there was no particular connection between Zen and tea other than the fact that, like the Buddhist priests of the Heian period, the followers of Zen used tea as a medicine and as a means to keep awake during meditation.

The Spread of *Matcha*

Apart from changes in the manner of making and drinking tea that accompanied the introduction of *matcha* to Japan in the early Kamakura period, tea continued to be used, as before, primarily for its practical value. We should also note, however, that in medieval times tea drinking spread outward from the Buddhist temples to other realms of society. A good example of this diffusion can be found in the practice of *obukucha*.

Obukucha refers both to the offering of tea to the Buddha and to the tea itself. The following case of Saidaiji Temple reveals that during the medieval age, which witnessed an acceleration of the merger of Shinto and Buddhism that had begun much earlier in Japanese history, tea was also offered to the *kami* of Shinto.

Sometime about the mid-thirteenth century a tea gathering called *ōchamori* was begun at Saidaiji by Eison, the restorer of the temple's fortunes. We learn that the gathering was instituted by having the priests of the temple drink tea that had been offered at the Chinju Hachimangū Shrine on the last day of the Buddhist mass known as *shūsei-e* in the first month of 1239.[14] Later, the practice was expanded to include the townspeople of the vicinity, and today it has become a great celebration in which tea is given to all comers. These days a large tea bowl forty centimeters in diameter is used, but the bowl was evidently somewhat smaller at the end of the Tokugawa period.

The method of handling tea in *obukucha* is also followed in *ōbukucha*, which is held at Rokuhara Mitsuji Temple and elsewhere among the people of Kyoto. Tradition has it that Kūya, upon hearing that Emperor Murakami was ill, presented him with tea and forthwith cured him. Thereafter the emperor recommended that people begin the year by drinking tea for their health. But this tale is apocryphal. The true beginnings of *ōbukucha* were rooted in the simple practice of people drinking together the tea presented to the Buddha and distributing it to others, a practice that began not in Kūya's day in the mid-tenth century but probably during the medieval age.[15]

Thus we see that *ōchamori* at Saidaiji and *ōbukucha* at Rokuhara Mitsuji both had their origins in the partaking of tea at banquets held at the conclusion of religious ceremonies in temples. These practices then spread outward from the precincts of the Buddhist temples. Interestingly, the two temples at the center of the practices, Saidaiji and Rokuhara Mitsuji, both were institutions closely associated with folk beliefs. A "thousand cup" grinder, said to have been used to distribute tea to people, has even been preserved at Gokurakuji Temple, a branch of Saidaiji, at Kamakura.

The Popularity of Tea Contests

Accompanying this expansion in tea drinking was a spread in the cultivation of tea. Two of the earliest tea fields we know of were those at the imperial palace, laid out in the early ninth century, and at Yakuōji Temple in Mikawa province, which was observed by a literatus who visited the temple in the late tenth century.[16] For the most part, tea was cultivated at temples, even after Eisai brought *matcha* back from China. The tea fields Eisai founded after his second return from China—the Fushun field at Senkōji Temple on Hirado Island, where he landed, and the field at Tendaijiin in the Seburi Mountains (on the border between Chikuzen and Hizen provinces), which he visited later—are still in existence.

Eisai also gave tea to Myōe of Kōzanji Temple in Kyoto, and it was this tea which, thriving in the mountain setting of Toganoo, earned a great reputation and became known as *honcha* (real tea). People of the early medieval age treasured *honcha* to the point of labeling the tea produced in other regions *hicha* (non-tea). It is said that the tea of Uji, which replaced Toganoo as the premier tea-producing region later in the Muromachi period, was also first planted by Myōe.

We know that tea was cultivated at Shōmyōji Temple in Kanazawa in Musashi province at the end of the Kamakura period and was collectively drunk by the priests of the temple from a large bowl. In the documents of the period we even see references to the fact that tea fields were spreading throughout the country.

This spread of tea fields into the provinces is mentioned in *Isei Teikin Ōrai*, which was compiled during the Nambokuchō (Northern and Southern Courts) and early Muromachi periods.[17] According to this source, the principal fields were still those at temples, but so-called peasant tea fields had also begun to appear. This development was accompanied by the rise of tea tribute. Just like rice and other products, tea became the object of feudal levy, and documents concerning the buying and selling of tea began to be seen. Tea was produced in Kyoto, and stores materialized to sell it.

Tasting contests to discern different teas, which began at the end of the Kamakura period and were known as *tōcha*, emerged as a result of the great expansion in tea cultivation and the concomitant spread of tea drinking in this age. In contrast to the Chinese practice of judging tea by its quality, the *tōcha* of Japan were competitions aimed at distinguishing among teas according to the regions where they were grown. Although originally the purpose was simply to differentiate between Toganoo tea and all others, there finally evolved, after experiments with various possibilities, the contest of "four kinds and ten cups." This contest called for drinking three cups each of three kinds of tea and one cup of a fourth kind, known as "guest tea" (evidently because contestants were given only one chance to identify it). This was precisely the same procedure as the one followed in identifying incenses, and indeed we read in the *Nijō-Kawara Rakusho*, which satirized the new government of the Kemmu Restoration, that tea and incense contests were greatly popular not only in Kamakura but also in Kyoto during this age.[18] As the wagers increased, the value of *tōcha* as entertainment grew correspondingly. *Tōcha* became known as "tea affairs of excess or extravagance *(basara)*" and were even singled out for prohibition. *Basara*, connoting an extravagance that transcended social status, was a voguish term reflecting the trend toward *gekokujō* during the Northern and Southern Courts period.[19]

With the evolution of tea rules, *tōcha* gradually declined. But the basic attraction of this form of tea entertainment can be observed in the fact that during the Tokugawa period it became a kind of tea gathering called *cha kabuki*. *Kabuki*, conveying the same meaning as *basara*, originated in the *kabuki* of the theater of that name, which became popular in the late Provincial Wars and early Tokugawa periods.

SPECIAL FEATURES OF *CHANOYU*

Conditions for *Chanoyu*

The most significant feature of the history of tea drinking in Japan has been the development of *chanoyu*. Yet, as we have seen, *chanoyu* is not simply a matter of consuming tea: It is an art form based on the act of tea drinking. What, then, was the minimum condition necessary to give rise to *chanoyu*? It was *sarei*—tea rules or codification of the way in which tea was drunk. *Sarei* were first established in the mid-fourteenth century—the Nambokuchō and early Muromachi periods—and it is no accident that *chanoyu* as a historical term also first appeared at that time.

Although the existence of *sarei* was the minimum condition needed for its creation, *chanoyu* was given concrete form, historically speaking, by three things: discrimination (*mono-suki*), behavior (*furumai*), and the setting of the tea room (*chashitsu*). The original meaning of *mono-suki*, for our purposes, was an "attachment to things (utensils)"; but in *chanoyu* it also suggested the development of a particular aesthetic based on the relationship between people and things. Indeed the later aesthetic of *wabi* can be explained in terms of this relationship. *Furumai*, on the other hand, refers to the principles of behavior evolving from the personal association among people at a tea gathering (*cha-yoriai*) and from the ethical sentiment of such a session as expressed in the phrase *ichigo ichie* (one time, one meeting).

Let us turn now to the tea room. Just as *sarei*, *suki*, and *furumai* were not established at any particular time but evolved with the passage of the years, the tea room as the setting for *chanoyu* was not created at once. Rather, it emerged from developments in the architecture of room construction whereby the *kaisho*, designed as a general gathering place for people, became, on the one hand, the *shoin* room and, on the other hand, the *sōan chashitsu* ("hutlike" tea room).[20]

Rules and Etiquette of Zen Temples

Many of us are apt to believe, on the basis of the phrase "tea and Zen have the same flavor," that *chanoyu* and Zen Buddhism are one and the same; and in fact there is a popular line of argument that accepts this proposition, a priori, as true. Yet a moment's reflection makes us realize that the vast number of people in China and elsewhere in the world who drink tea have no connection whatsoever with Zen. Even in Japan, a history of tea drinking unrelated to Zen evolved from the early Heian period on. Yet even if we set aside "tea and Zen have the same flavor" as an idea lacking in historical validity, it is still undeniable that *chanoyu* has had a deep association with Zen. To put the matter another way, why was it that neither the old sects of Heian Buddhism nor the new sects of Kamakura Buddhism, although they had their ties with tea, gave rise to *chanoyu?* The reason, I believe, is that Zen possessed special rules for drinking tea that were not to be found in other sects.

Zen was introduced to Japan in the early Kamakura period first by Eisai (Rinzai Zen) and then by Dōgen (Sōtō Zen). I shall not discuss the way in which Zen was received as a new sect of Buddhism at this time. The usual reason given for its spread among the warrior clans is that Zen, which insisted that enlightenment was to be achieved by direct transmission from mind to mind or by seated meditation, appealed to the sentiments of the samurai, who as warriors were obliged constantly to face death. I do not deny this reason for Zen's spread. But a more important reason, to my mind, was that the regulated group life found in the societies of Zen temples attracted the attention of the samurai class and was found congenial. Rules known as *shingi* were established in these temples and became the basis for a form of communal life that governed the typical day of the priests from the time they arose in the morning until they retired at night. A work dealing with *shingi* that exerted great influence in Japan was *Ch'an-yüan ch'ing-kuei* by Tsung I of the Sung dynasty.[21]

Shingi were not, however, drawn up and put into practice immediately in the Zen temples of Japan. Eisai, although interested in such rules, produced nothing that can be truly likened to them. But Dōgen compiled *Eihei Shingi* based on the *Ch'an-yüan ch'ing-kuei*,[22] and Enni Ben'en, the founder of Tōfukuji Temple, wrote rules for that temple modeled on the same work after his return from Sung China. Yet the real advocates of the introduction and implementation of *shingi* were the Chinese priests who came to Japan. Lan-ch'i Tao-lung (Rankei Dōryū), who arrived in 1246, was especially zealous. It is said that, as a result of the Sung-style rules he codified at Kenchōji, rules were established at Zen temples throughout the country.

Ch'ing-cho Cheng-ch'eng (Seisetsu Shōchō), who came to Japan in 1326, compiled *Ta-chien ch'ing-kuei (Daikan Shingi)*.[23] During the course of a career that took him to such temples in Kyoto and Kamakura as Kenchōji, Jōchiji, Engakuji, Kenninji, and Nanzenji, Ch'ing-cho criticized the priests of Japan for not accepting the views of Chinese priests but, instead, adhering to the old ways of their own country. Insisting that the procedures for the Zen sect must be entirely in accord with those of China, he reformed the rules of the Zen temples of Japan.

Shingi were adopted at Zen temples primarily during the mid-fourteenth century—the time of transition from the Kamakura period to the early age of the Northern and Southern Courts and the Muromachi Bakufu. Among these *shingi* were rules dealing with the drinking of tea (that is, *sarei*). *Chanoyu* was created at the same time, as the Zen sect was being adopted by the warrior houses and others in Japan and procedures governing tea were being established by means of the *sarei* of the Zen temples. In this sense, *chanoyu* emerged from the *sarei* of Zen.

The earliest form of the *chakai*, or tea gathering, was the meeting known as *yotsugashira* (four hosts). We know of this type of gathering from such sources as volume thirty-three of *Taiheiki*, where Sasaki Dōyo and other *"basara daimyō"* in Kyoto met daily to drink tea *(cha-yoriai)*. The setting for these meetings is described as a room decorated with treasures from both China and Japan, where "people lined up at the seats of the four hosts."[24]

Tea gatherings based on the *sarei* of Zen temples are still held today at Kenninji and Tōfukuji in Kyoto and at Engakuji in Kamakura. According to an account in *Kissa Ōrai* that describes one of the gatherings of the early Muromachi period, the four hosts used chairs in a form of conduct known as "upright etiquette" *(ryūrei)*.[25] Later, in the mid-fifteenth century, when envoys from Ming China were received at the Muromachi Bakufu, chairs were also provided and tea was served. This was known as "Chinese etiquette." Upright etiquette became "seated etiquette"—that is, the etiquette of sitting on the floor on *tatami*—during the Muromachi period with the evolution of *shoin*-style interior construction *(shoin-zukuri)* and the covering of floors with *tatami*. This was the beginning of *shoin sarei*, or rules for behavior in the *shoin* room setting.

THE STRUCTURE OF *SHOIN CHANOYU*

The Taste for *Karamono*

The *shoin* form of *chanoyu* evolved in conjunction with the *shoin* room. Essentially, it was a set of rules for handling tea established primarily within the society of the military aristocracy. An important aspect of this form of *chanoyu* was the emergence of a special discrimination or taste called *karamono suki* (taste for Chinese objects of art and craft). Two characteristics of *shoin chanoyu* were the decoration of the *shoin* room with *karamono* and the preparation of tea using *karamono* utensils.

As noted in the last section, there was a close relationship between the Zen sect of Buddhism and *chanoyu*. Not only did tea rules emerge from the rules of Zen temples, but such things as scrolls of calligraphy, paintings, and Buddhist implements used in the communities of Zen priests were taken directly into *chanoyu* and became its distinguishing features. Most of these things were, of course, *karamono* imported from abroad.

The importation of *karamono* owed much to the trade between Ming China and Japan that was begun by the shogun Ashikaga Yoshimitsu in the early fifteenth century. It would be incorrect, however, to regard *karamono suki* as something created by this trade, since Japanese and Chinese Zen (Ch'an) priests journeying to and from the continent had already brought *karamono* in great numbers to Japan in the late Kamakura period. Most of these *karamono* were originally acquired for religious purposes and were used in Zen temples.

Because of the Mongol invasions of 1274 and 1281, relations between Japan and China were strained during the late Kamakura period. Yet even at that time Japanese commercial ships were allowed to go to Yüan China and engage in trade. Moreover, numbers of Zen priests seemed to be going to China every year. It was also during the late Kamakura period that the *shingi* were transmitted to Japan.

As we know from the index of items of Butsunichian at Engakuji in

Kamakura, the transmission of *shingi* was accompanied by the accumulation at Zen temples of many things of Buddhism, including paintings, scrolls of calligraphy, and *tenmoku* tea bowls.[26] What interests us, however, is whether these things were immediately sought after by the people of Japan and became objects of aesthetic appreciation. Kanazawa Sadaaki, who held the important position of *shikken* (shogunal regent) in the Bakufu, wrote at the end of the Kamakura period in a letter addressed to his son in Kyoto that "the popularity of *karamono* and tea grows ever greater" and urged his son to bring *karamono* back from the imperial capital.[27] It is interesting to note that tea and *karamono* are mentioned together in Sadaaki's letter. In the miscellany *Tsurezuregusa* (Essays in Idleness), written by Yoshida Kenkō in the early part of the Nambokuchō period, there is a passage criticizing the taste for "treasures imported from afar."[28] *Karamono suki* was in fashion at this time in both Kyoto and Kamakura, among both priests and laity, and became a principal cause for the rise of a trend toward extravagance *(basara)*.

Advent of the *Tokonoma*

The growth of *karamono suki* inevitably gave rise to the need for a setting in which to display these treasures imported from abroad. In the *Kissa Ōrai* description of a tea-drinking pavilion, paintings of Shaka and Kannon were hung on the front wall and portraits of Monju and Fugen were placed to the sides of them. On the opposite wall were picture scrolls of Kanzan and Jittoku.[29] In all, the effect was one of overdecoration. We also know from the records of this age that a number of folding screens were set up around the interiors of rooms and Chinese picture scrolls were hung over them. Apparently the purpose was to use these Chinese picture scrolls more as decorative furnishings than as objects for purely artistic appreciation. In any case, we can observe here one manifestation of the taste for Chinese paintings during this period. And indeed it is understandable, given the trends of the time, that "Chinese paintings" done by Japanese artists using the subject matter and style of the Chinese originals (and regarded as copies rather than fakes) were also prized.

The growth of *karamono suki* also brought about changes in residential architecture, one of which was the development of the *tokonoma* (alcove). Three installations that had previously been used independently—a *shoin* writing desk, shelves, and a decorative platform (on which an incense burner, vase, and candleholder were placed)—were combined into a set and used for the display of writing objects, paintings, calligraphy, and the like. Thus a new kind of interior space was created—and along with it the need to consider the decoration of its installations (the *shoin* writing desk, *chigaidana* or asymmetrical shelves, and the *tokonoma*).

Among those in attendance upon the shogun at the Muromachi Bakufu were the *dōbōshū* (companions), including such men as Nōami, Geiami, Sōami, and Sen'ami, who performed various functions in the shogunal palace. They were responsible for *karamono* and were entrusted with the care of Chinese pieces collected by the shogun's family. Their duties included evaluating the quality of *karamono*, handling the finances related to them, and, in the case of pictures and scrolls, having them mounted. Moreover, they were concerned with room decoration using *karamono*, and in the course of carrying out their duties they devised rules for this decoration based on their own experience. These rules were placed in writing in *Kundaikan Sōchō Ki*.[30] Although the original of this work has not survived, we have copies of it attributed to Nōami and Sōami.

Kundaikan Sōchō Ki is divided into three parts. The first part lists more than one hundred and fifty painters, centering on those of the Sung and Yüan dynasties in China, ranks the painters as artists, and itemizes their favorite artistic subjects. The second part discusses, with illustrations, the decoration of the *shoin* room and its alcove, shelves, and writing desk. The third part is a collection of illustrations and explanations of articles of pottery, porcelains, and lacquerware. Of the three parts of *Kundaikan Sōchō Ki* the first, containing the list of painters, is especially handy as a means for learning about the taste for *karamono* that was then so popular, and hence it has often been separated from the others and used by itself. But since articles of craft as well as paintings were integral elements in the decoration of the *shoin* room, *Kundaikan Sōchō Ki* should be taken in its entirety as a text on this kind of decoration.

Kundaikan Sōchō Ki also contains a discussion of flower arrangement, dealing with such matters as the display of flowers on and below the *chigaidana* shelves, in hanging vases, and in vases hung on pillars. From this discussion evolved the theory of flower arrangement, which in the sixteenth century took the form known as *rikka*.

Thus *Kundaikan Sōchō Ki* is truly a record of the aesthetic tastes of life
in the medieval age.

The *Kaisho* Room as a Setting

Shoin chanoyu had several distinguishing characteristics: It was held in
a room, essentially as described above, decorated with karamono and
it employed *karamono* as utensils. The room in question still had not
evolved into the tea room, however.

During the early Muromachi period, structures called *kaisho* began
to appear in the shogun's palace and at the residences of powerful
warrior chieftains. These structures were not formally appointed settings for public rituals and the like; rather, they were situated in gardens and intended mainly for purposes of entertainment.

The emergence of the *kaisho* accompanied a growing interest in the
arts within elite warrior society. Gatherings for *waka* and *renga* (linked
verse) poetry, *chanoyu*, and other activities were frequently held by the
samurai chieftains, and, at the Bakufu, get-togethers for enjoying the
arts and entertainment were arranged on a monthly basis. As these
gatherings became more frequent, *kaisho* were increasingly required to
accommodate them. From the period of Yoshimitsu to Yoshimochi
the number of *kaisho* at the shogunal palace proliferated, and by
Yoshinori's time they were abundant. Elected by lot to be shogun,
Yoshinori imposed despotic rule over the Muromachi Bakufu and was
greatly feared. But he was also exceedingly interested in the arts, and
shoin chanoyu was formally established during his term as shogun—
that is, sometime in the mid-fifteenth century.

Kaisho literally means a place where people gather. At first the
kaisho was a room in a larger building rather than an independent
structure, and it possessed no distinctive architectural features. But as
it evolved in warrior society, the *kaisho* adopted the structural elements of the new *shoin* style of residential architecture (instead of the
traditional, courtier style of *shinden* construction). We noted in the
last section the creation of the *tokonoma* in *shoin* architecture. It was
not until later that the *shoin* room took on its full shape and structure,
including the installation of upper, middle, and lower-level floors as a
means of indicating feudal status differences.

Shoin chanoyu was *chanoyu* held in a *kaisho* room done in the *shoin* manner. No hearth was built into the room. Sometimes a burner was placed in a corner and tea was prepared behind a folding screen. But most often the tea was made in a separate room or hallway and brought into the main room by a *dōbōshū* or young servant. The room used for making tea was called the "place of tea," but this meant the place where tea was prepared and did not refer to a true tea room (*chashitsu*). At the historical stage of *shoin chanoyu*, the *chashitsu* as a room designated especially for tea did not exist. Stated another way, the place where host and guests gathered to drink tea was only an occasional tea room, employed for the purpose of *chanoyu* when needed.

Junji Chakai

We have just examined the characteristics of *shoin chanoyu*, particularly as it evolved at the Muromachi Bakufu. But this was simply the central line in the evolution of tea drinking. During the same age—the fourteenth and fifteenth centuries—tea was also consumed in various other ways at different levels of Japanese society.

Courtiers, for example, did not develop rules for tea drinking to the extent that the warrior aristocrats did and hence were essentially free from the dictates of *sarei*. At tea gatherings known as *junji chakai* (tea gatherings by turns) at the Fushimi Palace in southern Kyoto, the palace's master, Prince Sadafusa (the father of Emperor Gohanazono), and the courtiers and samurai associated with the palace took turns being host and arranging the gatherings for certain days. On one occasion at the end of the second month and the beginning of the third month of 1416, a three-day gathering was held.[31] Two elegant chests were placed in a room and, in addition to various appetizers and refreshments, were stocked with fine prizes for a tea-tasting contest.

The room was decorated with a pair of folding screens with a triptych of Kannon flanked by monkeys hung over it and, in front of the triptych, a pair of ceramic flower vases. After the serving of sake and appetizers, the contest was held and the winners were awarded prizes. This brought the tea gathering to an end; but the assembled group then turned to drinking and feasting, and others who had not partaken of tea joined them and helped divide up the remaining prizes by lot. With the sake flowing freely, many became drunk. The group played music and danced, enjoying themselves until late into the night.

Apart from this elegant form of tea gathering, "kitchen tea gatherings" (*daidokoro chakai*) were held at Fushimi Palace. Although not directly related to the *junji chakai*, these gatherings too were conducted by people who took turns preparing for them. The participants were maids and other people of the lower orders who came to the palace. Any place served as a setting, and there were no particular room decorations. The tea was a crude kind known as *unkyaku*, a fact that led to gatherings of this sort being labeled *unkyaku chakai*. There was also a game played at the palace called *unkyaku semefuse*—a form of *monoawase* (comparison of things) in which people analyzed Chinese characters. The winners received *unkyaku* and the losers sake, and there was great enjoyment in having the winners consume six or seven bowls of *unkyaku*.

Rinkan Chanoyu

Another species of tea gatherings devoted to pleasure were the *rinkan* (summer bath) parties held at a later period—during the time of the Ōnin War (1467–1477)—by the Furuichi, a warrior chieftain family of Yamato province. While bathing, people at these parties composed *waka* and *renga* and partook of both food and sake. Since the principal purpose of the parties was to drink tea, they were called *rinkan chanoyu* or "summer bath tea gatherings." The bath was prepared either by servants or young samurai of the Furuichi family. Host and guests soaked in the water, drank tea, ate food, and consumed sake. On 1469:5:23 some one hundred and fifty people of the Furuichi family and retainers from the vicinity bathed,[32] and at another party on 7:10 of the same year all the nearby villagers gathered to watch.

Having a cup of tea after one's bath must have been refreshing. Indeed, at a later time both Toyotomi Hideyoshi and Matsudaira Fumai engaged in this practice. The teahouse used for the purpose was a rough structure made of logs. Although this kind of party was a rather loose form of entertainment, in terms of elegance it was considerably advanced beyond the *junji chakai*. And indeed we can even catch a glimpse in it of the aesthetics of the *sōan* (hut) form of *chanoyu* that was soon to appear.

THE AESTHETIC OF *SŌAN CHANOYU*

The Changing Character of *Suki*

In ranking poets by their artistic merit, Shōtetsu, writing in *Shōtetsu Monogatari*, the mid-fifteenth-century critical work on *waka*, also remarked on men of tea (*chajin*). According to Shōtetsu, a person who has "tea discrimination" is one "who keeps his tea utensils in beautiful condition, and who loves and possesses, according to his own tastes, such utensils as *tenmoku* tea bowls, kettles, and water buckets."[33] These remarks give us an idea of the nature of *karamono suki* from the Kamakura age until Shōtetsu's time.

However, a great change in the aesthetic of *suki* occurred during the brief period that elapsed between the writing of *Shōtetsu Monogatari* and Murata Shukō's "Letter of the Heart" (*Kokoro no Fumi*), which is thought to have been composed shortly after the Ōnin War. The "Letter of the Heart" contains information about *chanoyu* that Shukō addressed to his disciple Furuichi Chōin, a chieftain of Yamato province. In it Shukō admonishes Chōin to avoid the faults of pride and self-assertion in *chanoyu* and explains how to develop a taste for fine utensils on the basis of one's own ability. The precise year of the "Letter of the Heart" is not known, but it was probably composed around the same time—approximately 1488—when Chōin was also given *Shinkei Sōzu Teikin*, a text about *renga*, from Shinkei's disciple Inawashiro Kensai.[34] Both writings make essentially the same points.

The "Letter of the Heart" devotes particular attention to explaining how one should regard the utensils of tea, and indeed it is remembered especially for its injunction that one should "harmonize Japanese and Chinese tastes." It is wrong, however, for the inexperienced to delight vainly in such Japanese pieces (*wamono*) as Bizen and Shigaraki ware because they possess the qualities of being "cold and withered" and "cold and emaciated." We can deduce from this that it was then popular to seek Bizen and Shigaraki ware for precisely these qualities. Cold and withered or emaciated are qualities in the realm of *kotan kanjaku* (the plain and simple) and the beauty of the crude and imperfect. In other words, they suggest the same aesthetic sphere as that evoked by the comment attributed to Shukō: "The moon is not pleasing unless partly obscured by a cloud."[35]

Here we see a clear movement away from *karamono suki*, whose ideal was to possess fine utensils (*karamono*) in accordance with one's tastes, to the *wabi* aesthetic and *wamono suki* (taste for things Japanese), which favored the crude and imperfect. Considered from the standpoint of the kind of *karamono suki* that had prevailed until this time, the idea of "harmonizing Japanese and Chinese tastes" might be rephrased to mean a "shift from *karamono* to *wamono*."

We must note, however, in regard to the development of this *wabi-wamono* aesthetic, that *karamono suki* and *wamono suki* were not diametrically opposing tastes. It is true that *karamono* were considered at the time to be objects of richness and perfection and were contrasted with the rough and simple beauty of *wamono*. But since many *karamono* were used in Zen temples to suggest the Zen state of enlightenment, it is dangerous to say there were no aesthetic correspondences between *karamono* and *wamono*. Indeed, it appears that in some sense the aesthetic of *wamono* simplicity was nurtured within the long tradition of *karamono suki*.

It is common knowledge that the wares of local Japanese kilns—for example, the pottery of Shigaraki, Ise, and Bizen—were taken into *chanoyu*. But in the second half of the fifteenth century these wares were limited to flower vases and water waste jars and did not include *wamono* tea bowls. In fact, as we enter the sixteenth century and the period when records of tea gatherings *(chakai-ki)* were kept, we learn that the number of Korean pieces (Kōrai *mono*) employed in *chanoyu* was increasing yearly. Not until the time of Rikyū did *wamono* tea bowls come into common use.

A second point to note concerning the development of the *wabi-wamono* aesthetic was a change in the meaning of the word *suki*. No longer did it mean simply to covet or wish to possess. It now took on the added sense of contrivance and artifice. *Zenpō Zatsudan*, which contains Shukō's remark about the moon, states that although *karamono* utensils are splendid they lack "feeling." Ise and Bizen pieces, if interestingly contrived, could be superior to them.[36] In this kind of discrimination *(suki)*, even cracked Bizen pottery might be seen as better than *karamono*. The notion that the beauty of the crude and imperfect could, by means of clever contrivance, be revitalized gave greater depth of meaning to *suki*, a word that hitherto had implied only attachment to things. The time had arrived in history when people truly understood the aesthetic mix necessary for *chanoyu*.

The third point to note in the development of the aesthetic sense of *wabi* and *wamono* is the great influence exerted upon it by the works of poetic criticism. We have observed that the points made in Shukō's "Letter of the Heart" were almost identical with those of *Shinkei Sōzu Teikin*. This was because Shukō was influenced by Shinkei, and the "Letter of the Heart" is, conceptually at least, almost a product of Shinkei's critical writing on poetry.

A linked verse master of the fifteenth century, Shinkei espoused the aesthetic associated with "the cold and withered." This aesthetic had not only become dominant in the worlds of *waka* and *renga* poetry, it had also powerfully influenced the other arts. Artists of different kinds readily took this aesthetic and applied it to their own fields. The period of the late fifteenth and early sixteenth centuries was a time when theories of art were established for all artistic pursuits. *Chanoyu* was no exception, and we find both Shukō and Takeno Jōō, who was a *renga* master until age thirty, constantly seeking to endow *chanoyu* with the aesthetic that Shinkei advanced in the phrase "the withered, stunted, and cold."

Setting of the Dōjinsai

The same aesthetic change we have just noticed in utensils also occurred in the setting in which *chanoyu* was held. An example of this correspondence is the reduction in size of the *shoin* which, although not used exclusively as a tea room, was a place where tea was drunk. We can actually see one such *shoin* in the Dōjinsai, a room in the Buddha hall of the Tōgudō located on the Higashiyama estate built by the shogun Ashikaga Yoshimasa. Yoshimasa, who died at the end of the fifteenth century, has been labeled a failure as a ruler, but he possessed exceptional talent of an artistic kind. And although he constructed the Higashiyama estate as a retreat from the world of politics, the construction was itself achieved by means of his authority as shogun. Hence the extent of Yoshimasa's power should not be underestimated.

There are two differing views of the role of Yoshimasa in the history of the way of tea. The first, found for example in the early Edo (or Tokugawa) period treatise on painting *Tōhaku Gasetsu*, notes that Yoshimasa gathered to himself the famous *karamono* of the country and argues that his period was the high point of the *shoin* style of *chanoyu* based on *karamono suki*, which had been in vogue since Kamakura times.[37] According to the second view, the Dōjinsai room of the

Tōgudō, which is outfitted with a *shoin* writing desk and *chigaidana* asymmetrical shelves (although it lacks the *oshiita-toko*, or decorative platform), is an early example of the four-and-a-half mat tea room and Yoshimasa should therefore be ranked with Shukō as an originator of *wabicha*. Both views have merit, in fact, and Yoshimasa is probably best regarded as a representative of the transition from *shoin chanoyu* to *wabicha*. But one point that deserves our particular attention is the origin of the four-and-a-half mat "small *shoin*" room.

Ever since the Edo period it has been generally thought that the Dōjinsai is the oldest extant four-and-a-half mat tea room, even though architectural historians have argued that it was not a tea room but a study. When the Dōjinsai was dismantled for repairs, however, it was discovered that a sunken hearth had been constructed in it at an earlier time and that the room was called "the place of the sunken hearth."[38] These facts tended, of course, to strengthen the popular theory that the Dōjinsai was used for drinking tea. In any case, the main question to resolve is why the Dōjinsai was constructed as a small *shoin*, a four-and-a-half mat room. For it was in the late fifteenth century, when the Dōjinsai was built, or the early sixteenth century that the small room (*kozashiki*) made its appearance.

When Sanjōnishi Sanetaka, a courtier associated with Yoshimasa, purchased a tiny six-mat house in 1502:6 and moved it to a corner of his estate, for example, he had it reconstructed to four-and-a-half mat size. We know from the details given by Sanetaka in his diary that the house was in the *shoin* style of architecture and the purpose in reconstructing it was clearly to transform it into a four-and-a-half mat structure.[39]

One of Sanetaka's acquaintances, Toyohara Sumiaki, built a "mountain village hut" (*yamazato-an*) under a pine tree at the rear of his garden and composed this poem:

> A place to escape to
> When one cannot ease one's cares in the mountains.
> The hut beneath the pine within the city.[40]

According to this poem, Sumiaki's hut constructed in Kyoto was a retreat for moments when he could not unburden his cares by going to a mountain village. Although the construction and layout of this mountain village hut is not precisely known, presumably it was a *shoin-zukuri*, four-and-a-half mat edifice.

The nature of a mountain village within Kyoto becomes clearer at a later time, during the period of Murata Sōju, Shukō's successor. Sōju, who lived in the bustling southern (Shimogyō) part of the city, where the homes of craftsmen and merchants were clustered, was called the Shimogyō man of tea. The teahouse he built was said to be most tasteful, having the appearance of a dwelling from the mountain, and Sōju himself was thought to be like "a hermit in the city." But in this case too it is not certain that the structure in question was really in the style of a teahouse. And very likely its architecture was *shoin-zukuri* rather than a countrified form of construction.

By tracing the cases of Yoshimasa, Sanetaka, Sumiaki, and Sōju, we can see the significance of the appearance of the small *shoin*. First, when contrasted with the large-scale *shoin* construction, the small, four-and-a-half mat room implied a rejection of differences in social status. In this regard it is interesting to note that the name Yoshimasa chose to have inscribed on the plaque for his room—Dōjin—means that sages consider all people to be the same, without distinguishing among those of high and those of low status. And second, the space of four-and-a-half mats had, from much earlier times, been that of the hermit and hence signified the desire to reject mundane, worldly existence. The fact that Sumiaki called his *sōan* the mountain village hut informs us that he was inspired by the hermit's way of thinking.

"A Mountain Place Within the City"

Although Sumiaki's poem spoke of a mountain village, it was not a village separated from the urban centers in which most people lived; rather, it was a village constructed in just such a center. In this sense, it differed fundamentally from the mountain villages of Saigyō and Kamo no Chōmei.

Even Saigyō, having retired from the world, composed poems speaking of the suffering caused by his inability truly to forsake the world; and, like Chōmei, he continued to socialize with people of quality even after taking Buddhist vows. In one respect, taking Buddhist vows and forsaking the world can be regarded as a means of smoothing one's relations with people in everyday life. The fact remains, however, that one has abandoned one's status in everyday life.

Since the mountain villages in question were refuges in the city, they served a purpose quite contrary to that of the mountain villages of such earlier people as Saigyō and Chōmei. The desire of these earlier *inja* (those who withdraw from everyday life) to seek the way was transformed into the aesthetic of the *suki* person, who wished to enjoy the realm of the tranquil in the worldliness of the city.

This aesthetic developed against the background of an age of strife. It emerged from the conspicuous prospering of Kyoto in the wake of the destruction of the Ōnin War and from the tastes, supported by this prospering, of the city's inhabitants. Urban retreats and mountain villages were artificial creations of time and space sought within the hustle and bustle of everyday life: They were components of a man-made world of aestheticism.

Thus the phrase "a mountain place within the city" became a voguish expression among the *suki* people of the capital. At a later time, the Jesuit missionary João Rodrigues, commenting on the spread of *chanoyu* among the wealthy townsmen of Sakai, observed that these townsmen sought small dwellings in the city because they regarded their construction in the mountain village style to be superior to the real places of retreat in the mountain villages themselves.[41] This observation supports the notion that the mountain village within the city was essentially an aesthetic construct. *Chanoyu* was itself a classic product of urban culture. In the preface to this essay I remarked on the artificiality of *chanoyu*. It was during this age that the concept of artificiality first arose.

We have already observed that the miniaturization of room size to a scale of four-and-a-half mats occurred within the evolution of *shoin* construction. It is not clear, however, precisely when the four-and-a-half mat *sōan* or hut—that is, the *sōan* tea room—appeared, although, as stated above, it obviously evolved from the small *shoin*. From the standpoint of architectural style, there was no continuity in this transition from *shoin* construction to *sōan* construction. But inasmuch as the two forms of construction shared the notion of a mountain village, especially a mountain village within the city, there was in fact a continuity. I believe that, just as in the case of taste for *karamono*, it is only when we have completely grasped the relationship between continuity and discontinuity in the evolution of the tea room that we can understand the special characteristics of *sōan chanoyu* and its historical significance.

The Aesthetic of *Wabi*

Sōan chanoyu appears to have evolved, as noted, about the mid-sixteenth century and took its essential form during the Tenmon era (1532–1554). If we place the creation of the *shoin* form of *chanoyu* in the mid-fifteenth century, then *sōan chanoyu* required approximately a century to appear. During this time, the course of *chanoyu* shifted direction from the warrior aristocracy to the townsmen *(machishū)*.

I believe from the facts adduced that—at least insofar as *chanoyu* is taken as a measure—the period of so-called Higashiyama culture was entirely transitional. Indeed, for our purposes, Higashiyama culture is not a meaningful concept. We would do much better to compare Tenmon culture to that of the Kitayama epoch.[42]

In any event, proof that *chanoyu* had become a form of urban culture can be observed in the records of tea gatherings that appeared one after another with the advent of the Tenmon era. These included the *Matsuya Kaiki*, a record of three generations of tea men of the Matsuya family of Nara, the *Tennōjiya Kaiki*, kept by three generations of tea men of the Tsuda family of Sakai, and the *Imai Sōkyū Chanoyu Nikki Kakinuki*, also kept by a Sakai tea man.[43] Since all of these records were begun during the Tenmon era, they have generally been called *Tenmon Chakai-ki*. Their appearance was both a quantitative index of the spread of *chanoyu* among townspeople and a qualitative sign of the establishment of forms for the handling of tea that made possible the gatherings recorded—not only the rules but also the use of certain utensils, the *roji* garden, and the tea room necessary for the holding of *chakai*.

Thus *chanoyu*, having been adopted by the warrior and courtier elites, became popular also among townsmen. As a result, the cultivated taste for utensils expanded to a scale beyond compare with earlier times. As we have seen, however, this was also the period of the development of a taste for *wamono*—that is, the rise of interest in a plain and unpolished beauty—and it is important to note that growth of the aesthetic of the cold and withered corresponded to the spreading practice of collecting utensils and to the cultivation of taste for them.

Thus the aesthetic of the plain and simple *(kotan kanjaku)* constituted not an abandonment of the interest in "things" (such as utensils) but rather a searching for their true essence—that is, a deepening of the taste for them. Seen from this perspective, the significance of the emergence of *wabi* as the aesthetic of *chanoyu* following the quest for beauty in the "cold and withered" *(hiekareru)* and the "cold and lonely" *(hiesabiru)* is abundantly clear.

The noun *wabi* derives from *wabu* (to be wretched) or *wabishii* (wretched) and originally referred to the miserable feeling that comes from material deprivation. *Wabi* became a meaningful aesthetic term in the world of *waka* poetry at the end of the ancient age and the beginning of medieval times, when Saigyō and other *inja* emerged and voluntarily pursued lives of loneliness and deprivation, forcing themselves to deal with *"wabishii"* living conditions. Fujiwara no Shunzei and his son Teika also played significant roles in the development of the aesthetic of *wabi* at this time. Thus we see that *wabi* was not just associated with *chanoyu* but was used as well in the realm of poetry as a term related to *sabi* (loneliness).

Wabi was taken into the world of *chanoyu* and made its aesthetic because, at the height of the craze for *mono-suki* (the taste for material things), *chanoyu* encountered *wabi* as an aesthetic based on things. *Wabi* was, indeed, the final point in the development of *mono-suki*. Yet we have noted that *wabi* originally implied a lack of things. The point, however, is not to be completely bereft of material possessions (since there would then be no need for an aesthetic): *Wabi* does not mean to deny things, but rather to penetrate as far as possible to their true essence and therein to discern beauty. In the beauty of the plain lies the ultimate sense of beauty that the Japanese have discovered. It is a beauty of restraint. *Wabi* goes beyond the aesthetics of things and becomes a state of mind.

One Time, One Meeting *(Ichigo, Ichie)*

To examine this state of mind, it is necessary to inquire into the meaning of *furumai* in *chanoyu*. The basic sense of *furumai* (in its form as the verb *furumau*) is to act or behave; but, in terms of personal relations, it came also to mean entertaining people and, finally, providing them with a feast. This is the kind of *furumai* we find in the record of a tea gathering. Obviously the record gives the setting, the participants (host and guests), and the various utensils used at a tea gathering held on a particular day. These matters are set down in the record under the heading of *suki*. Following the description of *suki*, it is customary to have a discussion of *furumai*. Here *furumai* refers to the meal served at the tea gathering. In other words, the typical tea gathering consists of *suki* (the presentation of tea) and *furumai* (the serving of food).

The meal served as *furumai* is also known as *kaiseki*. The true meaning of *kaiseki* is a gathering of people—in other words, a tea gathering. But it is also common to refer to the food served at such a gathering as *kaiseki*—a fact that suggests the great significance of food in *chanoyu*. According to *Yamanoue Sōji Ki*, it is the *kaiseki* that demands the most creative attention in *chanoyu*.[44]

At the same time that *furumai* is given concrete form as a meal, the spirit behind it is carefully investigated. Thus *Yamanoue Sōji Ki* speaks of the attitude of the host and the guests and the spirit that binds them as a group (*ichiza*) sitting together.[45] In order to have a successful meeting of this kind, it is necessary to imagine that the group as constituted may only come together once in a lifetime (even though, in fact, its members see each other every day) and to give oneself to it with utter sincerity. This is the basis of the notion of "one time, one meeting."

We have seen, then, that *chanoyu* is based on the everyday act of drinking tea and developed within the context of the gathering of people for the purpose of pleasure. Yet what we discover during the course of *chanoyu*'s development is not only the creation of the aesthetic of *wabi*, emerging from the extreme liking for "things," but also the crystallization of an ethic of the gathering expressed in the phrase "one time, one meeting." The aesthetic of *chanoyu* is to be sought in the relationship of people to things; its ethic is to be found in the relationship between people and people. I believe that once *wabi* and *ichigo*, *ichie* were discovered, *chanoyu* was established in both name and fact. The time of this discovery was on the eve of the rise of Sen no Rikyū.

IN CONCLUSION

Chanoyu is often called a composite art. This is because in the evolution of tea drinking various arts and crafts, such as painting, calligraphy, landscape gardening, and architecture, were made part of *cha-noyu* or became intimately related to it. I doubt that there is any other form of artistic conduct that is so indulgent and extravagant. But it is not just a matter of accumulating things. A major feature of *chanoyu* is the arranging of these things—that is, the suitable display of them according to the time, place, and people involved. In other words, the artistic conduct of *chanoyu* is closely related to the ethic of entertaining people, and in this sense *chanoyu* cannot simply be categorized as an art.

If we regard *chanoyu* in this light, it becomes an exceedingly difficult task to comprehend it in overall, composite terms. For one thing, it is necessary to be informed about the various fields of art and craft that I have mentioned. One cannot present a thesis of *chanoyu* simply by piling up fragments of information about points related to it; one must have a knowledge that transcends the various genres of art and craft associated with *chanoyu*. The best way to overcome this difficulty of understanding *chanoyu* is to examine its historical evolution. And indeed such an approach should not be restricted to *chanoyu*: All things reveal their true nature under historical analysis. With this thought in mind, I have in this essay traced the history of *chanoyu* up to the appearance of Sen no Rikyū—or, to be more precise, the history of *chanoyu* before it became *chanoyu*—and have attempted to abstract the essentials of *chanoyu* as they can be understood by such means.

NOTES

1. Okakura Kakuzo (Tenshin), *The Book of Tea* (New York: Fox Duffield, 1906), p. 3.
2. Chin'a, comp., *Chadō Hayagaten*, in *Nihon Kyōiku Bunko*, vol. 12 (*Eisei oyobi yūgei*) (Tokyo: Dōbun-kan, 1911), p. 410.
3. Nambō Sōkei, *Nampōroku*, in Sen Sōshitsu, ed., *Chadō Koten Zenshū*, vol. 4 (Kyoto: Tankōsha, 1956), pp. 319–320.
4. There is a theory that the "mountain tea" (*yamacha*) that even today is seen growing in remote, mountainous places is natural and autogenetic. But botanists and plant breeders, judging the characteristics of this form of tea, believe that it was originally cultivated and hence did not simply appear in nature.
5. *Nihon Kōki*, in Kuroita Katsumi, ed., *Shintei Zōho Kokushi Taikei* (Tokyo: Yoshikawa Kōbunkan, 1975), 815:6.
6. See Lu Yü, *Ch'a Ching*, in Sen Sōshitsu, ed., *Chadō Koten Zenshū*, vol. 1 (Kyoto:

Tankōsha, 1957). See also the translation by Francis Ross Carpenter, *The Classic of Tea* (Boston: Little, Brown, 1974).

7. *Nihon Kōki*, in Kuroita Katsumi, ed., *Shintei Zōho Kokushi Taikei*, 815:4.

8. The Shishinden was the main ceremonial building of the emperor's residential compound *(dairi)*. During Saga's time, tea for these seasonal readings of the sutras was grown on the Daidairi (Greater Imperial Palace) field, located in the northeastern corner of the palace enclosure. We know from later records that other tea fields functioned under the management of the Tenyakuryō (Office of Medicines).

9. Ryōgen's twenty-six interdicts can be found in Hayashiya Tatsusaburō, *Zusetsu Chadō Shi* (Tokyo: Tankōsha, 1981), p. 89.

10. Kondō Heijō, ed., *Kaitei Shiseki Shūran*, vol. 26 (Tokyo: Shiseki Shūran Kenkyū Kai, 1968), pp. 649–814.

11. Eisai returned from his two trips to China in 1168 and 1191.

12. Eisai, *Kissa Yōjōki*, in Hanawa Hokiichi, ed., *Gunsho Ruijū*, vol. 19 (Tokyo: Zoku Gunsho Ruijū Kansei Kai, 1958), p. 13.

13. Ibid., p. 858.

14. Also *shūshō-e*—a mass held annually in the first month at the temples of various sects to celebrate the beginning of the new year.

15. Nagashima Fukutarō, *Chadō Bunka Ronshū*, vol. 1 (Kyoto: Tankōsha, 1982), p. 343. The term *ōbukucha* is a corruption of *obukucha*.

16. Kuroita Katsumi, ed., *Shintei Zōho Kokushi Taikei*, vol. 29, pt. 2 *(Honchō Monzui, Honchō Zoku Monzui)* (Tokyo: Yoshikawa Kōbunkan, 1965), p. 242.

17. *Isei Teikin Ōrai*, in Sen Sōshitsu, ed., *Chadō Koten Zenshū*, vol. 2 (Kyoto: Tankōsha, 1958), pp. 200–203.

18. The *Nijō-Kawara Rakusho* or "Scribblings at the Intersection of Nijō and Kawara" are contained in the *Kemmu Nenkan Ki* in Hanawa Hokiichi, ed., *Gunsho Ruijū*, vol. 25 (Tokyo: Zoku Gunsho Ruijū Kansei Kai, 1960), pp. 503–504. See also the translation of the *Rakusho* in David Lu, ed., *Sources of Japanese History*, vol. 1 (New York: McGraw-Hill, 1974), pp. 149–150.

19. *Gekokujō* ("those below overthrow those above") was a term used to describe social upheaval during the medieval age.

20. The *kaisho* evolved about the early fifteenth century as a room where people met and socialized. Later in the century we see the emergence of the major elements of *shoin*-style interior construction and decoration: *tatami* floor matting, *shōji* sliding doors, the *tokonoma* (alcove), the *shoin* installed desk, and *chigaidana* (asymmetrical shelves).

21. Sōtōshū Zensho Kankō Kai, ed., *Sōtōshū, Shingi* (Tokyo: Sōtōshū Shūmu Chō, Sōtōshū Zensho Kankō Kai, 1931), pp. 1–63.

22. Dōgen, comp., *Eihei Shingi*, in Takakusu Junjirō, ed., *Taishō Shinshū Daizōkyō*, vol. 82, *Zoku shoshū bu* 13 (Tokyo: Taishō Shinshū Daizōkyō Kankō Kai, 1965), pp. 319–342.

23. Ch'ing-cho Cheng-ch'eng, comp., *Ta-chien ch'ing-kuei (Daikan Shingi)*, ibid., vol. 81, *Zoku shoshū bu* 12, pp. 619–623.

24. Gotō Tanji et al., *Taiheiki*, vol. 3 in *Nihon Koten Bungaku Taikei*, vol. 36 (Tokyo: Iwanami Shoten, 1962), pp. 443–444.

25. *Kissa Ōrai*, in Hanawa Hokiichi, ed., *Gunsho Ruijū*, vol. 19, p. 860.

26. Yabe Ryōsaku, ed., *Chadō*, vol. 8 (Tokyo: Sōgensha, 1936), pp. 697–709.

27. *Kanazawa Bunko Komonjo* (Yokohama: Kanazawa Bunko, 1952), no. 279, p. 85; no. 329, p. 99.

28. Donald Keene, trans., *Essays in Idleness* (New York: Columbia University Press, 1967), p. 101.

29. *Kissa Ōrai*, in Hanawa Hokiichi, ed., *Gunsho Ruijū*, vol. 19, p. 859.

30. *Kundaikan Sōchō Ki* can be found in Hanawa Hokiichi, ed., *Gunsho Ruijū*, vol. 19.

31. Ōta Tōshirō, ed., *Kanmon Gyoki*, vol. 1 (Tokyo: Zoku Gunsho Ruijū Kansei Kai, 1958), pp. 6–9.

32. *Keikaku Shiyō Shō*, in Hayashiya Tatsusaburō, *Zusetsu Chadō Shi*, p. 203.

33. *Shōtetsu Monogatari*, in Hisamatsu Shin'ichi and Nishio Minoru, eds., *Karon-shū Nōgaku-shū*, in *Nihon Koten Bungaku Taikei*, vol. 65 (Tokyo: Iwanami Shoten, 1961), p. 230.

34. *Shinkei Sōzu Teikin* can be found in *Zoku Gunsho Ruijū*, vol. 17, pt. 2 (Tokyo: Zoku Gunsho Ruijū Kansei Kai, 1924).

35. Kitakawa Tadahiko, ed., *Zenpō Zatsudan*, in Hayashiya Tatsusaburō, ed., *Kodai Chūsei Geijutsu Ron* (Tokyo: Iwanami Shoten, 1983), p. 480.

36. Ibid., p. 494.

37. Akai Tatsurō, ed., *Tōhaku Gasetsu*, in Hayashiya Tatsusaburō, ed., *Kodai Chūsei Geijutsu Ron*, p. 707.

38. Kyōto-fu Bunkazai Hogoka, *Kokuhō Jishōin Tōgudō Shūri Kōji Hōkoku Sho* (Kyoto: Kyōto-fu Bunkazai Hogoka, 1965).

39. Sanjōnishi Sanetaka, *Sanetaka-kō Ki*, vol. 4, pt. 1 (Tokyo: Zoku Gunsho Ruijū Kansei Kai, 1935), pp. 23–24.

40. Toyohara Sumiaki, *Shōkashō*, in Wakashi Kenkyū Kai, ed., *Shikashū Taisei*, vol. 6, *chūsei* 4 (Tokyo: Meiji Shoin, 1976), p. 691.

41. João Rodrigues, *Nihon Kyōkai Shi*, in *Daikōkai Jidai Sōsho*, vol. 1 (Tokyo: Iwanami Shoten, 1967), p. 608.

42. The Higashiyama epoch may be regarded as the second half of the fifteenth century (the age of Yoshimasa), or, more narrowly, the time span from the end of the Ōnin War in 1477 until Yoshimasa's death in 1490. The Kitayama epoch was the age of Yoshimitsu: roughly the last quarter of the fourteenth century and the first decade of the fifteenth.

43. *Matsuya Kaiki* can be found in vol. 9 of *Chadō Koten Zenshū*, *Tennōjiya Kaiki* in vol. 7, and *Imai Sōkyū Chanoyu Nikki Kakinuki* in vol. 10.

44. Yamanoue Sōji, *Yamanoue Sōji Ki*, in Sen Sōshitsu, ed., *Chadō Koten Zenshū*, vol. 6 (Kyoto: Tankōsha, 1958), p. 93.

45. Ibid.

TWO

SEN NO RIKYŪ:
INQUIRIES INTO HIS LIFE AND TEA

Kumakura Isao
Translated by Paul Varley

SEN no Rikyū was born in the city of Sakai, Izumi province, in 1522 and as a child had the name of Yoshirō. The earliest reference in the records to this young Rikyū appears in 1535 in an account called *Nembutsu Sachō Nikki* and reads: Imaichi Town; Master Yoshirō, Sen.[1] Rikyū was then fourteen, and his family, the Sen, which established its residence in the town of Imaichi in Sakai, were middle-level merchants dealing in fish.

Sakai in those days was a city of tremendous wealth that refused to submit to the control of any *sengoku daimyō* (Provincial Wars daimyo). Much like the free cities of Europe, it was autonomously governed by a coalition of merchant families. The bulk of Sakai's economic wealth derived from the flow of goods from overseas, but it was also supported by the manufacture of muskets and other weapons essential to the Provincial Wars daimyos. Sakai's prominent merchant coalition, the *egōshū*, made use of its wealth to produce an opulent culture. Surrounding themselves with luxuries from abroad, the rich merchants of Sakai invited linked verse masters, painters, priests, and various entertainers from all over the country to visit them, enabling Sakai to surpass even Kyoto as a cultural center.

Chanoyu, an excellent pastime for bringing people together, became especially popular among the townsmen of Sakai, and the round of social gatherings held during the year by the Sakai townsmen was no doubt greatly enhanced by participation in it. Within *chanoyu*, moreover, was a world of beauty based on appreciation of the country's *meibutsu*, or famous works of art and craft. These *meibutsu*, as symbols of wealth, apparently helped satisfy the insatiable craving of Sakai's merchants for the power obtainable through money. As a newly emerging art, *chanoyu* was ideally suited to the newly emerged city of Sakai. Among the Sakai townsmen who rose as noted tea men, the most representative were Takeno Jōō and his disciple, Sen no Rikyū.

THE LIFE OF RIKYŪ

Sen no Rikyū was probably in his early twenties when he took the Buddhist name of Sōeki and first distinguished himself as a man of tea. While studying under the master Jōō, he often surprised his mentor with his original methods in the way of tea. Thus we find written in a certain work on tea: "Although Sōeki is reasonably well off, he does not have sufficient wealth to obtain even one *meibutsu*. He favors a piece known as Shiribukura, and selects for his use simple but fine utensils. With no desire for ostentation, he cuts his own bamboo and achieves a deeply *wabi* effect. For this reason, Sōeki is much appreciated by Jōō."[2] Rikyū's wealth was evidently far inferior to such other famous tea men as Tsuda Sōgyū of the Tennōjiya. But Rikyū had new methods for handling utensils and a discerningly artistic eye, and by the time he reached manhood he had established himself as a practitioner of tea.

Chanoyu was also a symbol of new wealth and culture for the warlords of the Provincial Wars period who aspired to go up to the capital and unify the country. These daimyos vied with one another to invite tea practitioners and hold tea gatherings. We find, for example, the master of Tamonzan Castle in Nara, Matsunaga Hisahide, summoning Rikyū to such a gathering on the twenty-ninth day of the first month of 1565.[3] Water was brought for the occasion from the area of Uji Bridge, famous for its waters, and the tea was of the highest quality from the noted Mori fields of Uji. Hisahide even displayed his prized caddy, the *meibutsu* known as Tsukumonasu, at the gathering. Rikyū was forty-four at the time.

Three years after the Tamonzan affair a new unifier emerged: Oda Nobunaga. With his forceful nature, Nobunaga tried to transform *chanoyu* into his own possession. Confiscating Tsukumonasu from Matsunaga Hisahide and taking possession of the caddy Hatsuhana, a Higashiyama period treasure, Nobunaga forced the city of Sakai to surrender a number of *meibutsu* pieces to him in what became known as the *meibutsu* hunt (*meibutsu-gari*). The pieces thus acquired were *meibutsu* of the realm worthy of Nobunaga as lord of the realm. It was only natural that Nobunaga should also seek out masters of tea who were befitting of such *meibutsu*. Under him there emerged three great tea masters: Sen Sōeki (Rikyū), Imai Sōkyū, and Tsuda Sōgyū, all of whom were merchants of Sakai.

In a letter from Nobunaga addressed to Rikyū, there is this note of thanks for a thousand musket balls:

> As I was leaving for Echizen, a thousand musket balls arrived. I was most pleased to receive this gift from afar. I will have Harada, the Governor of Bitchū, convey my thanks.

> To Hōsensai [Rikyū]
> 1575:9:16
> Sincerely, Nobunaga[4]

From this note we learn that Rikyū served Nobunaga not only as a master of tea, but also in his role as a Sakai merchant. This role, however, was slight compared with that of Imai Sōkyū and Tsuda Sōgyū. Rikyū was more truly a practitioner of his art who rendered service by means of the way of tea.

When Nobunaga was assassinated in 1582, Toyotomi Hideyoshi emerged as his successor. Politically, Hideyoshi continued the course set by Nobunaga. At the same time, with respect to *chanoyu*, he took possession of Nobunaga's cherished tea pieces and retained Rikyū as a master. Rikyū was already sixty-one and, having reached this landmark age, was thought by the standards of his day to be a fairly old man. But during the next ten years, until 1591, he ignited explosions in every aspect of *chanoyu*. This is an astounding fact. And as Rikyū's tea became ever more individualistic and moved beyond the reach of others, it also became isolated and, when viewed from the outside, even appeared heretical. Yet it was during the last decade of his life that Rikyū brought his way of tea to perfection.

On 1585:10:7 tea was served to Emperor Ōgimachi in the imperial palace.[5] Never before had tea been formally presented to an emperor. But, because of Hideyoshi's extreme infatuation with *chanoyu*, arrangements were finally made to hold a gathering for that purpose. No doubt Hideyoshi wished to demonstrate a more intimate coming together of the chrysanthemum (the court) and the paulownia (his own house) at a time when he was launched on the road toward national unification. Presumably he also wanted to use the palace tea gathering as a means, first, to give thanks for his accession to the office of regent (kampaku) and, second, to bring about the anticipated conferral upon him of the post of great minister of state (dajō daijin) and the surname of Toyotomi.

We learn that Hideyoshi arrived at the palace at ten in the morning on the seventh day of the tenth month. The emperor, after receiving Hideyoshi in audience, went to the Kogosho, where the hegemon prepared tea and served it to him. Nearly all the utensils used by Hideyoshi were new, and the chrysanthemum crest was engraved on his natsume caddy and his kettle.[6] The only meibutsu he had were the Nitari no Nasu caddy, a hanging scroll, and a tea storage jar. After Hideyoshi, Rikyū prepared tea at a seat in the corner and served it to the courtiers who were present. Rikyū's place was equipped entirely with meibutsu.

The palace gathering was a great public occasion for Rikyū as Hideyoshi's tea master, and thanks to it his position was firmly established as the foremost practitioner of tea in the country. Rikyū, however, did not have court rank and office; and it was necessary, in order to be admitted into the palace, either to have such high rank and office or, alternatively, to assume the status of a priest who transcended lay distinctions. Thus Rikyū took the priestly designation of koji (Buddhist layman). He was given the Buddhist name of Rikyū and was formally designated Rikyū Koji.

There have long been two theories about the name Rikyū. Was it created at the time of the palace tea gathering for Emperor Ōgimachi, or had Rikyū held this name from an earlier period?[7] I subscribe to the second theory and believe that the name was selected for Rikyū in his youth, perhaps by Dairin Sōtō. It is my opinion that when Dairin bestowed the name upon Rikyū he intended it merely as a gashō (elegant appellation). But because the occasion of the palace tea gathering called for a koji name, the gashō of Rikyū was taken to serve that purpose. Pursuing this line of speculation further, I would suggest that when the emperor issued his decree about the koji name it was Kokei Sōchin and Shun'oku Sōen who urged that "Rikyū" be used. I say this because even before the palace tea gathering Kokei wrote a letter to Rikyū congratulating him upon his receipt of the koji name and because Rikyū himself wrote a record of the gathering and sent it to both Kokei and Shun'oku.[8]

Let us now inquire into the meaning of the designation Rikyū. A number of Zen priests have expressed their opinions on this matter. Typical of these are the "Verse on the Name Rikyū" composed by Sengaku Sōtō at the request of Rikyū's adopted son Shōan and Shun'oku Sōen's verse on the subject in his collection *Ichimoku Kō*.[9] In the opinion of Haga Kōshirō, the words "ancient awl" in Shun'oku's verse most fully convey the true meaning of the Rikyū designation.[10] In the manner of an awl that is worn out, dull, and useless, one reaches a point where one's sharpness (*ri*) is lost. Then there is an awakening (*satori*) and one enters a state of no-mind, a state which in Zen terms can be referred to as a great idiocy of the most common variety. This is the essential meaning of "Rikyū."

Having served as tea master at the palace gathering, Rikyū became in fact as well as in name the leading tea practitioner in the land. He was not, however, simply first in the land as a tea man but also held power behind the scenes as Hideyoshi's confidant. Ōtomo Sōrin, who in the fourth month of 1586, the year after the palace gathering, came from Kyushu to Osaka Castle seeking an audience with Hideyoshi, wrote about this fact to his chief retainer (*karō*) immediately upon learning about relations among the people around Hideyoshi, relations he could never have imagined back in his native place of Kyushu. When Sōrin called upon Hideyoshi's younger brother, Hidenaga, he was sumptuously entertained in the temporary dwelling Hidenaga was occupying while his regular residence was under repair. And as Sōrin was about to depart, Hidenaga purposely took his hand and said before many people: "Since I am here, you have nothing to worry about. Rikyū will take care of all personal matters and I will handle the official business. Hence there should be no problems."[11] Sōrin was exceedingly moved—not only by the actions of Hidenaga, in whom Hideyoshi placed great trust, but also by his words to the effect that, since he was on hand, there was no need to worry.

But the words we should particularly note are those indicating that Rikyū would handle personal matters and Hidenaga would take care of all the official business. Continuing the story to his chief retainer, Sōrin wrote: "I was next met by Rikyū Koji, and entertained in a way I have difficulty describing in words. It was something I am never likely to forget. As I observe things here, I realize that no one can say a word to the lord Kampaku (Hideyoshi) without first going through Rikyū. . . . It is clear that now and henceforth I must take care not to alienate Hidenaga or Rikyū, but must devote myself to cultivating their friendship." Thus Sōrin recorded with astonishment how Rikyū went to great trouble to entertain him, how one could say nothing to Hideyoshi without going through Rikyū, and how unreservedly intimate Hidenaga was toward Rikyū. This intimacy of Hidenaga and Rikyū and the tea master's position of power signify that the time, about the years 1585 and 1586, was the honeymoon period in the Hideyoshi-Rikyū relationship.

In the ninth month of 1587 the Jurakudai residence in Kyoto, which Hideyoshi had ardently desired, was completed. Soon the people close to him were building residences nearby. Rikyū, for example, constructed a house in front of Motoseiganji Temple in Ashiya-chō. In this house were a hall (*hiroma*), a long five-mat room, a colored nine-*ma shoin*, a four-and-a-half mat room, and a two-mat tea room. It is said that the Zangetsutei at the present Omotesenke preserves the form of the original *shoin* room of Rikyū's Jurakudai home. Apparently the hall and the *shoin* were constructed in preparation for a formal visit by Hideyoshi.[12]

Although Rikyū's *shoin* possessed the essential characteristics of the *shoin* style of room, it also revealed a sense of *wabi* originality in its layout. It was constructed, for example, of plain wood, and the ceiling over the raised portion of the floor was lowered to five *shaku* seven *sun* in order to convey an intimate *wabi* feeling. The room was constructed in the formal (*shin*) style of *wabicha*.

The year the Jurakudai was completed, 1587, was also a time when Rikyū's world began to change rapidly. This was the result of a major shift in Hideyoshi's attention to Korea and from there to the continent proper. So long as Hideyoshi had his main bases of operation in Kyoto and Osaka and so long as the Shimazu of Kyushu showed no sign of submitting to him and the Hōjō family remained ensconced, as before, in the Kantō, the importance of Sakai as a center of the countrywide circulation of goods was great indeed. Even Hideyoshi was of necessity obliged to recognize the power of the Sakai merchant group, including Rikyū. But a change occurred that at a stroke brought about the collapse of Sakai's position, which was based on a particular set of power relations. The occasion of the change was Hideyoshi's campaign to subjugate Kyushu.

Hideyoshi attacked the Shimazu on the seventh day of the fifth month of 1587. Upon forcing them to capitulate, he returned on the third day of the sixth month to Chikuzen province, where he established his headquarters at Hakozaki Shrine. Summoning the merchants of Hakata, Hideyoshi passed about a month at Hakozaki absorbed in the pursuit of *chanoyu*. We learn from *Sōtan Nikki* that Rikyū held a tea gathering at the Tōrōdō of the shrine, inviting to the affair Kamiya Sōtan, Shimai Sōshitsu, and Shibata Sōjin. Here is a description of the setting and contents of the tea room Rikyū used: "three thick *tatami* mats; a thatched roof; green thatched walls; a new *ubaguchi* kettle; and a metal brazier."[13] We are told that Rikyū served tea directly on the mats without using a small board *(koita)*. The tea room was very likely one hastily erected near the Tōrōdō. In any case, its walls of green thatching appear to have given it a cool feeling. Placement of the brazier for the preparation of tea directly on the mats was a rustic touch.

While based with his army at Hakozaki, Hideyoshi summoned Sōtan, a representative of the merchant group of Hakata, twice for tea. He treated this guest with great cordiality, even pushing open the sliding door for him and personally calling him to his seat. With Kyushu under his wing, Hideyoshi was no doubt conjuring up plans to extend his conquest to Korea. In any such plans Hakata would hold a key position. Therein lay the reason for the cordial treatment extended to Sōtan and the other Hakata merchants. An invasion of Korea would, on the other hand, inevitably lead to a decline in the position of the Sakai merchants, especially Rikyū, whose intimacy with Hideyoshi was premised on Sakai merchant power.

After returning from his Kyushu campaign, Hideyoshi ordered the staging of a tea gathering on an unprecedented scale and announced that it would be held in the forest at Kitano in Kyoto for a ten-day period beginning on the first day of the tenth month. The notice read as follows:

Proclamation

Item: It is ordered that, weather permitting, a tea gathering will be held in the forest at Kitano for a period of ten days beginning on the first day of the tenth month. All of the Kampaku's *meibutsu*, without exception, will be placed on display. This event is being held so that devotees of *chanoyu* can view the collection.

Item: Devotees, whether they are military attendants, townspeople, farmers, or others, should come, and each should bring a kettle, a water bucket, a drinking bowl, and either tea or *kogashi*.

Item: Since the seating will be in a pine field, two mats should suffice for each person. *Wabi* persons, however, may use either mat covers or coarse straw bags.

Item: In order to allow people from distant places to see the *meibutsu* collection, the event will be extended from the first until the tenth of the tenth month.

Item: In regard to what has just been said, the Kampaku has made these arrangements for the benefit of *wabi* persons. Accordingly, those who do not attend will henceforth be prohibited from preparing even *kogashi*. This prohibition will extend also to persons who visit those who do not attend.

In addition: Lord Kampaku has declared that he will personally prepare tea for all persons who attend, not only those from distant places.[14]

Thus all of Hideyoshi's *meibutsu* were to be placed on display for viewing by devotees of *chanoyu*. Moreover, these devotees, whether military attendants, townspeople, farmers, or others, were invited to attend and were obliged to bring with them only a few things for their personal use. It was fitting that no social distinctions were to be drawn, since Hideyoshi himself had risen to power on the crest of the *gekokujō* upheavals of the age.[15] The grand scale on which the affair was intended to be held can be clearly observed in the following words, which were also contained in the proclamation: "Not only Japanese, but all connoisseurs of *chanoyu*, even Chinese, should attend." Yet we must not forget that the proclamation also reflected Hideyoshi's despotic side in the pronouncement that "those who do not attend will henceforth be prohibited from preparing even *kogashi*." This meant that if one attended it would be all right, but if one did not attend one would not be permitted to perform anything resembling *chanoyu*, even if one used only crude tea.

Rikyū was kept busy. After he returned from Kyushu and moved to his Jurakudai residence, there were preparations to be made for the great tea gathering at Kitano. In the ninth month the decision was made to have courtiers attend the gathering, and it became necessary to construct on short notice more than eight hundred tea stalls for them within the Kitano grounds. Rikyū also wrote a letter to the tea men of Sakai, saying that since "the Sakai group will be gathered together in one place in the pine grove at Kitano,"[16] the tea men should bring all their prized kettles, water buckets, and caddies.

On the day of the gathering, tea was served in four groups chosen by lot. Those who drew lots for the first group drank tea at Hideyoshi's place. Rikyū, Tsuda Sōgyū, and Imai Sōkyū were responsible respectively for the second, third, and fourth groups. In one day, more than eight hundred people received tea. Rikyū's utensils included a picture of wild geese by Yü Chien, the caddies Shiribukura and Narashiba, the Semehimo kettle, and the Sutego jar. During the afternoon, Hideyoshi walked around visiting the tea stalls that were set up here and there. According to the record of Kubo Risei, who came from Nara, a *wabi* person named Ikka was highly praised when, burning pine needles, he served *kogashi* to Hideyoshi.[17] Although the great tea gathering was scheduled to last for ten days, it came to an end after only one.

THE DEATH OF RIKYŪ

Among Rikyū's disciples was a man named Yamanoue Sōji. About twenty years younger than Rikyū, Sōji was the possessor of a free and unconventional spirit much like that of Sakai during the Provincial Wars period. Upon Rikyū's recommendation, he was engaged as a tea master by Hideyoshi. But Sōji's sharp tongue incurred the wrath of the hegemon, and he was banished and reduced to a life of wandering. Eventually he was taken in by the Hōjō of Odawara. Inasmuch as the Hōjō were the only family that still opposed Hideyoshi's hegemony and remained outside his sphere of control, it is fitting that they should harbor someone banished by him. But Hideyoshi had no intention of overlooking the Hōjō or the power of the Kantō and Tōhoku regions which, with the Hōjō as a shield, opposed his will. In 1590 he rose up to attack the Hōjō and thereby complete the overall job of national unification. Pouring into Odawara like a raging wave, Hideyoshi's army surrounded the Hōjō castle and commenced a war of attrition that was a Hideyoshi specialty.

The army's encampment became a place of leisure to which such people as artists, tea men, and even courtesans were brought from Kyoto. And on a certain day Yamanoue Sōji, who had secretly escaped from Odawara Castle, was led to Hideyoshi. At first the hegemon, no doubt encouraged by Rikyū, permitted Sōji's return to his service. But the return did not end happily, for once again Sōji spewed words that incited Hideyoshi's great wrath and, after having his ears and nose cut off, Sōji was executed at Odawara. Sōji's character was assessed this way in *Chōandō Ki*: "In Sakai, as a person skillful in *chanoyu* and well versed, he was someone who could not be ignored; but he had a bad manner and was evil-tongued, and thus was disliked by others."[18]

Yamanoue Sōji revered Rikyū as his teacher. But Sōji's frank manner of expressing himself has also left us with an accurate and objective view of Rikyū's tea. In his book *Yamanoue Sōji Ki*, Sōji remarked: "Sōeki's tea is like a deciduous tree in early winter. It is not for the ordinary person."[19] And in regard to Rikyū's having been the first to construct a tea room of the virtually minimum size of one-and-a-half mats, Sōji wrote: "Although unusual for the time, it was useless for the ordinary person. It is interesting that Sōeki, as a *meijin* (master), freely transformed mountains into valleys, changed west to east, and broke the rules of *chanoyu*. But if the ordinary person were simply to imitate him, there would be no *chanoyu*."[20] This is a candid assessment of Rikyū by a contemporary that would not exist except for Sōji, who was firm in his ways and opinions to the point of eccentricity.

To elaborate on Sōji's view, we see that Rikyū's tea was sharply different and not popular in society as a whole. Surely his conduct—freely breaking the rules of society and shaking the very foundation of the aesthetic order—was too much in the spirit of the Provincial Wars age of *gekokujō*. An emotional gulf seems gradually to have grown between Hideyoshi, who was at the apex of the order of the day, and Rikyū, who would not acknowledge authority. The Odawara campaign came at the point when the gulf between the two men was nearly unbridgeable. And after Hideyoshi's victory at Odawara—that is, his attainment of unification of the country—the antagonism between him and Rikyū led to catastrophe.

The suicide of Sen no Rikyū by disembowelment was one of the central events in the history of the way of tea in Japan. Yet its cause remains ever a mystery. Various theories have been advanced, but of

course there was no single cause. There simply came a point, after a
number of developments that constituted "causes," when it suddenly
became Rikyū's fate to commit suicide. What sort of developments
were these? Let us look first at the political setting. It is clear, on the
basis of the document by Ōtomo Sōrin cited above, that Rikyū was a
trusted confidant to Hideyoshi and held considerable behind-the-
scenes power. Yet one after another problems arose that threatened
Rikyū's political position. One was the emergence, after the end of the
Kyushu campaign in 1587 and Hideyoshi's completion of national
unification, of the invasion of Korea as a new item on the political
agenda of the Hideyoshi administration.

The promoters of this invasion plan are said to have been the group
of direct vassals, headed by Ishida Mitsunari, who were in Hideyoshi's
personal service. As a result of Mitsunari and his group's having made
Korea the next objective after unification, Hakata in northern
Kyushu was suddenly brought into the limelight as a strategic base.
Conversely, the status of Sakai, which had until then been the principal city for the production of military weapons, was abruptly reduced.

Within the Hideyoshi administration, Rikyū stood at a distance
from Ishida Mitsunari, Maeda Gen'i, and their allies and instead was
on close terms with Maeda Toshiie, Tokugawa Ieyasu, and other military leaders. This was evidently a fact well known to everyone.
Indeed, there was even a rumor after Rikyū's suicide that his wife and
daughter were subjected by Maeda Gen'i to an ordeal of snakes.[21]

So long as Hideyoshi's younger brother Hidenaga was alive, the
opposition under Hideyoshi between Mitsunari and the personal service group on the one hand and Tokugawa Ieyasu and the great
daimyo group on the other actually afforded a measure of stability for
the administration. But no sooner did Hidenaga die in the first
month of 1591 than the situation changed. The opposition was
brought into the open and, as the two groups clashed, Rikyū was
offered up as a blood sacrifice. We can interpret the burying of Rikyū,
who had lost Hidenaga's protection, by Mitsunari and his group as a
rejection of Maeda and Tokugawa influence in the Hideyoshi administration.[22]

No doubt the immediate reason for Rikyū's suicide was the wooden
statue of him shod in straw sandals that was placed atop the gate of
Daitokuji Temple. But there were also rumors at the time that it was
because Rikyū had lined his pockets or because his daughter had

refused to enter Hideyoshi's harem. Judging from the *Sen no Rikyū Denki* in the *Gongen Sama Go-Nenpu,* which was written by Rikyū's great-grandson Kōshin Sōsa in response to questioning by the Tokugawa Bakufu, the Bakufu officials were aware of these rumors and asked: "There is a story that Rikyū's suicide was because of his daughter. Is this true?" Sōsa denied the fact, replying: "Although it is popularly believed that this was the case, I know nothing of it."[23] If the rumor were true, the daughter would have been the widow of Bandaiya Sōjo. But Sōsa told the Bakufu officials: "Although it concerns my family, nothing has been passed down to me about it." In fact, in this account Sōsa gave the incident of the Daitokuji gate as the cause of the suicide.

Let us assume, then, that the Daitokuji gate incident was indeed the main cause of Rikyū's suicide. What motive did Rikyū have in undertaking construction work on the gate? As is well known, the Daitokuji gate was rebuilt by the linked verse master Sōchō, but this was only a one-story structure. Rikyū decided to add the splendid second-story tower that we see at Daitokuji today. He did so to celebrate the fiftieth anniversary of the death of his father, Itchū Ryōsen (Yohyōe), whom he had lost at age nineteen.

For the young Rikyū, who had lost both his father and grandfather, succeeding to the Sen family business could hardly have been pleasant. There was a rumor, found in the *Tennōjiya Kaiki,* that Rikyū fell into difficult straits.[24] Since the date of the rumor was 1568, when he was forty-seven, it could not have been related directly to the deaths of his father and grandfather. Nevertheless, for Rikyū, the family fortunes were not flourishing and he was in low circumstances. There remains a verse by him in the possession of the Fushin'an called the "Ryokutai calligraphy," which was done on the occasion of the seventh anniversary of the death of his grandfather, Dōetsu. In this verse Rikyū says he thought of holding a memorial service for his grandfather but, because he had "no money," could do nothing but shed tears before Dōetsu's grave.[25] It is not clear how old Rikyū was at the time of the seventh anniversary of his grandfather's death, but the event may have coincided with the period when he was in financial distress. In any case, Rikyū obviously regretted not having the money to hold a proper memorial service.

When the fiftieth anniversary of his father's death arrived in 1589, however, Rikyū was at the height of his prosperity as Hideyoshi's tea master. It was an especially fine opportunity to use his considerable influence to undertake construction on the Daitokuji gate—both as a memorial to his father and as a means of repaying his indebtedness to the Zen teacher Kokei Sōchin. Rikyū made up his mind. While waiting for the year 1589 to arrive, he made arrangements with the Jukōin for a permanent family memorial;[26] then, with the coming of spring, he rushed into construction on the gate. In the seventh month Kokei Sōchin, who had been exiled after arousing Hideyoshi's anger, returned to Kyoto, and Rikyū was able to call upon him to serve as head priest for the memorial service. It was then necessary only to await completion of the gate. But when fall came, it appeared that the work was not progressing as Rikyū had hoped. The fiftieth memorial service had been set for the eighth day of the twelfth month, the anniversary of his father's death. If construction could not be completed by the early part of the twelfth month, Rikyū's plans would be spoiled. Hence Rikyū became impatient and, in a letter he wrote to Arima Chūmu dated the twenty-second day of the eleventh month, called upon Arima to send "help for the stone wall of the gate" in the form of twenty laborers with ten spades and hoes.[27] Evidently, with just a few days remaining before the originally scheduled completion of the construction, Rikyū boldly—and in an act that overstepped his authority—sought to requisition labor from a daimyo.

At last the gate was completed. A Buddhist mass was held on the fifth day of the twelfth month, with Shun'oku Sōen officiating, to celebrate the completion. Three days later, on the eighth, the long-awaited fiftieth memorial service for Itchū Ryōsen was grandly carried out by Kokei Sōchin at the gleaming vermilion-colored Kinmōkaku at Daitokuji. This was the service that Rikyū had long hoped to hold for his father, and the construction work on the gate was his offering for the service.

It is not clear whether the erection of a wooden statue of Rikyū atop the gate as an expression of appreciation for his work was the wish of Rikyū himself or the idea of Daitokuji. Perhaps there were other cases of decorating a gate, at the time of its construction, with a wooden statue of a contributor to or administrator of the project. This may have been the case, for example, some years later when the gate at Nanzenji was adorned with a statue of Gomi Kin'uemon, who administered its building.[28] But who could have imagined that the statue of Rikyū would lead to his death?

There was an intercalary first month in 1591, and it appears that the wooden statue of Rikyū on the Daitokuji gate somehow managed to become an issue during that time. In the preceding month, as noted, Hidenaga, Hideyoshi's younger brother by a different father, died. With Hidenaga gone, there were few people in Hideyoshi's circle who could defend Rikyū; and by the time the succeeding second month arrived, Rikyū's position had rapidly changed for the worse. Ordered into house confinement on the thirteenth, he went down to Sakai. The famous incident in which Hosokawa Sansai and Furuta Oribe saw Rikyū off at the bank of the Yodo River occurred on this occasion of his departure for Sakai.[29]

After more than ten days in Sakai, Rikyū was summoned back to Kyoto on the twenty-sixth (or perhaps the twenty-fifth). It was clear that he had already been officially condemned to death. Rikyū's Jura-kudai residence was surrounded by three thousand soldiers, who guarded it so closely that not even a mouse could get in or out. This was presumably done because of rumors that certain people might try to save the popular Rikyū.

On the twenty-eighth day of the second month Kyoto was struck with a violent thunderstorm accompanied by hail. In the journal of the family of Shinto priests at the Shōbaiin in Kitano, the size of the hailstones that fell that day was recorded in thick black ink. If we are to believe this record, the stones reached a diameter of no less than one and a half centimeters.[30] The sky itself seemed to be plunged into agitation in anticipation of a momentous event.

Rikyū, who had already received word of the sentence of disembowelment (*seppuku*) from a soldier who was his disciple, was prepared for death and awaiting the arrival of the official assigned to serve as witness. After he and the official drank tea together, Rikyū adeptly committed suicide.

The story of Rikyū's suicide is well known, and there is little I could add to existing theories by discussing the details here. Surprisingly, however, scant attention has been given to the particular form of the suicide: *seppuku*. There is special significance to the fact that Rikyū came to a violent, untimely end by disembowelment. And the suicide itself has exerted an important influence upon the later course of *cha-noyu* by giving rise to the deification of Rikyū, a subject that Paul Varley discusses in Chapter 6. Let us examine here some of the attitudes and sentiments of the premodern Japanese that shaped the way in which Rikyū was transformed after his death into a veritable god of *chanoyu*.

One of the questions most frequently asked by foreigners is: Why do the Japanese commit suicide by disembowelment? This unique method of self-destruction is surely the expression of a basic way of thinking. According to Chiba Tokuji's *Seppuku no Hanashi*, the most frequently consulted book on *seppuku*,[31] the Japanese believe that the source of life lies in the stomach. Indeed, they have evolved a number of phrases indicating the great importance they attach to this part of the body. Here are a few examples:

> *hara ga dekita hito* (literally, people who have acquired stomachs)—broad-minded people
>
> *hara no suwatta hito* (literally, stomach-seated people)—people who are respected
>
> *haraguroi hito* (literally, black-stomached people)—evil people

Moreover, to talk to another person with a sincere heart is to "open one's stomach and speak" *(hara o watte hanasu)*. This means that when one is misunderstood by another person and cannot convey one's sincere feelings to him, it becomes necessary to make known with one's very body the "purity of that body's stomach." Thus one "opens the stomach and shows it." The feeling of mortification implied in this phrase gave rise to suicide by *seppuku*. Later, when *seppuku* was formalized as the *bushi*'s way of death, to cut open the stomach was called *munenbara* (suicide in mortification) and became, in fact, an act of defiance. But originally *seppuku* was simply an expression of mortification and symbolic of an untimely death.

What happened to the spirits of those who suffered such untimely deaths? In Japanese history the person best known for having come to an untimely end—although he did not commit suicide—was Sugawara no Michizane. When faced with death, Rikyū thought of Michizane. We are told, for example, that on the thirteenth day of the second month, as he departed from Kyoto for Sakai, he wrote this note and gave it to his daughter Kame: "I, Rikyū, am indeed a person of fortune. To think that I will become one with Sugawara no Michizane!"[32] The original text of this writing no longer exists, and in Rikyū's death poem, which has been preserved at the Dairyūji Temple in Wakayama, the phrasing is slightly different.[33] I believe that the death poem was written on the twenty-fifth of the second month—the so-called day of Tenjin-san (Michizane). What Rikyū sought to convey in his death poem was something like this. Although people felt sorry for him, he was grateful to think that, by suffering the same fate as Michizane (who, having been slandered, died in a remote place), he would become a god. This was not Rikyū's formal death poem, of course, but a verse intended as a kind of joke. Presumably Rikyū did not expect to become a "god" like Michizane, but the fact remains that he compared himself to the great Heian period writer and states-man. And when the public heard of Rikyū's death, there must have been more than a few who recalled the story of Michizane.

The foregoing entry in the journal of the Shōbaiin about violent thunder on the day of Rikyū's *seppuku* also calls to mind the account of Michizane's vengeful spirit, which became a thunderbolt and struck the imperial palace. Let us inquire, then, into the concept of vengeful spirits.[34] The Japanese believe that the spirits of those who suffer untimely deaths inflict various ills upon people. When an epidemic rages or a natural disaster occurs, it is attributed to the work of someone's vengeful spirit—whereupon the spirit is designated an "honored spirit," prayers are said for it, and a festival (*matsuri*) is held to console it. The Kitano Shrine, for example, was built to revere Su-gawara no Michizane, and we can observe other cases, apart from Michizane's, of festivals held to give consolation to honored spirits. The Gion festival of Kyoto evolved from just such a celebration. If a vengeful spirit is pleased with acts of devotion, he will bestow his favor upon people and serve them as a powerful deity. (An example of faith in honored spirits in modern times can be observed at the Yasu-kuni Shrine, where not vengeful spirits but those of men who died in battle have been resurrected as gods of war.)

Rikyū was well qualified to be both a vengeful and an honored spirit. In 1599, nearly ten years after his death, Furuta Oribe and oth-ers held a flower-viewing party at Yoshino and erected a portable tea-house with a plaque inscribed "The Departed Soul of Rikyū."[35] People must have been struck with a sense of awe by these words, as though Rikyū's spirit had somehow been called forth by the miraculous power of the flowers.

But the true resurrection of Rikyū as an honored spirit and the guardian deity of the way of tea was achieved in the *Nampōroku*, whose existence was made known to the world at the time of the hundredth anniversary of Rikyū's death. In the final section of *Nampōroku* it states that if, following the death of Rikyū, someone should appear—even after a hundred years—who could truly succeed to his *wabicha*, Rikyū's bones would be blessed and he would be reborn: His departed spirit would rejoice and he would surely become "the guardian deity of the way of tea."[36] I am convinced that it is the shocking manner of Rikyū's death that explains why his *chanoyu* has been so rigorously preserved and transmitted, almost as an object of faith. Belief arose in the "honored spirit of Rikyū," and in death he greatly captured the minds of the people as the guardian deity of tea.

Rikyū was dead, the wooden statue of him was crucified at Ichijō Modoribashi in Kyoto, and his family was disbanded. Those who mourned him could do so only within their own hearts. The gravity of the situation had been anticipated at Daitokuji, and Kokei Sōchin made a stout defense of Rikyū when the messenger bearing Hideyoshi's reprimand arrived.[37] But this fact is well known and need not be discussed here. Allow me, in concluding this section, to add a few comments about Rikyū's graves.

Three such graves are known.[38] The most famous is the monument in the center of the gravesites of generations of the Sen family at the Jukōin subtemple of Daitokuji. Brought by Rikyū's grandson Sōtan from Funaokayama, its middle stone has been hollowed out to provide a place for a candle, thus making it a lantern. We are told that this lantern was built by Rikyū himself in 1589. Abandoned for a time following the suicide, it was evidently returned to its original place and reerected there by Sōtan after the reinstatement of the Sen family.

The second of Rikyū's graves is the one constructed at Nanshūji Temple in Sakai during the Genroku era (1688–1703). The third, which is not well known, was built behind the tombstone of the founder of the main quarters at Daitokuji. Since reference to this last grave appears as early as the collected poetry of the priest Takuan and the grave is thus known to have been in existence within some twenty or thirty years after Rikyū's death, it is by far the oldest of the three Rikyū burial sites. Rikyū's death date and name are inscribed on a small pagoda. But the most unusual feature of the grave is its placement directly behind the grave of Daitō Kokushi (Shūhō Myōchō), the founder of Daitokuji. Since Takuan recorded that Rikyū's grave was next to that of the founder of Daitokuji, it appears that its site has never been altered. The founder's grave is atop a foundation of piled stones, and Rikyū's is at the base of this foundation, unobtrusively situated in a small opening between it and the mud wall of Shinjuan. We have absolutely no idea why, when, and by whom this grave was built.

Nevertheless, if we give free reign to our imaginations, we can interpret the selection of the site for Rikyū's grave at Daitokuji—in a hidden place behind the eminently secure gravesite of the temple's founder and arranged so that it is not even visible from the front—to mean that at the time of its construction services still could not be openly held for Rikyū. Accordingly, the grave must have been built in the Bunroku era (1592–1595), before the reinstatement of the Sen family. If this was the case, then the person most likely to have dared to do it was Kokei Sōchin himself. Daitokuji could not very well have turned its back on Rikyū, who was a great patron and met death for the crime of having repaired its gate. It appears, then, that the present grave at the main quarters of Daitokuji was the grave secretly built for Rikyū, in a way that would not incite Hideyoshi's anger, after Daitokuji took custody of his remains. In this too we can discern a great, dark shadow lying across the unusual death of Rikyū.

RIKYŪ'S CHANOYU—
CREATION OF THE NIJIRIGUCHI

What were the precise characteristics of the *wabicha* perfected by Sen no Rikyū? Let me begin by considering, first, the creation of the *nijiriguchi* or "crawling in" entrance found in the *sōan* (hut) form of tea room. The unique entranceway known as *nijiriguchi* was conceived by Rikyū during the process of completing the tea-room style of architecture, and it became virtually mandatory that a *nijiriguchi* be installed in all tea rooms four-and-a-half mats or less in size. This tiny entranceway, a bare sixty-six centimeters square, is unquestionably an inconvenience that might irritate not only the critics of tea but others as well. Nevertheless, it is the *nijiriguchi* that gives the narrowly restricted space of the tea room its unlimited possibilities.

The traditional explanation for the origin of the *nijiriguchi* is given in this anecdote in *Chadō Shiso Densho*: "Finding it to be tasteful and interesting that one must crawl into and out of the boats at the dock

Plate 1. *Fishing Village at Twilight.* Thirteenth-century *karamono* painting attributed to Mu Ch'i. National Treasure. Nezu Institute of Fine Arts, Tokyo.

Plate 2. Early *shoin*-style room called Dōjinsai (Room of Mutual Benevolence), located in the Tōgudō Buddha hall at Jishōji Temple (better known as Ginkakuji, or Temple of the Silver Pavilion), Kyoto. The room has an installed desk *(shoin)* and asymmetrical shelves but no alcove. National Treasure.

Plate 3. *Karamono* celadon vase known as Sensei (Thousand Voices). Important Cultural Property. Yōmei Bunko Foundation, Kyoto.

Plate 4. Matsuya "shouldered" *(katatsuki)* tea caddy, a *karamono* utensil once the property of Shogun Ashikaga Yoshimasa. Important Cultural Property and *ō-meibutsu*. Nezu Institute of Fine Arts, Tokyo.

Plate 5. Old Seto ware, Japanese-style *(wamono)* tea caddy known as Ōsaka. Sixteenth century. *Chūkō meibutsu*. Nezu Institute of Fine Arts, Tokyo.

Plate 6. Scene from a Namban (Southern Barbarian) folding screen. Momoyama epoch. Namban Bunkakan, Osaka.

Plate 7. Scene from the *Takao Kampū Zu* (Maple Leaf Viewing at Takao) folding screen by Kanō Hideyori. A man sells cups of tea at left. Momoyama epoch. National Treasure. Tokyo National Museum.

Plate 8. Detail of the *Chōba Zu* (Horse Training) folding screen. A man preparing tea can be observed at right. Momoyama epoch. Important Cultural Property. Taga Shrine, Shiga Prefecture.

Plate 9. Sen no Rikyū. Portrait by Kan'ei Sōtan (1611–1672) based on an earlier painting by Hasegawa Tōhaku (1539–1610). Konnichian of Urasenke Foundation, Kyoto.

Plate 10. Tea room Zangetsutei in Fushin'an at Omotesenke, Kyoto. Rebuilt in 1909, the original is believed to have been moved from Sen no Rikyū's house near Toyotomi Hideyoshi's Jurakudai residence in Kyoto. Displayed in the alcove is a *karamono* painting of a mountain village by Yü Chien.

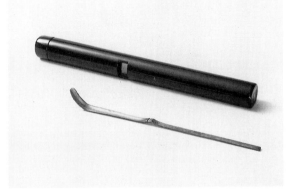

Plate 11. Bamboo flower vase called Onjōji, made by Sen no Rikyū. Tokyo National Museum.

Plate 12. Tea scoop Namida and its case. Sen no Rikyū made the scoop and Furuta Oribe the case. *Meibutsu.* Tokugawa Reimeikai Foundation, Tokyo.

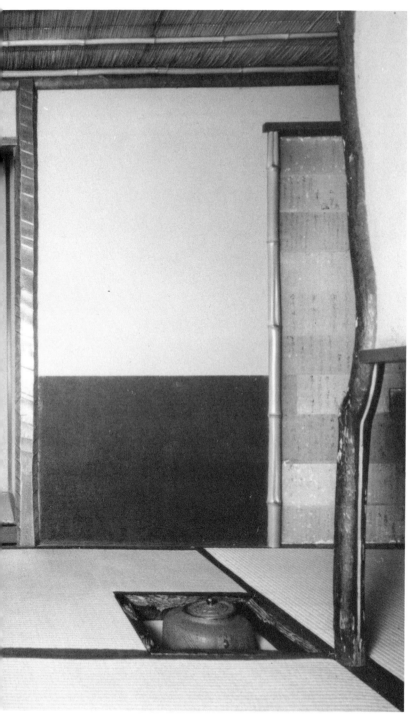

Plate 13. Nineteenth-century replica of the tea room Ennan of Furuta Oribe. The attendants' seating area *(shōbanseki)* can be seen at left. Important Cultural Property. Yabunouchi Ennan Foundation, Kyoto.

Plate 14. Kinmōkaku gate at Daitokuji Temple, Kyoto, the gate upon which a wooden statue of Sen no Rikyū was placed. Important Cultural Property.

at Hirakata in Osaka, Rikyū began to use such a passageway in the small tea room."[39] As the anecdote informs us, Rikyū was taken with the passageway of a riverboat, which was small and had a certain *wabi* feeling about it—whereupon he adapted this passageway to the tea room. Yet it was not simply the form of the passageway that intrigued Rikyū. Those who board a boat enter another realm where they share a common fate apart from the rest of the world. Perhaps Rikyū thought of this when he was attracted to the configuration of the passageway of the boat at Hirakata.

As I have discussed elsewhere, the concept of the *nijiriguchi* may also have been suggested by the wicket entranceway to theaters.[40] The reason for the *nijiriguchi*'s rapid and widespread acceptance, I believe, was the existence of a similar structure elsewhere that made the *nijiriguchi* readily comprehensible to people of the Azuchi-Momoyama epoch. The entranceway to theaters that we see pictured in genre paintings of the period were exceedingly small apertures, appropriately named "mouse wickets," that resembled *nijiriguchi*. By crawling through the mouse wicket, people entered a world of the theater separate from the everyday space in which they usually moved. They entered, indeed, a world of dramatic space. Thus the mouse wicket was the dividing line that prevented the "ordinary" of one place from merging with the "extraordinary" of another.

In earlier times the *nijiriguchi* was called a "pass-under" or "pass-through" *(kuguri)*, and the idea of stooping to pass through a very small passageway immediately calls to mind a type of rite: *tainai-kuguri*, a rite of Shugendō, the "mountain religion," which involves crawling through a small space among rocks (the literal meaning of *tainai-kuguri* is "to pass from or through the womb"). There is no need to cite the tales of *Nezumi no Jōdo* and *Tōgenkyō* in which passing through an infinitesimally small hole leads to the opening up of a different world on the other side.[41] The rite of passing through was a means for gaining new life force, even rebirth. It also served as ingress to utopia, and in this sense both the tea room and the theater can be regarded as utopias of a kind.

The *nijiriguchi* pass-through seems clearly to have had the same function as the mouse wicket and the *tainai-kuguri* rite. But this is not sufficient to explain its creation. I believe the true origin of the *nijiriguchi* was in the narrow openings cut into mud walls *(tsuiji)*. Records suggesting the *nijiriguchi* or pass-through can be found from a relatively early period before the evolution of *chanoyu*. There is, for example, this excerpt, dated 1462:3:12, about a tea gathering in *Hekizan Nichiroku*:

> The twelfth day. I was invited to stay with Eian. Every effort was expended to entertain me lavishly. . . . Later we left Eian's house and walked a short distance. We came to an extremely small gate in a wall and had to squeeze our bodies in order to get through. On the other side we found a room made of fine wood and other excellent materials. Landscapes were painted on the four walls, and in the middle was a picture of a gathering of birds by Mu Chi. On the cushion in the alcove there were utensils, all of which were from China. Tea from the south of Uji was prepared.[42]

In the year 1462 *shoin daisu* tea was still evolving and Murata Shukō, the putative founder of *wabicha*, had not yet made his name in the world. I may be criticized for probing back more than a century for the origin of the *nijiriguchi*. But it is a mistake to associate the *nijiriguchi* just with *wabicha*. The idea of establishing a division between the outside world and the world of tea was very likely born the moment it was realized that tea could be made into a performing art.

The style of tea setting referred to in the preceding excerpt from *Hekizan Nichiroku* was one of *karamono* magnificence, just as described in *Kundaikan Sōchō Ki*. But what sort of gateway was the narrow opening through which the people were obliged to crawl? Evidently it was a gateway constructed as an entrance to the *roji* or tea garden—that is, a gateway within a residential compound designed for crawling into the special realm of *chanoyu*. If this was the case, then we can regard the gateway as a pass-through cut low and narrow into a wall or other partition surrounding the four sides of a tea garden. It appears from the excerpt that this was the only such gateway; there was no special entrance to the tea room itself. Nevertheless, the gateway suggests the creation of the *nijiriguchi*.

I contend, therefore, that the earliest *nijiriguchi* was not designed exclusively for the tea room. Rather, it was built as a narrow entranceway separating the realm of tea, including the tea garden, from the outside world of everyday life. Upon going through this entranceway, one entered a utopia conceived as another world in the mountains, much like the "mountain place within the city" described by Rodri-

gues in *Nihon Kyōkai Shi*,[43] a place which, although in the city, gave
the appearance of remote mountains and deep valleys.

The pass-through that served as an entranceway to the *roji* did not
immediately become the *nijiriguchi* of the tea room. There are, in fact,
various other structures that reveal the process whereby the pass-
through evolved into the tea room *nijiriguchi*. One of these is an intermediate pass-through located inside the entrance to the *roji*—situated
by itself in the very center of the *roji*—that exactly resembles the wall
of the teahouse into which the *nijiriguchi* was ultimately built. We find
an intermediate pass-through of this sort in the *roji* of today's
Fushin'an at Omotesenke. According to tradition, the original layout
of Fushin'an was done to the taste of Furuta Oribe. But the place
seems to have a genealogy dating back before Oribe. We find, for
example, this interesting entry, dated 1587:6:19, in *Sōtan Nikki*:

> The morning of the nineteenth day of the sixth month. The Lord
> Kampaku held a tea gathering at Hakozaki camp, inviting Sōtan and
> Sōshitsu. The *sukiya*-style teahouse consisted of a three-mat room,
> without veranda, that was entered through a two-*shōji* doorway and
> had a sky window. There was a six-*shaku* display shelf. In order to enter
> the *roji*, one had to crawl through a passage from the outside. Beyond
> there were stepping-stones and, under a pine tree, a washbasin.[44]

Intermediate pass-throughs like the one at Fushin'an existed in
Hideyoshi's time. And since 1587 was during Rikyū's last years, when
we can assume that the *nijiriguchi* had already been devised, we cannot regard the passageway mentioned in this entry in *Sōtan Nikki* as a
forerunner of the *nijiriguchi*-style entranceway. Nevertheless, we see
that here also a narrow pass-through had been built into the entrance
to a *roji*; and since it is described as the kind of opening one "crawled"
through, we know that it required bending the body and pulling oneself through with the hands. This was the only place in the layout,
however, that had a narrow pass-through. Beyond it were, once again,
stepping-stones and a hand basin under a pine tree. Because there was
no veranda, one entered directly into the teahouse simply by opening
the *shōji*.

In the next stage of development of the *nijiriguchi*, the pass-through
that had been constructed in the middle of the *roji* was moved up to
the teahouse, where it became part of the dirt-floored room under the

eave. Finally, the pass-through was made an annex of the house's wall. Although it is from a later time, the Teigyokuken teahouse favored by Kanamori Sōwa at the Shinjuan subtemple of Daitokuji incorporates this kind of structure and provides us with a piece in the puzzle of the evolution of the *nijiriguchi*.

When viewed from the outside, the *nijiriguchi* at Teigyokuken appears quite ordinary. But on the inside one finds stepping-stones; and although the space is small, there is a hand basin. It is very much like the world of the inner *roji*. Also, curiously, the entrance to the main tea room has two *shōji* and no veranda, and thus it resembles in appearance the tea room used by Hideyoshi in 1587. It sufficed to have the pass-through or *nijiriguchi* in one spot. And thus, when the intermediate pass-through that had been constructed in the middle of the *roji* was moved up to the teahouse and an eave was extended from the teahouse to cover the space between it and the wall of the intermediate pass-through, the kind of teahouse found at Teigyokuken came into being. Moreover, once the pass-through had been brought in this close, it was a simple matter to incorporate it into the wall of the teahouse itself.

What is the significance of the development of the *nijiriguchi*? This type of opening is clearly an obstruction to entering an area. Originally it had been the entranceway to the entire space that contained the garden and various buildings used in *chanoyu*. But gradually it was shifted inward and was eventually integrated as part of the teahouse. This does not necessarily mean, however, that the opening to the *roji* and the intermediate pass-through totally disappeared. During the course of the development of *wabicha*, the masters of tea came to conceive of a restricted space to seal off the smaller space of the teahouse itself. At first, the larger space included the entire *roji*; but when the double *roji* was evolved, the gateway known as the intermediate pass-through was built. In this way, two interior worlds were created, the first by the original opening to the *roji* and the second by the intermediate pass-through. The most restrictive entranceway of all, which could be used only by crawling, was finally built into the teahouse. His body cleansed, the guest passes from one world to another and, with a sense of keen awareness increasing at each step of the way, finally arrives at the teahouse, whose interior has become less the realm of the connoisseur than a sacred space.

How was the interior of the teahouse constructed? As we can tell from the old word "enclosure" (kakoi), the space used for chanoyu was created by partitioning and enclosing open space. Use of the peculiar entranceway known as nijiriguchi inevitably limited the size of the tea room, reducing it to four-and-a-half mats or less. Because of its small size and restricted character, the tea room placed great restraints upon the actions of people in it. Conduct became ritualized and, by means of refined conversation and movements, people came to experience an increase in awareness and an uplifting of the spirit. Rikyū had transformed a setting from everyday life into a unique place of cultural creativity. And thus the mundane act of drinking tea was elevated to a splendid culture of living.

RIKYŪ'S KAISEKI

Let us turn now to the second distinctive feature of Rikyū's tea: the kaiseki meal. One reason why chanoyu has evolved into such a high form of culture lies in its creation of a new kind of social banquet as part of the tea gathering. The meal that later became known as kaiseki has, in particular, exerted a great influence upon the overall development of Japanese cuisine.

What were banquet meals like before the kaiseki was contrived for wabicha? Rodrigues' Nihon Kyōkai Shi informs us that the European missionaries in Japan during the Azuchi-Momoyama epoch observed four kinds of banquet meals.[45] The first was called the "three-tray" meal, because three formal trays of food were placed separately before each guest; the second, which used two additional trays, was called the five-tray meal. In the third kind of banquet meal, all was done with the greatest formality, and the meal was truly a solemn affair. No less than seven trays of food were given to each guest. It was a meal that had always been presented by people of the highest social status. When such people entertained others of equally high status, the occasion was a means by which they could welcome their guests warmly and show their respect for them. The fourth kind of banquet meal was given when tea was drunk.

The first three kinds of banquet meals observed by the missionaries were evolved by the warrior chieftains of the Muromachi period for purposes of social entertainment and entailed the decorative presentation of a variety of dishes on seven, five, or three trays. Rodrigues, however, also indicated that in recent times—that is, in the latter part of the sixteenth century or the age of Nobunaga and Hideyoshi— there had occurred a great change in the banquet meal. He was referring, of course, to the meal for *chanoyu:*

> The fourth kind of banquet meal, begun during the time of Nobunaga and Hideyoshi, is now in great favor and has spread among people everywhere, high and low. Since then there have been many changes. Superfluous and troublesome things have been eliminated, and old customs have been altered. From the banquet meal to the everyday partaking of food, Japanese cuisine has been greatly reformed.[46]

What was meant by this reform of cuisine? It meant "rejecting food that was served solely for its decorative appearance and rejecting cold food. In their places, trays of warm and amply prepared food were to be served at appropriate times. Like the tea in *chanoyu,* the food was to be of high quality."[47] Here we have the true essence of the newly evolved *kaiseki* meal.

As Rodrigues also mentioned, this new style of cuisine developed along with *chanoyu. Kaiseki* was originally written with the characters for a "seat at a gathering." The *chanoyu* characters for the word, meaning literally "bosom" and "stone," were adopted with reference to the fact that in the same way that Zen monks, during the course of their austerities, placed warm stones in the bosoms of their robes to stave off hunger, this was a simple meal intended to help people bear hunger pangs. Usage of the term with these characters dates from the middle of the seventeenth century.

The cuisine of *chanoyu* was not always like the food of the later *kaiseki* meal: The *kaiseki* meal was perfected at the same time that *wabicha* was brought to perfection by Rikyū. Before this, the cuisine of *chanoyu* followed a long, shifting course until it was finally able to reject the lavish banquet food served on trays. If we consult *Chōka Chanoyu Monogatari,* which is said to have been written by Ashikaga Yoshimasa's cultural adviser Sōami (but is actually thought to be an account from the mid-sixteenth century), we find that the method for preparing tea and handling a gathering of guests was essentially the same as in the later *chanoyu.* But the meal was by no means a *kaiseki.* In *Chōka Chanoyu Monogatari,* the young participants in the tea room gobbled up the fish and fowl, grabbing the food with bare hands, and poked about with their chopsticks at the vegetables that were arranged delicately on a tray. They gnawed on the hard bones and brandished their chopsticks, clutching them to the point of breaking. They also drank sake.[48] If this tale was written to criticize disgraceful behavior at tea gatherings, its portrayal is probably quite exaggerated. Nevertheless, before the rise of Rikyū the meals that were part of *chanoyu* were more like drinking parties than *kaiseki*.

Wabicha divorced itself from the disordered tea gathering and also took its own distinct position about cuisine during the time of the two masters Jōō and his disciple Rikyū. Jōō, in his teaching, said: "Although there may be novelty in the *kaiseki*, it should conform to *chanoyu* and not exceed one soup and three dishes."[49] Yet when we look at the records of tea gatherings, we find that it was in the gatherings of Rikyū rather than Jōō that the menu of one soup and two dishes or one soup and three dishes was established. Someone at a later time put it correctly when he observed:

In the old days people of high social status served two or three different kinds of soup. But after Rikyū reformed the *kaiseki*, even the aristocratic and wealthy limited themselves to one soup and three dishes or to one soup and two dishes. *Wabicha* people finally reduced it to one soup and one dish. Since the number of dishes was limited, the expression of personal likes and dislikes was prohibited.[50]

Let me give an example of one of Rikyū's *kaiseki*. Here is the menu for a tea gathering held by Rikyū on the evening of 1590:9:21 with Hideyoshi, Mōri Terumoto, Shiyakuin Zensō, and Tsuda Sōgyū as guests:

Broiled salmon
Soup with vegetables
Sake-marinated sea bream
Oborodōfu
Rice
Sweets: *funoyaki*, roasted chestnuts, *irikaya*[51]

First, sake-marinated sea bream and soup and rice were brought out together on *oshiki* trays. When the lids of these bowls and the rice bowls were removed, vermilion sake cups and pourers were brought out. Next the broiled salmon and the *oborodōfu* were passed around. In the records of tea gatherings the word *hikite* was used for this passing of food. *Oborodōfu* is *tōfu* in a soft state just before it is placed into a mold and set. The sweets were of three kinds, made like crepes from chestnuts and torreya nuts braised with *miso* and baked.

Thus the menu had one soup and three dishes: the sea bream, the cooked *oborodōfu*, and the broiled salmon. The menu was not limited to one soup and three dishes because of an insufficiency of food, however, but rather to allow for better appreciation of the taste of the food that was served. It was a humanistic meal.

Instead of humanistic, perhaps it should be called an early-modern type of meal. I say humanistic because *kaiseki* cuisine was the first cuisine to reflect a sense of season and a sensitivity to human feelings. There is a story that illustrates what I mean.

Between Kyoto and Osaka is a place named Moriguchi, where a certain *wabi* tea man lived. Upon meeting Rikyū, this man of tea asked the master to visit his house to drink tea. Late one night in winter, when Rikyū was returning to Kyoto, he passed through Moriguchi. Thinking suddenly of this *wabi* tea man, he got the idea of visiting him. The tea man was overjoyed that the most famous master in the country, Rikyū, had unexpectedly deigned to call upon him late at night. He showed Rikyū into his tea room, and Rikyū was pleased to observe the scrupulous care with which the head of the house had arranged things. Noticing someone outside the window, Rikyū saw by the dim light of a lantern the figure of the tea man taking some citrons from the garden with a bamboo pole. He appeared to take two of these fruits. Indeed, thought Rikyū admiringly, how in keeping with the spirit of *wabi* to do this late at night when one is not likely to have made preparations. The tea man presented Rikyū with sake and the freshly picked citrons dipped in *miso*. While enjoying the fragrances of the evening, Rikyū drank his sake. Next the tea man brought in a bowl of splendid sliced *kamaboko*, saying it had just arrived from Osaka. But the *kamaboko* was not only improper to the season, it was a luxury unsuited to *wabicha*. Moreover, it was false to have said the *kamaboko* had just arrived from Osaka. His interest suddenly dissipated by the tea man's words, Rikyū brushed aside the man's efforts to detain him and returned to Kyoto.[52]

This story, found in *Chawa Shigetsu Shū*, expresses the notion that food in *chanoyu* is less important for its taste than as a means of communion between the guest and his host. The *kaiseki* attaches significance to the sentiment of hospitality conveyed by the food rather than to how luxurious it is.

WABI, ZEN, AND RIKYŪ

If we regard Murata Shukō as the founder of *wabicha,* then we must take particular note of his "Letter of the Heart" (*Kokoro no Fumi*), which was preserved by the Matsuya family of lacquerers in Nara and which Rikyū constantly praised. *Chadō Shiso Densho* says that Shukō owed much of his fame to Rikyū.[53] And indeed it was because of his love of Shukō's *wabicha* as expressed in the "Letter of the Heart" that Rikyū elevated the earlier master to the position of patriarch of this form of *chanoyu.* The "Letter of the Heart" says: "In pursuing this way of tea, extreme care should be taken to harmonize Japanese and Chinese tastes."[54]

In Shukō's time the highest form of tea was the tea of "*karamono* magnificence," which involved objects imported from China. Shukō, however, understood also the beauty of the "cold and withered," as found in *renga,* and the beauty of the imperfect and incomplete. He perceived this latter beauty in such *wamono* (Japanese things) as Shigaraki and Bizen ceramic ware, which, when compared to the art and craft of China, was imperfect and rough. Shukō sought to discover a new beauty in the contrasting tastes of *kara* (Chinese) perfection and *wa* (Japanese) crudeness and imperfection. To the people of his age, the injunction to "harmonize Japanese and Chinese tastes" probably called to mind the mixed form of Chinese and Japanese poetry that was then popular. It appears that Shukō attempted to apply to *chanoyu* the artistic principles used in this mixing of the poetry of China and Japan.

Rikyū, however, did not stop at harmonizing and mixing. Dynamically he interpreted the idea of blending Japanese and Chinese tastes as a quest for beauty not possessed by either. This was the beauty of "Korean things" (*Kōrai-mono*), which had a warmth unknown to the works of China and a delicacy of texture and craftsmanship not found in Japan. It was a beauty that accorded with the ideal of *wabi.*

Ceramic ware of the Yi dynasty was imported to Japan in great quantity in Rikyū's time. Yet if we examine the Ido incense burner that Rikyū cherished, we find that it was by no means of the finest Yi dynasty quality. On the contrary, it was a crude piece of work. Nevertheless, it had a deep warmth that was like the warmth in the palms of Rikyū's hands.

Rikyū appreciated the tastes of the three kinds of "things," Japanese, Chinese, and Korean, and the ultimate beauty he sought in them was that which could be expressed with the word *wabi*. What, then, are the characteristics of the *wabi* form of beauty?

The beauty of *wabi* has both a positive side and a negative side. *Wabi*'s purpose is not to compete with the tea ways and precious objects of people like the Ashikaga shoguns and the hegemons Nobunaga and Hideyoshi. On the contrary, it has always rejected the "*karamono* magnificence" and *meibutsu* perfectionism that these people commonly pursued. But since *meibutsu* could not be entirely ignored, *wabi* sought a new harmony of taste by setting a few of these treasures against cruder utensils. I believe this is what led Shukō to create *wabicha*. Among the words attributed to him are these: "It is fine to have an excellent horse tethered to a straw-thatched hut." According to Shukō, the appeal of *wabicha* lay in the startling contrast we find here between a hut and an excellent horse.

But this, surely, is a negative sort of *wabi*. The person who first asserted *wabi* in a positive sense as an independent form of beauty was Takeno Jōō. It was also Jōō who linked the term *wabi* to *chanoyu*. He gave *wabi* specific meaning as a new way of regarding the objects and things of *chanoyu*—a way based on the principle of "disguising" (*yatsushi*) true value. Let us, for example, look at the tea room. The setting for *chanoyu* decorated in the aristocratic manner with *karamono* was the *shoin*. Such a setting required that, along with the *oshiita* (decorative platform), there must be a papered alcove. In the four-and-a-half mat room Shukō constructed in the *shin* (formal) style, there was also a papered alcove. But the paper on the walls of the alcove was not adorned with pictures; it was plain white.[55]

Jōō did away with even the white paper and left the alcove walls unadorned, thus thoroughly implementing the principle of *yatsushi*. And whereas the frame of the alcove was traditionally painted with heavy lacquer, Jōō either used thin lacquer or dispensed with the lacquer entirely and kept the wood plain. The beauty of *yatsushi* lies in the plain and unadorned. Jōō discovered this fact, and Rikyū used it to perfect the aesthetic of *wabicha*.

The water container used in *chanoyu* is normally either a Chinese metal vessel or a ceramic vessel. But Jōō, on a certain occasion when he prepared tea in a novel manner in the dressing chamber of a bathhouse, used a plain wooden bucket from the bathhouse.[56] Rikyū went further and used the beauty of plain wood in his everyday practice of tea. It was from his time, for example, that bentwood utensils, with their beautifully textured grains, were widely employed. Bamboo utensils appeared as articles of tea in the period of Jōō, but these too were not given truly high status as utensils until Rikyū. Cutting his own bamboo, Rikyū made flower vases and prepared lids for them; at other times, he took what bamboo was at hand and made tea scoops.

Utensils made of plain wood and objects of bamboo were traditionally used only once—perhaps they were even prepared on the spot—and discarded. Yet within the brevity of this one-time-only usage can be discerned the beauty of *yatsushi*. Indeed, it is no exaggeration to say that in the effort to sense directly the beauty of workmanship in these hastily contrived, handcrafted articles lies the sense of *wabicha*.

Rikyū instilled *chanoyu* with a new kind of *wabi* taste. And if there is one aspect of this taste that comes most readily to mind as something Rikyū alone discovered and nurtured, it is the beauty of *raku* pottery. The earliest authenticated works by Chōjirō of the first generation of *raku* makers were not tea bowls but "lion tiles," purportedly unearthed in the vicinity of Nijō Castle in Kyoto. From a close comparison of these tiles and Chōjirō's later red *raku* and other pottery, we can deduce that Chōjirō's original occupation was that of tile-maker. Obviously Rikyū's interest in Chōjirō was captured not by the methods of a specialist in the making of receptacles for food but by the clay and glazing used by a tile-maker. Just as he preferred not to put a final coat of lacquer on the walls of his tea rooms but to allow the texture of the materials to show through, Rikyū sought not to conceal the qualities of the clay with glazing but, by means of a low firing, to deposit the glaze like a skin on its surface.

When did Rikyū begin to use Chōjirō's bowls? As earlier scholars have pointed out, a "tea bowl with flaring mouth" appeared at a gathering held by Rikyū on 1580:12:9 and was recorded in *Tennōjiya Kaiki*.[57] Very likely this was a red *raku* bowl such as Kōtō. In any case, the liking for Chōjirō's bowls came to Rikyū rather late in life.

An example of a bowl in Chōjirō's manner designed by Rikyū can be detected in *Matsuya Kaiki* for 1586:10:13, which refers to a "Sōeki-style tea bowl."[58] Some people believe that this bowl was actually designed by Chōjirō. But later, when "modern style" bowls suddenly appeared, Rikyū himself made frequent use in tea gatherings of bowls, such as the one named Kinamori, that were done like those of Chōjirō. We can assume, then, that Rikyū in fact designed the bowl mentioned in *Matsuya Kaiki* and had it baked at Chōjirō's kiln. In its plain black and red coloring and its simplicity of form, the beauty of *raku* is one with the severely restrained taste of *wabi*.

If Rikyū brought the taste of *wabi* to perfection, the spiritual means by which he did it was Zen Buddhism. As often stated, *wabicha* is inseparably linked to Zen. Indeed, it was when Shukō studied with Ikkyū Sōjun that he created this new form of *chanoyu*. Realizing that Shukō had attained enlightenment, Ikkyū gave him as formal certification a scroll of calligraphy by Yüan-wu K'o-ch'in (Engo Kokugon). A passage in *Yamanoue Sōji Ki* informs us that Shukō's use of this scroll inaugurated the practice of hanging calligraphy at tea gatherings.[59] From this, then, we know that the Yüan-wu scroll was the first to be used in *chanoyu*. Today it is held in the highest regard and is considered to be the forebear of all such scrolls.

From these facts we know that Shukō brought Zen into *chanoyu* and sought to make it the spiritual basis of tea. Jōō also worked to further the merger of tea and Zen. Jōō studied Zen under Dairin Sōtō and, as Haga Kōshirō notes in Chapter 7, was given this injunction by his teacher: "Realize that the taste of tea and the taste of Zen are the same and absorb the wind in the pines. Then will your mind be undefiled."[60] This is not the same as saying that "tea and Zen are one," but it is worth noting as a statement by a Zen priest that derived from similar thinking. The foundation of Jōō's tea, in fact, was *renga*. Advancement to the unequivocal concept that tea and Zen are one had to await Rikyū.

Many tea men of Sakai became close to the Daitokuji line of Zen, as we can observe in the cases of both Jūshiya Sōgo, who studied Zen under Kogaku Sōsen, and Jōō, whose teacher was Dairin Sōtō. Such ties between tea men and Daitokuji became especially intimate after Miyoshi Nagayoshi (Chōkei) built Nanshūji Temple in Sakai with Dairin Sōtō as its founder. Rikyū studied under Dairin's successor, Shōrei Sōkin.

The historical document *Busso Seiden Shūha*, which is in the possession of Omotesenke, is a genealogy of transmission of the law which records how various lines of Buddhist teachings were passed down through the generations.[61] At the end, under Shōrei Sōkin, is an entry that contains the name of Rikyū Sōeki and the date of the eighth day of the fourth month (the Buddha's birthday) of 1545. This document, whose author was purportedly Shōrei himself, is of particular interest because it sheds light on the question of when Rikyū received the name by which he is best known. We may question whether Shōrei actually wrote *Busso Seiden Shūha*, but the lines of transmission it contains are generally reliable. Rikyū was twenty-four in 1545 and, although still young, had evidently undergone considerable Zen training. *Nampōroku* states that "in *chanoyu* held in a small tea room, it is primarily by means of Buddhism that practice is undertaken and the Way is achieved."[62] Clearly Rikyū, in his tea, sought to achieve the Way through Buddhism.

After Shōrei Sōkin's death, Rikyū became a devoted follower of Shōrei's successor, Kokei Sōchin. Kokei was a member of the Asakura family and, although ten years Rikyū's junior, was greatly admired by Rikyū for his abilities. It is said that when Kokei became head abbot of Daitokuji in 1573, Rikyū bestowed upon him the unprecedented sum of one hundred *kanmon* as a congratulatory gift.

An event that well illustrates the trust between Kokei and Rikyū is the tea gathering held by Rikyū on 1588:9:4. The guests were Kokei's senior disciple Shun'oku Sōen, Gyokuho Jōsō, Kokei, and one other person; the place was a four-and-a-half mat room in Rikyū's Jurakudai residence.[63] Beneath Kokei's name in the account of the gathering is written: "At the time when, having incurred the Taikō's wrath, he is going to the western provinces." From this we learn that the gathering was held on the occasion of Kokei's exile to the western provinces after angering Hideyoshi. Rikyū somehow managed to arrange a farewell gathering for the disgraced Kokei, ironically holding it at his Jurakudai residence right under Hideyoshi's nose. The boldness of Rikyū's purpose was revealed in his selection of objects to display during the gathering, for in the alcove he hung a scroll of calligraphy by Hsü-t'ang Chih-yü, who was popularly known as Ikushima Kidō.

This calligraphy by Ikushima, which was treasured as a *meibutsu* of the realm, belonged in fact to Hideyoshi. It was in Rikyū's possession simply because Hideyoshi had directed the tea master to see to the repair of its mounting. But because the words of the calligraphy were ideally suited to Kokei's exile and journey to a distant place, Rikyū daringly decided to hang the scroll as a farewell gift for his friend. Of course, he was obliged to keep this secret not only from Hideyoshi but also from his attendants.

Rikyū risked his life to hold the tea gathering for Kokei. His repair of the Daitokuji gate, which was the cause of his suicide, also arose from a deep feeling for this priest. And the will that Rikyū is said to have drawn up at the end of his life was addressed to Kokei. In all manner of things, including instruction in Zen and assistance in day-to-day affairs, Kokei was the person to whom Rikyū turned.

Kokei placed equal trust in Rikyū. At the time in 1589 when Rikyū held services for the fiftieth anniversary of his father's death, Kokei delivered the eulogy. The apparent draft of his eulogy shows signs of much polishing to make the language as eloquent as possible.[64] And when Rikyū was granted the title of *koji* by the emperor, Kokei spoke of him as "my friend of thirty years." Kokei also admired Rikyū's deep understanding of Zen.

IN CONCLUSION

After Rikyū's suicide, the Sen family was disbanded. His son Dōan, his adopted son Shōan, his grandson Sōtan, and his daughters and other relatives dispersed into exile and waited for Hideyoshi's anger to subside. In fact, permission for reinstatement of the family was given surprisingly soon, although we still do not know the precise time. It is believed that Shōan, who took shelter with Gamō Ujisato of Aizu, received—through the mediation of Tokugawa Ieyasu and Ujisato—a document of reinstatement in the early part of the Bunroku era (1592–1595). When Shōan, the successor to Dōan as head of the Sen family, returned to Kyoto, he decided to situate the family residence at the head of the small stream, Ogawa, where Omotesenke and Ura-senke are presently located. Rikyū rated the strength of Dōan's *cha-noyu* highly, and indeed Dōan evolved many fine ways of tea. But we know little about the last half of his life. It is said that he died in Sakai after roaming through Shikoku and Kyushu. But it is also possible that he and his sisters carried on the tradition of the Sen family line in Sakai.

Upon Shōan's death on 1614:9:7, his son Sōtan succeeded to the Sen headship. As a youth, Sōtan had served at Daitokuji, where he practiced Zen under Shun'oku Sōen. But when Shōan undertook to revive the family fortunes, Sōtan returned home. For Sōtan, transmission of the tea tradition of the Sen and succession to the family headship were extremely serious responsibilities.[65] Having witnessed Rikyū's suicide and the dispersal of the family, Sōtan laid his plans with great care. Recognizing that a change in overlords or the whim of a particular overlord could result in his family's disbandment, he personally declined to serve anyone. Instead, he positioned himself outside the arena of power politics and adopted the strategy of placing other Sen family members in the service of various overlords. Thus he sent Kōshin Sōsa, the third son of his second wife, to the Tokugawa family of Kii, Sensō Sōshitsu, his fourth son, to the Maeda family of Kaga, and Ichio Sōshu, the second son of his first wife, to the Matsudaira family of Takamatsu. In this way Sōtan created an arrangement whereby at least one member of the Sen could be expected to preserve the family tradition of tea no matter what ill fate might befall the others. Sōtan's sons became, in fact, the founders of today's Omotesenke of Fushin'an, Urasenke of Konnichian, and Mushanokōji Senke of Kankyūan.

In concluding I wish to comment on one final point: the fact that the tradition of Rikyū's *chanoyu* has been preserved to the present day. The study of Rikyū is not limited to analysis of a legacy; it seeks also to exert a positive influence upon the contemporary practice of *chanoyu*. Put differently, Rikyū and his *chanoyu* are continuously sustained as living things among those who study tea. Fresh interpretations are always being advanced, amplified, and regenerated. The image we have of Rikyū today emerges from the sum total of all we have learned about the way of tea during the four hundred years since his death. From the time of his suicide until the present day, countless tea men have studied Rikyū and written books about him. Among these books, the one that has exerted a decisive influence on how we now regard Rikyū is *Nampōroku*.

If Tachibana Jitsuzan had not compiled *Nampōroku* on the occasion of the hundredth anniversary of Rikyū's death, our impression of the great master would be far less clear than it is. What Jitsuzan has given us in his words is not, of course, based directly on Rikyū as he actually lived in history. A retainer of the Kuroda domain of Hakata, Jitsuzan saw Rikyū through the eyes of a samurai of the Genroku epoch. His achievement was to bring together, in a lucid manner, the ideals of *wabicha* as reflected in his own practice of tea. And indeed we have learned a great deal from *Nampōroku*.

Jitsuzan, who was drawn into a dispute within the Kuroda family, came to an even more pitiable end than Rikyū. In *Bonjisō*, the journal he wrote in jail, using his own blood when he could not get ink, Jitsuzan tells of calling upon the Sen family in Kyoto during the course of one of the regular visits of the Kuroda daimyo and his retinue to Edo.[66] We must realize that the Sen line of tea has been preserved also by people like Jitsuzan, a man of provincial origins who fiercely believed in Rikyū. We ourselves, in our turn, must seek the very best means for clarifying our impression of Rikyū and thus advance research both into the history of the way of tea and, especially, into Rikyū. Here, I believe, lies the special purpose of our historical study of *chanoyu*.

NOTES

1. Hayashiya Tatsusaburō, *Zuroku Chadōshi* (Kyoto: Tankōsha, 1980), fig. 289.
2. Yabunouchi Chikushin, *Genryū Chawa*, in Sen Sōshitsu, ed., *Chadō Koten Zenshū*, vol. 3 (Kyoto: Tankōsha, 1956), p. 463.
3. Kumakura Isao, *Yon Dai Chakai-ki* (Tokyo: Sekai Bunka Sha, 1984), pp. 52–53.
4. Kumakura Isao, *Sen no Rikyū* (Tokyo: Heibonsha, 1978), p. 18, fig. 39.
5. There is a theory that this tea gathering in the imperial palace was held on 1585: 9:7, but the correct date is the one given in *Kanemi Kyoki* (10:7).
6. Hideyoshi used new utensils because of the tradition that all objects handled by the emperor must be clean and uncontaminated by others. The utensils were meant for a single occasion and were not to be used again even by the emperor himself.
7. For a representative version of the theory that Rikyū received his name at the time of the palace tea gathering, see Kuwata Tadachika, *Sen no Rikyū* (Tokyo: Tōkyōdō Shoten, 1978). For a discussion of the theory that he possessed the name before the palace tea gathering, see Sugimoto Hayao, *Sen no Rikyū to Sono Shūhen* (Kyoto: Tankōsha, 1970).
8. Rikyū's letter to Shun'oku Sōen in which he described the palace tea gathering is in the possession of the Fushin'an of Omotesenke (see Kumakura Isao, *Sen no Rikyū*, p. 54, fig. 118). The letter to Kokei Sōchin is quoted in Sen Sōshu, *Rikyū Koji no Chadō* (Tokyo: Tōkyōdō Shoten, 1943), p. 94.
9. Sengaku's verse can be found in Haga Kōshirō, *Sen no Rikyū* (Tokyo: Yoshikawa Kōbunkan, 1978), p. 165, and Shun'oku's verse in *Ichimoku Kō* (Tokyo: Sangen-in, 1960), p. 35.
10. Haga Kōshirō, *Sen no Rikyū*, pp. 157–177.
11. *Ōtomo Sōteki Shojō*, in Takita Manabu, ed., *Ōtomo Shiryō*, vol. 2 (Ōita: Kinyōdō Shoten, 1938), p. 253.

12. The colored nine-*ma shoin* was an eighteen-mat room with paint added over the plain wood posts and lintels. The paint was meant to give the *wabi* appearance of older wood even though the lumber was new. In a tea gathering held by Sen Shōan on 1608:2:25 as recorded in *Matsuya Kaiki* (*Chadō Koten Zenshū*, vol. 9, p. 236), Shōan remarked that the *shoin* room was designed on the pattern of the room in which Rikyū had entertained Hideyoshi when the latter paid him a visit. This room was presumably a replica of the colored nine-*ma* room in Rikyū's Jurakudai residence; that is, it was the original form of the present Zangetsutei at Fushin'an.

13. Kamiya Sōtan, *Sōtan Nikki*, in Sen Sōshitsu, ed., *Chadō Koten Zenshū*, vol. 6, (Kyoto: Tankōsha, 1958), p. 228.

14. *Kitano Ō-Chanoyu Ki*, in Sen Sōshitsu, ed., *Chadō Koten Zenshū*, vol. 6, p. 3.

15. *Gekokujō* means "those below overthrow those above."

16. "Rikyū Jihitsu Shojō," in Kuwata Tadachika, *Teihon Sen no Rikyū no Shokan* (Tokyo: Tōkyōdō Shoten, 1971), p. 378.

17. *Chōandō Ki*, in Sen Sōshitsu, ed., *Chadō Koten Zenshū*, vol. 3, p. 360.

18. Ibid., p. 365.

19. *Yamanoue Sōji Ki*, in Sen Sōshitsu, ed., *Chadō Koten Zenshū*, vol. 6, p. 102.

20. Ibid., pp. 102–103.

21. Yoshida Kanemi, *Kanemi Kyōki*, 1591:3:8.

22. Asao Naohiro, "Toyotomi Seiken Ron," in *Iwanami Kōza Nihon Rekishi*, vol. 9 (Tokyo: Iwanami Shoten, 1963), pp. 196–198.

23. *Sen no Rikyū Denki*, in Murai Yasuhiko, ed., *Chadō Shūkin*, vol. 3 (Tokyo: Shōgakukan, 1982), pp. 298–304.

24. *Tennōjiya Kaiki*, in Sen Sōshitsu, ed., *Chadō Koten Zenshū*, vol. 7 (Kyoto: Tankōsha, 1959), p. 144.

25. The "Ryokutai calligraphy," owned by the Fushin'an of Omotesenke. See Kumakura Isao, *Sen no Rikyū*, p. 77, fig. 112.

26. *Jukōin-ate Sen no Rikyū Shojō*, in Murai Yasuhiko, ed., *Chadō Shūkin*, vol. 3, p. 257.

27. Kuwata Tadachika, *Teihon Sen no Rikyū no Shokan*, p. 488. Professor Kuwata believes that this letter was written before 1588, but I think it dates from 1589 when the repair work was being done on the Daitokuji gate.

28. For information about this work on the Nanzenji gate, see Hayashiya Tatsusaburō, ed., *Kyōto no Rekishi*, vol. 5 (Kyoto: Kyōto-shi Shi Hensanjo, 1972), p. 220.

29. When Hideyoshi ordered him into house confinement in Sakai on 1591:2:13, Rikyū sadly departed Kyoto as a "criminal." But when his boat reached the Yodo River and stopped at the Yodo Dock, much to his surprise he discovered that Hosokawa Sansai and Furuta Oribe had secretly come to see him off. Unable to bid their master farewell in Kyoto, these two disciples had come to Yodo during the night for their final parting with Rikyū. This story is contained in a letter Rikyū wrote to Hosokawa Sansai's leading vassal, Matsui Sado no Kami. See Murai Yasuhiko, ed., *Chadō Shūkin*, vol. 3, p. 70, fig. 87.

30. *Kitano Shake Kiroku*, in *Shiryō Sanshū*, vol. 4 (Tokyo: Zoku Gunsho Ruijū Kankō Kai, 1973), p. 283. See also Kumakura Isao, *Sen no Rikyū*, p. 71, fig. 153.

31. Chiba Tokuji, *Seppuku no Hanashi* (Tokyo: Kōdansha, 1972).

32. Murai Yasuhiko, ed., *Chadō Shūkin*, vol. 3, pp. 298–304.

33. Kumakura Isao, *Sen no Rikyū*, p. 4, fig. 2.

34. For a good discussion of vengeful spirits in Japanese thought, see Higo Kazuo, "Heian Jidai ni okeru Onryō Shisō," in *Nihon Bunka* (Tokyo: Kōbundō, 1939).

35. *Matsuya Kaiki*, in Sen Sōshitsu, ed., *Chadō Koten Zenshū*, vol. 9 (Kyoto: Tankōsha, 1957), p. 197.

36. Nambō Sōkei, *Nampōroku*, in Sen Sōshitsu, ed., *Chadō Koten Zenshū*, vol. 4 (Kyoto: Tankōsha, 1956), p. 267.

37. See Murai Yasuhiko, ed., *Chadō Shūkin*, vol. 3, pp. 298–304.

38. See Kumakura Isao, "Rikyū no Haka," in Murai Yasuhiko, ed., *Chadō Shūkin*, vol. 3, pp. 287–289.

39. *Chadō Shiso Densho*, revised by Kumakura Isao (Kyoto: Shibunkaku, 1974), p. 54.

40. Kumakura Isao, *Chanoyu: Wabicha no Kokoro to Katachi* (Tokyo: Kyōikusha, 1977), pp. 26–28.

41. *Nezumi no Jōdo* ("The Pure Land of Mice"): Seki Keigo, ed., *Nihon Mukashibanashi Taisei*, vol. 4 (Tokyo: Kadokawa Shoten, 1978), pp. 117–149. *Tōgenkyō*: T'ao Yüan-ming, *Tōkagen no Shi, Narabi ni Ki*, in Ikkai Tomoyoshi, ed., *T'ao Yüan-ming*, in *Chūgoku Shijin Senshū*, vol. 4 (Tokyo: Iwanami Shoten, 1958), pp. 141–146.

42. *Hekizan Nichiroku*, in Kondō Heijō, ed., *Shiseki Shūran*, vol. 25 (Tokyo: Shiseki Shūran Kankō Kai, 1902), p. 256.

43. João Rodrigues, *Nihon Kyōkai Shi*, vol. 1 in *Daikōkai Jidai Sōsho* (Tokyo: Iwanami Shoten, 1967), p. 608.

44. Kamiya Sōtan, *Sōtan Nikki*, in Sen Sōshitsu, ed., *Chadō Koten Zenshū*, vol. 6, p. 229.

45. João Rodrigues, *Nihon Kyōkai Shi*, vol. 1, p. 547.

46. Ibid.

47. Ibid., p. 552.

48. *Chōka Chanoyu Monogatari*, in *Chadō Bunka Kenkyū*, vol. 1 (Kyoto: Konnichian Bunko, 1974), pp. 89–100.

49. *Jōō Montei e no Hatto*, in Sen Sōshitsu, ed., *Chadō Koten Zenshū*, vol. 3, pp. 50–51.

50. Yabunouchi Chikushin, *Genryū Chawa*, in Sen Sōshitsu, ed., *Chadō Koten Zenshū*, vol. 3, p. 438.

51. *Rikyū Hyakkai Ki*, in Sen Sōshitsu, ed., *Chadō Koten Zenshū*, vol. 6, p. 415.

52. Kusumi Soan, *Chawa Shigetsu Shū*, in Sen Sōshitsu, ed., *Chadō Koten Zenshū*, vol. 10 (Kyoto: Tankōsha, 1961), p. 205.

53. *Chadō Shiso Densho*, p. 86.

54. Murata Shukō, *Kokoro no Fumi*, in Sen Sōshitsu, ed., *Chadō Koten Zenshū*, vol. 3, p. 3.

55. For changes in the structuring of the tea room, see Nambō Sōkei, *Nampōroku*, in Sen Sōshitsu, ed., *Chadō Koten Zenshū*, vol. 4, pp. 52–53.

56. For more about Jōō's novel preparation of tea in a bathhouse, see *Chōandō Ki*, in Sen Sōshitsu, ed., *Chadō Koten Zenshū*, vol. 3, pp. 362–363.

57. *Tennōjiya Kaiki*, in Sen Sōshitsu, ed., *Chadō Koten Zenshū*, vol. 7, p. 327.

58. *Matsuya Kaiki*, in Sen Sōshitsu, ed., *Chadō Koten Zenshū*, vol. 9, p. 125.

59. Yamanoue Sōji, *Yamanoue Sōji Ki*, in Sen Sōshitsu, ed., *Chadō Koten Zenshū*, vol. 6, p. 72.

60. Kumakura Isao, *Sen no Rikyū*, p. 13, fig. 25.

61. Ibid., p. 51, fig. 115.

62. Nambō Sōkei, *Nampōroku*, in Sen Sōshitsu, ed., *Chadō Koten Zenshū*, vol. 4, p. 3.

63. Suzuki Hancha, ed., *Sen no Rikyū Zenshū* (Tokyo: Gakugei Shobō, 1943), p. 212.

64. Kumakura Isao, *Sen no Rikyū*, p. 50, fig. 111; p. 54, fig. 119.

65. In *Chanoyu-teki Den* it is written that the main line in the transmission of tea was "Shukō, Jōō, Rikyū, Shōan, and Fushin (Sōtan)"; ibid., fig. 168.

66. Tachibana Jitsuzan, *Bonjisō*, in *Zen-cha Roku*, vol. 3 (Fukuoka: Enkakuji, 1971), p. 103.

THREE

CHANOYU AND MOMOYAMA:
CONFLICT AND TRANSFORMATION
IN RIKYŪ'S ART

Theodore M. Ludwig

THE brief Azuchi-Momoyama epoch is generally regarded as one of the most important periods in the long history of *chanoyu*. During these years masters like Sen no Rikyū, Imai Sōkyū, Tsuda Sōgyū, and many others—including even Toyotomi Hideyoshi—brought the tea art to a perfection which is recognized as a fulfillment of *chanoyu* development up to that time, particularly in the form generally known as *wabicha*.

But why Azuchi-Momoyama? This would seem to be an unlikely atmosphere for the perfecting of a gentle, humane art like *chanoyu*. The struggle for the unification of Japan involved the use of power and violence of almost unbelievable proportions, and the very patrons of *chanoyu* were the instigators of this power and violence— that is, Nobunaga, Hideyoshi, and many other powerful daimyos. The contradictions cut several ways. Why were these men of power attracted to the tea art to such an extent that they not only amassed hoards of valuable tea utensils but also immersed themselves in the discipline and practice of *chanoyu*? And why did the leading masters of the art, like Rikyū, drawn to the centers of power, willingly serve in positions and places that seemed even to some contemporaries to contradict the basic values and ideals of *chanoyu*? These contradictions have led to the assumption of a sharp dichotomy between the simple, unrestrained art known as *wabicha* and the flamboyant, luxurious practice that has been called daimyo tea. The problem is that the same daimyos and *wabi* masters (Hideyoshi and Rikyū, for instance) were deeply involved in both.

These questions involve many complex factors. Studies of Nobuna-

ga's and Hideyoshi's attraction to *chanoyu* have generally focused on
their need to impress others with their cultural accomplishments,
given their lack of distinguished pedigrees—Nobunaga came from an
upstart family which rose to control Owari province, while Hideyoshi
was the son of a farmer and part-time soldier from a small village in
Owari. Moreover, the value of using the *chanoyu* masters in political
and economic negotiations has often been pointed out. But the use of
chanoyu as a *ritual process* in the context of the new societal structuring
was also an important element in the sudden rise of this art during the
Azuchi-Momoyama epoch. Ritual, whether religious, quasi-religious,
or secular, has essential public functions in societies: It communicates
values and structures, it reduces conflict by affording a means of
mutual recognition, and it dramatizes consensus regarding roles and
thus motivates actions for healthy intragroup bonding.[1] Further,
social rituals provide crucial occasions for those tightly conscripted by
structural roles to find relief in the experience of equality and *communitas* outside the societal structures.[2] In attempting to understand
the popularity of *chanoyu* in the powerful places of Azuchi-Momoyama, attention must be given to the ritual function of this art within
Momoyama society.

Why the tea masters allowed their aesthetic ideals to be bifurcated
into the seeming incompatibility of *wabi* values and parvenu pursuits
likewise involves complex factors. One of the major problems in
studying Rikyū in his aesthetic ideals and in his relations with
Nobunaga and Hideyoshi is the fact that he himself left no *chanoyu*
diaries or essays about his own understanding of the tea art. Consequently, our picture of his artistic stance must necessarily be constructed on the basis of contemporary tea records jotted down by his
fellow masters (and, to some extent, rivals), together with interpretations heavily colored by the lenses of succeeding generations. Perhaps
it is *Nampōroku*, more than any other classic of tea literature, that has
influenced our picture of Rikyū as the consummate master of *wabicha*,
bringing to perfection the *wabi* tendencies begun by Murata Shukō
and transmitted by Takeno Jōō. *Nampōroku* tells us that Rikyū in his
heart rejected the elegant *shoin-daisu* tea ceremony with its display of
formality and riches, teaching rather that just enough food and shelter—and tea—epitomizes both the way of the Buddha and the way of
tea.[3] The ideas of *Nampōroku* are obviously significant in attempting
to understand Rikyū and his *wabicha*, just as, for example, the Gospel

of John is valuable in attempting to understand the life and teaching of Jesus of Nazareth. But it must be recognized in both cases that the system of interpretation stems from needs and experiences accumulated in nearly a century of living tradition in drastically changed circumstances, and thus one can hardly expect more than an echo of the *ipsissima verba* of the master. Perhaps the lines were drawn too tightly by *Nampōroku* in describing the contrast between *wabicha* and its antithesis; in the contemporary tea records Rikyū appears more complex and his art more encompassing.

Modern Japanese scholars have done a great deal of research on the *chanoyu* of this period and on Rikyū's art in particular,[4] and one must review this research to understand Rikyū's aesthetic achievements in this phase of the development of *chanoyu*. Of significance for understanding Rikyū's art will be, first of all, the major sources upon which he drew in developing the basic contours of his own *chanoyu* practice. Then, on the basis of contemporary records, we will review the main tendencies of his artistic practices in relation to Nobunaga and Hideyoshi. Finally, we will interpret some of the transformations he effected in the art of *chanoyu*, whether in conflict with the powers that impinged upon him or in some sense transcending them.

SOURCES OF RIKYŪ'S *CHANOYU*

The notion of Rikyū's achievement as a "transformation" comes from the history of *chanoyu* itself. From the beginning of the ritual drinking of tea in China, a tradition was accrued; tea men in each new era focused on certain elements of that tradition, reordering and thus transforming the total configuration of the art in response to the needs of their age. This traditioning process reached a culmination of sorts in the elegant tea ceremony practiced during the Higashiyama epoch, when *chanoyu* was moved from the monastery hall and the tea pavilion to the reception room *(kaisho,* later *shoin)* setting, and the formal ceremony using the *daisu* stand focused on the aesthetic display of Chinese art objects. A different sort of transformation was effected by Murata Shukō and his disciples; deliberate cultivation of the astringent nature of tea led to an aesthetic of the "cold and withered" *(hiekareru)* and a corresponding reshaping of the art toward simple and frugal settings and common utensils.[5]

Tea tradition asserts that Rikyū's *chanoyu* was a transformation of these two basic currents in the development of the art. *Nampōroku* singles out two masters as Rikyū's teachers: Jōō, who studied with Shukō's disciples Sōchin and Sōgo, and Dōchin, who learned the Higashiyama style of *chanoyu* in the tradition of Nōami.[6] The historical reality, of course, is somewhat more complex. The Higashiyama tradition and the Shukō tradition were not so clearly delineated in Rikyū's training, and at least several other basic influences went into the making of Rikyū's art. One such influence was his relationship with other Sakai tea men. Another crucial influence in Rikyū's development was his lifelong association with Zen Buddhist masters and his practice of Buddhist discipline. The precise effect of these influences on his development is difficult to measure, for there is little historical information on his early training. But there are enough data to suggest that in a comprehensive interpretation of his aesthetic outlook each of these influences must be taken seriously.

Tea tradition puts forth the Higashiyama tea school, with its formal *daisu* style and display of valuable Chinese articles, as a major source of Rikyū's art; and it relates him to it in a number of ways. First there is a family connection. *Sen no Rikyū Yuishogaki* asserts that Rikyū's grandfather was Tanaka Sen'ami, who was a member of Ashikaga Yoshimasa's *dōbōshū* and later retired to Sakai after the Ōnin War (1467–1477).[7] If this tradition is correct, we can surmise that the *chanoyu* art of the Higashiyama school was maintained in the Tanaka family even in Sakai. Although there is no record showing that Rikyū's father, Sen Yohyōe, was involved in *chanoyu*, a Sen Sōkyū appears on numerous occasions in Tsuda Sōtatsu's *Chayu Nikki*.[8] This may have been an otherwise unknown older brother or uncle, suggesting, in any case, a deep involvement of the Tanaka-Sen family in *chanoyu*, possibly going back to Sen'ami.[9]

Tea tradition makes a second link between Rikyū and the Higashiyama tradition through the Sakai tea man Kitamuki Dōchin. *Nampōroku* reports:

As for Sōeki's teachers, Jōō was not the only one. Nōami had a page by the name of Ukyō, who when grown up received instruction in tea from Nōami. Afterward he renounced worldly life and, taking the name Kūkai, resided in Sakai, where there also lived the recluse Dōchin. They often conversed familiarly together, and it is said that he transmitted the way of tea to Dōchin in great detail. . . . Sōeki was then called Yoshirō, and from age seventeen he was principally attracted to tea, receiving training from Dōchin. . . . *Shoin, daisu,* and so forth he learned for the most part from Dōchin.[10]

It is not possible to verify this supposed transmission of *shoin-daisu chanoyu* from Nōami via Kūkai to Dōchin and thus to Rikyū, particularly in view of the disparity in time—Dōchin could not have been an *inja* or eremite in Sakai until at least fifty years after Nōami's death. But he no doubt was influenced by the Higashiyama tradition; he became a well-known master in Sakai, and *Yamanoue Sōji Ki* describes him as a connoisseur who possessed a number of valuable tea articles.[11] He appears frequently in the tea records in Sakai between 1542 and 1560 and was, according to the records, particularly close to Tsuda Sōtatsu and Imai Sōkyū, members of a circle which Rikyū also entered both as guest and host.[12]

Tea tradition makes a third link to the Higashiyama tea style through the Shukō school to which Jōō and Rikyū attached themselves. Shukō, it is said, knew Nōami and through him became tea master to Yoshimasa after the shogun's retirement to Higashiyama.[13] As in the case of Dōchin and Kūkai, it seems unlikely that Shukō was actually associated with Nōami, who died long before Yoshimasa's retirement to Higashiyama, but he could have had contact with other *dōbōshū.* That Shukō's tea style, new and simplified though it was, contained strong elements of the *shoin-daisu* tradition of *chanoyu* is suggested by *Nampōroku's* description of Shukō's four-and-a-half mat tea room decorated in the *shoin* style.[14]

The net result of these three traditional links between Rikyū and Higashiyama *chanoyu* is fairly convincing. True, the links are oversimplified and are recorded as personifications of what was undoubtedly a complex web of association between the earlier Higashiyama tradition and the developing tea style of the Sakai masters, as the newly wealthy merchants of Sakai learned the refined arts from the once-monied cultured class which found its way to Sakai. But the importance of the *shoin-karamono* aesthetic attitude in Rikyū's own development is not to be doubted.

A second significant source in Rikyū's art was the Shukō *sōan* (hut) tradition. The importance of Shukō's approach to tea in Rikyū's training and development is amply attested in the tea writings. *Yama-*

noue Sōji Ki traces Rikyū's style of tea through Jōō back to Shukō's secret teachings,[15] and *Nampōroku* notes that Rikyū's teacher Jōō studied with Shukō's disciples Sōchin and Sōgo.[16] Shukō, influenced by his participation in popular tea gatherings in Nara and also by his association with the Zen master Ikkyū of Daitokuji Temple in Kyoto, developed a tea style which centered on a "cold and withered" aesthetic and moved in the direction of the *sōan* setting and use of common utensils, emphasizing honesty of heart in the *chanoyu* art.[17] While Shukō remains shrouded in the mists of history, some of his disciples further developed the practice of tea in hermit hut settings with crude utensils. Sōshu, for example, built a *sōan* in lower Kyoto that was praised by many, including the *renga* master Sōchō.[18] And Sōgo cultivated the sense of restraint and poverty to the extent of discarding the use of valuable tea articles altogether, earning the comment in *Yamanoue Sōji Ki* that he "did not discriminate."[19]

Shukō's tradition thus gave rise to the practice of *chanoyu* in the *wabi* sense. *Wabi* had been used in the poetic recluse tradition to express religious discipline as a life on the bare edge of survival in a thatched hut in the midst of nature. As an aesthetic term, *wabi* expressed the sense of the pithy beauty of things prior to human civilization and in contrast to extravagant beauty.[20] Although it is not clear when this term came to be used in *chanoyu*, Jōō defined it as "a strong sense of respectful self-control in integrity, living one's life without extravagance." Jōō's experience as a *renga* poet, however, led him to stress the creation of fellowship rather than solitude as the ideal aesthetic experience, viewing the tea gathering as "a single occurrence once in a lifetime."[21]

Thus the sense of *wabicha* that developed in Shukō's school changed the focus of *chanoyu* by delighting in simplicity of setting and genuine communion of the guests; an example is Zenpō, who had but one kettle for tea and all other needs.[22] No doubt Rikyū was also influenced by some of these authentic *wabi* people who perhaps were looked upon as oddities but who were respected for embodying aesthetic ideals. Starting with his first undoubtedly historical tea gathering in 1544,[23] when he used a tea bowl and incense burner associated with Shukō, Rikyū revealed in his tea ensembles that he deliberately aspired to possess and use articles connected with the Shukō tradition.

A third source in Rikyū's art was related to *chanoyu*'s broad popularity among the merchant class in general and those merchants living in Sakai in particular. This was the era of rapid upward movement of certain commoner families, not only among the military but also among those engaged in the rapidly expanding commerce and trade. These newly rich merchant families were attracted to *chanoyu* for a variety of reasons, including the benefits to be derived from trading in valuable tea articles, the social prestige of a refined art associated with Higashiyama culture, the leveling of distinction between commoner and noble in this art, the socializing and entertaining possibilities of *chanoyu*, and the discipline and self-refinement required of those who practiced tea. In the bustling port city of Sakai, merchants mixed freely with military leaders, nobles, and ranking priests. Free of feudal control, Sakai was governed by a council of townspeople (*egōshū*) and maintained a sometimes precarious relationship with the various daimyos by reason of its commercial power. The spirit of the townspeople was frequently noted by visitors to the city, who mentioned the feelings of pragmatism and materialism, the excitement of unloading ships from China, the peace and quiet maintained by the citizens.[24] Especially among the merchant families who owned and ran large warehouses for commerce, much interest in *chanoyu* developed. Jōō, for example, was from a merchant family which had risen by trading in leather goods. The Tennōjiya family was especially prominent among these merchants, and both Tsuda Sōtatsu and his adopted son Sōgyū became influential tea masters.

As the fourth general source for Rikyū's *chanoyu* art we can point to the influence of Buddhist ideas and discipline. It is not necessary here to spell out the close association of tea with Buddhism in a continuous way from ancient times in China down to the Momoyama epoch. It should be noted, however, that this association was not limited to Ch'an/Zen but extended to various other Buddhist schools. For example, Eisai promoted a somewhat esoteric (*mikkyō*) interpretation of the benefits of tea drinking, and the Ritsu priests Ninshō and Eison used tea in their wide travels.[25] Further, the Buddhist values cultivated by recluse poets like Saigyō and Kamo no Chōmei contributed to the *wabi* ideals which later influenced *chanoyu*.[26] But it is also true that ritual tea drinking found an important place in the communal life of Ch'an monasteries in China and, correspondingly, in Zen monasteries in Japan, as monastic codes (*shingi*) incorporated "tea ceremony" rules (*sarei*) for many important occasions.[27] As Murai Yasuhiko has explained in Chapter 1, the monastic *sarei* were fundamental in the development of the formal tea ceremony using the *shoin* room and *daisu* stand in the Higashiyama epoch.

Thus it hardly needs to be said that Buddhist thought and discipline strongly influenced the development of *chanoyu*. But since *chanoyu*, particularly in the Azuchi-Momoyama epoch, was associated with politics and merchant pursuits, the extent of Buddhism's influence on Rikyū's development can be debated. Perhaps Buddhism was simply part of the cultural milieu and had only a marginal effect on the artistic pursuits of Sakai. The indications are, however, that the development of Rikyū's art of *chanoyu* was inseparably intertwined with Buddhist practice. It was not just an accruement of the age but served as a wellspring of inspiration. Shukō, for example, had been a Buddhist monk before wandering off to popular tea gatherings; and it appears that the concept of his new type of *sōan* tea came from involvement in the circle of artists who associated with the Zen master Ikkyū. Later, the Sakai circle of *chanoyu* seems to have been motivated by the Buddhist practices taught by Ikkyū's successors at Daitokuji and the related Nanshūji Temple in Sakai.

Thus four principal sources of Rikyū's art were the Higashiyama school, the Shukō tradition, the values of the Sakai merchant class, and Buddhist discipline. In the fertile years at the close of the Muromachi period, these four influences commingled in a creative way as Rikyū and his fellow tea masters of Sakai practiced the discipline of their art, collected valuable tea articles, involved themselves in the affairs of their family businesses, worked out city problems by participating in the *egōshū*, and developed *chanoyu* as an art of daily life in their frequently held tea gatherings. But when Nobunaga marched into Kyoto in 1568 and inaugurated the brief but explosive Azuchi-Momoyama epoch, a new situation was thrust upon the Sakai tea men and before long they found their art of *chanoyu* at the vortex of the struggle for the centralization of power in Japan.

CHANOYU IN PUBLIC AND POWERFUL PLACES

It is striking that almost all the available records of Rikyū's *chanoyu* practice stem from the last two decades of his life—in fact, most of them relate to his last eight years when he was associated with Hideyoshi. Since it is somewhat questionable to interpret an artist's life-work by relying on material so one-sidedly from his sixties, the scanty records of earlier *chanoyu* activity become invaluable in attaining a perspective. As Kumakura Isao has observed in Chapter 2, the explosive years with Hideyoshi evoked a burst of creativity from the nearly septuagenarian Rikyū. But the tendencies of his discipline and ideals had surely been forged in earlier years.

Sōeki Among the Tea Masters of Sakai

The years in Sakai before Nobunaga's entrance onto the scene show Rikyū and his fellow tea men in frequent tea gatherings, hosting and being hosted reciprocally. The merchant tea men were attracted to valuable tea articles, particularly those from China, and they displayed these articles in formal tea gatherings in four-and-a-half mat rooms, although larger sessions for tea and other entertainment were also occasionally held.[28] When Rikyū invited his teacher Jōō to a gathering in 1544, just seven months before Jōō's death, he used a Korean tea bowl, a kettle with a pattern of clouds and dragons, a Hotei incense container, a Kinrinji tea caddy, and a water jug of Shigaraki earthenware, and displayed a painting by Mu Ch'i with his own inscription in the alcove.[29] These were all suitably valuable articles to show that Rikyū was in the first rank of Sakai tea men. A decade later Rikyū hosted a gathering with Imai Sōkyū as the only guest, and Sōkyū's account shows that Rikyū continued to collect and use famous and valuable articles; he placed a Semehimo kettle in the hearth, narcissus flowers in the highly-prized Tsuru no Hitokoe flower vase, and used a Shigaraki water jug, a Korean tea bowl, and the celebrated Narashiba Katatsuki tea caddy which had been beloved by Torii Insetsu and was afterward passed to Shimai Sōshitsu of Hakata and, finally, to Hideyoshi.[30] The available records thus make clear that Rikyū from an early age shared with the other Sakai tea men a liking for the collection and display of valuable articles, and he developed his aesthetic sense in accordance with his training in the Higashiyama tradition.

It is significant that in Rikyū's first undisputed appearance in the available records, in 1544, Matsuya Hisamasa recorded his name not as Yoshirō but as "Sen Sōeki of Sakai."[31] Sometime before the age of twenty-three, Rikyū involved himself in Buddhist training and re-

ceived this name. Tea tradition says that after Dōchin introduced
Rikyū to Jōō, Rikyū first entered Daitokuji, shaved his head, received
the name Sōeki from the head priest, and came to his first tea gathering with Jōō dressed as a monk to show his fervor.[32] While it is more
likely that he received this name from Dairin Sōtō of Nanshūji in
Sakai, there is in this traditional account an indication that Rikyū
began to practice Buddhist discipline under the guidance of the masters of the Daitokuji school. The influence of Daitokuji guidance in
this period can perhaps be seen concretely in Rikyū's preference for
hanging in the alcove the calligraphic scrolls of Zen masters, such as
those of Yüan-wu K'o-ch'in (Engo Kokugon) and Shūhō Myōchō.[33]

Rikyū's gathering for Matsuya Hisamasa in 1544 is significant also
for its first indication of Rikyū's high regard for the Shukō tradition
of *chanoyu*. Visiting Sakai with Hisamasa was Ejunbō, head priest of
Shōmyōji in Nara, the temple with which Shukō had been associated.
For the visit of these two Nara tea men, Rikyū used a Shukō tea bowl
and a Segai incense burner. The bowl, according to descriptions by
Tsuda Sōgyū and Yamanoue Sōji, was a *karamono* celadon porcelain
of a simple, *wabi* style preferred by Shukō;[34] Rikyū often used this tea
bowl during these years.[35] The incense burner was also associated
with Shukō.[36] Further, beginning with his gathering for Tsuda
Sōtatsu and two others in 1562, Rikyū frequently displayed the valued calligraphic scroll by the famous Sung master Yüan-wu K'o-ch'in
(Engo Kokugon) which, according to *Yamanoue Sōji Ki* and *Sōtan
Nikki*, had been given to Shukō by his Zen master Ikkyū and was
thought to be particularly expressive of Shukō's tea spirit.[37]

The influence on Rikyū of the new attitude of the Sakai merchant
class is hard to pinpoint, but some traces of a free spirit and a somewhat flamboyant style can be detected in several records. At a gathering hosted by Totoya Ryōkō in 1567, "in front of the guests Sōeki
pounded in a peg and hung" a calligraphic scroll of the Sung master
Ch'ih-chüeh Tao-ch'ung (Chizetsu Dōchū).[38] Several months later,
when Rikyū was hosting Matsuya Hisamasa and others from Nara at
his residence in Imaichimachi, he displayed the famous Tsuru no
Hitokoe flower vase—but with no flowers, only water, in it.[39] Matsuya
Hisamasa's diary is of particular interest, for with each of his extended
visits to Sakai he recorded tea gatherings on successive days, as he
made the rounds of the residences of the leading tea men.[40] From
these records it is clear, first of all, that many more tea gatherings were

customarily held in Sakai than are recorded in the *Tennōjiya Kaiki* in this period and, secondly, that Rikyū's circle of Sakai tea men was much larger than other records indicate.

Several intriguing but obscure references in Tsuda Sōgyū's diary suggest something of the ups and downs of masters in Sakai's tea circles. Describing one of Rikyū's gatherings in the winter of 1568, Sōgyū noted obliquely that this winter Rikyū was "slipping into poverty," apparently hinting at troubled times for him.[41] And Sōgyū mentioned that Tennōjiya Dōshitsu hosted Matsue Ryūsen, Rikyū, and himself on 1569:12:18 specifically as "entertainment to mend the relations between Ryūsen and Sōeki." Apparently it worked, for Rikyū hosted a gathering for the same group six weeks later, and Matsue Ryūsen invited them to his gathering a week after that.[42] From this type of evidence, one is justified in assuming a great deal of interaction among the tea men of Sakai, some of it fraught with conflict, and in concluding that this interaction contributed to Rikyū's style and ideals in *chanoyu* which were being developed and honed in these three decades among the tea men of Sakai.

Chanoyu and Azuchi: Tea Master to Nobunaga

Rikyū never attained such importance with Nobunaga as either Imai Sōkyū or Tsuda Sōgyū, perhaps because his merchant family was not as powerful in Sakai. References to his serving tea at Nobunaga's gatherings in 1570 and 1573 are dubious. His first indisputable *chanoyu* contact with Nobunaga was at the tea gathering hosted by Nobunaga in the third month of 1574.[43] Like the other masters, Rikyū involved himself in Nobunaga's military and political endeavors.

But of interest here is not so much the involvement of the tea men in military and political affairs but the role of *chanoyu* itself in the new developments under Nobunaga. The new ruler clearly saw the possession of valuable *chanoyu* articles and the *chanoyu* gatherings as important in establishing his claims of hegemony and ritualizing his position. At a victory celebration after establishing peace in Kaga and Echizen provinces in 1575, for example, Nobunaga turned to *chanoyu* and hosted a deluxe gathering at Myōkōji Temple, inviting seventeen tea men from Kyoto and Sakai to display and use his many treasured tea articles. Rikyū's role in this sumptuous ceremony is indicated in

Shinchō Kōki by the phrase "*sadō wa* Sōeki," showing that Rikyū acted as tea master for Nobunaga.[44] And when Nobunaga visited Sakai in the fall of 1578, the large formal tea gatherings at the residences of various tea men had to do with ritualizing Nobunaga's authority over Sakai—thereby cutting off the Sakai merchants' relations with Ishiyama Honganji Temple.[45] *Chanoyu* was becoming a national ritual, a means of dramatizing consensus for Nobunaga's hegemony.

Not much is known of Rikyū's art in this period apart from his involvement in Nobunaga's extravaganzas, but a number of tea gatherings were recorded which suggest further development of his inclination toward *wabi* sensitivities. In the summer of 1577 he held a gathering to open his tea room, probably in Sakai, and invited Matsue Ryūsen, Tennōjiya Dōshitsu, and Tsuda Sōgyū; apart from the Koshima bowl, all his tea articles were common and plain, and the meal *(kaiseki)* was quite simple.[46] The next year he again held a simple gathering in his small room *(kozashiki)*.[47] He continued also to host tea gatherings at which he used the *daisu* stand,[48] but by 1580 it is clear that he had developed a strong *wabi* style. Hosting Tsuda Sōgyū and Yamanoue Sōji at a morning gathering, he displayed the somber Tung-yang Te-hui (Tōyō Tehi) calligraphic scroll in the alcove, hung a *kata no taretaru kama* (kettle with a drooping shoulder) in a spontaneous fashion in the hearth, and used a *hata no soritaru chawan* (tea bowl with the mouth spreading out).[49]

With Hideyoshi: The First Years

While there is little indication that Nobunaga understood or appreciated the *wabi* side of Rikyū's tea aesthetics, Hideyoshi provided circumstances that enabled Rikyū's creativity to soar to new heights in the last decade of his life. It is convenient to divide these years into two periods: Rikyū as "the tea master Sōeki" prior to the tea meeting in the imperial palace in 1585 and Rikyū as "Rikyū Koji" in the ebullient period after that significant event.

With Hideyoshi in control, the political use of the leading tea masters continued, and Rikyū played a central role. This can be seen from his letters of 1584 and 1585, which show he was well informed of Hideyoshi's plans in the campaign against Oda Nobukatsu's and Tokugawa Ieyasu's forces and the Etchū campaign against the Sassa, took a deep interest in these military affairs, and was even given responsibility in the custody of Osaka Castle.[50] But what did *chanoyu* mean to Hideyoshi? He no doubt acquired his interest in *chanoyu* from Nobunaga, from whom he received valuable tea articles; and probably he took his initial tea instruction from Tsuda Sōgyū, whom he hosted at a gathering in 1578 during the siege of the castle of Miki.[51]

Hideyoshi quickly showed his intention to continue Nobunaga's flair for displaying famous utensils at extravagant tea gatherings. Returning in triumph from the battle against Shibata Katsuie in 1583, he hosted a victory celebration gathering at Sakamoto in Ōmi province and displayed the valuable tea articles he had been collecting. On this occasion Tsuda Sōgyū referred in his diary to the "tea master" Sōeki, indicating that Rikyū acted as tea master for this victory celebration just as he had for Nobunaga's celebration in 1575.[52] Four months later Hideyoshi hosted Rikyū, Tsuda Sōgyū, Matsui Yūkan, Araki Dōkun, and Mozuya Sōan at a tea gathering, having ordered them to bring their own valuable utensils for *dōgu soroe*, an inspection of collected articles. Tsuda Sōgyū listed the principal articles and their owners in his diary, revealing a magnificent accumulation of great value.[53] A year later, in the fall of 1584, Hideyoshi paused in the middle of his stand-off campaign against Nobukatsu and Ieyasu to return to Osaka Castle to host a great assembly of twenty-nine tea masters. Each master prepared and served tea, and with each of them Hideyoshi had a cup of tea—twenty-nine tea masters on parade![54] Five months later Hideyoshi presented the great tea affair at Daitokuji. Twenty-five tea men from Sakai and fifty from Kyoto brought their own tea articles for this splendid occasion. Hideyoshi's collection of articles was on display in specially constructed huts, one in Rikyū's charge and the other in the care of Tsuda Sōgyū.[55] Such extravagant public display and elaborate ritual were clearly important in Hideyoshi's, as they had been in Nobunaga's, drive to establish authority, and now Rikyū played a leading role in this use of *chanoyu*.

But under Hideyoshi during these first few years a number of new developments took place in which Hideyoshi moved beyond Nobunaga's precedent in the use of *chanoyu*. For one thing, Hideyoshi began to turn to *chanoyu* for the ritual reception of powerful daimyos and other notable visitors. In 1583, for example, he hosted an all-day gathering, apparently for some of his generals and their close retainers, with Rikyū and Tsuda Sōgyū as tea masters.[56] And in 1585, during Nobukatsu's five-day visit to Osaka Castle following the conclusion of peace negotiations, among banquets, *nō* drama, and other entertainment, a central event was Hideyoshi's tea gathering for Nobukatsu in the *yamazato* (mountain village) small tea room, with Rikyū and Tsuda Sōgyū as fellow guests. Hideyoshi himself served tea to Nobukatsu.[57]

The high position Rikyū had achieved by the middle of 1585 can be observed in the fact that when the head of Honganji came to visit Osaka Castle, he received a *chanoyu* reception—but Hideyoshi did not come to the tea room, only Rikyū.[58] *Chanoyu* receptions were becoming significant in ritualizing the new structure of relationships between Hideyoshi and the various daimyos and other figures of importance, and Rikyū played a leading role in these receptions, even acting as Hideyoshi's representative.

Hideyoshi trained thoroughly in the art of *chanoyu*, first with Tsuda Sōgyū and then with Rikyū, and often hosted gatherings in which he himself served tea, not only to daimyos but often to his own tea masters. In the fall of 1582, soon after Nobunaga's death, Hideyoshi hosted Tsuda Sōgyū, Imai Sōkyū, and Rikyū and Yamanoue Sōji at Yamazaki, using a variety of valuable utensils; tea was prepared first by Hideyoshi and then by Tsuda Sōgyū.[59] A few months later Hideyoshi hosted the leading tea masters again at Yamazaki.[60] Even Hidenaga, Hideyoshi's half-brother, demonstrated an interest and ability in *chanoyu* and hosted the tea masters at his own gatherings.[61] Such tea meetings, in which Hideyoshi's tea masters were the only guests, went beyond the political use of *chanoyu* and suggest that Hideyoshi and Hidenaga had penetrated into the aesthetic meaning of the art itself.

Also new in Hideyoshi's attitude toward *chanoyu* was the obvious appreciation he developed for small, *wabi*-type tea rooms in contrast to the lavish settings which had been customary. Hideyoshi's tea meetings for his masters at Yamazaki in 1582 and 1583 may have been in the small, two-mat Taian tea hut in Myōkian which Rikyū is said to have planned for Hideyoshi, although the number of guests Hideyoshi had on these occasions makes that unlikely. Hideyoshi's liking for the Taian tea hut is not to be doubted, however, and was accompanied by an attraction to the *wabi* feeling it embodied.[62] While historical proof is lacking, it appears that Hideyoshi had a small, two-mat, hut-style "mountain village" tea room constructed within the Yamazato-maru in Osaka Castle. This was probably planned, under

Rikyū's guidance, in the tradition of the "mountain village hermit-age" which Toyohara Sumiaki built in his garden. Hideyoshi is reported to have hosted the "tea room opening" of the *yamazato* tea room with Rikyū and Tsuda Sōgyū as guests on 1584:1:3 and frequently used this room thereafter.[63]

Another development in Hideyoshi's early years in power was the cultivation of *chanoyu* as a complete way of life, not only for the tea masters but for Hideyoshi himself. Hideyoshi began to pause for small tea meetings in the midst of campaigns and had his tea masters visit him when he was encamped in the field.[64] Small tea gatherings apart from official receptions became frequent. For example, Hideyoshi moved into Osaka Castle in 1583 and hosted his first gathering there in 7:2, with Rikyū and Tsuda Sōgyū as guests. And beginning on 7:7 there was "everyday *chayu*" for an entire week with Rikyū and Tsuda Sōgyū acting as tea masters.[65]

In the first month of 1585 Hideyoshi took Rikyū, Tsuda Sōgyū, and Yamanoue Sōji along on a pleasure trip, since the negotiations with Ieyasu had been successful, and went to the hot baths at Yūshima, where they held many *chanoyu* gatherings.[66] Here *chanoyu* was not for public display and ritualization of authority, but simply for Hideyoshi and his tea masters, who pursued it as an aesthetic mode of life.

Rikyū Koji with Hideyoshi: At the Summit of Power

In the fall of 1585 the rise of *chanoyu* to the status of a national sacrament reached its culmination. Hideyoshi's success in unifying the country brought him new positions and titles from the emperor, and in the seventh month of 1585 he was elevated to the office of regent (*kampaku*). The next month he triumphed in the Etchū campaign against Sassa and completed negotiations for peace in Shikoku. Standing on the threshold of unified national power, Hideyoshi turned to *chanoyu* to ritualize his new status and claim to political dominance, taking the completely unprecedented step of hosting a tea gathering for the emperor and courtiers in the imperial palace. The story of this gathering is given in Kumakura Isao's essay on Rikyū in Chapter 2.

The second act of this ritual process took place a number of months later, when Hideyoshi returned to the imperial palace to serve tea once again to the emperor on 1586:1:16. What stirred particular interest on this occasion was the golden tea room (*ōgon chashitsu*) which Hideyoshi had dismantled and transported from Osaka Castle and set up in the palace for this event. Afterward he displayed it for public viewing. Although the golden tea room was apparently completed in time to show to retainers from the Mōri family who visited Osaka Castle the previous month,[67] it seems clear that Hideyoshi constructed it especially for use at the imperial palace for this important ritualization of his position by the emperor. According to descriptions by Yoshida Kanemi, Ōtomo Sōrin, and Kamiya Sōtan (who saw it or a similar one in 1592), the golden tea room was fabulous; its posts, walls, ceiling, and even its utensils (except the linen cloth, the bamboo whisk, and the wooden ladle) were of gold. Yet it was a small three-mat room—a golden hermit's hut![68]

Much has been written about Hideyoshi's ostentatious display of wealth and power in constructing the golden tea room, which was surely antithetical to the ideals of *wabi*. But, as indicated, the golden tea room was planned as part of Hideyoshi's ritualization of his position by hosting *chanoyu* in the imperial palace, serving tea to the emperor in the room's brilliant golden light. After its use in the imperial palace, the golden tea room was virtually regarded as sacred. Hideyoshi often guided visitors to inspect it, just as he allowed them to inspect his famous tea utensils, and he used the room to display his fabulous collection of *meibutsu*.

Although records of the 1586 tea gathering at the imperial palace do not expressly mention Rikyū, the fact that he was deeply involved in preparing the earlier gathering at the imperial palace suggests he also played a central role in planning this second ritual gathering. Moreover, when Hideyoshi showed the golden tea room to visitors to Osaka Castle, Rikyū was also in attendance, serving them tea and showing them Hideyoshi's other famous articles.[69]

When retainers of the Mōri family visited Hideyoshi in the twelfth month of 1585, they were shown the golden tea room by him, instructed in *chanoyu* by Rikyū, and invited to tea gatherings hosted by Hidenaga and by Hideyoshi himself (in the small *yamazato* tea room).[70] Ōtomo Sōrin visited Osaka Castle in 1586. After an audience, Sōrin was shown the golden tea room by Hideyoshi and was served tea first by Rikyū and then by Hideyoshi. After this, Sōrin inspected the five famous tea rooms in Osaka Castle. He was hosted in these rooms by Tsuda Sōgyū, Imai Sōkyū, Sen Jōan (Rikyū's son, later called Dōan), and Rikyū himself, who presided over two rooms.[71] When Ieyasu's envoy Sakakibara Yasumasa visited in the sixth month of 1586, *chanoyu* was the central ritual: Rikyū hosted him at a gathering on 6:7, and Hideyoshi served him tea in a large room in the castle on 6:8, displaying the famous Ikushima Kidō calligraphic scroll, which was the work of Hsü-t'ang Chih-yü (Kidō Chigu). On 6:9, the tea meeting was held in the *yamazato* tea room with Hidenaga also participating; Rikyū acted as master (*sadō*), and Hideyoshi performed the *temae*.[72] When Tokugawa Ieyasu visited Hideyoshi in the tenth month of 1586, the hegemon and Rikyū received him first with tea at Azuchi. After a formal reception, Rikyū hosted him and Hideyoshi with tea in the Osaka tower.[73]

When Hideyoshi successfully completed his campaign against the Shimazu family in Kyushu, Shimazu's retainer Ijūin Tadamune visited him at Osaka Castle in the tenth month of 1587, and Hideyoshi received Tadamune with a gathering in the small *yamazato* tea room.[74] Such receptions reveal that not only was *chanoyu* used ritually to establish Hideyoshi's relationship with the imperial court, but powerful daimyos were brought into proper hierarchical relationship with the regent through the national sacrament of *chanoyu*.

The broad public use of *chanoyu* was continued, as well, in the form of great displays and lavish tea gatherings. The public display of the golden tea room has been mentioned. When visiting Jesuits had an audience with Hideyoshi in 1586, they were guided to this tea room and also met "Soyequi, master of chianoyu."[75] And when Kamiya Sōtan, a wealthy merchant tea man of Hakata, visited Osaka Castle in the first month of 1587, he was so impressed by an opulent tea gathering hosted by Hideyoshi in a large room that he described it at length in his diary: Many of Hideyoshi's famous tea articles were displayed, and a large number of people received tea from the different masters.[76]

Such tendencies toward large tea gatherings and lavish displays culminated in the great tea meeting in the Kitano pine grove in the fall of 1587. The Kitano gathering, described in Chapter 2, was a very complex affair bringing together many of the tendencies that had been developing in Hideyoshi's and Rikyū's *chanoyu*, combining both *wabi* ideals and the display of riches and power. It is clear, however, that one of the central purposes of the gathering was the public ritualization of Hideyoshi's position as unifier of the nation. For by this point

Hideyoshi had completed his victorious Kyushu campaign and moved into his Kyoto castle, Jurakudai.

In keeping with the great significance of *chanoyu* in Hideyoshi's consolidation of authority and the public acceptance of his rule, Rikyū's role in advising and negotiating for him continued to grow. Ōtomo Sōrin's comments about Rikyū are well known, as he relayed to his retainers how Hidenaga told him that "confidential matters are known by Sōeki, public matters by the counselor (Hidenaga)," with Sōrin's added comment that "I think there is none other than Sōeki who can say even a word to the regent."[77] Although these comments are usually interpreted to refer to Rikyū's role in secret negotiations, as in the Date affair during the Odawara campaign,[78] Rikyū's power and authority lay primarily in his role as master of the ritualization of Hideyoshi's status vis-à-vis the daimyos. In particular, Rikyū's activity as *chanoyu* instructor played a part in his relations with various daimyos and thus contributed to his value as confidential adviser to Hideyoshi. For example, the joint letter of Rikyū and Hosokawa Yūsai to Ijūin Tadamune, the Shimazu retainer, involved a master-disciple relationship.[79] It appears that Rikyū also instructed Ōtomo Sōrin, since Hideyoshi questioned Rikyū concerning Sōrin's ability in *chanoyu*.[80] And when the retainers of the Mōri family visited Hideyoshi in the last month of 1585, Rikyū gave them instruction in tea prior to their attendance at their host's gathering.[81] Daimyos and retainers from various regions thought of Rikyū as "first in the realm" (*tenka ichi*) as a master of *chanoyu*, and his aesthetic judgment on matters pertaining to all aspects of the art was widely sought.[82]

Apart from these tendencies to use *chanoyu* in various ways in order to dramatize the hegemon's status, authority, and power, Hideyoshi and Rikyū continued to deepen their aesthetic enjoyment of *wabicha*. After Rikyū met Sōtan for the first time at the grand tea gathering in Osaka Castle in the first month of 1587, Sōtan recorded a long description of a simple *wabi* gathering that Rikyū held for him in a three-and-a-half mat tea room a week later, followed the next month by Hideyoshi's own *wabicha* gathering in the *yamazato* tea room.[83]

Returning in triumph from the Kyushu campaign in the sixth month of 1587, Hideyoshi and his tea masters relaxed in Hakozaki for several weeks and entertained each other with spontaneous, simple tea meetings. Kamiya Sōtan recorded some of these meetings in his diary. On the morning of 6:13, for example, Tsuda Sōgyū hosted

Hideyoshi in a *sukiya* in the style of a seaside salt hut thatched with miscanthus—and received much praise from the regent for his inventiveness. The next day Rikyū held a morning gathering for the three tea men from Hakata, Kamiya Sōtan, Shimai Sōshitsu, and Shibata Sōjin, in a deep, three-mat hut thatched with miscanthus and enclosed with fresh green miscanthus on the walls. In the Korean flower vase he arranged bamboo and flowers of *yakumo* grass. After Rikyū's tea ended, Sōtan and Sōjin went to a noon gathering hosted by Jōan (Dōan) in a two-and-a-half mat hut, thatched with rush like a boat, with green pine leaves on the wall. On 6:19 Hideyoshi hosted tea for Sōtan and Sōshitsu in a three-mat hut in which he used simple utensils and a flower arrangement of *enoko* grass. Sōtan himself hosted Hideyoshi and others on 6:25, using a two-and-a-half mat hut thatched with fresh miscanthus.[84] Here at Hakozaki the whole emphasis was on *wabi*; the tea meetings were held in temporary huts constructed from materials at hand. Apparently a great deal of freedom and inventiveness was in evidence.

Hideyoshi's appreciation of *wabi* was no mere show. Several weeks later he hosted a tea gathering with a distinctively countryside flavor in a hastily built *sukiya* at the Yamazato quarter in Osaka Castle. Sōtan and Tsuda Sōgyū were guests.[85]

In the last three years of his life—after the climactic grand Kitano tea gathering—Rikyū seems to have been less pressured by the demands for great public displays of *chanoyu*, perhaps because Hideyoshi's status and authority were sufficiently established by then. Rikyū continued to make use of the formal *daisu temae*, as, for example, when he hosted a farewell gathering for Kokei Sōchin, who was exiled by Hideyoshi in 1588. But his distinct preference for *wabicha* is seen particularly in the records of the *Hyakkaiki*, a fairly reliable account of the tea gatherings he hosted in the last half year of his life. For these gatherings Rikyū frequently used small tea rooms and simple utensils even when hosting important chieftains like Maeda or Hideyoshi himself or—in his last recorded gathering—Tokugawa Ieyasu.[86] Yamanoue Sōji noted in 1588 that Rikyū went so far in his preference for small, *wabi* tea rooms as to build a one-and-a-half mat tea room in Kyoto.

Even when he was approaching seventy, Rikyū's *chanoyu* continued to demonstrate a sense of innovation. For example, Tsuda Sōbon recorded an incident at Hideyoshi's tea gathering on 1590:9:23, when

Rikyū was acting as tea master. Rikyū displayed a scroll from Mu Ch'i and used a Jōō *tenmoku* bowl, but the guests were surprised to see the formal setting disrupted—the tea canister was in the *tenmoku* bowl, and in between was a stalk of wild camomile *(nogiku)*. When Rikyū entered, he rather nonchalantly drew out the flowers and placed them sideways over the alcove before proceeding with the tea ceremony.[87]

Particularly impressive is the evidence from the *Hyakkaiki* of the extent to which *chanoyu* had become Rikyū's entire life. In the eleventh month of 1590, for example, he hosted tea gatherings twenty-six times, occasionally having three in one day, morning, noon, and evening. And in the first month of 1591 he hosted twenty-five tea gatherings. Thus it is not surprising to read in the tea tradition that his *seppuku*, approximately one month after his last recorded tea gathering, was performed in the setting and style of a final *chanoyu* ritual. One gets the feeling that he acted out the ritual of *seppuku* as the terminating flourish to his creative, aesthetic, *chanoyu* mode of life.

Rikyū's association with Buddhist ideas and practices continued in these last years of his life. His Buddhist title, Rikyū Koji, was related to the specific occasion of the tea gathering in the imperial palace in 1585. But Rikyū did not treat it as a temporary name for a specific occasion; he continued to use it, possibly indicating an involvement in religious discipline toward the goal expressed in this name, which is discussed by Kumakura Isao in Chapter 2.[88] In the first month of 1589 he had a Buddhist service performed for his parents, his dead child, and also for himself and his wife.[89] His close association with Kokei Sōchin continued, and he went to some pains so that Kokei could return from exile.[90] He hosted the priests from Daitokuji and consulted with them.[91] And he showed his interest in the Daitokuji tradition by making a sizable donation for building the upper story of the Daitokuji gate. Finally, the poem he composed with Kokei in his last days and his own death poems are eloquent testimony to Buddhist sentiments about life and death which had penetrated his own aesthetic pursuit of life.[92]

RIKYŪ'S TRANSFORMATION OF *CHANOYU*

Transformation is part of every living tradition, as new generations reinterpret the tradition's dominant symbols in the context of their

own experience.[93] Joseph Kitagawa has pointed out that the reinterpreted tradition then becomes a kind of "grammar" which structures new expressions and experiences.[94] It is important, therefore, to
discover the nature of Rikyū's reinterpretation of the tea tradition in
order to understand the aesthetic "grammar" which guided his practice of *chanoyu*.

There is wide agreement that the fundamental transformation
effected by Rikyū was the reinterpretation of both the elegant *shoin-
daisu chanoyu* of the Higashiyama school and the inchoate *sōan-wabi
chanoyu* of Shukō's tradition. Studies of Rikyū's recorded tea gatherings, as well as extant tea articles and tea rooms associated with him,
have clearly revealed the contours of *wabi* as the dominant symbol of
his aesthetic system.

Wabi is usually understood in *chanoyu* as the negation of all luxury,
extravagance, and power, producing aesthetic forms of simplicity, frugality, poverty, and the common. These aspects of *wabi* can be
highlighted in Rikyū's career by using a model of conflict: conflict
between simplicity and extravagance, between the *yamazato* small tea
room and the golden tea room, or, more fundamentally, between the
wabi master Rikyū and the regent Hideyoshi. Karaki Junzō, in his
insightful study of Rikyū, comes to this conclusion. In making his
point, Karaki cites Rikyū's use of Fujiwara no Ietaka's poem:[95]

Hana o nomi	To those who await
Matsuran hito ni	Only the cherry blossoms,
Yamazato no	How I would like to show
Yukima no kusa no	The patches of green springtime
Haru o misebaya.	Through the snow of the mountain village.

Karaki sees the *yamazato* of the poem as a reference, in Rikyū's mind,
to the *yamazato* tea room, and he interprets Rikyū's feelings in this
way: "Precisely because Rikyū had the unpleasant experience of serving as tea master in the golden tea room, he was all the more anxious
to stress '*yamazato*'. . . . With this poem constantly on his tongue,
Rikyū always experienced deeply the contrast of the *yamazato* and the
golden tea room, the patches of green through the snow and the
cherry blossoms."[96] In Karaki's view, Rikyū lived in constant conflict
between the unpleasant duties of Hideyoshi's extravaganzas and the
relief of practicing his own style of *wabicha*.

Haga Kōshirō, in his brilliant study of Rikyū's career and aesthetic

outlook, has also penetratingly analyzed the conflict between Hideyoshi and Rikyū. According to Haga, Hideyoshi was the despot whose
sense of being "almighty" drove him to conquer and subdue. Rikyū
was the artist whose practical sense as a merchant led him to cooper-
ate but who, in his pride, refused to allow his artistic sense to be mas-
tered. Such conflict could only be resolved by the death of one of
them.[97] Although this is a compelling picture of the struggle of wills
between despot and artist, Kuwata Tadachika points out that the roles
of ruler and servant were so determined by the social forces of the sixteenth century that such a dramatized conflict may simply reflect a
modern interpretation of medieval realities.[98]

Haga also extends the conflict of wills between Hideyoshi and
Rikyū into the aesthetic arena. He points out that Rikyū's aesthetic
system was very complex in that he was not a real *wabi-inja* artist but
lived in rich and powerful surroundings. Even so, his fundamental
sense of *wabi*, according to Haga, contradicted the type of beauty
favored by Hideyoshi: "Hideyoshi's idea would have been a golden
hiroma (large room), for he would stop at nothing. But it was probably
Rikyū's sensitivity and guidance which caused this to be altered into a
three-mat *kozashiki* (small room). It is ultimately unthinkable that
Rikyū approved this golden tea room in his heart and that he actually
promoted it." Thus, Haga holds, when Rikyū used Fujiwara no Ietaka's *Hana o nomi* poem, he was thinking of the "new age" aesthetic
values being espoused by Hideyoshi and other daimyos who were
looking for sensual beauty; he was pained that they did not understand the traditional beauty of *wabi*.[99]

Karaki, Haga, and other scholars have thus placed Rikyū's *wabi*
understanding in sharp contrast to the type of beauty represented
especially by Hideyoshi's golden tea room, and in the process they
have highlighted the contradictions in which Rikyū, as Hideyoshi's
tea master, was involved. But this "other side" of Rikyū deserves more
consideration. When one looks through the tea records, it is surprising how little historical evidence there is of a fundamental aesthetic
conflict between Rikyū and Hideyoshi.

The records do not show that Hideyoshi preferred only glittering
beauty, while Rikyū was happy only with monochromatic *wabi* types
of beauty. On many occasions Hideyoshi hosted and served tea in rustic huts with very simple utensils. Certainly he had a taste for extravagant beauty. But it is also clear that he was deeply influenced by
Rikyū and took a genuine interest in *wabi* aesthetics even after

Rikyū's death.[100] Conversely, there is no evidence that Rikyū felt particularly uncomfortable serving tea and displaying *meibutsu* at Hideyoshi's lavish receptions or exuberant public tea gatherings, or even that he had basic reservations about the golden tea room. Using a model of conflict as the basic frame of reference for Rikyū's aesthetic outlook would lead ultimately to the conclusion that Rikyū must have had a hidden split aesthetic personality—that the basic conflict was within himself, between his own sense of *sōan-wabicha* ideals and his drive to pursue his *chanoyu* art in public and powerful places. This reasoning suggests further that Rikyū failed his own ideals when he served tea in Hideyoshi's grand displays—or at best, as some have suggested, that he willingly compromised his ideals in order to spread the good news of *chanoyu* to the masses by means of his powerful position.[101]

Surely great tensions existed in Rikyū's art and life. But within these tensions Rikyū was a creative artist who transformed the meaning of *wabi* and integrated new elements into the symbolic world of *chanoyu*. Rikyū's achievement as an artist of *chanoyu* was based on freshness, vitality, and freedom. In expressing admiration for Fujiwara no Ietaka's *Hana o nomi* poem, for example, he pointed to the experience of a new, powerful beauty that was possible in *chanoyu*. In contrast to people who have eyes only for cherry blossoms in full bloom, Rikyū wished to create the *wabi* experience—but not the usual *wabi* with autumn-winter images of the "cold and withered." He longed to show them the *wabi* of a mountain village in the early spring, as the greening grass strains to push through the snow, to reveal an image of potential beauty and suggest a feeling of pent-up spring eruption, a fresh and vital source of creativity.[102] The sense of urgency and eruption of strength must have been crucial in Rikyū's aesthetic perceptions, for his final poems are deeply imbued with this motif. Together with Kokei Sōchin, Rikyū in his last days put his feelings into words full of Zen connotation: "On a clear day, in the blue sky, angrily erupting flashes the lightening."[103] His Japanese death poem is replete with a sense of urgency. And connotations of inner strength, freedom, and the immediacy of enlightenment are expressed in his Chinese death poem (given here in the well-known translation by D. T. Suzuki):

> Seventy years of life—
> Ha ha! and what a fuss!

> With this sacred sword of mine,
> Both Buddhas and Patriarchs I kill![104]

Rikyū's *seppuku* was a final flourish in an artistic mode of life which, according to this poem, took seriously the words of the Ch'an master I Hsüan: "Kill the Buddha if you happen to meet him. Kill a patriarch or an arhat if you happen to meet them. . . . Only then can you be free."[105] These were, of course, Rikyū's death sentiments expressed in traditional form, but they show the motif of immediate strength and freedom, deeply rooted in Zen conceptions, which must have been central to his sense of life and art.

Several years before Rikyū's death, Yamanoue Sōji wrote an interesting judgment of him: Rikyū took liberties to the extent that he "made mountains into valleys and west into east, breaking the rules of *chanoyu* with freedom."[106] While there is implied criticism in Sōji's tone here, his words point to Rikyū's achievement in transforming the aesthetic experience of *wabi* in the *chanoyu* art. In this light we can understand Rikyū's display of the flower vase without flowers, the wild camomile incident, the one-and-a-half mat tea room, the spontaneous use of country articles and materials at hand. We can also understand his use of *meibutsu* and big displays, the mixture of *wabi* and grandeur at Kitano, even, perhaps, the three-mat golden tea room. With his reinterpreted aesthetic "grammar" of *wabi*, Rikyū transformed the art of *chanoyu* with freshness and creativity, not only perfecting the ideals of *sōan-wabicha* but extending the compass of this form of *chanoyu* to every aspect of his life.

This aesthetic attitude placed *chanoyu* squarely in the middle of life itself. Amid the tensions and ambiguities of the Momoyama epoch, Rikyū did not have a split aesthetic personality. He did not withdraw from the demands of human civilization to create a special art world apart from society and culture—which perhaps would have been the *wabi* ideal. Moreover, he did not slavishly follow traditional rules and aesthetic ideals. Thoroughly immersed in his *wabi* mode of life, he was able to make *chanoyu* into an aesthetic cultivation of common human activities and cultural creations.[107] Thus Rikyū's *chanoyu* became a microcosm of Momoyama life, drawing the outside world into his tea room and there integrating the ordinarily discrete aesthetic, religious, political, and social dimensions of human existence.

These aspects of Rikyū's *chanoyu* helped to make this art of daily life central for Hideyoshi in his struggle for power and authority. As mentioned earlier, rituals have crucial functions in society: communicating structures, reducing conflict, and promoting consensus. Because *chanoyu* was able to integrate the disparate areas of human concern within a traditional ceremony, it became a fitting art for the ritualization of the structures developing in Momoyama society. It responded to an age's need to find ritual integration of the religious and the secular, the traditional and the new, the hermit ideal and the urban reality, the nobility and the emerging classes. It was a traditional ceremony transformed with new meanings and became, for a while, a national ritual ushering in a new age.

But something more needs to be said, for the daimyos and their tea masters also immersed themselves in *wabicha* almost as a way of life apart from political ends. Here Victor Turner's concept of the ritual creation of *communitas* is suggestive. Turner points out that, in tightly structured societies, certain rituals offer a liminal experience which provides relief from structural commitments. Such a ritual often involves seclusion; people who are ordinarily involved in struggle and rank are stripped of their structural attributes, approximate a condition of poverty, and experience complete equality. The ritual represents a "timeless" condition. And the heart of the experience is the showing of the *sacra* (the traditional sacred objects), the secretive rehearsing of the sacred history, and the transformative actions of the ritual.[108] For the powerful men of Momoyama society, participating in a *wabicha* gathering involved some of these elements of liminality. They gathered in a small hut close to nature in the "one-timeness" (*ichigo, ichie*) of the tea ceremony; they symbolically left behind their status and power, experiencing true equality in the atmosphere of poverty (*wabi*); the *sacra* (valued tea articles) were shown and their history rehearsed; and through the *temae* of the tea masters and the responsive ritual actions of the guests the liminal experience of *communitas* was created. From this point of view, *wabicha* provided men in the tightening structures of Hideyoshi's new society with an opportunity to sit in fellowship outside the system. Thus they could partake of an "antistructure" which at the same time encouraged consent for the formal new structures that were being put into place.

NOTES

1. See, for example, the essays in James Shaughnessy, ed., *The Roots of Ritual* (Grand Rapids: Eerdmans Publishing Co., 1973), and the essays in *Philosophical Transactions of the Royal Society of London*, ser. B, vol. 251 (1966), pp. 247–524.

2. Victor Turner, *Dramas, Fields, and Metaphors: Symbolic Action in Human Society* (Ithaca: Cornell University Press, 1974), pp. 231–270.

3. In Sen Sōshitsu, ed., *Chadō Koten Zenshū (CKZ)* (Kyoto: Tankōsha, 1956–1962), vol. 4, p. 3.

4. See, for example, Kuwata Tadachika, *Sen no Rikyū Kenkyū* (Tokyo: Tōkyōdō Shoten, 1976); Kuwata Tadachika, *Teihon Sen no Rikyū no Shokan* (Tokyo: Tōkyōdō Shoten, 1971); Haga Kōshirō, *Sen no Rikyū* (Tokyo: Yoshikawa Kōbunkan, 1972); Karaki Junzō, *Sen no Rikyū* (Tokyo: Chikuma Shobō, 1979); Horiguchi Sutemi, *Rikyū no Cha* (Tokyo: Kagoshima Kenkyūsho Shuppankai, 1970); Murai Yasuhiko, *Sen no Rikyū: Sono Shōgai to Chanoyu no Imi* (Tokyo: Nihon Hōsō Shuppan Kyōkai, 1971); Sugimoto Hayao, *Sen no Rikyū to Sono Shūhen* (Kyoto: Tankōsha, 1970); Kumakura Isao, *Sen no Rikyū: Wabicha no Bi to Kokoro* (Tokyo: Heibonsha, 1978).

5. For the early history of *chanoyu*, see Haga Kōshirō, *Wabicha no Kenkyū* (Tokyo: Tankōsha, 1978); Harada Tomohiko, *Chadō Seisuiki* (Tokyo: Kadokawa Shoten, 1967); Murai Yasuhiko, *Cha no Bunkashi* (Tokyo: Iwanami Shoten, 1979); Hayashiya Tatsusaburō, *Zuroku Chadōshi: Fūryū no Seiritsu* (Kyoto: Tankō Shinsha, 1962); H. Paul Varley and George Elison, "The Culture of Tea: From Its Origins to Sen no Rikyū," in George Elison and Bardwell L. Smith, eds., *Warlords, Artists and Commoners: Japan in the Sixteenth Century* (Honolulu: University of Hawaii Press, 1981), pp. 187–222; and Theodore M. Ludwig, "Before Rikyū: Religious and Aesthetic Influences in the Early History of the Tea Ceremony," *Monumenta Nipponica* 36 (1981), pp. 367–390.

6. Nambō Sōkei, *Nampōroku*, in *CKZ*, vol. 4, p. 4.

7. There is some evidence for such a Sen'ami at Higashiyama, although the link with Rikyū's grandfather cannot be proved; see Murai Yasuhiko, *Sen no Rikyū*, pp. 50–64; Kuwata Tadachika, *Sen no Rikyū Kenkyū*, pp. 39–40.

8. See, for example, *Sōtatsu Chayu Nikki Takaiki*, entries for Tenbun 21:3:13; Kōji 3:12:4; *Sōtatsu Chayu Nikki Jikaiki*, Tenbun 20:2:231; 21:5:19; 22:11:10; 24:9:30 (cited from *CKZ*).

9. Haga Kōshirō, *Sen no Rikyū*, pp. 30–35.

10. *CKZ*, vol. 4, pp. 4–5.

11. *Yamanoue Sōji Ki*, in *CKZ*, vol. 6, p. 97.

12. *Matsuya Hisamasa Chakaiki*, Tenbun 11:intercalary 3:9; Eiroku 2:3:22; *Sōtatsu Chayu Nikki Takaiki*, Tenbun 19:2:2; 22:intercalary 1:29; Kōji 3:3:18; 4:6:24; *Imai Sōkyū Chayu Nikki Nukigaki*, Kōji 4:1:5.

13. *CKZ*, vol. 6, pp. 51–53.

14. *CKZ*, vol. 4, p. 52.

15. *CKZ*, vol. 6, p. 53 ff.

16. *CKZ*, vol. 4, p. 4.

17. See *Shukō Furuichi Harima Hōshi ate Isshi*, in CKZ, vol. 3, pp. 3–4; also Haga Kōshirō, *Wabicha no Kenkyū*, pp. 30–53.
18. *Sōchō Shuki*, Daiei 6; quoted in Haga Kōshirō, *Wabicha no Kenkyū*, p. 162.
19. CKZ, vol. 6, p. 96.
20. See especially Haga Kōshirō, *Wabicha no Kenkyū*, pp. 124–149; Ishida Yoshisada, *Inja no Bungaku* (Tokyo: Koshobō, 1968), pp. 246–250; Kazue Kyōichi, *Wabi: Wabicha no Keifu* (Tokyo: Tsuru Shobō, 1973); and Mochizuki Shinjō, *Wabi no Geijutsu* (Osaka: Sōgansha, 1974).
21. These teachings attributed to Jōō may reflect later interpretations: Kuwata Tadachika, ed., *Shinshū Chadō Zenshū* (Tokyo: Shinjūsha, 1956), vol. 8, pp. 17–18; and CKZ, vol. 3, p. 29.
22. CKZ, vol. 6, p. 53. According to *Yamanoue Sōji Ki*, Zenpō was a disciple of Shukō; CKZ, vol. 6, pp. 52, 96.
23. *Matsuya Hisamasa Chakaiki*, Tenbun 13:2:27. Kuwata Tadachika, *Sen no Rikyū Kenkyū*, p. 43, believes the "Yoshirō" who held a *chakai* for Matsuya Hisamasa in Kyoto on Tenbun 6 (1537):9:13, as recorded in *Matsuya Hisamasa Chakaiki*, was the youthful Rikyū at sixteen; but Murai Yasuhiko, *Sen no Rikyū*, p. 78, thinks this is unlikely.
24. See Toyoda Takeshi, *Sakai: Shōnin no Shinshutsu to Toshi no Jiyū* (Tokyo: Shibundō, 1957); Murai Yasuhiko, *Sen no Rikyū*, pp. 83–91; and V. Dixon Morris, "The City of Sakai and Urban Authority," in Elison and Smith, *Warlords, Artists and Commoners*, pp. 23–54.
25. See Haga Kōshirō, *Wabicha no Kenkyū*, pp. 11–12; and Hayashiya Tatsusaburō, *Zuroku Chadōshi*, pp. 55–59.
26. See Ishida Yoshisada, *Inja no Bungaku*.
27. See the discussion in CKZ, vol. 1, p. 371 ff.
28. Murai Yasuhiko, *Sen no Rikyū*, pp. 79–80.
29. *Imai Sōkyū Chayu Nikki Nukigaki*, Tenbun 24:4:1.
30. Ibid., Eiroku 9:10:18; see Haga Kōshirō, *Sen no Rikyū*, p. 76.
31. *Matsuya Hisamasa Chakaiki*, Tenbun 13:2:27.
32. Kuwata Tadachika, *Sen no Rikyū Kenkyū*, p. 46.
33. *Sōtatsu Chayu Nikki Takaiki*, Eiroku 5:5:27; *Sōgyū Chayu Nikki Takaiki*, Eiroku 9:11:28; 13:2:3.
34. *Sōgyū Chayu Nikki Takaiki*, *Dōgu Haiken*, Eiroku 9:12:9 (CKZ, vol. 7, p. 207); *Yamanoue Sōji Ki*, in CKZ, vol. 6, p. 63.
35. *Sōtatsu Chayu Nikki Takaiki*, Tenbun 24:1:6; Kōji 2:12:19; *Matsuya Hisamasa Chakaiki*, Eiroku 2:4:23.
36. *Sōgyū Chayu Nikki Takaiki*, *Dōgu Haiken*, Eiroku 9:11:28 (CKZ, vol. 7, p. 206); *Yamanoue Sōji Ki*, in CKZ, vol. 6, p. 68; see Kuwata Tadachika, *Sen no Rikyū Kenkyū*, pp. 47–48.
37. *Sōtatsu Chayu Nikki Takaiki*, Eiroku 5:5:27; 6:12:1; *Sōgyū Chayu Nikki Takaiki*, *Dōgu Haiken*, Eiroku 9:11:28 (CKZ, vol. 7, p. 206); see *Yamanoue Sōji Ki*, in CKZ, vol. 6, p. 72; and *Sōtan Nikki*, Tenshō 15:1:12.
38. *Sōgyū Chayu Nikki Takaiki*, Eiroku 10:10:17.
39. *Matsuya Hisamasa Chakaiki*, Eiroku 10:12:26.
40. Ibid., entries for Tenbun 13:2:18–27; Eiroku 2:4:18–25; 10:11:29 ff.

41. *Sōgyū Chayu Nikki Takaiki*, Eiroku 11:11:12.

42. Ibid., 12:12:18; 13:2:3; 13:2:11. See Murai Yasuhiko, *Sen no Rikyū*, p. 96.

43. *Sōgyū Chayu Nikki Takaiki*, Tenshō 2:3:24. The entries in *Imai Sōgyū Chayu Nikki Nukigaki*, Eiroku 13:4:1 and Tenshō 1:11:24, contain errors and contradictions; see Haga Kōshirō, *Sen no Rikyū*, pp. 93–97.

44. Kuwata Tadachika, ed., *Shinchō Kōki* (Tokyo: Jimbutsu Ōraisha, 1965), Tenshō 3:10:28, p. 187. Interestingly, Sōgyū's diary does not mention Rikyū on this occasion.

45. See Haga Kōshirō, *Sen no Rikyū*, pp. 102–104; *Sōgyū Chayu Nikki Jikaiki*, Tenshō 6:9:30.

46. *Sōgyū Chayu Nikki Takaiki*, Tenshō 5:intercalary 7:7; see Murai Yasuhiko, *Sen no Rikyū*, pp. 120–121.

47. *Sōgyū Chayu Nikki Takaiki*, Tenshō 6:6:27.

48. See, for example, *Sōgyū Chayu Nikki Takaiki*, Tenshō 7:4:22.

49. Ibid., Tenshō 8:12:9.

50. See the convenient summaries of this material in Kuwata Tadachika, *Sen no Rikyū Kenkyū*, pp. 89–92, 102–108; Haga Kōshirō, *Sen no Rikyū*, pp. 130–131, 138–142.

51. *Sōgyū Chayu Nikki Takaiki*, Tenshō 6:10:15.

52. Ibid., Tenshō 11:5:24.

53. Ibid., Tenshō 11:9:16. Another such exhibition was held two months later (11:11:14).

54. Ibid., Tenshō 12:10:15.

55. Ibid., Tenshō 13:3:5. Note that Imai Sōkyū did not have a tea hut in his charge.

56. Ibid., Tenshō 11:12:10; the details of this large *chakai* are not clear.

57. Ibid., entries for Tenshō 13:2:20–25; the *chakai* was on 2:24.

58. See Haga Kōshirō, *Sen no Rikyū*, p. 138.

59. *Sōgyū Chayu Nikki Takaiki*, Tenshō 10:11:7.

60. Ibid., Tenshō 11:intercalary 1:5.

61. Ibid., Tenshō 13:2:8.

62. Karaki Junzō, *Sen no Rikyū*, p. 74; Karaki says of this tea room, still preserved today, "The Taian is the 'north pole' of *wabi*." See Horiguchi Sutemi, *Rikyū no Chashitsu* (Tokyo: Iwanami Shoten, 1968), pp. 374–458.

63. *Sōgyū Chayu Nikki Takaiki*, Tenshō 12:1:3. *Sōtan Nikki*, Tenshō 15:2:25, provides a long description of this tea room.

64. *Sōgyū Chayu Nikki Takaiki*, Tenshō 11:3:26; Tenshō 6:10:15.

65. Ibid., Tenshō 11:7:2; 11:7:7 ff.

66. Ibid., entries for Tenshō 13:1:17–2:1.

67. Haga Kōshirō, *Sen no Rikyū*, p. 182.

68. *Kanemi Kyōki*, Tenshō 14:1:16; *Sōtan Nikki*, Tenshō 20:5:28; see Haga Kōshirō, *Sen no Rikyū*, pp. 187–189.

69. Haga Kōshirō, *Sen no Rikyū*, pp. 182–188.

70. Ibid., pp. 182–183.

71. See Kuwata Tadachika, *Sen no Rikyū Kenkyū*, pp. 133–135.

72. See Rikyū's letter describing this gathering; Kuwata Tadachika, *Teihon Sen no Rikyū no Shokan*, no. 110, pp. 263–265, and *Sen no Rikyū Kenkyū*, pp. 141–142. In

the sixth month of 1586, Kamisugi Kagekatsu, governor of Echigo, was received by Hideyoshi and Rikyū at a *chakai* in Jurakudai, then under construction; see Haga Kōshirō, *Sen no Rikyū*, pp. 193–194.

73. This is according to *Sen no Rikyū Yuishogaki*; see Haga Kōshirō, *Sen no Rikyū*, pp. 195–196, and Murai Yasuhiko, *Sen no Rikyū*, pp. 185–186.

74. *Sōtan Nikki*, Tenshō 15:10:21.

75. See Beatrice M. Bodart, "Tea and Counsel: The Political Role of Sen Rikyū," *Monumenta Nipponica* 32 (1977), p. 56, nn. 47–48.

76. *Sōtan Nikki*, Tenshō 15:1:3.

77. See Kuwata Tadachika, *Sen no Rikyū Kenkyū*, pp. 134–135.

78. Bodart, "Tea and Counsel," pp. 56–64.

79. Ibid., pp. 53–54; Kuwata Tadachika, *Teihon Sen no Rikyū no Shokan*, no. 84, p. 200.

80. Kuwata Tadachika, *Sen no Rikyū Kenkyū*, p. 133.

81. Ibid., p. 128.

82. Ibid., pp. 179–180; Haga Kōshirō, *Sen no Rikyū*, pp. 223–224.

83. *Sōtan Nikki*, Tenshō 15:1:12, 2:25.

84. Ibid., entries for these dates.

85. Ibid., Tenshō 15:10:14.

86. *Rikyū Hyakkaiki*. See Haga Kōshirō, *Sen no Rikyū*, pp. 311–312.

87. *Sōbon Chayu Nikki Takaiki*, Tenshō 18:9:23.

88. See the extensive discussion of this name in Haga Kōshirō, *Sen no Rikyū*, pp. 150–177; Kuwata Tadachika, *Sen no Rikyū Kenkyū*, pp. 108–121; Sugimoto, pp. 28–39; and Murai Yasuhiko, *Sen no Rikyū*, pp. 167–179.

89. Kuwata Tadachika, *Sen no Rikyū Kenkyū*, pp. 201–202; and Murai Yasuhiko, *Sen no Rikyū*, pp. 116–117.

90. Haga Kōshirō, *Sen no Rikyū*, pp. 230–233.

91. See, for example, *Hyakkaiki*, Tenshō 18:9:14.

92. See Kuwata Tadachika, *Sen no Rikyū Kenkyū*, pp. 256–266.

93. See Peter Slater, *The Dynamics of Religion: Meaning and Change in Religious Tradition* (New York: Harper & Row, 1978), pp. 1–46.

94. Joseph M. Kitagawa, "The Japanese *Kokutai* (National Community): History and Myth," *History of Religions* 13 (1974), p. 224. See also Joseph M. Kitagawa, "The Buddhist Transformation in Japan," *History of Religions* 4 (1965), p. 319.

95. *Nampōroku*, in CKZ, vol. 4, pp. 16–17.

96. Karaki Junzō, *Sen no Rikyū*, pp. 83–85.

97. Haga Kōshirō, *Sen no Rikyū*, pp. 299–308.

98. Kuwata Tadachika, *Sen no Rikyū Kenkyū*, pp. 228–230, 295–303.

99. Haga Kōshirō, *Sen no Rikyū*, pp. 191–192, 313–316.

100. See his favorable comments about Rikyū's style of *chanoyu*: *Sōtan Nikki*, Tenshō 20:10:last day; letters 39 and 42 in Adriana Boscaro, ed., *One Hundred and One Letters of Hideyoshi* (Tokyo: Sophia University, 1975).

101. See, for example, R. Castile, *The Way of Tea* (New York: Weatherhill, 1971), p. 74.

102. For this interpretation of *wabi* in this poem, see Haga Kōshirō, *Wabicha no Kenkyū*, pp. 155–156.

103. Kuwata Tadachika, *Sen no Rikyū Kenkyū*, pp. 259–260, discusses the Zen background of this poem.

104. Kuwata Tadachika, *Teihon Sen Rikyū no Shokan*, no. 262, p. 611; translated by D. T. Suzuki, *Zen and Japanese Culture* (Princeton: Princeton University Press, 1970), p. 319. See Kuwata Tadachika, *Sen no Rikyū Kenkyū*, pp. 260–266; and Karaki Junzō, *Sen no Rikyū*, pp. 127–129.

105. Translated by Wing-Tsit Chan, *A Source Book in Chinese Philosophy* (Princeton: Princeton University Press, 1963), p. 447.

106. *Yamanoue Sōji Ki*, in CKZ, vol. 6, pp. 102–103.

107. On this interpretation, see Shuichi Kato, *Form, Style, Tradition: Reflections on Japanese Art and Society*, trans. John Bester (Berkeley: University of California Press, 1971), pp. 151–163.

108. Turner, *Dramas, Fields, and Metaphors*, pp. 231–270.

FOUR

THE EARLY EUROPEANS AND TEA

Michael Cooper

WHEN, on 14 November 1584, the Japanese youths representing the three Christian daimyos of Bungo, Arima, and Ōmura were received in audience by Philip II in Madrid, they apologized to the king for the poor quality of their gifts. The haste in which their expedition had been organized, they explained, had obliged them to leave Japan without bringing suitable presents. Among their gifts was a drinking vessel, and Diogo Mesquita, the Jesuit priest accompanying the embassy, remarked that the cup was intended for wine:

> "How is that? Don't they drink hot water?" asked the king. The priest replied that they did but that they also made wine. The king then asked, "Do they drink the hot water only in winter?" The priest told him that they drank it all the year round, at which the king was greatly astonished.[1]

Philip II was not the only European astonished by the Japanese custom of drinking "hot water," or tea, throughout the year, and the habit had been expressly noted as early as 1565 by the Jesuit chronicler Luis Frois in a letter he wrote in Miyako (the capital, Kyoto).[2] Such nonalcoholic beverages as hot tea, coffee, and cocoa were still unknown in Europe or, at best, regarded as exotic drinks, so it is hardly surprising that both the Jesuit writers in Japan and their readers in Europe were intrigued by the Japanese propensity for drinking tea.

EARLY EUROPEANS IN JAPAN

Although European traders first reached Japan in 1542, the mysterious island of Cipangu, as described in Marco Polo's hearsay account,

101

had long attracted considerable European attention, not least because of the Venetian traveler's colorful but fictitious description of the island's wealth in gold. Within a few years of the European traders reaching Japan, Christian missionaries also arrived when Francis Xavier and two Jesuit companions stepped ashore at Kagoshima in 1549. In due course, more missionaries, usually Spaniards, Portuguese, or Italians, arrived to propagate their religion, and it was they who began to reveal Japan to the West by sending back to their native Europe long letters and reports about the country, its people, and its culture.

With one or two exceptions the European traders did not bother to commit to paper their impressions of Japanese life.[3] Most of them stayed only a matter of months, did not speak the language, seldom strayed beyond Nagasaki and its surroundings, and were probably not interested in the country or its people. Japan, for them, was just one of many Asian countries they visited to conduct trade. If they had any desire to describe Japan to their fellow Europeans, this could be done by word of mouth on their return to India and Europe.

The position, and therefore the attitude, of the missionaries was somewhat different. Since the great majority of them never returned to Europe, their only means of communication was the written word. Their commitment to Japan was total and lifelong, and many of them learned to speak Japanese with varying degrees of fluency. Further, in the course of their apostolic labors they traveled widely throughout Kyushu and, in a more restricted way, throughout Honshu. Frequent communication between Jesuits working in the mission field was officially encouraged, and an instruction dated 1553 exhorted them to write detailed accounts about "the weather, the degrees of longitude, the dress, food, housing, numbers, and customs of the inhabitants" of the countries in which they were working.[4]

This instruction had a twofold aim—to foster fraternal union among the missionaries working in distant lands and to promote interest in the missions among the faithful in Europe. The Jesuits in Japan and, later, in China, set to work with a will to keep Europe informed not only about the progress of their mission but also about the country and the people among whom they were working. And there was a great deal to write about, for the Europeans found in Japan a highly civilized and cultured country, untouched, at least directly, by Western influence, a country which differed radically from Europe in outlook, religion, social structure, government, customs, architecture, food, and drink. Alessandro Valignano went so far as to observe: "They have rites and customs so different from those of all other nations that it seems they deliberately try to be unlike any other people. The things they do in this respect are beyond imagining and it may truly be said that Japan is a world the reverse of Europe."[5]

One further observation may be made. The European visitors' position vis-à-vis the Japanese was different from that obtaining in other Asian and South American countries, where the Spaniards and, to a lesser extent, the Portuguese had arrived as conquistadores and therefore tended to look down on the native population and ignore and sometimes destroy the indigenous culture. The situation in Japan was far different. Here the Europeans were accepted as guests and visitors, welcomed or at least tolerated, and they were obliged to conduct themselves accordingly. It was now the Europeans' turn to be regarded as uncouth barbarians until they could prove to the Japanese that cultural differences did not necessarily imply cultural superiority on the one hand or cultural inferiority on the other. It was a salutary lesson for the Europeans to have to deal with Asians on an equal footing, possibly for the first time in East-West relations, but it may be doubted whether more than a handful of the Europeans in Japan were sufficiently enlightened to be able to overcome their ethnocentrism and view the situation objectively.

EUROPEANS AND TEA

The first European reference to tea drinking in Japan seems to have been made by the merchant Jorge Alvares, who spent some months in Kagoshima in 1546, three years before the arrival of the missionaries in the country. In his perceptive report, drawn up on his return to India, Alvares noted that the Japanese ate sparingly, their staple diet being rice. They drank an arrack made from rice, and "there is also another drink which both the nobles and ordinary people take." He went on to describe this drink by remarking: "They drink water mixed with herbs in winter, although I never learned what these herbs were. Neither in the winter nor in the summer do they drink cold water."[6]

The references to tea as "hot water" persisted for many years. Writing in 1561, Juan Fernandez, one of Xavier's original companions, praised the fervor of Damien, a young Japanese convert, and recounted how the man helped around the Jesuit residence:

> This Japanese has many jobs in the residence, and he has the task of always having a kettle of hot water ready, which he gives to all the visitors and to those in the residence who want it. This is the custom of the country. This task requires that the man who does it must always be very neat and polite on account of the dealings he has to have with everybody. . . .[7]

Four years later Frois reported from Miyako: "In winter and summer they always drink hot water, as hot as they can stand it."[8] This observation was confirmed more than twenty years later by Valignano: "They always drink hot water at the end of every meal, both in summer and winter; the water is so hot, in fact, that it can be drunk only by sips."[9] With this flow of reports reaching Europe about the Japanese drinking "hot water," it is hardly surprising that Philip II should have thought that this was the sole drink of Japan. Yet one can understand why the early Europeans initially described tea as "hot water." The foreign guest might easily fail to notice the tea powder being spooned into his cup and would see only the boiling water being added; in any case, the hot, clear beverage might well have appeared to the foreign palate as so much hot water with some slight flavoring added. As far as can be discovered, the earliest documentary reference to tea as such can be attributed to the veteran missionary Luis de Almeida who, perhaps on account of his earlier medical training, gave a precise description of the brew in a letter dated 25 October 1565. Almeida noted that there was "a certain boiled herb, which is called *cha* and which is tasty to anybody getting used to drinking it."[10]

With the passing of time the missionaries began to take a more lively interest in tea drinking, which was then very much in vogue among the nobility and wealthy merchant class, and to realize its pivotal role in Japanese etiquette. In his efforts to encourage missionaries to adapt themselves to Japanese life and manners, Valignano placed tea drinking firmly in the Jesuit sphere of activity. Valignano came to Japan three times in his capacity as "Visitor," or inspector, of the mission, and it was during his first stay in the country (1579–1582) that he laid down detailed regulations concerning the use of tea. As Visitor, Valignano was the religious superior of all the Jesuit missionaries in Japan during his stay in the country and was therefore authorized to issue any directives that he saw fit for the good of the mission. Not content with general rules, the strong-willed Valignano normally spelled out his regulations in considerable detail, and the case of tea is no exception. His far-sighted urging of the need for adaptation to the Japanese way of life is remarkable in that, at the time of writing, he himself had spent little time in Japan. Yet for all his lack of direct experience of Japanese customs, the Visitor intuitively saw the need for greater assimilation if the missionaries were to work with maximum effectiveness. In this campaign, Valignano was encouraged by conversations he had with two friendly Kyushu daimyos, Arima Harunobu and Ōtomo Yoshishige (Sōrin): the latter made a particularly deep impression on him. The result was Valignano's treatise whose title can be rendered into English as "Notes and Advice About the Customs and Outlook of Japan."[11] In concrete detail, he directs how missionaries should conform to Japanese etiquette.

In the first chapter, Valignano lays down that all Jesuit residences in Japan were to have a *chanoyu*, using this term in its apparently current meaning of a tea room, as well as a *genkan* and *zashiki* in pure Japanese style, because "without such rooms made according to Japanese style, the guests who are received will be treated to many discourtesies and affronts."[12] Having stated the general principles, Valignano enters into greater detail in the following chapter and it is worth quoting his directive in full to show his appreciation of the importance of tea in Japanese life:

> All the [Jesuit] residences should have their *chanoyu*, kept clean and in good order. And there should be a *dojucu* (*dōjuku*, lay acolyte) or some other person in continual attendance there; he should know something about *chanoyu*, especially in places where a large number of nobles are liable to come. There ought to be two or three types of *cha*, one of very good quality and the other of lesser sort, in keeping with the rank of the people who come to visit. The man in charge of this *chanoyu* should not be employed in manual work, but should instead occupy himself in reading, writing, or grinding *cha* and doing other things connected with *chanoyu*. As soon as a person of quality or a messenger arrives, he should immediately inform the priest or brother in charge of dealing with Christians (visitors?) and then he must leave off everything else in order to welcome and entertain the visitors and to receive their messages without making them wait.[13]

Once more Valignano stresses the importance of observing as closely as possible Japanese customs and etiquette:

> It is very important to understand that if things are not done in Japan in the way the Japanese are accustomed, it often happens that, far from being welcomed, visitors are exposed to rudeness and bad manners. It is therefore necessary to pay much attention to this point—for example, to invite guests to drink and then to offer them bad wine or *cha* is rude and discourteous. . . . And so it is necessary always to have at hand good wine and good *cha* for visitors, and to pay much attention to these and similar matters.[14]

Valignano was not one to issue vague instructions during his visits of inspection, and as a result of his first tour of Japan, regulations for the smooth functioning of the mission were drawn up and circulated. This document, running to several thousand words, is divided into sections, each dealing specifically with some activity or office of the mission. There are precise rules governing preaching and gift giving, for example, as well as directives for guestmasters, sacristans, cooks, infirmarians, refectorians, and gatemen. A constant theme runs through these instructions—that of adaptation to Japanese life and customs—echoing the message expressed in his treatise mentioned above. We read, for instance, in the fifth section of the rules for *dōjuku:* "Let them be well instructed, and let them learn and observe the customs and *catangues (sic)* of Japanese good breeding, not only in their dealings with the fathers, brothers, and other people of the residence but also with outsiders, treating everybody with the respect and courtesy due to his station."[15] The guestmaster is also admonished to act in accord with the norms of Japanese etiquette and specifically to observe the Japanese canons of cleanliness:

> He should see to it that there is a man in the *chanoyu* who is both virtuous and skilled in that office. He should keep his house very clean, and the *dogu (dōgu,* utensils) of *chanoyu* and the different types of *cha* in good order. The *chanoyu* should not be a place for entertaining *ytazuramonos (sic)* who go there to drink and pass the time, talking about idle and unbecoming matters. Rather, its purpose is to welcome honored Christian visitors with edification and profit for their souls, as is only fitting in our residence. He should see to it that the *chanoyuxa (chanoyusha,* person of tea) observes his rules well.[16]

We have already seen that as early as 1561 Fernandez specifically mentioned a man appointed to welcome and serve tea to guests in the Jesuit residence. Now Valignano spells out in considerable detail the duties of the *chanoyusha*, the "person of tea" who served as an official in charge of the tea room:

He should rise when the morning bell rings, light the *andon* (lantern) of the *chanoyu*, and put charcoal in the *furo* (brazier) in order to heat the water, and then make his prayer while it is still getting light.

When the sun has risen and there is enough light by which to do it, he should carefully sweep all that pertains to him. With hot water he should wash the *cama* (kama, kettle) and the other *chaa* (sic) utensils. He should see to the *furo* just as it ought to be, and inform the man whose job it is to bring the water.

He should take care to check whether he has enough powdered *chaa* for two or three days, and if he has not, then he should advise the person whose job is to grind it if he cannot do it himself.

He will have all the *dogus* according to the list that they give him, and whenever the cleaning cloths, such as the *chaquin* (chakin), *zoquin* (zōkin), and *fucusamono* (fukusamono), as well as the cloth strainer, are torn or dirty, he will inform the person in charge so that he may provide.

He should give *chaa* to all the visitors in keeping with their station and with the order given by the brother, but he will not give *chaa* to those who are forbidden; instead, he will tell them not to enter or not to stay there.

At night, in accordance with the order given him by the brother, he will put all the *dogus* in good order and see to the fire so that no disaster may occur.

He will keep an inventory of all the *dogus* entrusted to him, so that, in conformity with this list, he may pass over everything when somebody else is appointed to take over his office. He will also have a public notice on which the following items are written:

Quinsey (Kinsei, prohibitions)

Nobody will touch the *chanoyu* or its *dogus* without the official's permission.

Nobody will remove hot water for another purpose without permission, or take some of the fire to light another one elsewhere.

Nobody will remove the *dogus* belonging to the *chanoyu* without permission.

Nobody will do any *saicu* (*saiku*, work) in the *chanoyu* house, nor place there any *dogus* not belonging to the *chanoyu*.

Nobody will sleep in the *chanoyu* without permission of the brother guestmaster.

The *dojucus* will not take their rest there, nor will any menial enter the *zaxiqi* (*zashiki*, sitting room).

There will be no games of *go* or *xogui* (*shōgi*, chesslike game), nor will there be any talk about unseemly matters.

No woman will stay there longer than it takes to deliver a message, nor will she remain there talking a long time.[17]

These regulations, with their quaint mixture of Japanese terms, are followed by a list of the utensils to be kept in the tea room:[18]

cama (*kama*, kettle)
canaburo (*kanaburo*, kettle brazier)
mizusaxi (*mizusashi*, water container)
mizucoboxi (*mizukoboshi*, waste water container)
futa uogui (*futaoki*, lid rest)
tansu (chest)
chaua (*chawan*, tea bowl) (5)
naccume (*natsume*, a type of tea caddy) (3 *dai*)
fiquidame (*hikidame*, a type of tea caddy) (1)
chaxen (*chasen*, tea whisk)
fixacu (*hishaku*, ladle)
chaquin (*chakin*, tea napkin)
cha vsu (*chausu*, tea mortar)
mizutago (water pail) (1)
suyeuoque (*sueoke*, water pail) (2)
chaccubo (*chatsubo*, tea jar)
chavataxi (*chawatashi*, ?)
vôguchi (*ōguchi*, wide-mouth vessel) (1)
tetodai (*tetōdai*, hand lamp stand) (1)
today (*tōdai*, lamp stand) (1)
andon (lamp) (1)
xuroboqui (*shurobōki*, broom) (2)
faiyre (*haiire*, ash container)
faisucui (*haisukui*, ash scoop)
ficaqui (*hikaki*, fire rake)
fucusamono (*fukusamono*, napkin)
sumitori (charcoal scuttle)
vozumitori (*ōsumitori*, large charcoal scuttle)

fibaxi (*hibashi*, fire tongs)
camasuye (*kamasue*, kettle stand)
zoquin (*zōkin*, floor cloth)
suino (*suinō*, water bag)
mizubixacu (*mizuhishaku*, water ladle) (2)

This list of tea utensils is surpassed by the number of *chanoyu* terms which appeared some years later in the celebrated *Vocabulario*, the Portuguese-Japanese dictionary (called *Nippo Jisho* in Japanese) published by the Jesuits at Nagasaki in 1603–1604. The main text and the supplement (which lists words either omitted in the main text or in need of more exact definition) contain no less than 32,978 entries, among which some 150 are related to *chanoyu*, thus reflecting the importance the compilers attached to the practice of tea.[19] About one-sixth of these tea terms are found in the supplement, either as additional words or more exactly explained, and among the words found in both parts of the dictionary is the term *chanoyu*. This word is first of all defined as a "place where water for *cha* is heated and prepared for drinking." The two following terms, *chanoyujo* and *chanoyunoma*, are marked "idem," thus appearing to indicate that the word *chanoyu* at that time referred to the place in which tea was drunk and not to the practice itself, and indeed the word often appears in this sense in Jesuit writings. But in the supplement of the *Vocabulario* we read "*Chanoyu:* Properly, the hot water with which *cha* is drunk," thus providing the literal translation of the term.[20]

Neither of these two definitions could be applied to the word *chanoyu* as the term is understood today. But it must be borne in mind that the Jesuit writers were living in Japan precisely at the time when tea drinking was developing into the aesthetic pastime we know today. For this reason I have avoided using the term "tea ceremony" when translating the Jesuit reports about tea drinking, as the use of this term would be misleading. Obviously Valignano and other Europeans recognized the special role that tea drinking played in Japanese etiquette and appreciated that the practice involved far more than a display of informal friendship and hospitality. This is clearly seen in the strict rules issued regarding the tea room in missionary residences and the prohibition of unseemly talk and behavior there. In this context, we note that Frois reports that traveling missionaries would often celebrate Mass in the tea room of a local Christian, thus indicating the exclusive and quasi-sacred character attached to the place.[21] But their reports indicate that the missionaries regarded tea as a drink offered formally to honored guests and requiring a variety of utensils to serve it in a room especially designated for this purpose—a far cry from the tea ceremony as developed by Sen no Rikyū and from the *chanoyu* we know today.

Valignano made three visits of inspection to Japan, and it was as a result of the third stay that he composed his last major work. In this unpublished treatise, "The Beginning and Progress of the Christian Religion of Japan,"[22] written in 1601, he returns once more to the subject of tea. It may be seen that his views on the subject have developed appreciably:

> Among other things that the Japanese greatly practice and hold in high esteem is a drink of hot water with a medicinal powder and stomachic powder, and this they call *cha*. This is so not only on account of its benefits but also because from ancient times it has been held in high esteem, and in this way they show their friendship and goodwill toward guests.[23]

Valignano then goes on to explain the value of tea drinking:

> There is a great deal to say about the use of this drink, as well as the method and ceremonies in which it is employed, for it is one of the things they most highly value in Japan. But in addition to what has already been said and the benefit to their health which they receive from this drink, the place appointed for its use is held in much veneration and esteem among the Japanese lords, although no sort of superstition is involved. While they are there, they deal with each other with great sincerity and decorum, regarding it as quite unpardonable to say or do there anything unseemly or improper.[24]

Clearly Valignano's attitude toward tea has matured considerably. From being a means for entertaining visitors, tea drinking has now taken on a special significance. The place where it is drunk in a formal way is regarded with a special aura of veneration, although no superstition is involved. This last point is of some significance for it allowed the missionaries and their Japanese converts to participate, with good conscience, in a traditional and thoroughly Japanese aesthetic pastime. Christian teaching was often accused of being divisive and even subversive regarding Japanese society, but in this ritual Christian and non-Christian could come together in a spirit of harmony without religious discord.

Although the missionaries residing permanently in Japan were in a better position to describe Japanese life than were the visiting merchants and laymen, the latter sometimes left pertinent accounts of considerable interest concerning, for example, the cultivation of the tea bush, the price at which its leaves were sold, and the wholesome and medicinal properties of the drink. Bernardino de Avila Girón was a Spanish trader who traveled around Japan in the 1590s and returned to that country once more in 1607. On one occasion he was given a tour of a noble's house, and he later left a description of the different chambers, gardens, and mural paintings. During the tour, Avila Girón was taken to see the tea room:

> From there we went to what they call the *chanoyu*, which is a room where they receive their visitors. In one corner they keep the utensils with which they prepare the *cha*. This is a dry herb which they grind into a powder, and then put about half a spoon of it into a little hot water and give it to the visitor to drink. The Japanese greatly value and esteem this for it has special qualities, chiefly for headaches, dispelling drowsiness, and soothing the brain. A *catty* of this herb costs a *real* and sometimes less. But this sort is of no account, for the good type costs three or four *mases (sic)*, and there is even some costing a *tael*, two *taels*, or even more for a *catty*, such as the best sort in Miyako.
>
> The herb is harvested only in the month of May and some parts of it are better than others, the best being the inner leaf. The tree from which it is picked is a small round bush, which has a leaf like a myrtle's although darker in color. But not to weary you, I will not continue with the many things that can be said about this. There is usually a manservant in this *chanoyu* house who has the task of sweeping it with a small broom with a long handle and serving the *cha* to visitors.[25]

Another layman in Japan to comment on the medicinal properties of tea was Francesco Carletti, a Florentine merchant who reached Nagasaki in June 1597. Carletti describes "a certain leaf they call *cha*":

> This leaf is produced by a plant that grows almost like that of the box tree, except that its leaves are three times as large and it remains green throughout the year. And it has a fragrant flower in the shape of a

damask rose. From its leaves they make a powder that they mix with hot water—which they continually have on the fire for this purpose, in an iron cauldron—and then drink it daily, more as a medicine than for its taste. It has a somewhat bitter flavor, so that one then washes out the mouth. Upon those who take it good and flavorsome, it produces a very good effect and relieves the stomach weakness because of its warmth. It marvelously assists digestion and is especially excellent for lightening and impeding the fumes that rise to the head. And for that reason it customarily is drunk immediately after the midday meal, when one feels full of too much wine; and drinking it after supper brings on sleep. In sum, the uses of drinking this *cha* are so many that one never enters a house without being offered it in a friendly way, out of good manners, as a matter of custom to honor the guest, as they do with wine in the regions of Flanders and Germany.[26]

EUROPEANS AND *CHANOYU* UTENSILS

Although a detailed account of *chanoyu* as it evolved in the late six-teenth century is lacking in the contemporary reports of the Europe-ans, references are made to the astonishing value which the Japanese nobility and wealthy merchants attached to prized tea utensils. The first account of any moment is dated as early as 1565, when Almeida wrote about his departure from the mansion of a rich Christian in Sakai:

I told Sancho (the host) that I wished to leave on the following day, and he said that since I wished to depart, he would like to show me some of his things. Now it is the custom of nobles and rich Japanese to show a guest, to whom they feel an obligation, some valuable possessions as a token of affection when he comes to take his leave. These things are utensils with which they drink a certain ground herb called *cha*, and anybody accustomed to drinking it finds it tasty and pleasant.

The way of drinking this is to pour half a nutful of this powdered herb into a porcelain dish and then drink it mixed with very hot water. And for this purpose they have very old iron kettles, some porcelain dishes, a small receptacle into which they pour the water with which they rinse the porcelain dishes, and a small tripod on which they place the lid of the iron kettle, for otherwise they would have to place it on the mats. The vessel into which they pour the *cha* powder, the spoon with which they pour it, the dipper with which they transfer the hot water from the kettle—all these utensils are regarded as the jewels of

Japan, much in the same way as we value rings, gems, and necklaces made of many costly rubies and diamonds. There are experts in this matter who can recognize these utensils and they act as brokers in their sale and purchase.

The best type of this herb is worth nine or ten crowns a pound, and to entertain their guests with it and to display their utensils, they first of all give a banquet in keeping with the means of each one. The place where this is held is a certain house which nobody enters except for this celebration, and it is quite astonishing to note the cleanliness therein.

At nine o'clock on the following day, a message was sent to me, to a Japanese brother, and to another man who looks after all our affairs in Japan—he is a wealthy man and a very good Christian. I was taken to the side of his rooms, where there was a small door through which one man could enter, and inside we went along a straight corridor. We then went down a cedar staircase and it seemed to be the first time men had ever used it, such was its indescribable workmanship. We emerged into a small courtyard about two fathoms long and wide, and proceeding along a veranda we entered the house in which we were to eat.

The house seemed to have been built by the hands of angels rather than by those of men. One side of it had a kind of cupboard, which is usual here, and there was also a hearth made of black clay about one yard around. This was something strange, for though it was blacker than pitch, it was as shiny as a limpid mirror. On this was a kettle of pleasant shape, placed very neatly on a tripod; the ash on which the live coals rested seemed like ground eggshells. All this was arranged with indescribable cleanliness and order, and it is not surprising that all their efforts are expended in this alone.

The man who accompanied me said that Sancho had skillfully bought the kettle for six hundred crowns, although it was worth a good deal more. I do not praise the food for Japan is very barren in this respect, but as for the service, order, neatness, and utensils—I believe that it would be impossible in the world to give a banquet with greater order and neatness than in Japan, for although a thousand men may be eating, the servants do not speak a word and everything is conducted in unbelievably good order.

After eating, we all knelt to give thanks to God Our Lord, for the Japanese Christians observe this good custom. Then, in front of many valuable utensils that he had there, he showed me a small iron tripod a little less than a span in circumference, on which is placed the lid of the kettle when they remove it. I took it in my hands, and it was so worn in many places on account of its age that it had broken in two places and had been soldered.

He told me that this was one of the most valuable utensils in Japan

and that it had cost him one thousand three hundred crowns, although
he himself valued it much higher. All these pieces were kept in rich silk
and damask bags and in costly boxes. He mentioned to me that he possessed other very valuable utensils which he would not show me then as
he did not have them in an easily accessible place from which he could
readily get them, but that he would show them to me on my return.

The value of these things is not surprising, for here in Miyako there is
a lord who possesses a small porcelain vessel, shaped like a small cup
and used to pour in *cha* powder. It is worth thirty thousand crowns; I
am not sure about the price they ascribe to it, but many princes would
give ten thousand crowns to buy it. There are many of this kind of
small vessel which are worth three, four, or five thousand crowns, and
they are often bought and sold.[27]

Almeida was not the only European to be astonished by the high
value set on choice utensils. Some twenty years later, Valignano left
on record his surprise at being shown some valuable pieces by Ōtomo
Yoshishige, daimyo of Bungo, and informed of their market price:

Throughout all Japan they are accustomed to use a drink made of hot
water and the powder of a herb called *cha*, which they regard very
highly. All the lords have in their residences a special place where they
make this drink, and as "hot water" in Japan is called *yu* and the herb is
called *cha*, the place assigned for this is *chanoyu*. This is the most
esteemed and venerated thing in Japan, and so all the leading lords
study very hard to make this drink. Sometimes they make it with their
own hands to show their affection for their guests and to pay them
honor.

As they make so much of this *chanoyu*, they highly esteem many
pieces and small vessels used in *chanoyu*, the chief of which is a kind of
iron pot, which they call *kwansu*, and some small iron tripods which
have no other function but to have placed on them the lid of the pot
when they make the aforesaid drink. They also have a kind of porcelain
cup in which they serve the *cha*, as well as some jars in which they keep
the said herb throughout the year. And there are other small jars in
which they keep the herb after it has been ground, and this they use to
make the said drink.

It is quite incredible how highly they esteem these utensils, which are
of a certain kind that only the Japanese can recognize. Often they give
three, four, or six thousand ducats and even more for one of these pots
or for one of these bowls or tripods. The king of Bungo showed me a

Plate 15. Hanging scroll by the Zen priest Yüan-wu K'o-ch'in (Engo Kokugon) written as a certificate of enlightenment (*inkajō*). Known as "Drifting Engo" from the legend that it drifted across the sea to Japan, the scroll is said to have been given to Murata Shukō by Ikkyū. National Treasure. Tokyo National Museum.

Plate 16. Ido tea bowl from Korea named Mino. Sixteenth Century. *Meibutsu*. Gotoh Museum, Tokyo.

Plate 17. Formal display of *karamono* on a *daisu* stand. Tokugawa Reimeikai Foundation, Tokyo.

Plate 18. Tea room known as Taian at Myōkian Temple, Kyoto, thought to have been built about 1582 by Sen no Rikyū. The illustration shows an alcove (*tokonoma*) and a sunken hearth (*ro*). National Treasure.

Plate 19. Sunken hearth of the Taian tea room. The kettle in the hearth is Old Ashiya with a "hailstone" pattern; the water container (right rear) is Shigaraki ware; the tea bowl (containing whisk and scoop) is a black *raku* ware piece named Shunkan and is attributed to Chōjirō; the bamboo scoop, called Urabari, is normally kept in a case inscribed by Kobori Enshū.

Plate 20. Reconstruction of a *kaiseki* meal served by Sen no Rikyū on 1590:9:21.
Photo by Yano Tatehiko.

Plate 21. Modern reconstruction of the portable golden tea room of Toyotomi Hideyoshi as it is thought to have been displayed at the Imperial Palace. MOA Museum of Art, Atami.

Plate 22. Middle gate *(chūmon)* separating the inner and outer gardens *(roji)* at the Urasenke Foundation, Kyoto.

small porcelain jar which among us would have no other use save to put into a birdcage as a water container. But he had bought this for nine thousand taels, which is about fourteen thousand ducats, although in all truth I myself would not have given one or two farthings for it.

One of our Christians in Sakai showed me a great treasure; it was one of these iron tripods, and, to add to its value, it had been repaired three times. He had bought it for nine hundred taels, or about one thousand four hundred ducats, although I would not have given any more for it than I would for the king of Bungo's small tripod.

And what is even more amazing is that although they manufacture a thousand small tripods and jars just like them, these things will enjoy no greater esteem and worth among the Japanese than they would among us. This is because the things which they value must be made by some ancient masters. And the Japanese have such understanding in these matters that they will immediately recognize the valuable pieces among a thousand similar utensils, just as European silversmiths can recognize and distinguish between false and genuine jewels. It seems that nobody from Europe can ever reach this understanding because, however much we may examine these things, we cannot determine in what consists the value and where is the difference.[28]

It is worth noting here that despite his colorful reference to a bird-cage and its water trough, Valignano is in fact making no value judgment. He is merely remarking that, owing to his European cultural background, he himself was unable to appreciate the value of such choice utensils, and in fact he doubts whether any European could ever reach a full understanding of Japanese aesthetic values. He does not deny the intrinsic worth of certain utensils, as may be seen in his reference to jewels: Although the layman would be incapable of distinguishing between false and genuine gems, an experienced European jeweler could do so at a glance. In this as in other cultural matters Valignano keeps an open mind. He does not condemn cultural differences between Westerners and Japanese but merely points them out.

Incidentally, the estimated worth of Ōtomo's tea jar, as quoted by Valignano, was quite accurate, as its subsequent sale was to prove. As a result of his military clashes with the armies of Satsuma as well as unrest in his own domain of Bungo, Ōtomo was obliged to appeal to Hideyoshi for military and financial aid, and in a letter written in

1585 Frois recounts Ōtomo's sale of his treasured Nitta Katatsuki, a tea caddy that had been salvaged after the fall of Sakamoto Castle. According to Frois:

> King Francisco (Ōtomo Yoshishige) became poor after the people of four kingdoms (Buzen, Chikugo, Chikuzen, and Higo) rose in rebellion and refused to obey his son, the prince (Yoshimune). And so he ordered that a utensil, very highly prized in Japan, should be sold in the city of Sakai. This was a small glazed porcelain cup shaped like a pomegranate, and it was used to hold certain leaves ground into a powder, which they drink with hot water on every occasion.
>
> Faxiba Chicugendono (Hideyoshi), lord of the greater and more important part of Japan, heard about this precious jewel and he yearned to obtain it for it was a very famous piece in Japan. He gave him fifteen thousand crowns for it, and to show his special favor, he ordered that the money should be carried overland, via the kingdom of Yamaguchi, to Bungo, which is a very long route.[29]

Traditional utensils such as iron kettles and porcelain cups were not the only items to fetch high prices. In the 1590s it was discovered that certain jars of Chinese origin and found in the Philippines had the property of preserving tea for long periods of time without the leaf losing its freshness. References to these so-called *rusontsubo* (literally, "Philippine jars") crop up quite often in the reports of the Europeans, for some of them were eager to make a profit by importing the jars into Japan. But hopes of making a fortune in this way were dashed when Hideyoshi ordered that all such jars were to be sold to his agents in Nagasaki and no private trading in them was to be permitted. Francesco Carletti learned about this ban even before he set foot on Japanese soil because his vessel was thoroughly searched by the Nagasaki port authorities:

> In the morning, before we set foot on the land, ministers of justice came by command of the governor of that region, so as to search among all the sailors, passengers, and merchants for certain earthenware vases that often are brought there from the Philippine Islands and other places in that sea. By order of Japan, these must, under pain of death, be shown by anyone who has them, as the king wishes to buy them all. Who ever would believe it? . . . Those cases are often worth five, six, or ten thousand scudos each, though ordinarily one would not say that

they were worth a giulo, and the reason is that they have the property of preserving unspoiled—for nine, ten, and twenty years—a certain leaf that they call *cha*. . . .

But to return to the aforesaid *cha*, besides the many special properties that they attribute to it, they say that the older the leaf the better it is. But they have great difficulty in preserving it for a long period and keeping it in prime condition, as they do not find containers, not even of gold or silver or other metals, which are good for this purpose. It seems a superstition, and yet it is true, that *cha* is preserved well only in the aforesaid vessels made simply of a clay that has this virtue. . . . These vases generally are found among those which they have made at a value of three or four soldi each, and many merchants have become rich on them, especially those who have profited from carrying some of the ones that have the virtue, or it may be a superstition, of preserving the *cha*. And it is the truth that the king of this Japan and all the other princes of the region have an infinite number of these vases, which they regard as their principal treasures, esteeming them more than anything else of value.[30]

As well as being the chronicler *par excellence* of missionary progress and current events in Japan, Luis Frois was also a keen observer of the cultural scene. In the introductory treatise to his history of the Japanese mission, he included a chapter titled, in English translation, "The Origin of the *Chanoyu* Utensils and Their Value and Reputation."[31] Only the list of chapter titles of this treatise has survived to the present day, however, so we have no means of knowing what Frois wrote about the subject. But if his other extant writings may serve as a guide, we can be reasonably sure that the meticulous and experienced Frois would have dealt with this topic with his customary thoroughness, and the loss of his cultural treatise can only be deplored. This consideration should give us pause lest it be assumed that only Valignano and a few other Europeans were knowledgeable about tea. While it is true that on the evidence of extant documents no more can be proved, it is highly probable that there were also other Europeans (such as perhaps Organtino Gnecchi-Soldi, resident in Miyako for more than twenty years) who knew a great deal about the subject but were too busy or disinclined to commit their knowledge to paper or whose writings have not survived to the present day.

In summary, then, we can say that the Europeans in Japan were well aware of the drink called *cha* and realized its important role in

Japanese etiquette; as a result, certain prized utensils were worth enormous sums of money, although it was impossible for the European eye to discern exactly wherein lay their intrinsic worth. Nevertheless, under Valignano's vigorous prodding, Jesuit residences were to be equipped with a tea room for welcoming visitors, and this room was to a certain extent set apart and not to be used for profane purposes.

So far there has been no description of a formal gathering specifically assembled to drink tea. As noted above, this may be because *chanoyu*, as we know it today, was still in a stage of development, and in any case tea masters would not be inclined to invite foreigners to participate in the intimate and esoteric atmosphere of a gathering whose finer points they could not appreciate. It is for this reason that although Valignano and others often refer to *chanoyu*, I have avoided using the term "tea ceremony" lest a mistaken impression be given. Now, however, we come to João Rodrigues, the outstanding Western exponent of the way of tea. Such is his contribution that early European accounts on this subject can be conveniently divided into two sections: pre-Rodrigues and post-Rodrigues.

JOÃO RODRIGUES AND THE TEA CEREMONY

João Rodrigues arrived in Japan as a boy in 1577 and spent more than thirty years in that country. He received most of his formal education there and learned to speak Japanese fluently—so fluently in fact that he became known as "Rodrigues the Interpreter."[32] In that capacity he dealt with many of the leading personalities of his day: Toyotomi Hideyoshi, Tokugawa Ieyasu, Maeda Munehisa, Takayama Ukon, Ōtomo Yoshishige, Konishi Yukinaga, to name but a few. And in the course of his work as missionary, interpreter, and trade negotiator he came into contact with some of the outstanding tea practitioners of the time, many of whom were Christian. Valignano may have encouraged the Jesuits to practice the custom of formal tea drinking, since the rite had no religious connotations and did not involve superstition. His efforts may help to explain, at least to a certain extent, the disproportionate number of tea men, such as Ōtomo Yoshishige, Hibiya Ryōkei, and Gamō Ujisato, who were Christians. Among Rikyū's Seven Disciples, no fewer than five were Christians. Among them was Takayama Ukon, who was regarded by Rikyū as one of his foremost disciples.[33] Ukon was often invited by Rikyū to his tea gatherings, at one of which, on 22 January 1590, he was the sole guest. On 8 February in the following year, Rikyū's two guests were Ukon and yet another Christian, Ōtomo Yoshimune; a week later, on 13 February, Ukon once more participated in Rikyū's tea session, only a matter of weeks before the master's enforced suicide on 21 April.[34]

Rodrigues knew Yoshimune, his father Yoshishige, and Ukon well,[35] and he noted how Ukon utilized his predilection for the tea ceremony to deepen his Christian faith, thus effecting a pleasing harmony between the newly introduced religion from the West and the traditional aesthetic pastime of the East:

> For example, Takayama Justus (Ukon) was unique in this art of the tea ceremony in Japan and as such was highly esteemed. . . . He was wont to say, as we several times heard him, that he found *suki* (the tea ceremony) a great help toward virtue and recollection for those who practice it and really understand its purpose. Thus he used to say that in order to commend himself to God he would retire to that small house (his teahouse) with a statue, and there according to the custom that he had formed he found peace and recollection in order to commend himself to God.[36]

An examination of Rodrigues' long account of the tea ceremony will leave no doubt that he was influenced by Rikyū's way of thought. Indeed, there arises the intriguing question whether the two men ever met, perhaps through the good offices of Ukon. If there was ever such a meeting, it could only have happened when Rodrigues accompanied Valignano as his interpreter for an audience with Hideyoshi. The party reached the capital on 27 February 1591 and was received by Hideyoshi in his Jurakudai palace on 3 March. Valignano then stayed in Kyoto for three weeks (during which time he and Rodrigues visited Gamō Ujisato, yet another outstanding Christian tea master), but Rodrigues, on Hideyoshi's insistence, remained in the capital until September.

Rikyū was certainly in Kyoto at the time and very possibly attended the audience on 3 March. According to Frois's account, Toyotomi Hidetsugu was present together with eight officials ("some of them powerful daimyos") and other nobles and officials. After the audience and a tour of the palace, Valignano's party retired to their lodgings, but Rodrigues was summoned back that evening and spoke with

Hideyoshi until a late hour. On the following day, Rodrigues was once more called to the palace and spent the rest of the day in the ruler's presence as Hideyoshi spoke about his plans to conquer China and made uncomplimentary remarks about Buddhist monks.[37]

This last point is of considerable interest, not because it necessarily represents Hideyoshi's true feelings about the Buddhist clergy but because of what Frois elsewhere records in a letter. He notes that Hideyoshi's secretary, Ai Fujiharu, and his physician, Seyakuin Hōin, were present, as well as "many lords from different kingdoms." One of those present remarked that there was a Jesuit in Osaka who wished to learn the arcane secrets of the Zen sect but he, the speaker, had urged him not to do so. When asked by Hideyoshi why he had given this advice, the man replied that Christians were against the Zen sect and thus it was not fitting that they should learn its secrets. Hideyoshi voiced his disagreement, observing that Christianity was far better than Zen.[38]

The accuracy of Frois's hearsay account does not greatly matter (Rodrigues may well have been his source of information), but the identity of the speaker is of interest. The standard Portuguese text in *Cartas* merely states that he was "one of those who were there." But this edited text appears to be missing a few words, presumably considered by the editors to be of no interest to European readers, and ironically we must turn to a contemporary Italian translation for a fuller version. In this latter account, the man in question was none other than "Soyequi, master of chianoyu"—in other words, Rikyū himself, attending court only six weeks before his suicide.[39]

The fact that the two men met, or at least were present in the same chamber, on this one occasion would hardly have produced a lasting effect on Rodrigues' thinking about the tea ceremony. But one must remember that the Jesuit was in frequent contact with Rikyū's disciples and it was through these men that he was undoubtedly influenced. Apart from the disproportionately long account he devotes to the subject in his treatise on Japanese life and culture, there is ample evidence to show that Rodrigues was deeply interested in tea. For example, in his *Arte Breve*, the revised edition of his Japanese grammar brought out in Macao in 1620, he urges students of the Japanese language to learn technical phrases relating to Japanese arts and crafts, naming *"cha or suki"* in the first place, before drama, poetry, and classical writings, so that when dealing with refined and cultured persons the Jesuits will understand what is being said and will "speak, whenever necessary even in sermons, without using unseemly words."[40]

Even more telling is the fact that Rodrigues had his own tea room in the Jesuit residence at Nagasaki. This the missionary Francisco Pires notes with more than a touch of disapproval in a letter written in 1612, two years after Rodrigues had been exiled to Macao:

> [Rodrigues] took over a part of the residence for his own use at the end of a corridor; this consisted of two rooms and he closed off the corridor with a door. There he remained at that end part of the house which he had taken over for himself. He also made an entrance, with a door and steps, to the outside, whereby lay people could enter. He set up for himself a *chanoyu*, which is an iron kettle in which water is kept boiling the whole day and a charcoal fire. This is a Japanese custom in the houses of the nobles.[41]

Rodrigues left a detailed description of the tea ceremony, together with an explanation of its ethos and purpose, and it is obvious that he based his account on firsthand experience obtained during his thirty-three years in Japan. This essay, which forms part of his treatise on Japanese culture, is readily available today in English, Spanish, and Japanese translations, but it has not, ironically, been published in Rodrigues' native Portuguese, the language in which it was written.[42] Admittedly the account is rambling and disorganized, for, as the elderly author pointed out in a letter, he lacked literary style owing to his departure from Europe as a boy. His purpose in compiling the report, he says, was merely to assemble disparate material for a more skillful editor to improve and polish. In all, he devoted four chapters (Chapters 32 to 35) to tea and the tea ceremony, plus a section of Chapter 12, which deals with Japanese methods of building. In the remainder of my essay, therefore, I will summarize what Rodrigues the Interpreter had to say, in his artless and repetitious way, about the way of tea.[43]

"Chapter 12: The Japanese Method of Building. Section 9: The House Called *Suki* Where They Give *Cha* to Their Guests to Drink"

The chief and most esteemed social custom among the Japanese is meeting to drink *cha*, and so they spare no pains in constructing a special building for this purpose. Emphasis is laid on a frugal and an apparently natural setting; nothing fashionable or elegant is used, but only utensils in keeping with a hermit's retreat. Social distinctions are not observed in this wholesome pastime, and a lower-ranking person may invite a lord or a noble, who on such occasions will behave as an equal. Although usually situated near a mansion or house, the tea-house should be located in a solitary and quiet place. In the surrounding garden there are stepping-stones, a pool of water, and a privy which is intended more for decoration than for actual use. The garden path runs naturally between bushes and trees (mostly pines), transplanted there with such elegance that they appear to have sprung up naturally.

The thatched *cha* house is small, from one-and-a-half to four mats in size, and is constructed of old wood; the ceiling is made of coarse woven reeds, smoke-dried to show age and lonely poverty. In the place of honor a recess is let into the wall and herein is placed an ancient picture, scroll, or a vase of flowers for the guests to contemplate. Everything is well ordered, spotlessly clean, and kept in good condition.

The guests enter the house and quietly view the surroundings without speaking loudly. When they have assembled, the host enters through an inner door, and greetings and salutations are exchanged. He then brings out small tables and places one in front of each guest, offering the visitors rice and wine. When they have eaten, the guests go out into the garden and wash their hands, while their host busily sweeps the little house and replaces the painting or flowers. He then summons the visitors in once more and they quietly drink *cha* in the little house. At the end of the gathering, thanks are exchanged and the guests quietly take their leave.

"Chapter 32: Their Manner of Entertaining with *Cha*"

Tea drinking is so common in Japan that water is always kept on the boil to prepare the drink at short notice, for this is the principal way in which they entertain their guests. *Cha* itself comes from a small tree or bush, rather similar to the myrtle bush. Its new leaves, which are used for the drink, are soft and delicate and must be protected from frost; at Uji, where the best tea is produced, straw awnings are erected over the bushes to protect the leaves. The best type of tea, used in the gatherings of nobles and rich men, is very expensive, while no value at all is attached to the wild bush because it yields a tough and bitter leaf.

The leaves are picked in March and are softened by being exposed to steam. Then they are placed in wooden trays and slowly roasted over a charcoal fire. The staff of the fifteen or twenty houses producing at Uji carefully superintend the operation to ensure that the leaves are roasted evenly. They then divide the leaves into four grades. Uji produces annually about three hundred piculs (about forty thousand pounds) of tea, which is distributed throughout the country. Lords and nobles patronize different houses and send their agents to make arrangements about the new tea. But no tea may be removed until the Lord of Tenka, or shogun, has sent his representative to collect the shogun's tea. Before removal, the tea is poured into caddies which bear the manufacturer's seal and name. These are packed into special boxes and then sent off to monasteries at the tops of mountains, where they are stored in cool surroundings until their owners send for them in October.

Both the Chinese and Japanese attribute various properties to *cha*. It aids digestion, expels drowsiness, and relieves headaches; it brings down fever, eases the heart, and relieves melancholy; it is conducive to chastity because it cools the kidneys, and it flushes out excess body fluids, thus bringing relief to pain caused by the stone. As a result of these healthy properties, plague and pestilence are seldom experienced in China and Japan, despite the densely populated nature of these two countries.

The Chinese have a different way of drinking tea; they do not observe any particular ceremony, nor do they set aside a special place for the pastime. They boil the leaves in the water, and in fact this way is also practiced in Japan by peasants and lowly people. In the mansions of the Japanese lords, a special room is assigned for tea drinking, and shaven men, called *dōbō*, look after the place. Water is always kept on the boil for unexpected guests, and all the necessary implements—caddy, bamboo spoon, cane brush for mixing, mortar for grinding, and so forth—are kept there. This is the usual Japanese way of drinking tea, and this is how they generally entertain their guests. But there is in addition a special rite with which they show visitors exceptional honor and welcome. This used to be called *chanoyu*, but is now known as *suki*.

"Chapter 33: The General Way in Which the Japanese Entertain with Tea"

This manner of entertainment differs greatly from ordinary social dealings, for much modesty, tranquility, and quietness are observed. Rather, it is a secluded exercise in imitation of solitary hermits who have retired from wordly concerns. The purpose of the gathering is not lengthy talk but the peaceful contemplation of the things of nature; everything employed in the pastime is rustic, rough, and unrefined, just as nature made it. They do not make use of spacious rooms or rich apartments for the occasion, nor do they use costly China dishes; there is no artistry or elegance, but only natural neglect and old age. The dishes are not made of silver or gold, but are of iron or clay without any polish or decoration that might incite the appetite to desire them for their luster and beauty. But although the small house and its utensils may appear rough, people spend large sums of money on them. Some earthenware utensils may be worth twenty thousand crowns—something which will appear as madness to other nations. In keeping with their melancholy disposition and with the purpose for which they collect such things, the Japanese find such mystery in these *cha* utensils that they attribute to them the value and esteem that other people place in precious stones and gems.

This pastime was much influenced by the shogun Ashikaga Yoshimasa, who on his retirement from office withdrew to a quiet life in Higashiyama in the eastern part of Kyoto. He built there a small house which was used exclusively for gatherings to drink tea. He assembled all the utensils needed for such meetings—a copper stove, a cast-iron kettle, a tea caddy, a cane brush, a small spoon, and porcelain cups from which to drink the tea. The house was only four-and-a-half mats in size and was constructed of drab materials; to compensate for this plainness, he chose the utensils carefully, insisting on special proportions, sizes, and shapes, and hung monochrome ink paintings in the alcove. It was he who set the fashion and he was called in to judge the suitability of various items, and this is how *chanoyu* began. Thus costly items of *chanoyu* started to acquire a high value, and the wealthy would not consider the expense when they found a choice piece. Anything that had been used by Yoshimasa became valuable and was considered a prize item.

Of the valuable utensils, pride of place is given to the *katatsuki*, or small foreign caddies; cast-iron kettles also have great value. Then there are the porcelain drinking cups, the scrolls, the flower vases, and the vessels for charcoal. Of special worth are the large caddies that have the property of preserving the *cha* leaf fresh from one year to the next.

In the course of time the Higashiyama way of presenting tea was modified and changed to the modern method called *suki*. The Zen sect has influenced this way of preparing tea, for Zen monks seek the First Cause through the contemplation of things and nature; they do not contend or dispute with arguments, but place emphasis on frugality and moderation, without any slackness, indolence, or effeminacy. Disciples of *chanoyu* try to imitate these solitary philosophers, and the pagan followers of the pastime join the Zen sect. But they do not take therefrom any superstition or religious ceremony, but merely imitate the resolution, alertness, and the lack of tepidity, softness, and sluggishness. They do not teach by words but rather by deeds. The purpose of *cha* is courtesy, breeding, moderation, peace of body and soul, humility, without pomp or splendor.

Suki, the new way of performing *chanoyu*, originated in Sakai, and the wealthy merchants there acquired many rich utensils. But because of the lack of space within the city, they made certain changes, such as reducing the size of the teahouse, and entertained their friends in these *cha* houses within the city itself. But to keep up their reputation, they laid down two conditions: Utter cleanliness had to be observed, and each participant had to acquire at least one good utensil, whether Japanese or foreign. And so the price of choice items continued to rise, especially as followers of tea refused to haggle over prices. They consider *suki* as a wealthy poverty and an impoverished wealth, because the things used therein are poor in appearance but rich in price. They see to it that such objects are more valuable than they look and do not possess any glitter, luster, or contrivance. The more precious the utensils and the less they show it, the more suitable they are. Hence the Japanese have come to detest any contrivance and elegance, any pretense, hypocrisy, or outward embellishment. Their ideal is to promise little but accomplish much, to use moderation in everything, and to desire to err by default rather than by excess.

Most of the people who practice *cha* are nobles or lords because the expense incurred therein is indeed great. For one thing, the utensils, however rough they may appear, are very expensive. And the *cha* house—although such a rough place might seem to cost next to nothing, it is incredible how much money is spent on choosing suitable material, the construction, and the skilled labor involved. Then there is the garden, for which they make search in remote areas for trees of certain shape and fashion; the stepping-stones too are expensive, for although they look as if they are there quite naturally, in fact they are sought for in distant places. Then, of course, there is the cost of the *cha* leaf itself, as only the finest quality may be served at such gatherings. Thus this poverty is in reality rich and wealthy, so much so that even the wealthy can maintain it only with difficulty.

Among those who practice the genuine *suki*, there is always one who is esteemed above the rest, and he is known as the *suki no oshō* (supreme tea master). This is traditional in Japan and is also true of other arts, such as poetry, chess, court football, perfume, swords, music, and acting. To be the head teacher of *suki* a man must have various talents and abilities. He must be of a resolute spirit, withdrawn from worldly trifles. He must possess a discerning eye for proportion and appearance, and thus he must know what is fitting in different times, places, and circumstances. He must also have the courage to invent new features as circumstances call for them and reject others hitherto in use. Anything artificial, refined, and pretty must be avoided, and it is necessary to imitate nature as closely as possible. For example, if you plant two trees of the same size and shape, and make them correspond to one another, they will end up causing boredom and tedium. But lack of artificiality and a note of naturalness (for instance, a tree whose branches point this way and that, just as nature intended) will never cause boredom. Finally, the master must have a good knowledge of traditional utensils, and he must be able to approve some, reject others, put a price on them, and grade them in a fitting manner. Such experts have a secret and arcane knowledge which ordinary people know nothing about. Thanks to their innate skill and experience, they may change the shape of a *cha* house, but it will always look good because of its pleasing proportions. Hence anything they make, however new it may be, will have a pleasing appearance because of the fitting proportions its parts bear to one another.

"Chapter 34: How Guests Are Especially Entertained with *Cha* in the *Suki* House"

In October the Japanese send for their caddies of *cha*, which have been stored in the cool mountains during the hot weather, and the opening of the caddies, called *kuchigiri*, is conducted with much ceremony. It is from this time of year that they entertain their friends and acquaintances with *cha*. Because of the small size of the house, only one, two, three, or at most four persons can be invited at one time. A formal letter is sent out inviting a person to attend a tea gathering at such an hour on such a day at such a place, and a formal acceptance is made either in writing or in person.

At the appointed hour each guest robes himself neatly and becomingly. The host unlocks the garden gate, bids the guests enter, and then leaves them while they change their sandals to avoid soiling the freshly sprinkled stepping-stones. After sitting in an arbor quietly contemplating the rustic scene, they walk along the path, taking in with pleasure all the things to be seen there—the paving stones, the trees and bushes, and the stone trough to wash their hands (in winter the water therein is warm).

When they reach the *cha* house, they deposit their daggers and fans in the cupboard outside, and one by one they enter through a small door, so low that one has to stoop to get through. Once inside, each guest goes to the alcove, or *toko*, to admire the flowers or scroll placed therein; he then inspects the stove, kettle, and the charcoal burning in the neatly arranged ash. Then after examining the house itself, its walls, ceiling, and windows, he quietly seats himself. When everyone is duly seated, the host enters through an inner door and thanks his guests for honoring his humble retreat; they in turn thank him for his invitation. They then converse gravely and modestly on wholesome topics for a short time. Then the host begins to place more charcoal on the fire, and the perfume in the ash gives off a pleasant smell.

The host disappears into the house, and then, beginning with the senior guest, places in front of each one small tables on which are neatly arranged rice, vegetables, and a dish of some prized fish or bird. The host then retires again into his house, leaving the guests to eat in silence; from time to time he reappears to see if they desire more to eat. He next serves warm wine, bidding them drink what they will but not pressing them to drink more. He then clears away the tables, serves some suitable fruit as dessert, and then retires from the scene. When they have finished, the guests collect the dishes, place them near the service door, and go out into the garden to wash their hands and mouths before they drink *cha*. As soon as they have left, the host enters, locks the door from the inside, sweeps the floor, and puts out fresh flowers; he then opens the door slightly, as a sign that all is ready, and retires.

The guests enter once more and again inspect everything in the *cha* house, especially the tea utensils. When they have quietly seated themselves, the host comes and asks them whether they wish to drink *cha*. They thank him and say that they do. He removes his prize caddy from a silken bag, sets it down, and then washes the cups. He puts a spoonful of tea in a cup, and humbly tells his guest that they had better drink the tea weak as it is very poor stuff. But they beg him to make it stronger as they know its excellent quality. He draws off hot water from the kettle with a suitable jug and pours it onto the powder in the cup. He then stirs it with a cane brush and places the cup in front of the guests. After an exchange of compliments in regard to who shall drink first, the senior guest lifts the cup, takes three sips, and then hands it to the second guest, and so the cup is passed around. Sometimes when a new caddy is opened, the host may ask permission to drink the tea first to see what it is like.

"Chapter 35: The End to Which They Aspire in *Suki* and the Benefits Therefrom"

There are two kinds of *suki*—the genuine and proper kind, called *hon no suki*, in which some costly item is used, and *wabizuki*, which even commoners of limited means may practice. The latter is a poor *suki*, but it serves a practical purpose because entertaining a person in this way does not involve so much expense. Whatever his rank, a guest is entertained soberly, honorably, and becomingly without pomp or ostentation. But both types of *suki* have the same end and purpose because they both imitate the same things.

Now everything used in the gathering—house, path, meal, utensils —must be adapted and matched to what *suki* professes, that is, the solitude and rustic poverty of a hermit. There should not be anything glossy or rich-looking; everything should be natural, comely, lonely, nostalgic, agreeable. Nature has endowed things with an elegance and grace which move the beholder to a feeling of loneliness and nostalgia, and a discernment of these qualities constitutes one of the main features of *suki*.

Moreover, there must be a mutual harmony in the size and proportions of the various parts. If the house is of a certain size, for instance, then the water jug, stove, kettle, and other utensils must be proportionate in size. This also applies to the parts of the house itself and to the wild trees in the garden. They work out the ideal proportions with respect to size and number of trees, their relation to one another, their position, and the distance between them. In all this they bear in mind what nature herself would do if she were to plant those trees there with natural grace and artlessness.

From this practice of observing the due relation and proportion of these things, the *suki* masters obtain a high degree of knowledge of things. If this is lacking, they cannot discern the hidden quality of things, such as *yowai*, feeble, weak; *tsuyoi*, strong, stable; *katai*, too strong (this is a defect); *nurui*, tepid, feeble, lifeless; *kedakai*, distinguished, dignified. They can distinguish between *tsuyoi* and *katai*, *nurui* and *kedakai*, and not everybody is capable of such discernment. The master must pay attention to the suitability of things, depending on the season, time of day, and the quality of the guests. Thus the principal science of *suki* lies in this ability to recognize the natural proportions and suitability of things, and it is in their serving *cha* that these men can demonstrate what they know and understand.

The guests take careful note of how a tea master serves *cha*, and afterward they say among themselves that the *suki* of so-and-so is *nurui*, or *taketa* (superior), or *jinjō* (average), or *niawanai* (unsuitable), for he shows his understanding and ability in his choice of trees, stepping-stones, in his preparation of the house and utensils, so that everything looks suitable and agreeable. It is not easy to acquire this discernment and not everyone who devotes himself to *suki* becomes a genuine master. Since masters do not teach by word but only by example, many people merely copy what they see without understanding the reason for it. And even among those who do obtain this knowledge there are higher and lower grades and different opinions.

Hence *suki* has three principal features. The first is the extreme cleanliness in everything, not only in what can be seen but also in what is not—for example, the preparation of the dishes in the *suki* kitchen. The second is the rustic poverty and solitude, the withdrawal from superfluous things of every kind. The third is a knowledge of the science of natural proportion and suitability and the hidden and subtle qualities inherent in natural and artificial things. The genuine master extends this knowledge to secular matters concerning honest and fitting customs, and he applies it to the end and purpose of each of these things. This had led them to reform ancient social customs, which were once observed at court but have now been found inconvenient and unsuitable. From this followed the reform of people as regards good breeding, modesty, outward humility, and the avoidance of hypocrisy and a host of useless things employed solely out of ostentation. The great nobles can mix with the lesser gentry without lessening their dignity thereby, for *suki* is a kind of rustic relaxation in the countryside.

This knowledge has been turned to artificial and secular affairs, whence they have conveniently improved some offensive and defensive weapons. It is a great help when applied to the proportions of buildings, courtyards, clothing, footware, and utensils. Thus they have improved many things with profit and advantage, especially in the reform of solemn banquets. These used to involve a great deal of expense even though the food was cold and tasteless, but now they are less expensive and hot and tasty and well-seasoned food is served.

This is enough about *suki* to understand why the Japanese think so highly of it and how the kingdom has benefited from the advantages resulting therefrom in customs and other features of social life.

Rodrigues in Retrospect

This sketchy summary of what Rodrigues has to say on tea scarcely does justice to his full report, but it conveys some idea of the breadth of his understanding and appreciation of the subject. While it is true that his account is rambling and idealized, modern tea masters have been astonished by his knowledge and discernment. Especially noteworthy is his extension of skill and ability in *suki* to other areas of Japanese life, thus showing that the way of tea has a wider application than is commonly realized. Some of his observations are remarkable for their insight and still retain their validity regarding the ideal and purpose of the pastime. For example: "Their ideal is to promise little but accomplish much, to use moderation in everything, and to desire to err by default rather than by excess. . . . The more precious the utensils and the less they show it, the more suitable they are."

The talented Rodrigues had firsthand experience of *chanoyu* in its formative period of development in the late sixteenth and early seventeenth centuries, and he personally conversed with some of the leading masters of the time. His sobriquet of Interpreter was given to him on account of his skill in the Japanese language, but it was equally merited for his work in explaining Japanese culture to the West. Certainly Europe's appreciation of the way of tea had advanced a long way from the early descriptions of *cha* as "hot water."

NOTES

1. Luis Frois, *La Première Ambassade du Japon en Europe, 1582–1592*, ed. Abranches Pinto et al., *Monumenta Nipponica* monograph, no. 6 (Tokyo: Sophia University, 1942), p. 88. Quoted by José Luis Alvarez-Taladriz in João Rodrigues, *Arte del Cha*, ed. José Luis Alvarez-Taladriz, *Monumenta Nipponica* monograph, no. 14 (Tokyo: Sophia University, 1954), p. 12, n. 44.
2. Miyako, 20 February 1565, in *Cartas que os Padres e Irmãos da Companhia de Iesus Escreuerão dos Reynos de Japão & China* . . . (Evora, 1598; Tenri Central Library Reprint, 1972), vol. 1, f. 172v.
3. Two exceptions come readily to mind: the merchants Jorge Alvares and Bernadino de Avila Girón. The shipwrecked Rodrigo de Vivero y Velasco also touches on various aspects of Japanese life in his report.
4. Instruction dated 13 August 1553, in *Monumenta Ignatiana, Epistolae et Instructiones* (Madrid: Monumenta Historica Societatis Jesu, 1907), vol. 5, p. 330; quoted in Michael Cooper (ed.), *The Southern Barbarians: The First Europeans in Japan* (Tokyo: Kodansha International, 1971), p. 99.
5. Alessandro Valignano, *Historia del principio y progresso de la Compañia de Jesus en las Indias Orientales*, ed. Josef Wicki (Rome: Institutum Historicum S.I., 1944), p. 142; quoted in Michael Cooper (ed.), *They Came to Japan: An Anthology of European Reports on Japan, 1543–1640* (Berkeley: University of California Press, 1965, 1981), p. vii.
6. Valignano, *Historia*, p. 191.
7. Bungo, 8 October 1561, in *Cartas*, vol. 1, f. 77v; quoted by Alvarez-Taladriz in Alessandro Valignano, *Sumario de las Cosas de Japon* (1583), ed. José Luis Alvarez-Taladriz, *Monumenta Nipponica* monograph, no. 9 (Tokyo: Sophia University, 1954), p. 191, n. 10.
8. See note 2 above.
9. Valignano, *Historia*, p. 146; quoted in Cooper, *They Came to Japan*, p. 193.
10. Fukuda, 25 October 1565, in *Cartas*, vol. 1, f. 163; quoted by Alvarez-Taladriz in Rodrigues, *Arte del Cha*, p. 1, n. 1.
11. Alessandro Valignano, *Advertimentos e Avisos acerca dos Costumes e Catangues de Jappão*, in Josef Fr. Schütte (ed.), *Il Ceremoniale per i Missionari del Giappone* (Rome: Storia e Letterature, 1946).
12. Ibid., p. 136.

13. Ibid., pp. 160–162.

14. Ibid., p. 172.

15. *Japonica-Sinica* series (Rome: Jesuit Archives), vol. 2, f. 99v.

16. Ibid., f. 102v.

17. Ibid., ff. 106v–107.

18. Ibid., f. 107v; quoted by Alvarez-Taladriz in Rodrigues, *Arte del Cha*, pp. 18–19, n. 57.

19. These words are conveniently listed by Alvarez-Taladriz in Rodrigues, *Arte del Cha*, pp. 96–106.

20. *Vocabulario da Lingoa de Iapam* (Nagasaki, 1603–1604; Tokyo: Benseidō reprint, 1973), ff. 46 and 339.

21. Luis Frois, *Historia de Japam*, ed. Josef Wicki (Lisbon: Biblioteca Nacional de Lisboa, 1976–1984), vol. 2, p. 265; quoted by Alvarez-Taladriz in Valignano, *Sumario*, p. 44, n. 112.

22. Alessandro Valignano, *Libro Primero del principio y progresso de la Religion christiana en Jappon . . .* (London: British Library), Add. MSS. 9875.

23. Ibid., f. 36; quoted by Alvarez-Taladriz in Valignano, *Sumario*, p. 43, n. 109.

24. Ibid.

25. Bernardino de Avila Girón, "Relacion del Reino de Nippon," in Doroteo Schilling and Fidel de Lejarna, eds., *Archivo Ibero-Americano*, vol. 37 (Madrid, 1934), p. 29.

26. Francesco Carletti, *My Voyage Around the World*, trans. by Herbert Weinstock (London: Methuen, 1965), p. 100.

27. Fukuda, 25 October 1565, in *Cartas*, vol. 1, ff. 163–163v.

28. Valignano, *Sumario*, pp. 43–46; Valignano, *Historia*, pp. 147–149.

29. Nagasaki, 20 August 1585, in *Cartas*, vol. 2, ff. 135–135v; quoted by Alvarez-Taladriz in Valignano, *Sumario*, p. 46, no. 121.

30. Carletti, *My Voyage*, pp. 99–102. For *rusontsubo*, see Rodrigues, *Arte del Cha*, p. 35, n. 101.

31. The work had a total of thirty-seven chapters, of which chap. 12 dealt with tea. The chapter titles are listed in Frois, *Historia de Japam*, vol. 1, pp. 11–13. But for the fact that Rodrigues' treatise on Japanese life was copied in the eighteenth century in Macao, this work too might never have survived since the original manuscript has perished.

32. Information about Rodrigues' life and career in Japan and China is given in Michael Cooper, *Rodrigues the Interpreter: An Early Jesuit in Japan and China* (Tokyo: Weatherhill, 1974).

33. Rodrigues, *Arte del Cha*, p. 40, n. 110.

34. Ibid., p. 78, n. 199.

35. Rodrigues may have met Yoshishige as early as 1578, since both were present at the battle of Mimikawa in Hyūga in December of that year.

36. João Rodrigues, *This Island of Japon: João Rodrigues' Account of 16th-Century Japan*, trans. Michael Cooper (Tokyo: Kodansha International, 1975), p. 296; and *Arte del Cha*, pp. 77, 80. See also João Rodrigues, *Nihon Kyōkai Shi*, trans. Doi Tadao et al. (Tokyo: Iwanami, 1967), vol. 1, p. 638.

37. Cooper, *Rodrigues the Interpreter*, pp. 75–84.

38. *Cartas*, vol. 2, p. 178.

39. Nishimura Tei, *Kirishitan to Sadō* (Tokyo: Zenkoku Shobō, 1948), p. 192. Utilizing microfilm in Tokyo, I have made a search among the letters preserved in the *Japonica-Sinica* series of the Jesuit archives, Rome, but have been unable to find the original letter.

40. João Rodrigues, *Arte Breve da lingoa Iapoa* (Macao, 1620), f. 4; quoted by Alvarez-Taladriz in Rodrigues, *Arte del Cha*, p. 94.

41. 20 March 1612, in *Japonica-Sinica* series, Jesuit archives, Rome, vol. 15 (II), f. 216.

42. The English, Spanish, and Japanese translations are contained in Rodrigues' *This Island, Arte del Cha*, and *Nihon Kyōkai Shi*. An unannotated and inaccurate Portuguese edition—João Rodrigues Tçuzzu, *Historia da Igreja do Japão*, ed. João do Amaral Abranches Pinto (Macao: Noticias de Macau, 1954–1956), 2 vols.—is no longer in print.

43. Rodrigues' account of tea in its English translation (in *This Island*) runs to about twenty thousand words and has been reduced to slightly less than one-fifth of its length in the following summary.

FIVE

KAN'EI CULTURE AND *CHANOYU*

Kumakura Isao
Translated by Paul Varley

THE term "Kan'ei culture" refers to a cultural epoch of approximately three-quarters of a century that was centered on the Kan'ei era of 1624–1643.[1] It began some twenty-five years before Kan'ei and ended about twenty-five years after. In other words, the Kan'ei cultural epoch extended from the opening years of the seventeenth century until around 1670. Commencing as a continuation of Momoyama culture, it faded into the shadow of the Genroku epoch, which began in the 1670s.

In dividing the Kan'ei cultural epoch into periods, I wish to designate the years from the Keichō era in the late sixteenth century (Keichō was 1596–1614) until the beginning of the Genna era (1615) as its first period. The second period was from about 1616 until the end of the Keian era (1651), and the third period spanned the years from the Jōō era (1652–1654) until the Empō era (1673–1680). Of course, cultural history cannot be separated as sharply into periods as political history. Let me briefly explain my reasons for suggesting this threefold division of the Kan'ei cultural epoch.

If the Momoyama epoch is viewed as the age of Toyotomi Hideyoshi, then it lasted until Hideyoshi's death in 1598. Yet surely the enforced suicide of Sen no Rikyū in 1591 was an important sign of the decline of Momoyama culture at least seven years earlier. A movement that emerged from the vigorous spirit of *gekokujō* (those below overthrow those above) and gave rise to a steady stream of aesthetic discoveries was brought to an abrupt halt by Hideyoshi's unification of the country. In establishing a centralized form of feudal rule and pursuing a policy of suppressing any tendencies toward *gekokujō*, Hideyoshi the hegemon was obliged to assert himself as an absolute power and authority in every sphere of activity. If in the cultural realm, for example, Rikyū possessed authority superior to Hideyoshi's, then he could no longer be permitted to exist. Here we have the real reason for Rikyū's penalty of death by suicide.

Yet, despite Hideyoshi's desperate efforts, it was no easy matter to cut the roots of *gekokujō*. One proof of this lies in the fact that the Toyotomi regime was unable in the end to prevent the *gekokujō* of Tokugawa Ieyasu. And although the establishment of the Tokugawa Bakufu created a government of power then unprecedented in Japanese history, in the realm of manners and culture the flames of *gekokujō* continued to blaze. Indeed the first period of Kan'ei culture was characterized by the spread of a fierce struggle between the politics of centralized power and the culture of *gekokujō*. The suicide in 1615 of Furuta Oribe, who symbolized the first period of Kan'ei culture, and the proclamation in the same year of the Laws for the Court and the Courtier Houses (*Kinchū narabi Kuge Sho Hatto*), which were designed to terminate opposition between the Imperial Court and the Bakufu, constituted a turning point that brought the transition from the first to the second period of Kan'ei culture. A major characteristic of subsequent Kan'ei culture lay in the fact that it was supported by a stable, centralized political power.

Kan'ei culture at its peak was a time of brilliance in virtually every field of endeavor. In architecture it produced the Katsura Detached Palace and the Yōmei Gate at the Nikkō Shrine; Tawaraya Sōtatsu and Kanō Tan'yū were among its leading painters; and the performing arts witnessed lively activity in *kabuki* and *nō* performances at Shijō and the Kamo riverbed in Kyoto. The leader in flower arrangement (*rikka*) was Senkō in the second generation of the Ikenobō family; and *chanoyu* produced Hon'ami Kōetsu, Kobori Enshū, Sen Sōtan, Kanamori Sōwa, Shōkadō Shōjō, and many others. In scholarship and the literary arts there were Hayashi Razan, Matsunaga Teitoku, and Kinoshita Chōshōshi. Among these brilliant men of culture, Kōetsu died in 1637 toward the end of the Kan'ei era, Shōkadō passed away in 1639, and Korobi Enshū's life came to an end at age sixty-nine in 1647. In the transition from the Shōhō era (1644–1647) to the Keian era (1648–1651) the character of Kan'ei culture changed.

Entering the 1650s, when the government of the Tokugawa shifted from military to bureaucratic rule and the period I have identified as the third and last stage of Kan'ei culture commenced, we find great alterations in customs described in such books as the *Mukashi-Mukashi Monogatari*.[2] This book tells of changes occurring in all manner of things—from women's fashions to customs in food—during the time from Meireki (1655–1657) to Kambun (1661–1672). As a result of the great Meireki fire of 1657, the entire city of Edo was transformed, and in Kyoto it was about this time that the upper class of townsmen (*machishū*), which had been granted special privileges by the Bakufu, began to die off. In its place there arose a new class of urban inhabitants: the *chōnin*.

The final flowering of Kan'ei culture, which occurred in the twilight of the epoch, was represented by the construction of former emperor Gomizunoo's detached palace (the Shūgakuin) and by Katagiri Sekishū's *chanoyu*. Yet even then a new culture was emerging with the appearance of the Genroku masters, who, among other things, benefited from the development of the publishing industry. The activities of Sen Sōtan and the other tea masters known as the "four famous disciples" (*shi-tennō*) of *chanoyu* were a product of this new culture, which ushered in the succeeding Genroku epoch.

RIKYŪ'S SEVEN SAGES AND THE *KABUKI* AGE

According to *Rekkō Kanwa*, Hosokawa Sansai once asked Rikyū: "If you should die, who will succeed you as the foremost master of *chanoyu* in the realm?" Rikyū replied: "My son Dōan performs *chanoyu* beautifully, but his background is poor. Hence he will not be able to succeed me as master of the realm. Won't the successor most likely be Furuta Oribe?"[3] And indeed, as Rikyū predicted, Oribe became the new master. The word "background" in Rikyū's reply meant social status. During the age of *gekokujō*, it was possible for a townsman like Rikyū to become the realm's leading master of *chanoyu*. But under a regime of centralized feudal power based on a rigid system of social status, it was important that the master be a member of the samurai class. The general feeling was that, in terms of ability, Sen Dōan was well qualified to be the master; but from the standpoint of social status, a daimyo like Furuta Oribe was more appropriate.

Rikyū's suicide marked the commencement of a new age dominated by Oribe, Hosokawa Sansai, and his other leading disciples. Among these men, seven warriors were identified as his "seven sages" (*shichi-*

tetsu). They were Gamō Ujisato, Takayama Ukon, Hosokawa Sansai, Shibayama Kenmotsu, Seta Kamon, Makimura Hyōbu, and Furuta Oribe.[4] The career of the model disciple among these, Furuta Oribe, exemplifies the special characteristics of culture and tea during the Keichō era.

Furuta Oribe was born in Mino province in 1544. A retainer of Oda Nobunaga, Oribe served as one of Nobunaga's deputies *(daikan).* He seems to have become seriously interested in *chanoyu* from about 1578 when he married the daughter of Nakagawa Kiyohide, the lord of Ibaraki Castle in Settsu province. Oribe first appears in a tea record *(chakai-ki)* in reference to an affair held on 1585:2:13.[5] It is also from approximately this time that the name Oribe Sasuke is to be found in the correspondence of Sen no Rikyū and that Oribe received instruction in *chanoyu* from Rikyū.[6] In the same year, 1585, Oribe was appointed to the junior fifth rank, lower grade, in the court ranking system and was designated Oribe-no-Kami. He also became the daimyo of Nishioka in Yamashiro province with an annual revenue of thirty-five thousand *koku* of rice. Thereafter Oribe was commonly known by the name "Oribe," and his formal given name was changed from Kageyasu to Shigenari. Oribe received the Buddhist name Kinpo from the Zen priest Shun'oku Sōen. His other Buddhist names were Sōoku and Insai.

The master-disciple relationship between Oribe and Rikyū was strong, and among Rikyū's preserved correspondence are a number of letters addressed to Oribe. These include the famous "Musashi Abumi no Fumi," which contains a story about a bamboo flower vase made for Oribe when he was fighting at various places in the Kantō out of the camp at Odawara.[7]

When Rikyū, immediately before his suicide, was ordered by Hideyoshi to go to Sakai, it was Oribe and Hosokawa Sansai who proceeded to the boat landing at Yodo to bid him farewell. In this way Oribe displayed to the very end the respect he held for his teacher. After Rikyū's death Oribe, as the leading connoisseur *(sukisha)* of tea in the country, was highly favored by both Hideyoshi and Tokugawa Hidetada, and his style of *chanoyu* became prized above all others. It was during this time that *Keichō Otazune no Sho,* a record of conversations between Oribe and his disciple Kobori Enshū, was compiled.[8] Nevertheless, for reasons that are not clear, Oribe—although an adherent of the Tokugawa—secretly communicated with the Toyotomi side at the time of the siege of Osaka Castle in 1615. After the siege he was ordered to commit suicide, and his family was exterminated. In meeting an untimely end, Oribe shared the fate of his teacher, Rikyū.

Considering Oribe from the standpoint of his role as a man of taste rather than as a samurai, we can see in his *chanoyu* a heterodox character that went against the trend of the times. Indeed, it possessed an inherent destructiveness that paralleled the political behavior which led to his physical destruction after the siege of Osaka Castle.

What were the special qualities of Oribe's *chanoyu?* It is recorded in his account of a tea gathering in 1585 *(Oribe Chakai-ki)* that he used a Seto tea bowl. Presumably this was a newly made bowl, since Oribe had no great liking for traditional *meibutsu* (famous works of art and craft) and was conspicuous in his use of new utensils. In this account, Oribe asserts: "If, using new utensils, we once enter the realm of discrimination, this can be called *wabi.*"[9] Herein is clearly revealed Oribe's aesthetic taste, which—contrary to the taste of others—gave preference to the newly-made. Yet "newly made" did not simply mean *wabi* utensils that were not *meibutsu.* It is well known, for example, that people regarded as "oddities" *(hyōgemono)* and "improperly baked" *(yakisokonai)* the eccentrically shaped tea bowls described in *Koshoku-kō Densho.*[10] Although the term "Oribe ware" was not coined until after Oribe's death, we can observe in these ceramics with bold design the tea style that was his.

In *Oribe Chakai-ki* we find written for 1603:7:3:

> In the alcove of the tea room was hung a scroll with the Buddhist name "Kimpo," written by Shun'oku Sōen. Lotus blossoms were placed in a basket for decoration.
>
> On the small shelf in the tea room was a metal ring for handling the kettle and a broom made of feathers. During the recess in the gathering, the scroll was left untouched and only the flowers were removed.[11]

The Kinpo calligraphy, given to Oribe by the Zen master Shun'oku Sōen, was neither a *meibutsu* nor an article of particular distinction. Oribe used it, moreover, while Sōen was still alive. This attests both to his intense devotion to Zen and to his free employment, unfettered by tradition, of the articles of *chanoyu.* Before Oribe, works of calligraphy by living people were scarcely ever used at tea gatherings, and it was conventional practice to display a calligraphic scroll in the first sitting of a gathering and flowers during the second. Oribe, however, used both calligraphy and flowers for decoration in the first sitting and removed the flowers for the second. Such radical handling of the things of *chanoyu* was typical of Oribe.

Oribe's aesthetic taste was based on the extremely deformed—for example, a misshapen tea bowl in which it was difficult to use a whisk or a water pitcher with large cracks which, although of extremely interesting shape, leaked when water was poured into it—and the need to destroy even the functional qualities of a tea article as a work of craft. Clearly his taste was in keeping with the *kabuki* preferences of the Keichō era in which he lived. (*Kabuki* derives from the verb *kata-buku* and means, literally, "not to stand straight.") The *kabuki* beauty of the crooked, the bent, and the radically altered appeared as the age of *gekokujō* expired. It represented, above all, the spirit of disenchanted youth. Groups called *kabuki-mono* (*kabuki* people), embracing unconventional styles and ways, esteemed pacts among companions that transcended feudal, leader-follower relations and opposed the existing order. These groups even revealed signs of forming secret societies. In a scene from the panoramic screen painting of the special celebration of the deity Daimyōjin at the Hōkoku Shrine in Kyoto that was held in 1604 on the occasion of the seventh anniversary of Hideyoshi's death, we find some young people with the look of *kabuki-mono* engaged in a brawl. On the sheath of one of their swords is inscribed: "Have I already lived to twenty-three? In the name of Lord Hachiman, I will never yield!"[12] We can interpret these as the words of a youth, born too late for the age of war, who still dreamed of *gekokujō*.

Furuta Oribe may also have wondered how he had lived as long as he had. Rikyū's death had brought the demise of the *gekokujō* spirit, which could not avoid destroying conventional sense and order as suggested in the words (from *Yamanoue Sōji Ki*) about "transforming mountains into valleys and changing west to east."[13] The rejection in 1591 of Rikyū's extreme form of *chanoyu* prefigured the ultimate rejection of Oribe's tea, which was deeply colored by the *gekokujō* spirit. During the quarter-century following Rikyū's death, Oribe appears to have presented the unconventional Rikyū style of *chanoyu* with ever greater intensity. In the same way that Rikyū's tea was regarded as heterodox and "not for the ordinary person," Oribe's too was looked upon as heterodox, and it was prophesied that he would meet a violent end.

The prophesy of Oribe's death appeared in *Rōdan Ichigon Ki*. According to this work, Matsudaira Ise-no-Kami Nobutsuna's father, Ōkōchi Kimbei, said: "Oribe will not die a normal death."[14] And, indeed, after the siege of Osaka Castle, Oribe was ordered to commit suicide as if in fulfillment of Kimbei's prophesy. When Kimbei was asked why he had made this prophesy, he replied in the following manner. Oribe was the kind of person who damaged the treasures of the realm. If, for example, he did not like the shape of a certain hanging scroll, he would deliberately cut it shorter. Or if tea bowls and caddies were perfect and without flaws, he would purposely break and repair them and declare the broken and repaired articles to be interesting. A person who thus damaged the treasures of the realm could not avoid meeting a violent end.

Of course, prophesies hold little value for the historian. Nevertheless it is intriguing to read this assessment of Oribe, which vividly describes him as one who, as noted, seemed fixed upon a course, both as a samurai in the service of the Tokugawa Bakufu and as a man of tea, that could only end in disaster. The story of Kimbei's prophesy also reveals that the concept of beauty had changed from the time of Rikyū and Oribe. In an age when the spirit of *gekokujō* thrived, it was permissible for one, in accordance with personal aesthetic tastes, freely to alter tea articles. But within the order of the early modern period, this license was regarded as immoral. And the retribution for immorality was destruction.

Oribe was not entirely opposed to the existing order of things nor was he completely like Rikyū. It is well known, for example, that he installed an attendants' seating area *(shōbanseki)* in the teahouse Ennan to accommodate the retainers of high-ranking guests. In contrast to Rikyū, who insisted that social distinctions be ignored and that all participants in a tea gathering sit together, Oribe took some recognition of these distinctions. And whereas Rikyū devoted himself to *wabicha* exclusively in the small room *(kozashiki)*, Oribe made use of a separate, "adjoining room" *(kusari-no-ma)*, where he permitted the pursuit of a more hedonistic form of *chanoyu*. In this sense, Oribe stood in opposition to what Rikyū represented.

Since Oribe served in the position of national tea master under the Tokugawa Bakufu, it was only natural that his tea should have been oriented more toward the military than Rikyū's. Yet Oribe's tea was distinguished not by the fact that it catered to the demands of the new military order but rather that it was kindred in spirit and aesthetic sensibility to the *kabuki-mono* of the age.

The *chanoyu* of Oda Uraku, who was also active at this time, tended in the same direction as Oribe's. The younger brother of Oda Nobunaga, Uraku loved *chanoyu* from his youth and also became a disciple of Rikyū. As a daimyo, Uraku served in the political realm as an intermediary between the Toyotomi and Tokugawa groups after the fall of the Oda house. The distinguishing features of Uraku's *chanoyu* are best revealed in the structure of the Joan tea room, a product of his later years. In the narrow space of the Joan are two regular *tatami*, a half-*tatami*, and a *daime* (a three-quarter-sized *tatami*). Moreover, a triangular piece of wood called *uroko ita* was installed next to the alcove, reflecting freedom and change in the handling of the room's passageway.[15] And in the use of windows in the Joan there is the unusual installation of a partition which, when viewed from the *nijiriguchi* ("crawling in" entrance), extends across from the *daime* post and has a window cut into it.

We cannot conclude, of course, that Uraku's *chanoyu* was of an entirely radical character. Rather, it appears in general to have been tranquil, as though reflecting Uraku's political role as a mediator. Using *Uraku-tei Chanoyu Nikki* as a source, we can observe in Uraku the growth of a daimyo style of tea focused on the handling of the calligraphy scroll *(bokuseki)*.[16] At the same time, we can note in his *chanoyu* the expression of a *kabuki* sentiment revealed in the structuring of his tea rooms. In short, Uraku's tea reflected aspects of both the military and the *kabuki* strains of *chanoyu*. Thus we may say that, for whatever reason, the Keichō era fomented even in Uraku a kind of heterodoxy, just as it gave birth to Furuta Oribe's tea.

THE WORLD OF TASTE
FOR "REFINED BEAUTY" (KIREI)

Ori Rikutsu	Oribe is disputatious,
Kirei kippa wa	Enshū has refined beauty
Tōtōmi	And a cutting blade.

| *Ohime Sōwa ni* | Sōwa is princess-like, |
| *Musashi Sōtan.* | And Sōtan squalid.[17] |

This crazy verse *(kyōka)*, apparently written in the late Tokugawa period, cleverly suggests the tastes of four tea masters: Furuta Oribe, Kobori Enshū, Kanamori Sōwa, and Sen Sōtan. By characterizing Oribe's *chanoyu* as "disputatious," the verse refers to the fact that in his tea Oribe was consistently unorthodox. His very manner of living revealed a single-minded unwillingness to compromise.

The tea style of Oribe's disciple, Kobori Enshū, is usually described, on the other hand, as *kirei sabi* (refined beauty and loneliness), and this is the aesthetic implied in the verse. *Kippa* seems to mean "cutting blade," and denotes the addition of a knifelike sharpness to the sensibility of *kirei*.

Discussions of Enshū's *chanoyu* usually approach it from two standpoints. One is the aesthetic of *kirei sabi* as reflected in the preceding verse; the second, typified in *Enshū Kakisute Bumi*, derives from the concept of "daimyo tea" based on Confucian ethical principles.[18] These two standpoints are not contradictory. Rather, I believe that in its complexity is revealed the comprehensive, synthetic character of Enshū's *chanoyu*.

Kobori Enshū was born in Ōmi province in 1579. He was known in his youth as Sakusuke and later received the name Masakazu. Enshū's father, Kobori Shinsuke Masatsugu, was of provincial gentry *(jisamurai)* origins and served the Asai daimyo house. Shinsuke was an able warrior who, after the fall of the Asai, entered the service of Hideyoshi and assumed a position as a leading vassal *(karō)* of Hideyoshi's younger brother Hidenaga. A man who had received instruction in *chanoyu* from Rikyū himself, Hidenaga was a chieftain of rich cultural training. The young Kobori Enshū served in Hidenaga's castle at Kōriyama in Yamato, and from this experience he was no doubt exposed at an early age to *nō* and *chanoyu*. From his teenage years Enshū came into association with Furuta Oribe and progressed in his study of tea. He also practiced Zen with Shun'oku Sōen of Daitokuji and was given the Buddhist name of Sōho. Upon the death of his father in 1604, Enshū succeeded to a domain of twelve thousand *koku* of rice revenue and became a daimyo. In 1608 he was given the junior fifth rank, lower grade, and was appointed governor of Tōtōmi province. From this appointment he acquired the familiar name of Enshū (an abbreviation for "Tōtōmi province").

As a warrior, Enshū served in a number of posts for the Tokugawa Bakufu, beginning with magistrate of Fushimi. But the position with which he is most closely associated is that of construction magistrate, a post that included responsibility for constructing castles and palace buildings and for laying out and superintending gardens. Enshū achieved great fame in architecture and garden construction. Typical of his gardens were those at the Nijō Palace and the palace of the retired emperor.

Although none has survived, many public structures, such as former emperor Gomizunoo's palace of retirement and the main compound *(honmaru)* and *yamazato* (mountain village) tea room of the imperial palace, were also the work of Enshū. Among his numerous private building projects were the Mittan tea room of the Ryūkōin at Daitokuji and the Bōsenseki tea room of the Kohōan at the same temple, both of which have been designated national treasures. Thus the ability of Kobori Enshū is well revealed in his architecture. He was quite influential in garden construction, as well, and can indeed be regarded as the founder of the early modern style in gardens.[19]

We have records of conversations about *chanoyu* between Enshū and Oribe from the Keichō era. In 1636 Enshū served tea to the shogun Iemitsu at the Shinagawa shogunal residence, and from that time on he was the shogun's master of tea. But Enshū's role was different from that of Oribe, who actually instructed Hidetada in *chanoyu*. Enshū simply served tea to the shogun, although even this function was sufficient to bring him recognition as the realm's leading *(tenka ichi)* tea master. In other words, even though the custom of having an instructor of *chanoyu* for the shogun (or national hegemon) was discontinued, Enshū was universally recognized after Oribe's death as the central figure in the world of warrior *chanoyu*.

Kobori Enshū hosted many tea gatherings during his life. The extant records of these sessions alone account for more than four hundred. Active also in designing tea utensils and in appraising old articles, Enshū remained a truly vital force in *chanoyu* until his death in 1647. Thereafter, his descendants in the Kobori house continued the Enshū line in the way of tea, transmitting it to the present day.

Now let us consider the main characteristics of Enshū's approach to *chanoyu*, using primarily the records of his tea gatherings. Enshū's tea records reveal the complex nature of his *chanoyu*. Here is an instance, as recorded in *Enshū Kuchigirichō*, of a gathering held on 1646:8:20:

> The morning of the twentieth day of the eighth month. The guests were Itō Naizen and four others.
>
> A scroll of calligraphy by a national teacher *(kokushi)* was placed in the alcove of the tea room.
>
> On the lower shelf of a small, two-level set of shelves was placed a steel ring used to remove and replace the kettle and a broom made of feathers for use in the charcoal *temae*. During the recess in the gathering, a round *tsubo*-shaped caddy called Tachibana was put on a lacquered tray with a whirlpool design, and the tray with caddy was placed on the lower shelf of the small set of shelves. The broom that had been on this shelf was transferred to the upper shelf.
>
> When the gathering was begun again after the recess, the calligraphy was removed from the alcove and replaced with a flower vase containing irises.
>
> A piece of Seto ware was used as the water container.
>
> The caddy was also a Seto piece, called Asukagawa, displayed in front of the water container. The ladle was put on the side of the mat.
>
> The tea bowl was Korean and slightly warped. The waste water bowl was also Korean, a metal utensil shaped like a hemisphere.
>
> The tea room was decorated in the foregoing manner.
>
> Here is the decoration of the *kusari-no-ma*:
>
> The picture display in the alcove was a scene of quails painted by the Sung dynasty artist Li An-chung. It was a set of three separate pictures.
>
> In another alcove was a painting of Han Shan (Kanzan) and Shih Te (Jittoku) by the Sung artist Liang K'ai.
>
> The remaining decorations were the same as those of gatherings on other days.[20]

The setting for the gathering was divided into two parts. First, a meal *(kaiseki)* and thick tea were served in the small room *(kozashiki)*. Then, in the adjoining room *(kusari-no-ma)*, refreshments and thin tea were presented in their various phases. The national teacher calligraphy in the alcove of the small room was the work of Shun'oku Sōen. As Konoe Iehiro, writing in *Kaiki*, observed: "Because Enshū makes great use of Shun'oku Sōen's calligraphy, it has become the fashion."[21] Enshū did indeed frequently use the calligraphy of Sōen, his teacher in Zen: He displayed Sōen's writings in one-sixth of all his tea gatherings whose records have been preserved.

Preference for calligraphy began with Rikyū and was continued by Uraku. Among the four hundred of Enshū's recorded gatherings, nearly four-fifths featured calligraphy.[22] It is no exaggeration to say that *Nampōroku*'s demand that "calligraphy should be given highest priority" was truly implemented for the first time by Enshū.[23] In attaching such importance to calligraphy, Enshū both preserved and furthered Rikyū's *wabicha*.

Rikyū forbade the holding of a "later sitting" in *chanoyu*. That is, he taught (in *Nampōroku*) that a banquet should not be given in a separately prepared room after the formal conclusion of a tea gathering.[24] As times changed, however, people became dissatisfied with only tea in the small room and demanded entertainment in a more spacious setting. This explains why the *kusari-no-ma* came into vogue as a place to assemble after the gathering in the small room. Created by Furuta Oribe, the *kusari-no-ma* was raised to its greatest popularity by Kobori Enshū. In the development of the *kusari-no-ma*, the practice of *chanoyu* was thus altered in the period between Rikyū and Enshū.

Turning to the decoration of the *kusari-no-ma*, we see the rise of painters like Li An-chung and Liang K'ai, who were among the Chinese artists most highly esteemed by the Japanese. Insofar as the works of such artists had been included among the Higashiyama collection of the shogun Yoshimasa, the decoration of Enshū's *kusari-no-ma* represented a revival of "*karamono* magnificence." If tea in the small room symbolized the tradition of Rikyū's *wabicha*, the way of the *shoin* style of tea from the earlier Higashiyama cultural epoch came, by means of decoration of the *kusari-no-ma*, to be joined to *wabicha*.

When we examine the decoration of the *kusari-no-ma* in *Enshū Kuchigirichō*, we note a particular style of arrangement in the *shoin* alcove that stands in contrast to *karamono* display. Here, for example, is an account of a tea gathering on 1645:11:1: "In the *shoin* alcove on the northern wall was hung a scroll by Fujiwara no Teika. On the asymmetrical shelves on the southern wall was displayed writing from *Ise Monogatari* in the hand of Fujiwara no Tameie."[25] Here we have an expression of traditional taste for courtier culture in the highlighting of Teika and Tameie, noted poets and authorities in *waka* scholarship from the courtly past, and in the use of passages from *Ise Monogatari* and a poetic anthology for room decoration.

Taste for ancient courtier culture has always been a powerful sentiment flowing in the background of Japanese cultural history. There was an especially strong renewal of interest in this culture from the late Momoyama epoch, an interest that became a major pillar of what I have defined as the Kan'ei cultural epoch. The surge of fascination with court culture can be seen, for example, in the following manifestations: the flourishing activity in the literary arts by members of the imperial and courtier families; the great demand for Fujiwara no Teika's calligraphy (in the practice of which Kobori Enshū was an expert); and the revival of the Yamato-*e* tradition of painting by Tawaraya Sōtatsu and Hon'ami Kōetsu. At the center of this renewal of interest in courtier culture was Enshū. Observing the decoration for the tea session cited above, we see in Enshū's *chanoyu* an amalgam of tastes from at least three ages: the ancient courtier age, the Higashiyama epoch, and the Momoyama epoch. One result of this amalgam was a clear assertion of the demand that *chanoyu* not be restricted to the small room of *wabicha* but be expanded to include the *kusari-no-ma*.

The combining of cultures of different historical lineages with *chanoyu* was not just a matter of random mixing. Behind the way they were combined was Enshū's aesthetic sensibility, a sensibility based on the *kirei* taste in beauty. Although the vocabulary was the same as that used to describe the *chanoyu* of Rikyū and Oribe, the character of the aesthetics involved was quite at variance. For example, a bowl listed in the tea gathering mentioned above was called a "warped" Korean piece (Kōrai *hizumi*). But this warped bowl was definitely not the roughly twisted, radically deformed ceramic ware we found in Furuta Oribe's *chanoyu*. Rather, it was "warped" in the sense of an emphasis given to the beauty of its flowing line achieved by gracefully bending the bowl's thinly constructed rim. Enshū's "warped" was clearly distinguished from Oribe's "warped" by the sense of *kirei*.

Kirei nearly became popular usage in Enshū's time. Not only Enshū, but many others, including courtiers, liked the term. In expressing admiration for the Ōwada villa of the Konoe family, for example, Prince Toshihito—the creator of the Katsura Detached Palace—said: "The refined beauty *(kireisa)* of the main building and teahouse . . . is dazzling."[26] Records exist that also bestow praise in the form of *kirei* on Katsura itself. And in *Matsuya Kaiki* Enshū's *temae* is assessed as *kirei* by Matsuya Gensaburō.[27] "Taste for refined beauty" is generally regarded as "Enshū taste"; but actually it was an aesthetic concept that was widely fascinating to people in this age. Enshū himself acquired his feeling for *kirei* from his study with courtiers. And through his work in constructing the ladies quarters at the imperial palace in Kyoto, Enshū had many opportunities to come into contact with courtier culture.

Enshū's relationship with Prince Toshihito became intimate from about 1618, when the prince first began work on a teahouse in Shimo-Katsura village. He deepened his *kirei* taste in particular through his tie to the prince.

I see three components in Enshū's *kirei* taste: first, a strongly ornamental brilliance and subtlety of expression taken to the point of delicacy; second, clear and sharp lines and coloring; and third, a symbolism that is found in the literature of China and Japan in all periods.

It is necessary, finally, to touch upon Enshū's role as a leader of architectural styling in the world of *chanoyu*. Let me cite some cases in which Enshū asserted leadership in this area. First, although no documentary proof has yet come to light that shows he gave direct guidance in the construction of the Katsura Detached Palace, it is clear from the circumstances surrounding Katsura's creation that Enshū exerted an influence upon it.[28] He was, moreover, responsible for supervising the construction, beginning in 1627, of the retired emperor's palace.

Letters written in response to inquiries by courtiers about tea articles indicate that Enshū had serious effect even upon *chanoyu* at the emperor's court.

In warrior society Enshū earned great fame as an administrator of such building projects as the shogun's residence at Shinagawa and was often involved in *chanoyu* with the shogun. He also had particularly intimate dealings with the Maeda house. For example, we read in the correspondence between Enshū and Maeda Toshitsune about a time when Toshitsune—inquiring about *temae*—asked whether it was necessary, in handling a *dai-tenmoku* (a *tenmoku* tea bowl on a stand), to place the tea caddy on a tray. Enshū replied that although there was a general rule that the caddy ought to be placed on a tray, the decision should be made in accord with the caddy's value.[29] Many detailed questions such as this appear in the letters Toshitsune sent to Enshū. For his part, Enshū performed the role of instructor of *chanoyu* by writing responses to the questions on the backs of the letters.

The records show that Enshū also provided instruction in tea to

Toshitsune's son Mitsutaka. Meeting with Enshū during recesses in official business at Edo Castle, Mitsutaka deluged the master with questions about *chanoyu*. Entries in the records state that, when queried about important points, Enshū lowered his voice and gave his replies in whispers.[30] In thus meeting the demands of daimyos like the Maeda, Enshū greatly enhanced himself as an instructor of *chanoyu*.

Enshū's firm position as a leader of *chanoyu* is well revealed, too, with regard to tea utensils and writings. The utensils known today as *chūkō* (literally, "restored") *meibutsu* were not so designated during Enshū's lifetime.[31] Rather, the designation was first adopted more than a century after his death by Matsudaira Fumai for purposes of classification in his *Kokon Meibutsu Ruijū*. The basis of the *chūkō meibutsu* was a collection of utensils selected by Enshū to meet the needs of various daimyos, townsmen, and others. For emergent tea masters who were no longer able to acquire *meibutsu*, Enshū created new ones. Thus, in his position as national leader of *chanoyu*, Enshū also served as an "enlightener" or arbiter of taste.

Sōjinboku, published in 1626, was the first tea book to be printed with wooden type. Although its author is unknown, part of it agrees with the transmitted writings of Enshū and hence it was probably compiled from these writings by a tea man of the Enshū school. Another part of *Sōjinboku* deals with Rikyū and Oribe.[32] Although Enshū himself may not have been involved with the book, the background of its publication reveals, in addition to the Enshū previously described as a leader in the world of tea, his role as an arbiter of taste. It is my conclusion that the special nature of Kan'ei culture lay in synthesis and the arbitration of taste, and in this sense Kobori Enshū was the personification of the Kan'ei cultural epoch.

REVIVAL OF THE SEN HOUSE

The fortunes of the house of Sen no Rikyū were revived by Sen Shōan sometime about 1594. (We do not know the precise date.) The fact that the Sen house's revival was permitted just a few years after Rikyū's suicide was a happy occurrence indeed for the tradition of *chanoyu*, since the tea Rikyū himself practiced still remained intact. We cannot, however, determine how the revival of the family which Shōan, Rikyū's adopted son, was allowed to undertake may have affected a similar revival by Rikyū's real son, Dōan. It is not beyond the realm of possibility that, while Shōan was formally taking charge of reconstruction of the Sen in Kyoto, Dōan, his wife (Rikyū's daughter-in-law), and others were continuing the family tradition as the Sakai line of the Sen. Quite likely there was a feeling of antagonism between Kyoto and Sakai. *Zuiryūsai Nobegami no Sho* states: "Moyuza Sōkan was to serve in *chanoyu* at the capital. He borrowed Rikyū's death poem but did not return it."[33] This failure of Rikyū's grandson Sōkan of Sakai to return the death poem may have resulted from a plan of opposition by the Sakai Sen to the Kyoto Sen, which inherited all of Rikyū's most valuable tea utensils and other belongings.

During the Genroku epoch, Rikyū's death poem was brought to Kyoto for a while and then was taken to Edo. After long and arduous work by Kawakami Fuhaku and others, the poem was finally returned from the Fuyuki family to Omotesenke in Kyoto in 1751. Inasmuch as the poem had been taken from Sakai in the Genroku epoch, it was probably then that the Sakai Sen line was terminated. In other words, the first period after the revival of the Sen house—from Shōan to Sōtan—was a crucial time when the family asserted its independence from the country's political authority and suppressed its Sakai line. In 1600, during the delicate political maneuverings involved in reestablishing the family, Sōtan succeeded his father Shōan as Sen family head.

Sen Sōtan, Shōan's son, was born in 1578. Shōan himself was Rikyū's adopted son. His real father was the *nō* master Miyaō Saburō Sannyū, and his mother was Sōon, who became Rikyū's second wife. It is not known precisely when Rikyū married Sōon. But since his first wife, Myōju, died in 1577:7, it was probably in 1578 or after. If this was the case, then very likely Sōtan had already been born at the time Rikyū and Sōon married. From the circumstances surrounding the relationship between Rikyū and Sōon, there has emerged the theory that Sōtan's mother (and Shōan's wife) was Rikyū's daughter Kame. But there is absolutely no proof for this theory. If, however, Kame was the mother, then Sōtan was Rikyū's real grandson—a possibility that would enable us to understand how Shōan and Sōtan became the revivers of the Sen house.

Sōtan served at a young age as a temple acolyte for Shun'oku Sōen in the Sangenin at Daitokuji. Later he entered the Buddhist priesthood. He appears to have left the priesthood and returned to his family at the time of the revival of the Sen house several years after Rikyū's death. Following the retirement in 1600 of his father, Shōan, Sōtan succeeded to the family headship; and in the next year, 1601, he received from Shun'oku Sōen the Buddhist name of Genshuku. Sōtan began to function prominently from this time as a tea man. (The first entry in his tea record is dated 1608.) His father, Shōan, died in 1614, and Sōtan married for the second time. He had two sons, Sōsetsu and Sōshu, from his first marriage, and two more, Sōsa and Sōshitsu, during his second. Sōtan's relations with his oldest son, Sōsetsu, were poor, and Sōsetsu, who on one occasion was even disinherited, did not succeed to the Sen family headship. Sōshu later built the Kankyūan at Mushanokōji and established the Mushanokōji Senke. As we shall see, Sōsa succeeded Sōtan as head of the main Sen line in 1645 and became the founder of Omotesenke. Sōshitsu, the youngest son, followed his father to his place of retirement and, in the same year, 1645, founded Urasenke at the Konnichian. Thus the three Sen lines were created by three of Sōtan's sons.

Now let us examine Sōtan's style of tea in terms of Sōtan the man. Here are the main points about Sōtan in *Fukō Chawa*, written by one of his leading disciples, Sugiki Fusai:

Having succeeded to the Sen house, Sōtan revived an abandoned tradition and clearly displayed the way of tea to the world. Those who praised him were legion: people from the cities and countryside, from far and near. They called upon him from morning until night to join together in *chanoyu*. Such was his popularity. The Sen house flourished as it had in Rikyū's day. Both the emperor and retired emperor admired Sōtan. He was frequently called by the Tokugawa shogun, but did not go. Upon reaching adulthood, Sōtan placed great importance on the true essence of *chanoyu* and took pleasure in tea. He was not attracted to *meibutsu* and settled for any utensils, enjoying those that simply came to hand. Sōtan was also disinterested in the past and unconcerned about the future. He named his small room Konnichian (meaning that only today—the present—matters) and lived with the thought of spending one more day with his aged body facing a tea kettle. His behavior was very similar to the priest who has entered the Zen state of enlightenment (*satori*). At times, Sōtan entertained himself by playing the *biwa* as he viewed the harvest moon through a window or by com-

posing poems in Chinese. His was truly a way of life that conformed to
the order of nature. Living this way, Sōtan died on 1658:12:19 at the
age of eighty-one.[34]

This is only a general sketch of Sōtan, who was known as "*wabi*
Sōtan" or "the beggar Sōtan." In the crazy verse given earlier in this
chapter, he was dubbed "Musashi Sōtan," a pun intended to convey
the image of him living a *wabi* life to the point of squalor (*musa-
kurushii*). Sōtan was frequently urged to accept official positions as tea
master but always refused. There is even the story that, unable to
ignore a summons from the Bakufu, he feigned illness and returned
home after going as far as the Osaka Pass.[35] Thus did Sōtan maintain
a thorough integrity, satisfied with genteel poverty and not mingling
with the grand and powerful. This is the familiar picture of Sōtan—
living the *wabi* life, ignoring *meibutsu* and using any utensils at hand
to enjoy his tea, gazing at the moon and reciting tales to the accompaniment of a *biwa*. It is the picture we are presented with in *Chawa Shigetsu Shū* and *Fukō Chawa*.

But a different picture of Sōtan emerges when we examine the more
than two hundred of his letters that have recently come to light at
Fushin'an (*Gempaku Sōtan Monjo*). Here is a Sōtan working indefati-
gably to gain employment for his sons in daimyo houses. We learn, for
example, that the reason Sōtan disinherited Sōsetsu, his oldest son by
his first wife, was because Sōsetsu repeatedly failed to make use of rec-
ommendations obtained at great effort to enter into daimyo service.

Kōshin Sōsa, the older of Sōtan's two sons by his second wife, was
twice made a *rōnin*—first, when the lord he served, Tarazawa Shima-
no-Kami, was dispossessed of his fief following the Shimabara Rebel-
lion in 1637; and second, when the house Sōsa next served, the
Ikoma, also lost its fief. Sōtan began a campaign to find new employment for Sōsa, and at the time wrote this in a letter to him: "So far as
employment for you with a daimyo house is concerned, it should be
in a domain in the region of the central provinces . . . you do not
need anything in a distant province. Indeed, if you cannot get an
appointment near the capital (Kyoto), you should come here [to the
capital] and make what arrangements you can."[36] This clearly reveals
Sōtan's concern to find daimyo service for one of his sons. Throughout his life Sōtan himself avoided such service; but far from prohibit-

ing his sons from entering into the employ of daimyos, he made every
effort to get them positions in daimyo houses.

Why did Sōtan thus avoid daimyo service himself while placing his
sons with daimyos? Since he was so insistent upon having his sons
serve daimyos, Sōtan's own avoidance of daimyo service cannot be
explained in terms of an aesthetic sensibility devoted solely to the way
of *wabi*. In the process of revival of the Sen family fortunes under
Shōan and Sōtan, deliberate efforts were made to establish the Sen
house independently of the political authority of the land. The story
of Rikyū was fresh in Sōtan's memory—how his grandfather had
become too deeply involved with the Toyotomi regime and had ultimately met destruction. He was determined that the Sen house not be
dispossessed again, and the safest way for him to ensure against dis-
possession was to avoid ties to power—that is, to live as a *rōnin* without accepting service with a military chief.

But from the Genna era (1615–1623), when Sōtan truly succeeded
his father (who died in 1614) as the head master of the Sen, strict sur-
veillance was imposed upon *rōnin* living in cities, and from time to
time orders were issued banishing them from the cities. Since the Sen
were not true samurai, they were not so severely regulated. Nevertheless, behind Sōtan's policy of declining daimyo service himself and living a life of reclusion while pressing his sons into such service lay the
desire to avoid the turmoil of *rōnin* roundups and to protect the Sen
house by having its head avoid association with the military powers.
Sōtan made this policy basic to the conduct of his affairs.

Nor should Sōtan's tea style be seen exclusively in terms of
wabicha. Sōtan had a broad range of acquaintances among daimyos,
members of the imperial family, and courtiers, and it was only natural
that his style of tea should share something of the *kirei* taste of Kan'ei
culture.

Among the Sōtan documents preserved at the Fushin'an are letters
that reveal a relationship in *chanoyu* between Sōtan and Tōfuku-
mon'in (Emperor Gomizunoo's empress), letters that confirm transmission from Sōtan of the idea of using a *tsumagure daisu* (a type of
daisu partly painted vermilion) and a vermilion *fukusa* (napkin). But
we can trace Sōtan's dealings with the Konoe house in even greater
detail. On a note by Sōtan kept with a tea caddy at the Tekisui Art
Museum is written "Sakura Gosho." Clearly the caddy was a gift from

the Konoe family, with which the name Sakura Gosho was associated. In this particular case Sakura Gosho was probably Konoe Nobuhiro. And in Nobuhiro's *Arima Tōji Ki* (dated 1643:1), among a catalog of gifts from the Arima, we find the following entries: "Sōtan; five bundles of Minato paper, bucket (*mentsū*), small hand ladle" and "Sōtan; a pair of *geta*, one ladle."[37]

Sōtan appears often in the diary of Hisatsugu, Konoe Nobuhiro's son and heir. And although many of the entries in the diary dealing with Sōtan are simple notations about his attendance at Hisatsugu's tea gatherings, an entry for 1651:5:12 is quite rich in content and therefore worth noting:

The twelfth day. Sky clear. I had a tea gathering in the afternoon attended by Sōtan, his son Sōsa, and others. Today's guest Sōtan is the grandson of Rikyū. I therefore used my treasured utensils:

Calligraphy: Chinese writing by Fan Chu-hsien.
Flower container: Chinese basket.
Tea scoop: Rikyū's.
Tea caddy: "crane's neck" *karamono*.
Tea caddy tray: *karamono*, an especially treasured piece; declared by
    Kobori Enshū to be a tray of the finest quality.
Kettle.
Brazier: *mayu* (eyebrow) brazier.
Water container: old Hizen washbasin (*tarai*) once owned by Rikyū;
    given to me by the lay priest [Oda] Uraku.
Incense box: *tsuishu* lacquerware; this too is an especially treasured
    piece of finest quality; old *karamono*.
Tea bowl: Korean.
Natsume: a Rikyū *natsume*.[38]

Although Konoe Hisatsugu had not, at this time, invited Sōtan frequently to tea gatherings, he deliberately took this occasion of the visit of Sōtan, Rikyū's grandson, to display to him his most treasured tea articles. Among these was a particularly noteworthy piece, a water container associated with Rikyū that was said to have been passed on from Rikyū to Oda Uraku and then to Hisatsugu.

Hisatsugu's diary clearly informs us that the reason Sōtan's own *chanoyu* attracted so many people was because he was the grandson and successor in the second generation of Rikyū and thus the principal transmitter of *wabicha*. The revival of the Sen house therefore established its base in Kan'ei culture.

THE *CHANOYU* SALON

Supporting Kan'ei culture were a great number of gatherings *(kai)*, both large and small. Among them were sessions devoted to *waka*, *renga*, and *haikai*. There were also gatherings for scholarship and divination, as well as flower arrangement, incense, and tea. In short, the calendar of events during the year witnessed an almost endless succession of gatherings that spanned the literary and other arts, scholarship, and the various accomplishments. These gatherings, moreover, were centered upon salons and were freely attended by a host of people from different classes and backgrounds, including courtiers, warrior chieftains, *rōnin*, townsmen, craftsmen, and priests. The various salons were joined together like the links in a chain by personal relations among the people who composed them. Among the pursuits that bore the character of a salon culture was *chanoyu*.

Matsuya Kaiki describes a tea gathering held by the Kyoto shogunal deputy *(shoshidai)* Itakura Shigemune on 1649:4:3 in which the alcove was decorated with two bamboo flower holders containing white double-blossom azaleas and wisteria.[39] According to the host, Shigemune, the flowers had been sent that morning from the retirement palace of the former emperor Gomizunoo. At length tea was prepared, using an Uji tea of the kind that was supplied to the shogun. The flowers used for side decoration had been given by the lord of Yodo Castle, Nagai Hisamasa. In the words of Shigemune, these gatherings "could not have been held in Kyoto or Nara." If feudal class relations had been strictly enforced, it would have been unthinkable for a mere Nara townsman like Matsuya to be invited to a daimyo tea gathering, there to drink tea intended for but not yet tasted by the shogun and to watch the *temae* of the Kyoto shogunal deputy performed before flowers supplied by a retired emperor and an important former Bakufu official. Yet the salon culture of Kan'ei times permitted this.

The Itakura shogunal deputy residence from which Itakura Katsushige and his son Shigemune governed Kyoto for half a century or so was the setting of a major salon in the imperial capital. Anrakuan

Sakuden, a disciple of Oribe and an intimate of Enshū, often participated in this salon; and indeed Sakuden's book *Seisuishō*, which is a
typical Tokugawa period work in *kokkei* (humorous) literature, is a
compilation of stories he told to the Itakuras. Sakuden, founder of the
Anrakuan in the precincts of Seiganji Temple, has also left a record,
entitled *Sakuden Oshō Sōtō Hikae*, of *kyōka* (crazy verse) exchanges
with various people. Among the many who appear often in the pages
of this record are Priestly Retired Prince Takeuchi Ryōjo, the courtiers
Karasuma Mitsuhiro and Nishinotōin Tokiyoshi, the *rōnin* Kinoshita
Chōshōshi, daimyos such as Kobori Enshū, and townsmen like
Yodoya Kaan and Matsunaga Teitoku.[40]

We note from this listing that the people in Sakuden's record represented a great variety of class statuses. Another person who appears—
twice—in Sakuden's record is Shōkadō Shōjō. Shōjō was a resident
priest at the Takimotobō priests' quarters of the Iwashimizu Hachiman Shrine. Distinguished in calligraphy, painting, and literature, he
was also a tea man who possessed many valuable tea articles of the
kind later called "Hachiman *meibutsu*." But Shōjō was not simply a
man of culture and taste. Contrary to what one might expect, he used
the salons of the time to play an important role in politics and society.
This can be observed, for example, in his part in the unprecedented
visit of Emperor Gomizunoo to the Nijō Palace when the shogun
Hidetada and his son Iemitsu visited Kyoto in 1626. It was Shōjō who
worked hard to bring about an understanding between Konoe Nobuhiro, representing the court party, and Tokugawa Yoshinao of Owari,
the spokesman for the warrior group. As a result, Nobuhiro went to a
tea gathering hosted by Yoshinao, and the two were able to discuss
the plans for the shogun's visit to Kyoto.

The salons of Kan'ei culture were linked together by means of *chanoyu* through the independent efforts of tea men like Shōjō functioning as intermediaries. Miyake Bōyō, one of Sen Sōtan's four famous
disciples, was another who performed the same role as Shōjō. Bōyō
had close ties to the courtier families of Ichijō and Kujō (he may even
have received certain stipends from these families, as Shōjō received a
stipend from the Konoe), and he served as an intermediary in court
society. Even Kanamori Sōwa was involved in such intermediating
activities. One of Konoe Nobuhiro's letters (Yōmei Bunko, *Konoe
Ōsan Shojō*), for example, informs us that Sōwa received flowers from
the retired emperor's palace through the good offices of Nobuhiro.

In discussing Kanamori Sōwa it is impossible to ignore his relationship with Nonomura Ninsei, the supreme craftsman in the history of Japanese ceramics. Sōwa was the oldest son of Kanamori Arishige, the lord of Takayama Castle in Hida, but left his family, became a *rōnin*, and earned fame as a man of tea. He recognized the talent of Ninsei, who had opened a ceramic kiln on the grounds of Ninnaji Temple in Kyoto, and, giving him instruction in design, made important use of Ninsei's ceramic ware—called *omuroyaki*—at his own tea gatherings. Meanwhile, Sōwa furthered the popularity of *omuroyaki* among the members of court society. The beauty of Ninsei's richly decorated ceramics was truly in keeping with the *kirei* taste of Kan'ei culture, and his creations became enormously fashionable with both the courtier and warrior elites of the country.

Essential to the spread of interest in Ninsei's ceramics among the various classes were tea men like Sōwa and the salons that comprised their tea gatherings. Sōwa's tea, behind which lay the elegance of Ninsei and court culture, has been characterized—for example, in the crazy verse cited earlier—as the tea of "*ohime* Sōwa" (literally, the tea of Sōwa of princess-like taste).

Along with Kanamori Sōwa and other *rōnin*, priests constituted focal points of Kan'ei culture. The intimate relationship of such Daitokuji priests as Kōgetsu, Takuan, and Gyokushitsu to *chanoyu* is well revealed in their collected sayings (*goroku*). Among the remaining records of salons by priests outside the Daitokuji line is the diary of Hōrin Shōshō of the Rokuon'in. Through this writing, the *Kakumeiki*, we learn of the nature of *chanoyu* at court and among the courtier elite. Within the courtly world there remained the tradition of an expansive, medieval kind of *chanoyu*—quite different from Rikyū's *wabicha*—that featured pleasure excursions by boat and outings to the hills and fields.

TOWARD THE GENROKU EPOCH

With the deaths of Kanamori Sōwa in 1656 and Sen Sōtan in 1658, virtually the entire generation of tea men who had lived in the historical shadow of Rikyū was gone. This left another generation, including the young Katagiri Sekishū and Sōtan's principal followers, known as the four famous disciples, as the leaders of the tea world.

Sekishū was acquainted with Sōtan, but the two men were not compatible in *chanoyu*. Behind this incompatibility was a challenge to Sōtan by Sekishū, who did not acknowledge the tradition of blood descent in Sōtan's Sen family line but, instead, stressed the principle of transmission of leadership in *chanoyu* from teacher to disciple. Sekishū's school of tea recognized the tradition passed on by Dōan as the mainstream of *wabicha*, and it exerted strong influence as a warrior form of *chanoyu* centered on the daimyo.

Sekishū moved in a direction similar to the generation of Sōtan's followers, represented by the four famous disciples. First, he emphasized receipt of instruction in *chanoyu* rather than blood lineage. Those in possession of such instruction should, while returning always to Rikyū's tea as a starting point, seek to create their own *chanoyu* by means of their own ability. There was no need to adhere to the Sen family line, which was based on succession by blood. Second, because he did not stress blood lineage, Sekishū transmitted instruction in tea in a way that was liberal when compared to the later *iemoto* (family headship) systems. Yet, apparently because of its rejection of blood lineage, the Sekishū school of *chanoyu* in fact produced many more branches than the Sen house. The school, of course, expanded widely among the daimyos, and its daimyo adherents often rejected the authority of the school's commoner powers and established their own *iemoto* lines. This appears indeed to have been a main reason for the division of the school into many branches. A third way in which Sekishū resembled Sōtan's followers was in his acceptance of support —in an age when the relaxation of class distinctions that had characterized the salons of Kan'ei culture was no longer possible—from various classes: from courtiers for courtiers, warriors for warriors, and townsmen for townsmen.

Sōtan's four famous disciples were one with Sekishū in the liberality of their approach to the transmission of tea instruction. They were also active in the writing of books on instruction, books which they either gave to their own disciples or had published and put up for sale. The production of this kind of liberated writing on tea reveals that there had arisen in the age of Sōtan's four famous disciples a great demand for instruction in the tea art. In short, with the approach of the Genroku epoch a new population—centered on the *chōnin* class—sought after *chanoyu*.

Former emperor Gosai's tea record is a uniquely valuable document. Not only is it the only such record by an emperor or former emperor, but it is also an account of considerable interest. Yet the participants in the tea gatherings Gosai recorded consisted of a mere handful of courtiers and princes who had taken priestly vows. We detect nothing of the relations among various classes of people that were observable in the tea gatherings of former emperor Gomizunoo. The same class distinctions inevitably appeared also in the *chanoyu* of Katagiri Sekishū and Sōtan's four famous disciples. Evidently the *chanoyu* salon that stood above the class system was no longer needed by the urban inhabitants who became the bearers of Genroku culture.

NOTES

1. The first to use the term "Kan'ei culture" was Hayashiya Tatsusaburō. See his "Kan'ei Bunka Ron" in *Chūsei Bunka no Kichō* (Tokyo: Tōkyō Daigaku Shuppan Kai, 1953).

2. *Mukashi-Mukashi Monogatari* can be found in *Nihon Seikatsu Shiryō Shūsei*, vol. 8, *Kenmon Ki* (Tokyo: Sanichi Shobō, 1969), p. 391.

3. *Rekkō Kanwa*, in *Dai Nihon Shiryō*, pt. 12, vol. 21 (Tokyo: Tōkyō Teikoku Daigaku, 1919), p. 99.

4. *Kōshin Gegaki*, in Sen Sōshitsu, ed., *Chadō Koten Zenshū*, vol. 10 (Kyoto: Tankōsha, 1961), p. 71, refers to this "group of seven among Rikyū's disciples." Some later writings include the name of Oda Uraku, instead of Furuta Oribe, as one of the seven.

5. *Tennōjiya Kaiki*, in Sen Sōshitsu, ed., *Chadō Koten Zenshū*, vol. 7 (Kyoto: Tankōsha, 1959), p. 408.

6. Kuwata Tadachika, *Teihon Rikyū no Shokan* (Tokyo: Tōkyōdō, 1971), p. 89.

7. Ibid., p. 554.

8. Ichino Chizuko, *Furuta Oribe Chasho*, vol. 1 (Kyoto: Shibunkaku, 1976), pp. 3–50.

9. *Furuta Oribe no Kami Dono Kikigaki*, ibid., p. 196.

10. *Koshoku-kō Densho*, in *Chadō Shiso Densho* (Kyoto: Shibunkaku, 1974), p. 84. The expressions *hyōgemono* and *yakisokonai* appear in *Sōtan Nikki* (in Sen Sōshitsu, ed., *Chadō Koten Zenshū*, vol. 6, p. 336) and *Oribe Chakai Ki* (gathering on 1601:1:24).

11. Ichino Chizuko, *Furuta Oribe Chasho*, vol. 2 (1984), p. 98.

12. Nakamura Hidetaka, "Keichō Nenjū no Sengo Seinen-tachi: Kabuki-mono no E Sugata ni Yosete," in *Rekishi to Jimbutsu* (Tokyo: Yoshikawa Kōbunkan, 1964), p. 385.

13. Yamanoue Sōji, *Yamanoue Sōji Ki*, in Sen Sōshitsu, ed., *Chadō Koten Zenshū*, vol. 6 (Kyoto: Tankōsha, 1958), p. 100.

14. *Rōdan Ichigon Ki*, in *Dai Nihon Shiryō*, pt. 12, vol. 21, p. 98.

15. *Uroko* means a triangular or half-diamond shape. The space for the *uroko ita* was created by cutting off a protruding corner to provide a view of the host's entranceway *(sadōguchi)* from any seat in the room.

16. *Uraku-tei Chanoyu Nikki,* in *Dai Nihon Shiryō,* pt. 12, vol. 39 (Tokyo: Tōkyō Teikoku Daigaku, 1958), pp. 170–230.

17. Horiguchi Sutemi, *Chashitsu Kenkyū* (Tokyo: Kajima Shuppan Kai, 1969), p. 252.

18. *Enshū Kakisute Bumi,* in Sen Sōshitsu, ed., *Chadō Koten Zenshū,* vol. 10, p. 137.

19. Mori Osamu, *Kobori Enshū* (Tokyo: Yoshikawa Kōbunkan, 1967), p. 194.

20. Kobori Sōkei and Tanaka Hiromi, *"Enshū Kuchigirichō,"* in Kumakura Isao, ed., *Chadō Shūkin,* vol. 4 (Tokyo: Shōgakukan, 1983), p. 301.

21. *Kaiki,* in Sen Sōshitsu, ed., *Chadō Koten Zenshū,* vol. 5 (Kyoto: Tankōsha, 1958), p. 28.

22. Kumakura Isao, "Daimyō Cha no Seiritsu," in *Chanoyu,* no. 1 (Kyoto: Shibunkaku, 1969).

23. Nambō Sōkei, *Nampōroku,* in Sen Sōshitsu, ed., *Chadō Koten Zenshū,* vol. 4 (Kyoto: Tankōsha, 1956), p. 10.

24. Ibid., p. 6.

25. Kobori Sōkei and Tanaka Hiromi, *"Enshū Kuchigirichō,"* in Kumakura Isao, ed., *Chadō Shūkin,* vol. 4, p. 293.

26. *Toshihito Shinnō Shojō,* in *Katsuranomiya-ke Monjo* (Kunai-chō, Shoryō-bu Zō).

27. *Jōshōin Shojō,* in *Katsuranomiya-ke Monjo.*

28. Kumakura Isao, "Katsura Rikyū—Sono Sakusha to Jidai," in *Katsura Rikyū* (Tokyo: Iwanami Shoten, 1984).

29. Tanaka Hiromi, "Maeda Toshitsune, Kobori Enshū Ōfuku Shojō," in Kumakura Isao, ed., *Chadō Shūkin,* vol. 4, pp. 286–287.

30. Kumakura Isao, "Kinsei Shotō ni okeru Daimyō Cha no Seikaku—Kobori Enshū to Kaga Maeda-ke," in *Nihon Bunka Shi Kenkyu* (Tokyo: Kasama Shoin, 1980), p. 190.

31. Kumakura Isao, *Kindai Chadō Shi no Kenkyu* (Tokyo: Nihon Hōsō Shuppan Kyōkai, 1980), p. 81.

32. Kumakura Isao, *"Sōjinboku* no Seiritsu," in *Chanoyu,* vol. 14 (Kyoto: Shibunkaku, 1978).

33. *Zuiryūsai Nobegami no Sho,* in Sen Sōshitsu, ed., *Chadō Koten Zenshū,* vol. 10, p. 122.

34. *Fukō Chawa,* in *Chadō,* Zenshū, vol. 11 (Osaka: Sōgensha, 1937), p. 711.

35. Masaki Atsuzō, *Hon'ami Gyōjō Ki to Kōetsu* (Kyoto: Unsōdō, 1948), p. 92.

36. Sen Sōsa, *Fushin'an Denrai Genpaku Sōtan Monjo* (Tokyo: Cha to Bi Sha, 1971), p. 47.

37. *Arima Tōji Ki,* Hongenjishōin-ki (Tokyo: Zoku Gunsho Ruijū Kansei Kai, 1976), p. 227.

38. *Hisatsugu Kōki,* Yōmei Bunko Zō.

39. *Matsuya Kaiki,* in Sen Sōshitsu, ed., *Chadō Koten Zenshū,* vol. 9 (Kyoto: Tankōsha, 1957), p. 447.

40. Kumakura Isao, "Kan'ei Bunka to Chishiki-jin Sō," in Aida Yūji, ed., *Chishiki-jin Sō to Shakai* (Kyoto: Kyōto Daigaku Jimbun Kagaku Kenkyūjo, 1978), p. 294.

SIX

CHANOYU: FROM THE GENROKU EPOCH TO MODERN TIMES

Paul Varley

DURING its long history *chanoyu* has been developed, influenced, and patronized by various classes and groups. In Chapter 1 Murai Yasuhiko discusses how *chanoyu* originated in the *shingi* or rules of Zen temples in the middle fourteenth century and how it assumed the form of *shoin chanoyu*, distinguished by the *shoin* room setting and the display and use of *karamono* (things Chinese), during the fifteenth century under the sponsorship of the military aristocracy of the Muromachi Bakufu.

From the late fifteenth century, leadership in the world of tea shifted to the elite merchant class *(machishū)* of such cities as Kyoto, Nara, Sakai, and Hakata, and *chanoyu* was shaped into *sōan chanoyu* (*chanoyu* in a hut setting) and *wabicha* (*chanoyu* based on the *wabi* aesthetic). The prominence of the elite merchant class in *chanoyu* in the sixteenth century was a reflection both of that group's economic power, which stemmed primarily from overseas trade, and its desire to advance itself in the realm of culture.

Wabicha reached a climax—perhaps even an untenable extreme, as Kumakura Isao suggests in Chapter 2—in the tea of Sen no Rikyū, a man of *machishū* background from Sakai. Meanwhile disciples of Rikyū, such as Yamanoue Sōji, established Murata Shukō, Takeno Jōō, and Rikyū as a trinity of gods of *chanoyu* whose achievements would remain the highest models for all tea masters who followed them.[1]

Two events near the end of the sixteenth century—the completion of unification of the country by Toyotomi Hideyoshi in 1590 and Rikyū's enforced suicide the following year—ushered in the next phase of *chanoyu*, one dominated to a large extent by daimyo masters such as Furuta Oribe, Kobori Enshū, and Katagiri Sekishū. Hideyoshi encouraged this trend toward daimyo-*cha* (daimyo tea) by calling upon Furuta Oribe, the heir apparent to Rikyū as the leading tea master of Japan, to make *chanoyu* more suitable for the warrior class.[2] And the second, third, and fourth Tokugawa shoguns—Hidetada, Iemitsu, and Ietsuna—furthered daimyo-*cha* by personally patronizing Oribe, Enshū, and Sekishū. Sekishū in particular enjoyed great success as a tea master among the higher echelons of warrior society, and many daimyos throughout the Tokugawa period followed the Sekishū school of tea.

Even as schools of *chanoyu* were founded by daimyo masters, interest in tea continued unabated among the upper-class merchants and spread as well into other social groups, including the courtier and imperial families in Kyoto and the Buddhist clergy. The Sen clan under Sōtan were the leading tea men among the *machishū*, which produced such other luminaries in the arts and culture of the early seventeenth century as Hon'ami Kōetsu and Tawaraya Sōtatsu. In Kyoto court society Emperor Gomizunoo was probably the leading patron of *chanoyu*, and among the Buddhist clergy Shōkadō Shōjō was the best-known master.[3]

Admiration for the *wabi* values of Rikyū's tea remained as strong as ever. But masters of the seventeenth century sought their aesthetic standards in other areas, as well. Furuta Oribe, for example, had a distinct liking for the eccentric and incorporated Namban (Southern Barbarian) tastes into his pottery designs. Kobori Enshū and Kanamori Sōwa were especially attracted to the classical aesthetics of court culture, joining other artists such as Kōetsu and Sōtatsu and, later, the Ogata brothers, Kōrin and Kenzan, in the powerful revival of interest in the Heian court tradition that occurred in the cultural world at this time. Still another variant in the aesthetics of seventeenth-century tea can be seen in the taste of Katagiri Sekishū, who chose Rikyū's predecessor Jōō as his primary model. Like others of his day, Sekishū rejected the extreme of Rikyū's *wabicha* and was drawn to the earlier *shoin* style of *chanoyu*.[4]

Both social and aesthetic diversity, then, characterized *chanoyu* on the eve of the Genroku epoch, the starting point of this essay. Genroku brought to the forefront still another group, the *chōnin* or townsmen, who constituted the urban merchant class as a whole, rather than just the elite *machishū*. From this time the *chōnin* became one of the principal agents of cultural development in Tokugawa Japan.

CHANOYU IN THE GENROKU EPOCH

Genroku can be understood, for the purpose of cultural history, as the period of about a half-century comprising the last quarter of the seventeenth century and the first quarter of the eighteenth. Some seven or eight decades of peace and economic growth brought great prosperity to the merchant class, and the Genroku epoch witnessed an efflorescence of *chōnin* activities in the arts—including prose literature (for example, the writings of Ihara Saikaku), the *kabuki* and puppet theaters, and genre art in the form of woodblock prints. The centers of *chōnin* culture were the pleasure quarters (*ukiyo* or "floating worlds") and the theater districts, particularly in the leading cities of Edo, Osaka, and Kyoto.

Accompanying this flourishing of the *chōnin* arts was another development of major importance: the rise of an enormous demand among all classes, samurai and peasants as well as merchants, for knowledge and training in the "elegant pastimes" (*yūgei*), such as *chanoyu*, flower arrangement, incense identification, the playing of musical instruments, dance, and theatrical chanting.

The masters of tea in the past certainly believed they were engaged in something more significant than an elegant pastime; but in fact the ordinary person could acquire skill in *chanoyu* sufficient to perform it as a host at least acceptably well. For this reason *chanoyu*, with its brilliant tradition, became one of the most popular—and popular can be understood here in the modern sense of having mass, commercial appeal—of these elegant pastimes from Genroku times on.

In *Nihon Eitai Gura* Saikaku wrote:

> Until age thirteen a person lacks discernment. From thirteen to twenty-four or twenty-five he is under the control of his parents. From then until forty-five he must work for himself and put his family in order. But thereafter he can devote himself without restraint to the quest of pleasure.[5]

Thus Saikaku presents the ideal of attaining, at the relatively young age of forty-five, access to unlimited pleasures, among them *chanoyu*, and elsewhere he describes numerous examples of men who threw themselves with abandon into such pleasant pursuits, often squandering their fortunes in the process. Although he wrote fiction, Saikaku had ample material from real life upon which to draw. We can deduce this, for example, from a book of stories and precepts (*kakun*) entitled *Chōnin Kōken Roku* that the commercial house of Mitsui compiled for the edification of its employees.[6] The book, written sometime about the 1720s and attributed to Mitsui Takafusa, third head of the Mitsui house, provides some fifty true tales of merchants who came to ruin for reasons that included the lending of money to daimyos and the pursuit of elegant pastimes.[7]

One merchant who squandered his wealth on amusement was Mitsui Saburōzaemon:

> From his father's time he had been brought up in style, and so he never had the merchant spirit. He lived in the grand manner and went in for fine tea utensils and tea rooms. . . . He was thoroughly extravagant in his tastes and put up all sorts of buildings and had tea gardens and tea rooms which surpassed those of other people in stylishness. . . . People still talk about him. . . . He took hardly any interest in business and spent his time in amusements.[8]

Another profligate merchant who immersed himself in pleasure was Satsumaya Shimbei:

> [He] became extraordinarily dissolute and spent money in abandoning himself to promiscuity. . . . Taking up the tea ceremony as his profession, he carried on just as he liked and finally went blind and died at the age of forty-two or forty-three. As his fortune gradually declined in view of these things, he pawned his utensils and so on and crashed when advances to daimyo were not repaid.[9]

The amount of wealth that some merchants were willing to expend on tea utensils is dramatically illustrated by the case of the Itoya family, which "possessed many fine household articles":

> One of these articles was the "Misoya Katatsuki" tea container, which was bought from Kameya someone or other for a thousand gold pieces. They say the purchase money was loaded on a cart and dragged around in broad daylight to make payment and take delivery.[10]

The great growth of interest in elegant pastimes was further stimulated by advances in printing and publishing. The first printed book on *chanoyu*, *Sōjinboku*, was issued in 1626.[11] By the Genroku epoch many tea masters, including Sen Sōtan's leading followers known as the "four famous disciples" *(shi-tennō),*[12] were publishing their writings to inform people about *chanoyu.* Japan had a long tradition, evolved during the medieval age, of *hiden*—essentially arcane information about the various arts that were transmitted in handwritten form from masters to their disciples. With the appearance of printed books in the seventeenth century, writings on *chanoyu* and the other elegant pastimes changed from secret transmissions to works intended to en-lighten people about all aspects of these pastimes. Authors sought to entice readers by pointing out, for example, that no one could afford to be totally ignorant of *chanoyu* and needed at least to know the proper conduct for a guest if invited to a tea gathering. Most of the books on *chanoyu* published from this time were, in fact, directed toward the uninitiated. Their contents typically dealt with such topics as tea history, the lines of the great masters, the decoration of tea rooms, how to prepare tea, and how to be a guest.

By its very intensity, the demand for training and participation in the elegant pastimes threatened to transform them into casual amuse-ments for the masses. One reaction to this danger in *chanoyu* was the rise of a movement to reaffirm, if not restore, its essential traditions, especially those associated with Sen no Rikyū.

THE RIKYŪ REVIVAL

Kumakura Isao has pointed out in Chapter 2 that the Sen family was reinstated quite soon after Rikyū's death in 1591. And before long tributes to the great master began to appear. Rikyū's letters, for exam-ple, were used for calligraphic display at tea gatherings, and the Sen family conducted periodic memorial services for him. But the real revival of Rikyū occurred in the Genroku epoch. Every school of *cha-noyu* claimed in various ways and to varying degrees a legitimacy of descent in its teachings from Rikyū. Sen Sōtan's four famous disciples pressed their claims of "descent" with particular force because of their special desire to meet the competition of Sōtan's blood descendants (that is, the heads of the three Sen branches, Omotesenke, Urasenke, and Mushanokōji Senke), who simply assumed they were the only proper successors to the Rikyū tradition by virtue of birth.

The case of the Yabunouchi school of tea illustrates the Genroku sentiment of revival and perpetuation of Rikyū's *chanoyu*. The school's founder, Yabunouchi Kenchū Jōchi, was a younger contemporary of Rikyū and a fellow disciple of Jōō. (The *"jō"* of Jōchi was taken from Jōō's name.) Although Rikyū was regarded as the principal successor to Jōō's *wabicha*, Kenchū inherited his collection of tea utensils. Kenchū was a personal admirer of Rikyū, as well, and established his school in the spirit of the Rikyū tradition.[13] This spirit was clearly retained during the following century, and in Genroku times we find Chikushin, the fifth head of the Yabunouchi school, declaring: "From the laws of tea to matters of taste and discrimination, the branches and leaves of Rikyū's *chanoyu* have been luxuriant and have borne both blossoms and fruit. This is because none of the other masters can attain his excellence even by standing on their toes. We cherish Rikyū and make him the source of our inspiration."[14]

The most important product of the Rikyū revival, however, was the "discovery" of *Nampōroku* which, despite its questionable historicity, has been accepted as the main scripture of Rikyū's tea. *Nampōroku's* discoverer was Tachibana Jitsuzan, a leading vassal *(karō)* of Kuroda Mitsuyuki, daimyo from Hakata in northern Kyushu. In 1686, while accompanying his lord on a procession to attend the shogun's court in Edo *(sankin kōtai)*, Jitsuzan received a letter from "a person from Kyoto." The letter inquired whether those retainers of Mitsuyuki who were known to be devoted practitioners of tea (Jitsuzan himself was a student of Kobori Enshū's school) would be interested in examining a copy of a secret book *(hiden)* in five volumes that transmitted the *chanoyu* of Rikyū. Accompanying the letter were excerpts from the book. Jitsuzan and his fellow devotees in Mitsuyuki's entourage replied that they would indeed like to see a copy of the book, and the following year, 1687, it was delivered to the Kuroda residence in Edo.[15]

The author of the book was Nambō Sōkei, a priest of Nanshūji Temple in Sakai who, if *Nampōroku* is to be believed, was an intimate disciple of Rikyū. Although nothing was known of Sōkei in the history of tea, Tachibana Jitsuzan tracked down a member of his family and, on another procession to Edo in 1690, obtained some tea utensils that had belonged to Sōkei and a copy of two more volumes of the *hiden*.

Nampōroku's first five volumes, the portion Jitsuzan received in 1687, were purportedly approved—at least tacitly—by Rikyū. But in a postscript to volume six, Rikyū requested that this volume be destroyed because it contained secrets (*hiji*) he did not wish to have openly transmitted.[16] In his own postscript, Nambō Sōkei stated that he could not bring himself to destroy volume six, which included things he had learned over many years from Rikyū, and therefore decided to go against the master's wishes and keep it without showing it to anyone else.[17] Volume seven was written after Rikyū's death.

Nampōroku is a compendium of Rikyū's thoughts and tastes. Often its passages comprise inquiries by the author and responses by Rikyū. Although *Nampōroku* deals with numerous aspects of *chanoyu*, its great underlying theme is the "spirituality" of Rikyū's tea—that is, *wabicha*. Rikyū's concept of *chanoyu* as a spiritual exercise reduced the elaborate procedures for preparing tea to a set of starkly simple actions, such as those described in *Nampōroku's* famous opening passage:

> First, we fetch water and gather firewood. Then we boil water and prepare tea. After offering some to the Buddha, we serve our guests. Finally, we serve ourselves.[18]

The importance of such simplicity of action is reiterated in another passage from volume one of *Nampōroku*, where we are told that Rikyū, in response to a certain man's request to be informed of the "great secrets" of *chanoyu*, replied:

> Manage to stay cool in the summer and keep warm in the winter. Use enough charcoal to bring the water to a boil, and make good tea. These are all the secrets there are.[19]

Much annoyed, the man observed that Rikyū had only told him what was obvious to everyone. Rikyū remarked that if the man could prepare tea as directed, he would visit him and perhaps become his disciple.

At the beginning of the final volume of *Nampōroku*, the *Metsugo* or "Posthumous" volume, we are again told there is nothing more to *chanoyu* than "lighting a fire, boiling water, making tea, and drinking it."[20] And later in the *Metsugo* volume there is this poem attributed to Rikyū:

> Know that *chanoyu*
> Is simply this:
> Boil water,
> Prepare tea,
> And drink—that is all.[21]

Yet we cannot suppose that Rikyū expected people to take literally his injunction that *chanoyu* consists only of boiling water, making tea, and drinking it. He enunciated an ideal for *wabicha*, but in his practice of *chanoyu* he also concerned himself with the manifold rules and procedures that encouraged people to aspire to become *meijin* (masters) in what was truly a complex art. Although Rikyū occasionally spoke of a *chanoyu* of ultimate simplicity, he apparently provided Nambō Sōkei with the vast wealth of lore that we find in *Nampōroku*.

As it happened, Tachibana Jitsuzan's discovery of *Nampōroku* coincided with the hundredth anniversary of Rikyū's death and the Rikyū boom of the Genroku epoch. These facts alone cast suspicion upon the discovery. Our doubts are further aroused when we read statements like the following in *Nampōroku* attributed to Rikyū:

> Within ten years the true way of tea will be abandoned. Yet even at that time, we can expect *chanoyu* to flourish in the world. . . . A person will appear in a later age who understands this way of tea . . . and even if a hundred years have elapsed, my bones will be reinvigorated, my spirit will be filled with joy, and I will surely become the patron deity of *chadō* (the way of tea).[22]

If Jitsuzan was in fact the true author of *Nampōroku*, he evidently sought to convey in this prophesy the idea that he himself was the person of a later age who would revive Rikyū's way of tea.

THE DAIMYO AS PATRON OF *CHANOYU*

The role of the daimyo in the development and spread of *chanoyu* during the Tokugawa period was by no means limited to the activities of those daimyos, such as Oribe, Enshū, and Sekishū, who became famous tea masters. Abiding by the first injunction of the *Buke Shohattō* (Laws Governing the Military Households) that "the arts of peace and war . . . should be pursued single-mindedly,"[23] daimyos aspired not only to be good administrators but also model rulers (*meikun*). The model ruler became a central image in Tokugawa history, especially after the transition from military to civil rule by the Bakufu from about the middle seventeenth century. The three daimyos most widely recognized as model rulers in the late seventeenth century were Hoshina Masayuki, Tokugawa Mitsukuni, and Ikeda Mitsumasa;[24] in the late eighteenth century, Matsudaira Fumai and Matsudaira Sadanobu gained great fame as *meikun*.

Model rulers fit a recognized mold: They encouraged frugality of living among all classes and were extremely solicitous of—even compassionate toward—the people (that is, the peasantry); they were scholarly themselves and promoted scholarship, especially Chu Hsi Neo-Confucian studies, among their vassals and others; and they were avid patrons of the arts, such as the *nō* theater and *chanoyu*.

Hoshina Masayuki was the younger brother of the shogun Iemitsu. He was adopted into the Hoshina family and became daimyo of the northern domain of Aizu-Wakamatsu, which had formerly been ruled by Gamō Ujisato, a noted general under both Nobunaga and Hideyoshi who was also known as one of Rikyū's "seven sages" (*shichi-tetsu*). When Iemitsu died in 1651, Masayuki was brought to Edo to serve as regent (*hosa*) for his young nephew, the new shogun Ietsuna. Noted for his sense of justice, his scholarly devotion to Neo-Confucianism, and his selflessness as an administrator, Masayuki was the dominant figure in Bakufu councils for the next decade.

Like Matsudaira Sadanobu a century later, Masayuki gained fame and prepared the way for his entry into Edo government through his policies as a domain (*han*) reformer. As lord of Aizu-Wakamatsu, he aided starving people in the winter and sick people on the highways and he built shelters for the homeless. He encouraged frugality, the opening of new fields, and the planting of cash crops. He was also among the first to prohibit the practice among samurai of *junshi*, "following one's lord in death."[25] The prohibition of *junshi* was one of the most conspicuous signs of the shift from military to civil rule about this time.

Before entering government service at Edo, Masayuki was a follower in *chanoyu* of Kobori Enshū, presumably because his brother Iemitsu patronized and engaged Enshū as official tea master to the Bakufu. But as regent for Ietsuna, Masayuki shifted his allegiance to the school of Katagiri Sekishū and was instrumental in attracting Ie-tsuna also to Sekishū and starting the trend which, as noted, made Sekishū *chanoyu* by far the principal school of tea among daimyos and other samurai.

Matsudaira Sadanobu, who admired Hoshina Masayuki as a model ruler in the past, lived in quite a different era.[26] By the eighteenth century, the Tokugawa Bakufu faced certain endemic problems that a series of reformers, including Sadanobu, were unable to correct. To a large extent these problems were financial. Because of commercial development with its accompanying monetary fluctuations and long-term inflation, the samurai, who received fixed stipends, and the peasants, who were burdened with heavy feudal rents and were frequently victimized by the disjunctions of commercial growth, found themselves sinking steadily into debt. The Bakufu, meanwhile, was increasingly unable to make income match expenditures. Calls for austerity and frugality, often in the form of sumptuary edicts, became a standard response to financial distress. Reformers and "model rulers" like Sadanobu characteristically couched these calls in moralistic terms, incorporating both Confucian and feudal ideas about restraining gross desires in the name of duty and service and rejecting the selfish pursuit of profit.

Sadanobu was a grandson of the shogun Yoshimune, sponsor of the first great reform of the eighteenth century, and distinguished himself as daimyo of Shirakawa domain in the Mutsu region of northern Honshu. So great was his success as a domain ruler—for example, he steered Shirakawa through a severe crop failure and famine from 1783 until 1787 without, it is said, a single life being lost—that many peple regarded him as a savior or "god."[27] He joined the Bakufu's Council of Elders (*rōjū*) in 1787 and, at the age of twenty-nine, became the chief minister of state in Edo. The reform that Sadanobu launched—known, after the year-period, as the Kansei Reform—was in large part a reaction against the policies of the notorious Tanuma Okitsugu, a parvenu official who had risen to great power in the Bakufu from the position of chamberlain (*soba-yōnin*) to the shogun Ieharu.

Sadanobu, as a devout Confucian, placed great store in the ethical qualities of rule, and his reforms included a restructuring and restaffing of the Bakufu bureaucracy with the primary intent of moral resuscitation. In his zeal to rectify what he regarded as the fallen moral state of the country resulting from the misrule of Tanuma Okitsugu,

Sadanobu even issued an edict in 1790 calling upon schools every-where to teach only the philosophy of Chu Hsi Neo-Confucianism and banning as heterodox all other systems of thought.

Sadanobu's importance in the history of *chanoyu* lies in his analysis of the art in Confucian terms in two brief tracts, *Sadōkun* and *Saji Okite*, which he wrote shortly after his retirement from the Bakufu in 1793. He was certainly not the first to discuss *chanoyu* from a Confu-cian standpoint—Kobori Enshū, for example, was strongly Confucian in his approach to tea.[28] But as a famous daimyo and Bakufu reformer, Sadanobu represented, at the highest level of Tokugawa society, the idea of using *chanoyu* to achieve social harmony and perhaps even to aid in rule.

Ascetic in his personal life, Sadanobu was ever the proponent of ethically proper and frugal behavior. We can see this clearly in the fol-lowing passage from *Sadōkun:*

> In using chipped tea bowls and cracked caddies in *chanoyu*, you will not convey the least sense of luxury beyond the ordinary. You should revere your elders, have compassion for the young, humble yourself before others, and be loyal to your lord and filial to your parents. Even though the cost of practicing *chanoyu* may be little, it comes from your stipend; and every *sen* and *tsubu* of that stipend is provided by your lord.[29]

On the conceptual basis of *chanoyu*, Sadanobu had this to say:

> Because [Murata] Shukō came from a background of Zen, he compared the ultimate truth of *chanoyu* to the Zen laws. Although *chanoyu* may not differ from Zen, it adheres more closely to the teachings of Confu-cianism, which I have received.[30]

Like Shukō, Sadanobu cautioned against willfulness *(gaman)* in the way of tea. He also opposed the ever-present tendency in *chanoyu* to covet "things" and insisted on the primacy of people over objects. He neatly characterized this primacy in remarks about scrolls of calligra-phy *(kakemono):*

> Admiration for a scroll of ancient writing lies in admiration for the writer. If you do not admire the sages of old or their ways, it is difficult to say that you have the proper spirit for appreciating such writing.[31]

Although himself a collector of tea *dōgu*, Sadanobu attacked people who wasted their money in acquiring them. It was far more important, he said, to use such money to serve one's lord or to bring comfort to the people of one's domain.[32]

Another distinctive aspect of Sadanobu's thinking about *chanoyu* was the importance he attached to conducting it according to one's social status *(bungen)*, a topic to which I will return.

THE FAMILY HEADSHIP *(IEMOTO)* SYSTEM

From earliest times the Japanese have organized themselves into schools or lines *(ryūha)* in their practice of the arts, in religion, and in other pursuits. Sometimes these schools have been based on blood relations; more often they have comprised unrelated members brought together in fictive kinship relations. The custom of leaders and followers associating as "parents" and "children" *(oyabun-kobun* in today's usage) is familiar to all students of Japanese social history. This custom was greatly strengthened in the medieval age with the development of feudal institutions, especially the lord-vassal relationship, which governed behavior among the samurai but also influenced people in the other classes of society.

Whether in the arts or other fields, schools shared common characteristics. The members of a school revered its founder and devoted great care to the transmission of the founder's philosophy and practices. Typically, such transmission was made from master to disciple (or "parent" to "child") both orally *(kuden)* and in secret writings (the *hiden* discussed above). The transmission of philosophy and practices, moreover, conveyed upon the disciple the status of master in his own right. In other words, a true disciple was thought to inherit the knowledge and authority of his master in their entirety *(kanzen sōden)* and thus to be entitled to have his own disciples, upon whom he in turn bestowed knowledge and, ultimately, authority.[33] In *chanoyu* such knowledge was transmitted, for example, from Rikyū to Furuta Oribe and from Oribe to Kobori Enshū.

The Rikyū revival was one reaction in *chanoyu* to the danger of diluting this art by widespread training and participation in the elegant pastimes and the publication of "enlightenment" books about them. An even more important reaction to the danger was the restructuring of *yūgei* schools by means of the *iemoto* (family headship) system.

The various schools of *yūgei* and the other arts have always had family heads, but the oldest reference to the term *iemoto*, which is widely used today among the *yūgei* to mean family head, is from 1757.[34] This date is about a quarter-century after the Genroku epoch, when the *iemoto* system began to take form.

Nishiyama Matsunosuke, the leading expert on this subject, contends that the main difference between the earlier practice of having family heads, whatever they may have been called, and the later *iemoto* system lies in the distinction between "complete transmission" *(kanzen sōden)* of the methods and authority of a school to its (that is, the family head's) disciples and "limited transmission" *(fukanzen sōden)*, which entails simply granting the right to give instruction on behalf of the school. Under the *iemoto* system, the *iemoto* has absolute authority to grant (or rescind) the right to teach the school's methods. This right is usually given in the form of the *natori* or "name-taking," the ceremony by which a student receives a professional name from the *iemoto* and becomes a teacher. The *iemoto* retains exclusive control over such matters as admission to the school and public performance, and only he can grant permission to use certain tangible and intangible properties of the school, including special utensils, costumes, rituals, and titles.[35]

Some general observations can be made about the *iemoto* system. First, it evolved, as noted, in response to a swelling demand for the arts, particularly *yūgei*. This demand came largely from amateurs, people who wished to engage in such pursuits as *chanoyu* as an avocation or merely to enrich themselves culturally. It was not uncommon for those who had the means to undertake training in two or more *yūgei*.[36] A second observation, related to the first, is that the *iemoto* system represented an attempt to harness—and profit from—the large new clientele for these elegant pastimes. The *iemoto*, once established, strictly controlled the revenue that came to his school and, as suggested by some scholars, became a capitalist in an age of impressive capital accumulation.[37]

Establishment of the *iemoto* system in *yūgei* during the eighteenth century was clearly an effort to fix the traditions of these arts and prevent heresies from arising among their followers. In the process, many *iemoto* assumed extraordinary powers. In receiving the *natori*, for example, students commonly accepted permanent subordination, even submission, to the *iemoto*, pledging never to open new schools or in any other way compete with their masters.

One line of *chanoyu*, however, did not undergo the imposition of this dominant *iemoto* system, and that was the Sekishū line. We have seen that the *chanoyu* of Katagiri Sekishū was particularly favored by the upper, daimyo level of warrior society. When daimyos became teachers of Sekishū *chanoyu*, they neither could nor would subject themselves to outside *iemoto* domination. These daimyos frequently became *iemoto* themselves and founded their own schools. This is one reason why the Sekishū line, compared to the other major lines of *chanoyu*, has proliferated into many schools.[38]

The *iemoto* system has often been criticized—especially after World War II, when *iemoto* were attacked as autocratic, feudalistic remnants of the past. Yet the system flourishes in many *yūgei* schools today and must be acknowledged even by its critics to have contributed greatly to the preservation of traditional arts and culture.

CRITICISM OF *CHANOYU*

The *iemoto* system is certainly not the only feature of *chanoyu* that has come under criticism. As Murai Yasuhiko observes in Chapter 1, *chanoyu* seems to be hounded by doubt and criticism because it has emerged from the everyday act of drinking tea. The expression of such doubt and criticism dates from the Genroku epoch, when *chanoyu* attained mass appeal.

One of the earliest and most severe critics of *chanoyu* was the Confucian scholar Dazai Shundai. Shundai was a samurai from Shinano province who was a follower of Ogyū Sorai and concentrated especially on economic thought. In his treatise *Dokugo*, Shundai describes a tea gathering in these terms:

> The host prepares the tea himself and presents it to his guests. Taking the single bowl in which tea has been prepared, the guest of honor drinks some and passes the bowl to the next guest in line. If there are three guests or five guests, all drink from the same bowl and the last guest finishes the tea. The empty bowl is then returned to the guest of honor, who takes it, examines it carefully, and praises it as a rare article

(*chinki*). He gives it to the next guest, who examines it and in turn passes it on until it reaches the last guest. After the last guest examines the bowl, he returns it to the host. The guests all bow and express thanks to the host for showing them the bowl. Next, the bag for the bowl is examined, then the caddy and the caddy's bag, and then the scoop. Even though none of these articles may be sufficiently unusual to warrant examination, it is proper etiquette to request to see them. And because much attention is given to preparing the charcoal in the hearth, the guests draw near and observe the host as he fixes the charcoal, praising what he does. They also praise the flowers placed in the flower vase. In short, the guests express admiration for everything they see the host do. It is flattery of the most blatant kind.[39]

Shundai had this to say about the setting—the *chashitsu* (tea room) —in which *chanoyu* is held:

Since only a small window is opened, it is dark even at midday, and in the summer it is exceedingly hot. The entranceway for guests is like one suitable for dogs. Obliged to crawl in on the belly, one has a suffocating feeling. In the winter it is unbearable.[40]

Shundai's remarks on the articles of *chanoyu* and the collecting of them are equally scathing:

Today's tea men take filthy and damaged old bowls, whose ages they cannot know, repair them with lacquer and other materials, and then use them. It is an unspeakably disgusting custom. . . .[41] People today who amuse themselves with *chanoyu* spend vast sums of money on ordinary ceramic objects that have nothing unusual about them and no distinctive merits—and regard them as priceless treasures! Insignificant bamboo tubes and shafts are purchased for a hundred pieces of gold and are thought to be extraordinary objects. It is all quite baffling.[42]

In summary, Shundai objected to the following practices: the unhygienic custom of drinking from the same tea bowl; the ceaseless flattering of the host at a tea gathering; the use of "filthy and damaged old bowls" and other objects; and the squandering of money on ordinary objects as though they were priceless treasures. The same criticisms of *chanoyu* were made by other critics in the late Tokugawa period.

But Shundai and other observers also went beyond this type of criticism, which essentially involved berating the practices of *chanoyu*.

They accused the world of tea—or at least part of it—of threatening the very order of Tokugawa society. According to their thinking, the sentiment of many tea masters, taken from that of Rikyū himself, was antithetical to feudal ethics since it encouraged the ignoring of class distinctions. (An atmosphere of classlessness at tea gatherings was no doubt particularly appealing to townsmen, who were officially consigned to a status of inferiority vis-à-vis the other classes of Tokugawa society.) Such critics also attacked *chanoyu*, particularly in its *wabicha* form, as a threat to feudal order within the aesthetic realm. As Kumakura Isao notes in Chapter 2, *wabicha* evolved from the *sengoku* (Provincial Wars) and Momoyama spirit of *gekokujō* and readily embraced unconventional aesthetic tastes. One conclusion we can draw from this line of criticism is that even after the passage of a century or more, which witnessed the firm establishment of the Tokugawa regime and the structuring of the society that supported it, outside observers were quick to condemn potential challenges to any aspect of the existing order.[43]

Criticism of still another kind was voiced from within *chanoyu* by a contemporary of Dazai Shundai: Yabunouchi Chikushin, who has already been quoted for his praise of Rikyū. Comparing the tea world of his day to a boat "lost in a sea of fog without a compass," Chikushin deplored the branching off of *chanoyu* since Rikyū's death into many schools—including those of Oribe, Enshū, and Sōtan's three sons and successors—and the concomitant divergence of these schools into various styles (*fūryū*) that were all perversions of the true way of Rikyū. It had reached the point, Chikushin claimed, where anyone could consider himself a master of *chanoyu* and introduce whatever novel practices he wished. Chikushin, in fact, saw himself as the man who would rectify the true way of Rikyū's tea.[44]

Chikushin was a Chu Hsi Confucian scholar who was adopted into the Yabunouchi family. In his prescription for the rectification of *chanoyu*, he said this to the people of his age about *chanoyu*'s importance:

People are apt to laugh when *chanoyu*, whose purpose is to enjoy unusual utensils and take pleasure in social intercourse, is compared to the teachings of Confucianism and Buddhism as a means of cultivating oneself, teaching people, and nourishing the heart. Yet the ways of Confucianism and Buddhism cannot be really understood without diligently reading books and practicing meditation. For ordinary people of the towns and villages in our country, the way of tea is superior to both Confucianism and Buddhism as a path for learning the way to serve one's lord and to associate with friends, a path designed to avoid defiling one's thoughts with mundane desires and, in accordance with the rules of the world, to maintain oneself frugally and keep one's heart honest (*sunao*).[45]

MATSUDAIRA FUMAI

Yabunouchi Chikushin was only one of many who sought to reform *chanoyu*. Among the leading reformers of the later Tokugawa period was Matsudaira Fumai, a contemporary of Matsudaira Sadanobu.

Fumai was born into a time when many, if not most, of the daimyos found themselves perpetually in financial straits—owing mainly to the inflation that accompanied steady commercial growth in an age of unbroken peace and the heavy cost of the alternate attendance system, which required traveling annually back and forth to Edo and maintaining full-time residences in the Tokugawa capital. Levies made by the Bakufu on Fumai's family domain (Matsue *han* of western Honshu) for repairs to Enryakuji Temple on Mount Hiei when Fumai was only a youth of eight or nine so impoverished the domain that it was pushed to the verge of bankruptcy. When Fumai became daimyo of Matsue at age sixteen, he devoted himself immediately and wholeheartedly to domain reform. In this effort he was ably assisted by his leading vassal, the elderly Asahi Tamba.

Fumai's reforms included the opening of new rice fields and flood control, the encouragement of local products such as ginseng and paper, and the restructuring of domain finances. Fumai also opened a *han* school for the encouragement of cultural studies, including Confucianism. A popular tale has it that one day, after the reforms had clearly been successful, Asahi Tamba showed Fumai the treasure house. It was filled with gold and silver, and Fumai was encouraged forthwith to begin purchasing and assembling what became one of the finest collections of tea articles in Japanese history.[46]

Fumai began his study of *chanoyu* as a student of the Enshū school but later shifted to the Sekishū school, thus joining the great majority of daimyos as an adherent to the teachings of Sekishū. In fact, Fumai was eclectic in his approach to *chanoyu*. While he followed the basic precepts of Sekishū, he remained, for example, devoted to Enshū's taste in tea articles and to Sen Sōtan's in tea gardens (*roji*).⁴⁷

Even before he began collecting tea articles in earnest, Fumai the *han* reformer expressed opinions about tea practice in his day that anticipated his role as a reformer of *chanoyu*. His principal critique of *chanoyu* is *Mudagoto*, which he wrote at age nineteen in 1770, three years after he became the daimyo of Matsue. Tradition has it that he produced *Mudagoto* to show his seriousness to Asahi Tamba, who had criticized him for his zealous devotion to *chanoyu*.

Fumai began *Mudagoto* with the statement: "When we examine the way of tea as it exists in the world today, we find that, because of the contrivances of later generations, there is ignorance of the true basis of the way."⁴⁸ He lamented the transformation of *chanoyu* into an "elegant pastime" that people everywhere could dabble in,⁴⁹ and he was particularly scathing in his claim that the way of tea had really become the way of tea articles (*dōgu*) with people competing madly to obtain at vast expense Dazai Shundai's "filthy and damaged old tea bowls" and the like.⁵⁰

Pursuing the line of criticism first set forth by Shundai, Fumai agreed with those who derided *chanoyu* not only because of its adherents' unseemly pursuit of *dōgu* and the convening of tea gatherings simply as an excuse to display these utensils but also because of the insincere lavishing of praise at a gathering on the host's every action.⁵¹ In truth, according to Fumai, *chanoyu* was the most serious of pursuits, ultimately to be used in governing countries. He spoke of creating peace and harmony by bringing people together for tea in the small room (*kozashiki*) and cited the example of Ieyasu, founder of the Tokugawa house, who, he claimed, employed the way of tea in structuring society—that is, in placing people in a proper hierarchical order.⁵²

Fumai's reference to social ordering and status is significant both as an affirmation of the enduring importance of such matters in Tokugawa Japan and as an indication of his own strong concern—in keeping, as noted, with Matsudaira Sadanobu's—with the social aspect of *chanoyu*. On the evidence of *Mudagoto*, we can, I believe, regard social concern as prior even to aesthetic considerations in Fumai's approach to tea.

Like virtually all others of his time, Fumai lavished great praise upon Rikyū as the spiritual father of *chanoyu*. He claims in *Mudagoto*

Plate 23. Black Oribe ware, "shoe-shaped" *(kutsugata)* tea bowl known as Waraya. Sixteenth century. Gotoh Museum, Tokyo.

Plate 24. Black *raku* tea bowl named Shichiri, made by Hon'ami Kōetsu. *Meibutsu.* Gotoh Museum, Tokyo.

Plate 25. Tea room Joan of Oda Uraku, presently situated in Inuyama City. The triangular piece of wood in the floor is known as *uroko ita*. National Treasure. Nagoya Railroad Company.

Plate 26. Kobori Enshū's tea room Bōsen, built in 1643 in the Kohōan subtemple of Daitokuji Temple, Kyoto. Important Cultural Property.

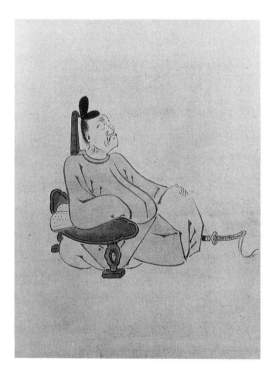

Plate 27. Kobori Enshū. Artist and period unknown. The inscription, dated 1609, is by Shun'oku Sōen of Daitokuji Temple. Kohōan subtemple of Daitokuji Temple, Kyoto.

Plate 28. Sen Sōtan. Artist unknown. Seventeenth century. Konnichian of Urasenke Foundation, Kyoto.

Plate 29. Yūin tea hut at Urasenke Foundation, Kyoto. Constructed by Sen Sōtan about 1653, it was destroyed by fire in 1788 and rebuilt the following year. Important Cultural Property.

Plate 30. Iga ware water container *(mizusashi)* called Yaburebukuro (Burst Bag). Seventeenth century. Important Cultural Property. Gotoh Museum, Tokyo.

Plate 31. Pair of tea bowls with overglaze enamels and gold and silver embellishments, made by Nonomura Ninsei in the seventeenth century. MOA Museum of Art, Atami.

Plate 32. Detail of the *Yūraku Zu*, a folding screen depicting the pleasure quarters. Ca. Kan'ei epoch. Tokugawa Reimei-kai Foundation, Tokyo.

Plate 33. Scene from the *Shijō-Kawara Yūraku Zu* (The Pleasure Quarters at Shijō-Kawara) folding screen showing a "mouse wicket" entranceway to a theater. Momoyama epoch. Important Cultural Property. Seikadō Bunko, Tokyo.

Plate 34. Matsudaira Fumai. Artist and period unknown. Gesshōji Temple, Matsue City.

Plate 35. Ii Naosuke. Portrait by Ii Naoyasu. Gōtokuji Temple, Tokyo.

that people fail to understand the true meaning *(hon'i)* of *chanoyu* because they do not know what is proper or sufficient *(taru koto o shirazu)*; and he speaks of *wabicha*, as perfected by Rikyū, in terms of taking pleasure in insufficiency *(fusoku)*.[53] On the face of it, this appears to be a conventional analysis of the *wabi* aesthetic and the spirit of *wabicha*. But from the overall content of *Mudagoto*, it is clear that Fumai was particularly interested in the "proper" or "sufficient" *(taru koto)* from the standpoint of social status. After criticizing tea men in general for inviting public ridicule by coveting tea utensils and paying enormous sums of money for them,[54] he says that one must use utensils commensurate in quality to the social status of one's guests. And since the better utensils necessary for the better people did not "rain down from the sky or boil up from the earth," it was essential to seek them out and buy them.[55]

Here we have a rationale for Fumai's own pursuit of *dōgu* and his accumulation of a great collection at considerable cost. But Fumai did more than expend wealth for tea articles worthy of socially prominent people. He based his collecting and classification of articles on scrupulously careful research. Partaking of the positivist scholarship of the Tokugawa period, he laid the groundwork for the modern study of *dōgu*.[56] This was, indeed, his principal contribution to the development of *chanoyu*.

Fumai's major work on the classification of *dōgu* was *Kokon Meibutsu Ruijū*. Assigning designations to tea articles such as *ō-meibutsu* (great *meibutsu*) or simply *meibutsu*, he provided a ranking of such articles, including both *karamono* and *wamono*, from the Higashi-yama epoch on. Above all, Fumai established the category of *chūkō* (restored) *meibutsu*, which, as Kumakura Isao notes in Chapter 5, comprised tea articles selected by Kobori Enshū in the seventeenth century in his role as arbiter of taste. Fumai's objective was to guide daimyos, townsmen, and others who could not hope to acquire *meibutsu* dating from the medieval age but wished to possess recognized *dōgu*. He based his ranking of *dōgu* on two criteria: personal examination and reliable written sources. If he could not himself examine an article and had no reliable written description of it, he merely listed it in *Kokon Meibutsu Ruijū* and left a blank space into which an entry could later be made.[57]

Fumai was aided in assembling his collection of tea articles, which was known as the Unshū (Izumo province) *meibutsu* collection, by the

fact that many financially troubled daimyos were willing to sell articles that had been in their families as heirlooms for generations. He
also received expert advice on collecting from prominent dealers in
tea articles in Edo, Kyoto, and elsewhere. In all, Fumai was able to
gather more than eight hundred high-quality articles (in the estimate
of modern scholars). Records in the care of the Gesshōji Temple in
Matsue list only five hundred and eighteen items, but this figure may
represent the articles Fumai regarded as worth recording for history.[58]
By Fumai's age the most valuable *dōgu* were not used in tea gatherings
but were kept safely in collections like his; other articles were displayed and used only on special occasions.

The items that Fumai treasured most in his collection were the
Engo calligraphy *(bokuseki)* and the caddy called the Aburaya shouldered *(katatsuki)* caddy. The Engo calligraphy was a sample of the
writing of the thirteenth-century Chinese Zen master Yüan-wu K'o-
ch'in (Engo Kokugon), which was given by the priest Ikkyū of Daitokuji to Shukō and was later used by Rikyū for display in the alcove
during a tea gathering. It is generally believed that this use of the
Engo calligraphy by Rikyū marked the beginning of the custom of
favoring calligraphy by Zen priests for alcove display. So highly did
Fumai regard the Aburaya shouldered caddy that he had it carried in
a special basket by a page who walked beside his palanquin during
journeys to and from Edo for attendance at the shogun's court.

JOSHINSAI AND KAWAKAMI FUHAKU

Probably the most significant development in *chanoyu* during the mid-
Tokugawa period was its extraordinary growth as a pleasurable pursuit, especially among members of the townsman class. Yabunouchi
Chikushin, although a harsh critic of tea practice since Rikyū's time,
was also one of *chanoyu*'s leading promoters and popularizers. An
even more prominent person in this regard was Chikushin's contemporary Joshinsai Tennen Sōsa, the seventh *iemoto* of Omotesenke.

Joshinsai succeeded his father as Omotesenke head at age twenty-
four in 1730 and held the position until his death at forty-six in 1751.
All three of the main Sen family schools—Urasenke and Mushanokōji Senke as well as Omotesenke—prospered from the steadily rising
interest in *chanoyu* among townsmen and others in the late seven-

teenth and eighteenth centuries. People were drawn especially to these schools because of the presumed authority of their *iemoto* as lineal descendants from Rikyū. Under Joshinsai, Omotesenke took the lead among the Sen schools in catering to the needs of the new, largely townsman clientele of the age, and in the process he effected major innovations in *chanoyu*. The aim of Joshinsai and the other *iemoto* of the Sen schools was to expand their practices in ways designed to attract new followers while at the same time adhering to the great traditions of *chanoyu* received from Rikyū.[59] Joshinsai was a leader, for example, in the cataloging of tea articles and secret writings (*hisho*) and in expanding the practice of *hakogaki*—the inscribing by *iemoto* and others of the boxes in which tea utensils are stored. *Hakogaki*, in particular, enabled the *iemoto* to draw new members to their schools and, at the same time, to advance themselves as personages of distinction in the world of tea.[60]

But the most important new practice in *chanoyu* introduced by Joshinsai was the *shichiji-shiki* or "seven exercises." These exercises, which may have been inspired by the "seven things" (*shichiji*) supposedly possessed by Zen masters, were intended to revitalize the teaching of *chanoyu*.[61] With the evolution of tea schools in the Tokugawa period, instruction in *chanoyu* had become standardized, in accordance with the special procedures of each school, into sets of graded lessons that students took under accredited teachers (that is, the holders of *natori* from the schools' *iemoto*). By Joshinsai's time in the eighteenth century, lessons in *chanoyu* had in many cases become so standardized—indeed conventionalized—that they were treated merely as opportunities for social intercourse.

The seven exercises, which Joshinsai formulated in consultation with others, including his younger brother Yugensai Ittō Sōshitsu, the eighth *iemoto* of Urasenke, and Mugaku Sōen of Daitokuji, Zen master to both Sen brothers, added variety to the teaching of *chanoyu*. At least one of the exercises, *ichi ni san* ("one, two, three"), involved evaluation of the tea preparation of others; another, *cha kabuki*, was modeled on the practice of *tōcha* or "tea competitions," which dated back to the late fourteenth century.[62]

Joshinsai was greatly helped in his work as a revitalizer—indeed, a modernizer—of *chanoyu* by the man who became his star pupil and, later, his closest confidant, Kawakami Fuhaku. Fuhaku was a samurai from a small domain in Kii province who relinquished his warrior status and, at age fifteen, entered the Omotesenke school in Kyoto to study under Joshinsai with the aim of becoming a professional tea master. In Fuhaku, Joshinsai found a kindred spirit. The two became particularly close through the study of Zen, and Fuhaku spent increasingly more time with his master. Although a student, he contributed to the development of the seven exercises. In 1749 Joshinsai displayed extraordinary trust in Fuhaku by revealing to him all the secret writings on *chanoyu* of the Omotesenke school.[63]

In 1750 Joshinsai sent Fuhaku to Edo for the purpose of establishing a branch of Omotesenke in that city. Fuhaku was obliged to return to Kyoto upon Joshinsai's death in the following year, however, and remained there until 1755 to help Omotesenke adjust to the administration of a new *iemoto*. But from then on Fuhaku lived in Edo, where he founded the Edo Senke school of tea. During the next half-century or more, Fuhaku worked tirelessly at expanding the following of the Edo Senke school and established himself as one of the great promoters of *chanoyu* in the Tokugawa period.

A RIVAL TRADITION: *SENCHA*

Chanoyu and *chadō*, the way of tea, invariably refer to the handling and drinking of *matcha* or powdered tea, which was introduced to Japan from Sung China during Japan's early medieval age and evolved into a great cultural tradition. But another form of tea drinking—*sencha*, steeped or infused tea—also developed in the Tokugawa period, to some extent as a reaction against *matcha* and *chanoyu*, and produced its own distinctive tradition.

The origin of the *sencha* tradition—that is, the self-conscious and idealized consumption of the beverage made by steeping green tea leaves in hot water—has been separately traced to at least two men. The first is the Chinese Zen monk Ingen, who came to Japan in 1652 and founded Manpukuji, a temple of the Ōbaku sect of Zen, at Uji. There, in the most famous of all tea-producing regions of Japan, Ingen grew the leaves for *sencha* in the form that was popular in China during the Ming and Ch'ing dynasties. The association of *sencha* with China, especially its literati (Japanese, *bunjin*) artists and scholars, became particularly important to the *sencha* tradition.

The second reputed "founder" of *sencha* was Ishikawa Jōzan, who was born into a warrior family of Mikawa province and entered the service of Tokugawa Ieyasu. After being rebuked by Ieyasu for his overzealous behavior at the siege of Osaka Castle in 1615 (which resulted in the destruction of the Toyotomi family), Jōzan renounced his warrior status and went to Kyoto, where he studied Chu Hsi Neo-Confucianism under the renowned scholar Fujiwara Seika. Later Jōzan, whose tastes also included poetry and *chanoyu*,[64] became an eremite *(inja)* and built a hutlike retreat *(sōan)* at the foot of Mount Hiei. He called this hut Shisendō and adorned it with portraits of famous Chinese poets. Here Jōzan lived the elegant life of a Chinese-style literatus, often inviting painters, poets, scholars, and others—including Hayashi Razan,[65] the noted Confucian adviser to the Tokugawa family—to socialize in a relaxed manner, to discuss culture and the arts, and to drink tea. No records remain, however, to prove conclusively that the tea consumed at Jōzan's social affairs was *sencha*, and indeed some scholars speculate that it was *matcha*.[66] Hence Jōzan's role as a founder of the *sencha* tradition cannot be confirmed.

One of the great popularizers of *sencha* was the eighteenth-century Ōbaku Zen priest Gekkai, who was also known as Chūkō Baisaō, a name that has the literal meaning of "revival" *(chūkō)* and "old man who sells tea" *(baisaō)*. Baisaō, who learned about *sencha* from a Chinese he met at Nagasaki, earned his sobriquet when, after leaving the Zen priesthood at age fifty-six in 1731, he became widely known as an itinerant seller of tea, a poet, and a philosopher of the "*sencha* spirit." Underlying Baisaō's idea of the *sencha* spirit was his rejection of what he regarded as the corrupted worlds of the Zen priesthood and *chanoyu* and his call for a revival of the sentiments of the Chinese poets of the T'ang period, when the first way of tea was formulated by Lu Yü, author of *C'ha Ching*.[67]

Sencha, particularly from the eighteenth century on, was popular for several reasons. First, as noted, *sencha* was attractive to artists and others who admired the Chinese literati way of life, which included steeped tea. *Sencha* also appealed to people who were disenchanted with *chanoyu*, or the partaking of *matcha*, because of the complex procedures and rules of etiquette that had come to govern it. Men of the arts especially enjoyed *sencha* as a beverage they could drink freely and casually in their private social gatherings. A third reason for the popularity of *sencha* can be found in the strong intellectual trend from the mid-Tokugawa period of seeking to recapture the past *(fukko)*—as, for example, in the Ancient Studies School *(kogakuha)* of Confucianism and the National Learning School *(kokugakuha)* of Shinto. Devotees of *sencha* called for a rejection of "Sung" tea *(matcha)* and a return to the "original way of tea"—that is, to the tea of Lu Yü in the T'ang dynasty.

Probably the most famous proponent of *sencha* was the National Learning scholar and prose writer Ueda Akinari, who is best remembered in Japanese history as the author of *Ugetsu Monogatari* (Tales of Rain and the Moon). Akinari's most important writing on tea is *Seifū Sagen*, which, like other books advocating *sencha*, praises the virtues of steeped tea in large measure by attacking *matcha* or *chanoyu*. Akinari criticized *chanoyu* for having become weighted down by forms and by its attachment to utensils; in his view, *matcha* had lost the "spirit" of tea. He also maintained that *matcha*, with its primary concern for taste, was in fact harmful to the body. *Sencha*, on the other hand, was beneficial both to one's spirit and to one's physical health.[68] (*Sencha* advocates stressed the importance of using only the finest, freshest water in preparing steeped tea.)[69]

In one sense, *sencha* was another form of criticism of *chanoyu* in the Tokugawa period—criticism which included the charge that *chanoyu* had abandoned higher culture and become no more than popular entertainment. Certainly *sencha* drew to itself a wide range of scholars, artists, and other representatives of the cultural elite. But perhaps most important, *sencha* was a reaction against the rigidities of Tokugawa society as a whole, including the restraints that had been imposed upon *chanoyu*, and sought to present an opportunity—if only a limited one—for freedom of expression and behavior.

II NAOSUKE'S WAY OF TEA

Kawakami Fuhaku died in 1807, Matsudaira Fumai in 1818, and Matsudaira Sadanobu in 1829. Their lives ended as a new age in Japanese history approached—an age when Japan was forced to abandon its seclusion policy of more than two centuries and enter into the affairs of a modern world dominated by the West. The political and social paroxysm that brought Japan into the modern world occurred during the so-called Bakumatsu (end of the Tokugawa Bakufu) period that lasted from 1853, when Commodore Matthew Perry of the United

States officially "opened" Japan to the world, until the Meiji Restoration of 1868. In fact, Westerners, including Russians, English, and Americans, had periodically been coming to Japan—for various reasons and under various pretexts—from at least the beginning of the century, and discussions had long been held in Japanese ruling circles about how best to deal with these unwanted foreign intrusions and violations of the seclusion policy. But foreign affairs did not become a critical issue until the Bakumatsu period.

The Bakumatsu period is important in the history of *chanoyu* because one of its leading actors, the statesman Ii Naosuke, who served as a chief official of the Tokugawa Bakufu from 1858 until his assassination in 1860, was a devoted student and practitioner of *chanoyu* and made a major contribution in his writing to the way of tea.

Born in 1815, Naosuke was the fourteenth son of Ii Naonaka, daimyo of Hikone domain in Ōmi province. The fates of the younger sons of a daimyo in the Tokugawa period were frequently unenviable, at least from the standpoint of their family origins. Some were adopted by other daimyos or by high-ranking feudal vassals. Others were simply set up in separate residences and consigned to lives of obscurity on meager stipends. At the time of his father's death in 1831, Naosuke, the fourteenth son, appeared to have no prospect whatever of succeeding to the family headship and was therefore obliged to move at the age of sixteen to a small residence outside Hikone Castle and accept a kind of banishment from the public life of the domain.

Naming his residence Umoreginoya (Dwelling of Buried Wood), Naosuke began a period of quietude that was to last for fifteen years. During this time he devoted himself to physical, mental, and spiritual cultivation through a variety of pursuits, including the martial arts, Zen, poetry, National Learning (*kokugaku*), and *chanoyu*. It is not known precisely when he began the study of *chanoyu*, but from documents in the possession of the Ii family we know that his principal teacher was Katagiri Sōen, the head of a branch of the Sekishū school of tea. As a member of a daimyo family that was close to the shogunal house, Naosuke no doubt gravitated readily to this school. He regretted that the Sekishū school had divided into so many branches; the reason he established his own branch, he said, was to pursue the original teaching of the school's founder, Katagiri Sekishū.[70]

Although it appeared that Naosuke had no hope for improvement in life, in 1846 he was suddenly vaulted into high prominence. By this time all of his brothers except the oldest, Naoaki, who was the Hikone daimyo, and Naomoto, the designated successor, had either entered other daimyo families or families of leading daimyo vassals. Thus after Naomoto died in 1845, Naoaki selected Naosuke (in 1846) as the new heir to succeed him as daimyo. And when Naoaki himself died in 1850, Naosuke became lord of Hikone.

The rise of Ii Naosuke to daimyo occurred within three years of Commodore Perry's arrival in 1853 and the commencement of the Bakumatsu period. In 1854 Perry secured a treaty of friendship between the United States and Japan, and three years later Townsend Harris, the first American consul to Japan, concluded a formal treaty of commerce between the two countries. The issue of ratification of the Harris Treaty caused a sharp political clash in Japan. On the one side were those, led by the daimyo of the Mito domain, Tokugawa (Mito) Nariaki, who wished to "expel the barbarians" (*jōi*); on the other side were those within the Tokugawa government who wanted to establish a working relationship with the Western powers while strengthening their control over both the Bakufu and the country. The ratification issue brought the appointment in 1858 of Ii Naosuke to the position of great elder (*tairō*), which was generally used only in times of emergency and then given to a daimyo of one of the more powerful hereditary (*fudai*) families, including the Ii.

Naosuke as Great Elder took decisive steps to ratify the Harris Treaty and suppress opposition to the Bakufu. He rounded up its opponents and even executed some of them, including the imperial loyalist from Chōshū domain, Yoshida Shōin. But his hard-line policy, known as the Ansei Purge, only stiffened loyalist opposition to the Bakufu, and in 1860 Naosuke was assassinated by samurai from the Mito and Satsuma domains.

Study of Naosuke's life was hindered in the years before the end of World War II because the Ii family, sensitive to the fact that many people regarded Naosuke as a traitor to the imperial court or a "bad minister," did not make public any of his records. However Naosuke may be viewed in the political history of his country, he assured himself a lasting place in the story of *chanoyu* through his authorship of *Chanoyu Ichie Shū*, a work which he revised and polished over a period of many years.

Whereas Matsudaira Fumai devoted himself primarily to the social and political aspects of *chanoyu* and to its aesthetics through the collecting and study of utensils, Ii Naosuke's main interest in tea was its spiritual foundation. *Chanoyu Ichie Shū*, which strongly reflects the sentiments of Sen no Rikyū, particularly as presented in *Nampōroku*,[71] begins with this famous statement:

> This book deals with the handling of a gathering for *chanoyu*, giving in detail the knowledge necessary for both host and guests. For this reason I have entitled it *Ichie Shū* (Collection for a Gathering). Great attention should be given to a tea gathering, which we can speak of as "one time, one meeting" *(ichigo, ichie)*. Even though the host and guests may see each other often socially, one day's gathering can never be repeated exactly. Viewed this way, the meeting is indeed a once-in-a-lifetime occasion. The host, accordingly, must in true sincerity take the greatest care with every aspect of the gathering and devote himself entirely to ensuring that nothing is rough. The guests, for their part, must understand that the gathering cannot occur again and, appreciating how the host has flawlessly planned it, must also participate with true sincerity. This is what is meant by "one time, one meeting."[72]

Ichigo, ichie, which has become one of the central terms of *chanoyu*, appeared first in *Yamanoue Sōji Ki*.[73] But it was given its classical definition by Ii Naosuke in *Chanoyu Ichie Shū*. Naosuke, whose approach to *chanoyu* was much influenced by Zen, conceived of the way of tea mainly in quietistic, contemplative terms. It is ironic that a man of such temperament was drawn into the maelstrom of post-Perry politics that brought his life to a violent end at the age of forty-five.

Naosuke's preference for the contemplative in *chanoyu* is most eloquently stated in another passage from *Chanoyu Ichie Shū*. This passage, entitled "Seated Alone in Meditation" *(dokuza kannen)*, is an elaboration of *ichigo, ichie*:

> After host and guests have expressed their feelings of regret *(yojō zanshin)* and after the final farewells have been said, the guests depart through the *roji*. They do not call out in loud voices, but turn silently for one last look. The host, moved, watches them until they are gone from sight. It would not do for him to rush about closing the *nakakuguri*, the *sarudo*, and the other doors, for this would make the day's entertainment meaningless. Even though it is impossible to see the guests returning to their homes, the host should not put things in order

quickly. Rather, he should return quietly to the setting of the tea gathering and, crawling through the *nijiriguchi,* seat himself before the hearth. Wishing to speak a while longer with his guests, he must wonder how far they have gotten on their ways home. This "one time, one meeting" has come to an end, and the host reflects upon the fact that it can never be repeated. The highest point of a tea meeting is, in fact, to have a cup of tea alone at this time. All is quiet, and the host can talk to no one but the kettle. This is a state in which nothing else exists, a state that cannot be known unless one has truly attained it oneself.[74]

THE MODERN AGE

The assassination of Ii Naosuke in 1860 ended the Bakufu's efforts to suppress opposition to its policies toward the West. Instead, it sought to encourage cooperation with the emperor's court and with powerful daimyos who had hitherto had no formal voice in national government. But the rush of events went against the Bakufu, and in 1867 it was overthrown by samurai loyalists, acting in the name of the young Emperor Meiji, who instituted the Meiji Restoration of 1868.

One of the most extraordinary aspects of the Meiji Restoration was the intense enthusiasm with which the Japanese, having rid themselves of the feudal Tokugawa regime, rushed to learn from the West. Although the idea of the Restoration was to retrieve valued forms from the past—for example, the bureaucratic form of government under the emperor that had been adopted from China in the late seventh and eighth centuries—in fact Japan promptly launched upon a course of all-out Westernization known as the movement for "civilization and enlightenment" *(bunmei kaika).* So determined was this movement, which embraced a wide range of activities from the aping of Western styles of dress to the adoption of Western forms of government, that it seemed Japan might abandon much of its cultural heritage and become simply another "Western" country.

The traditional arts were hit particularly hard by *bunmei kaika.* As it happened, Japanese art was, in general, in a state of creative decline at the time of the Meiji Restoration. Hence the traditional arts were even less well prepared than they might have been to withstand the flood of Western art that poured in with the Restoration. For a while, Western literature, theater, painting, architecture, and other arts virtually overwhelmed their Japanese counterparts, and there was a danger that certain native arts might be permanently lost. It was during this period that astute Westerners, such as Ernest Fenolossa, were able to purchase works of Japanese art—some of them national treasures—at extremely low prices. Many of these purchases subsequently formed the bases of collections of Japanese art in museums in Europe and the United States.

Chanoyu was badly neglected during this period. Its institutional structure—the *iemoto* system—was especially weakened by the loss of daimyo patronage, for the daimyo class was dissolved during the first few years of Meiji and the daimyo domains were divided up to form the modern prefectural structure. Although the daimyos as a group were generously recompensed by the new Meiji government, they no longer had reason to patronize tea masters, *nō* performers, and other artists. The damage caused by the loss of this patronage testified to the crucial role the daimyos had played in supporting the arts during the Tokugawa period.

Virtually all the tea masters of early Meiji, including the *iemoto* of the three Sen branches, found themselves in severe financial straits. The *iemoto* of Urasenke and Mushanokōji Senke were obliged to vacate their Kyoto residences; and the Urasenke *iemoto* even left Kyoto, the heart of the Sen tradition, and moved for a period to Tokyo.[75] In desperation, the *iemoto* and others in *chanoyu* sought to make ends meet by selling their treasured tea articles, but these brought little income. Like the native arts in general, they were no longer esteemed.[76]

But the *iemoto* were not content simply to sustain their schools. They also sought in innovative ways to adapt *chanoyu* to the tastes of the modern world. Gengensai, the eleventh *iemoto* of Urasenke, promoted the use of chairs at tea gatherings; Yūmyōsai, Gengensai's son and Urasenke's twelfth *iemoto*, was a leader in introducing *chanoyu* to school curricula, especially in women's schools. This innovation had a profound effect on the subsequent course of *chanoyu*. First, it launched the transformation of *chanoyu* from an almost exclusively male pursuit to one dominated, as it is today, by women. Women had occasionally participated in tea gatherings during the Tokugawa period; but some tea masters, such as Sugiki Fusai, one of Sen Sōtan's four famous disciples, banned them from *chanoyu*.[77] Second, the introduction of *chanoyu* to school curricula signified official recognition, so to speak, of *chanoyu* as the principal means for training young people, particularly women, in etiquette and deportment.

Chanoyu and the other traditional arts were aided by a major trend beginning in the 1880s against indiscriminate cultural borrowing from the West. There emerged a strongly conservative reaction to over-Westernization and a desire to save Japanese culture before it was swept away by the flood of *bunmei kaika*. In the Bakumatsu period, some Japanese thinkers had proposed the idea of "Eastern morals and Western technology"—that is, borrowing only the material elements of modern Western civilization while retaining Japan's spiritual values. The *bunmei kaika* movement of the 1870s, however, had in fact been one of "Western morals and Western technology"—in other words, unrestrained Westernization. The conservative reaction that started in the 1880s was part of a reversion in thinking, led by the Meiji government itself, back to the original "Eastern morals and Western techonology" concept.

The 1880s also witnessed the birth of a general movement to "preserve the national essence" *(kokusui hozon)*. This movement was an attack on Westernization based on the premise that nations and peoples, including Japan, should seek to advance—that is, modernize—not by rejecting all their traditional customs but by utilizing them, so far as possible, for the purpose of progress. In the world of culture, this movement rekindled interest in the traditional arts. Thus, for example, works of classical literature were published one after another. There was particular enthusiasm for the Genroku masterworks: Saikaku's prose writings, Chikamatsu's puppet plays, and Bashō's *haiku*.

The *nō* theater, *kabuki*, and *chanoyu* were other conspicuous beneficiaries of this revival of interest in the traditional arts. In the case of *chanoyu*, the revival coincided approximately with the steps taken to introduce it into the schools. *Chanoyu* also benefited greatly from its acceptance by leaders of modern industry, including Masuda Don'ō of Mitsui and Iwasaki Yanosuke, younger brother of the founder of the Mitsubishi combine. These wealthy industrialists became the major collectors of tea utensils in the modern age, and in their quest to acquire famous articles of the past they drove the prices of these recently scorned treasures to new heights. Don'ō, who was an intimate of the statesman Inoue Kaoru, is also well remembered in the history of *chanoyu* as organizer of the great tea gathering called Daishikai, which he held annually, beginning in 1895, at his Shinagawa residence in Tokyo.[78] This affair, reminiscent of the grand tea gatherings of the Azuchi-Momoyama epoch, once again demonstrated the value of *chanoyu* for social and even political purposes. It became one of the leading social events of the year and served as a model for similar extravaganzas that brought together prominent businessmen, industrialists, and others.

Confronted with the trauma of transition to the modern age, *chanoyu* demonstrated a vitality and adaptability—especially in attracting women to its ranks—that many would have doubted possible in early Meiji. Other contributors to this volume have commented on the prospects of *chanoyu* in the contemporary world. Perhaps most interesting are their remarks about the expansion of *chanoyu* outside Japan in recent years. Whether or not non-Japanese will ever engage in *chanoyu* (as participants) in significant numbers, there are strong indications that *chanoyu* as the way of tea is and will continue to be a major carrier of Japanese culture throughout the world.

NOTES

1. See, for example, *Yamanoue Sōji Ki*, in Sen Sōshitsu, ed., *Chadō Koten Zenshū*, vol. 6 (Kyoto: Tankōsha, 1958).
2. Kuwata Tadachika, *Furuta Oribe* (Tokyo: Tokuma Shoten, 1968), p. 190. See also Nishiyama Matsunosuke, *Iemoto no Kenkyū* (Tokyo: Kōsō Shobō, 1959), p. 362.
3. Shōkadō Shōjō was born into the Sakai merchant family of Kitagawa. Although he entered the Buddhist priesthood, he was active also in the world of the arts and culture, especially as a member of the salon of the Konoe courtier family in Kyoto.
4. Hayashiya Tatsusaburō, *Zuroku Chadō Shi* (Kyoto: Tankōsha, 1964), p. 62.
5. Ihara Saikaku, *Nihon Eitai Gura* (Tokyo: Meiji Shoin, 1975), pp. 112–113.
6. Kumakura Isao, *Mukashi no Chanoyu, Ima no Chanoyu* (Kyoto: Tankōsha, 1985), p. 150.
7. Most of *Chōnin Kōken Roku* was probably written by Takafusa's father, Mitsui Takahira. See E. S. Crawcour, *Some Observations of Mitsui Takafusa's Chōnin Kōken Roku*, in *Transactions of the Asiatic Society of Japan*, 3rd series, vol. 8 (Tokyo, 1961), p. 10.
8. Ibid., p. 70.
9. Ibid., p. 88.
10. Ibid., p. 40.
11. *Sōjinboku* is contained in Sen Sōshitsu, ed., *Chadō Koten Zenshū*, vol. 3 (Kyoto: Tankōsha, 1956).

12. The four famous disciples were Fujimura Yōken, Yamada Sōhen, Sugiki Fusai, and Kusumi Soan. Matsuo Sōji and Miyake Bōyō are sometimes added to this list of Sōtan's principal followers.

13. After Rikyū's death Kenchū, who married Furuta Oribe's younger sister, associated himself also with the new feudal style of *chanoyu* which was at that time being developed by Oribe. See Iguchi Kaisen, ed., *Nihon no Chake* (Kyoto: Kawara Shoten, 1983), pp. 143–144.

14. Yabunouchi Chikushin, *Genryū Chawa*, in Sen Sōshitsu, ed., *Chadō Koten Zenshū*, vol. 3, p. 403.

15. Kumakura Isao, *Nampōroku o Yomu* (Kyoto: Tankōsha, 1983), p. 373.

16. Nambō Sōkei, *Nampōroku*, in Sen Sōshitsu, ed., *Chadō Koten Zenshū*, vol. 4 (Kyoto: Tankōsha, 1956), p. 262.

17. Ibid., p. 263.

18. Ibid., p. 3.

19. Ibid., p. 8.

20. Ibid., p. 264.

21. Ibid., pp. 319–320.

22. Ibid., p. 267.

23. Ryusaku Tsunoda et al., *Sources of Japanese Tradition* (New York: Columbia University Press, 1958), p. 335.

24. Kuwata Tadachika, "Sannin no Daimyō Chajin," in Kuwata Tadachika, ed., *Cha ni Ikita Hito, Ge*, in *Zusetsu Chadō Taikei*, vol. 7 (Tokyo: Kadokawa Shoten, 1965), p. 190.

25. Ibid., pp. 191–192.

26. For a biography of Sadanobu in English, see Herbert Ooms, *Charismatic Bureaucrat: A Political Biography of Matsudaira Sadanobu, 1758–1829* (Chicago: University of Chicago Press, 1975).

27. Ibid., pp. 43–47. Ooms observes that the person most convinced of Sadanobu's godly character was Sadanobu himself.

28. Murai Yasuhiko, *Chajin no Keifu* (Osaka: Ōsaka Shoseki, 1983), p. 64.

29. Matsudaira Sadanobu, *Chadōkun*, in Hayashiya Tatsusaburō et al., eds., *Nihon no Chasho*, vol. 2 (Tokyo: Heibonsha, 1972), p. 214.

30. Ibid., pp. 214–215. "Confucianism" is given in the text as *gojō-gorin*, the five cardinal virtues and the five cardinal principles.

31. Ibid., p. 216.

32. Akimoto Nobuhide, "Matsudaira Sadanobu no Kyōkun-teki Chanoyu Ron," in *Chanoyu* 19 (1983), p. 39.

33. Nishiyama Matsunosuke, *Iemoto no Kenkyū*, p. 26. Professor Nishiyama notes that the *iemoto* system has remained a premodern, "prelegal" structure (p. 28).

34. Nishiyama Matsunosuke, "Iemoto Seido to Ryūha," in Murai Yasuhiko, ed., *Chadō Shūkin*, vol. 5 (Tokyo: Shōgakukan, 1985), p. 80.

35. Nishiyama Matsunosuke, *Iemoto no Kenkyū*, p. 20.

36. Kumakura Isao cites the case of an Osaka moneylender of a later time (the Meiji period) who planned to write a book about his twenty-one hobbies or pursuits (*shumi*) ranging from *yūgei*, such as tea, flowers, and *nō* chanting, to Confucianism, Buddhism, and Shinto. The man died, however, before undertaking the work. See *Mukashi no Chanoyu, Ima no Chanoyu*, p. 149.

37. Murai Yasuhiko, *Chajin no Keifu*, p. 130.
38. Kuwata Tadachika, "Shōgun-ke to Chadō Shihan," in Kuwata Tadachika, ed., *Cha ni Ikita Hito, Ge*, in *Zusetsu Chadō Taikei*, vol. 7, p. 78.
39. Dazai Shundai, *Dokugo*, in Hayakawa Junsaburō, ed., *Nihon Zuihitsu Taisei*, vol. 9 (Tokyo: Yoshikawa Kōbunkan, 1927), p. 240.
40. Ibid., pp. 240–241.
41. Ibid., p. 240.
42. Ibid., p. 243.
43. See Kumakura Isao, *Kindai Chadō Shi no Kenkyū* (Tokyo: Nihon Hōsō Shuppan Kyōkai, 1980), pp. 54–55. Kumakura also discusses (p. 52) *Chadōron* (Discussion of the Way of Tea), a book by Kawata Naomichi published in 1786 that is devoted entirely to criticism of *chanoyu* but follows essentially the same line of criticism as Dazai Shundai in *Dokugo*.
44. See Tsutsui Hiroichi, "Jōryū no Cha to Geryū no Cha," in Murai Yasuhiko, ed., *Chadō Shūkin*, vol. 5, p. 56.
45. Yabunouchi Chikushin, *Genryū Chawa*, in Sen Sōshitsu, ed., *Chadō Koten Zenshū*, vol. 3, p. 455.
46. Kumakura Isao, *Mukashi no Chanoyu, Ima no Chanoyu*, p. 159.
47. Kuwata Tadachika, "Sannin no Daimyō Chajin," in Kuwata Tadachika, ed., *Cha ni Ikita Hito, Ge*, in *Zusetsu Chadō Taikei*, vol. 7, pp. 204–205.
48. Matsudaira Fumai, *Mudagoto*, in Takahashi Baien, *Cha-Zen Fumai-kō* (Tokyo: Hounsha, 1944), p. 171.
49. Ibid., p. 172.
50. Ibid., p. 174.
51. Ibid.
52. Ibid., pp. 172–173.
53. Ibid., pp. 176–177.
54. Echoing the criticism of Dazai Shundai, Fumai expressed agreement with those who derided tea men for praising everything the host does at a tea gathering, for coveting old and dirty receptacles as tea articles, and for paying great sums of money for things whose original uses they cannot know and then pouring tea into them and giving them to others to drink. Ibid., p. 174.
55. Ibid., p. 175.
56. Kumakura Isao, *Mukashi no Chanoyu, Ima no Chanoyu*, p. 162.
57. Ibid., pp. 156–157.
58. Ibid., p. 159.
59. Nishiyama Matsunosuke, "Joshinsai to Fuhaku," in Kuwata Tadachika, ed., *Cha ni Ikita Hito, Ge*, in *Zusetsu Chadō Taikei*, vol. 7, p. 164.
60. Ibid., p. 163.
61. See "*Kagetsu* and the *Shichiji-shiki*," in *Chanoyu Quarterly* 48 (1986), p. 49. The seven things of Zen are: great capacity and great function, swiftness of intellect, wondrous spirituality of speech, the active edge to kill or give life, wide learning and broad experience, clarity of mirroring awareness, and freedom to appear and disappear.
62. For a description of the seven exercises, see ibid., pp. 49–52.
63. Nishiyama Matsunosuke, "Joshinsai to Fuhaku," in Kuwata Tadachika, ed., *Cha ni Ikita Hito, Ge*, in *Zusetsu Chadō Taikei*, vol. 7, p. 165.

64. Kuwata Tadachika, "Bunjin Shumi to Sencha," in Haga Kōshirō and Nishiyama Matsunosuke, eds., *Cha no Bunka Shi,* in *Zusetsu Chadō Taikei,* vol. 2 (Tokyo: Kadokawa Shoten, 1962), p. 224.

65. Ibid.

66. See, for example, Murai Yasuhiko, *Chajin no Keifu,* pp. 151–152.

67. Narabayashi Tadao, "Han-'Chanoyu' no Kishu-tachi," in Murai Yasuhiko, ed., *Chadō Shūkin,* vol. 5, pp. 250–251.

68. Kumakura Isao, *Kindai Chadō Shi no Kenkyū,* pp. 63–64.

69. The importance of water in *sencha* is discussed, for example, by Murase Kōtai, Ueda Akinari's Confucian teacher, who wrote the introduction to *Seifū Sagen.* See Murai Yasuhiko, *Chajin no Keifu,* p. 155.

70. Sen Sōshitsu, ed., *Chadō Koten Zenshū,* vol. 10 (Kyoto: Tankōsha, 1961), p. 423.

71. *Nampōroku* is quoted often in *Chanoyu Ichie Shū.*

72. Ii Naosuke, *Chanoyu Ichie Shū,* in Sen Sōshitsu, ed., *Chadō Koten Zenshū,* vol. 10, p. 331.

73. Yamanoue Sōji, *Yamanoue Sōji Ki,* in Sen Sōshitsu, ed., *Chadō Koten Zenshū,* vol. 6, p. 93. "Although it may be an ordinary tea gathering, from the time you enter the *roji* until you leave you should give respect to your host as though it were a meeting that could occur only once *(ichigo ni ichido no e no yō ni)*."

74. Ii Naosuke, *Chanoyu Ichie Shū,* in Sen Sōshitsu, ed., *Chadō Koten Zenshū,* vol. 10, pp. 414–415.

75. Kumakura Isao, *Mukashi no Chanoyu, Ima no Chanoyu,* p. 191.

76. Two extreme examples of the disregard for native art treasures can be seen in the sale of the five-story pagoda at Kōfukuji Temple in Nara for twenty-five yen and the donjon of Himeji Castle for one hundred yen. See Haga Kōshirō and Nishiyama Matsunosuke, eds., *Cha no Bunka Shi,* in *Zusetsu Chadō Taikei,* vol. 2, p. 232.

77. Murai Yasuhiko, *Chajin no Keifu,* p. 212.

78. This "Daishi" or "National Teacher" gathering was named after the great priest Kōbō Daishi, who flourished in the early ninth century. Masuda Don'ō had just acquired a work of calligraphy by Kōbō Daishi and displayed it at the first Daishikai.

SEVEN

THE *WABI* AESTHETIC
THROUGH THE AGES

Haga Kōshirō
Translated and Adapted by Martin Collcutt

CHANOYU seeks to embody a particular kind of beauty: *wabi*. Together with the concept of *yūgen* (mystery and depth) as an ideal of the *nō* drama and the notion of *sabi* (lonely beauty) in *haiku* poetics, *wabi* is one of the most characteristic expressions of Japanese aesthetic principles. This essay attempts to clarify the nature of *wabi* and the beauty it represents by looking at its historical development and the factors contributing to its refinement.

THE THREE ASPECTS OF *WABI*

Because *wabi* as an aesthetic brings together many diverse elements, it is difficult to encompass in a simple definition. It can, however, be likened to a three-sided pyramid. Let us briefly look at each of those three sides in turn.

Simple, Unpretentious Beauty

Wabi is a noun derived from the verb *wabiru. Wabiru* and its homophones can have several meanings. The meaning of *wabi* in its aesthetic sense is perhaps best defined by the author of the *Zen-cha Roku*, who wrote: "*Wabi* means lacking things, having things run entirely contrary to our desires, being frustrated in our wishes."[1] This is an extension of the meaning of *wabiru* as being disappointed by failing in some enterprise or living a miserable and poverty-stricken life. The original sense of *wabi*, then, embraces disappointment, frustration,

195

and poverty. The author of the *Zen-cha Roku*, in the section on *wabi*,
continues:

> Always bear in mind that *wabi* involves not regarding incapacities as
> incapacitating, not feeling that lacking something is deprivation, not
> thinking that what is not provided is deficiency. To regard incapacity as
> incapacitating, to feel that lack is deprivation, or to believe that not
> being provided for is poverty is not *wabi* but rather the spirit of a
> pauper.[2]

From this we can understand that instead of resenting disappointment or hating poverty and trying desperately to escape from it, *wabi*
means to transform material insufficiency so that one discovers in it a
world of spiritual freedom unbounded by material things. It means
not being trapped by worldly values but finding a transcendental
serenity apart from the world. This is the way of life of the true exponent of *wabi* and the best expression of *wabi* in action. Consequently,
although the beauty of *wabi* is not simply a beauty of mere poverty,
unpretentiousness, or simplicity, there are times when, at least superficially, it may seem to be such.

This seemingly unpretentious aspect of *wabi* is evident in the Taian
tea room in Myōkian Temple in Yamazaki, in the rustic style of the
Urasenke tea room known as Yūin, and in such tea bowls made by
Raku Chōjirō as Hinsō (Impoverished Monk). It is apparent, too, in
Takeno Jōō's preference for commonplace objects to use as tea utensils
—a bamboo kettlehook, a plain bucket-shaped water container (*mizusashi*), a bentwood washbasin-shaped bowl for used water (*kensui*), and
a bamboo lid rest; or in the Southern Barbarian (Namban) style rope
screen (*nawasudare*) or a taro-shaped *mizusashi*. This simple, unpretentious—at first glance even impoverished—sense of beauty is certainly
one of the more obvious features of the *wabi* aesthetic.

The artlessness of *wabi* beauty, however, should not be confused
with an empty simplicity, and its unpretentiousness or external rough-
ness should not be mistaken for mere poverty or coarseness. In this
connection it is worth recalling the injunction by Murata Shukō in
the *Yamanoue Sōji Ki*: "A prize horse looks best hitched to a thatched
hut."[3] Or as it says in the first of the "Ten Resolutions of the *Chanoyu*
Practitioner" (*Chanoyu-sha kakugo jittei*): "Truly, a rough and ready,
relaxed manner is superior, an overly regimented manner inferior"

and "Carrying things out in a relaxed, easy manner demonstrates good taste (*suki*)."[4]

From these injunctions we learn that *wabi* is a kind of beauty which stores a nobility, richness of spirit, and purity within what may appear to be a rough exterior. In offering an unpretentious appearance to the world, *wabi* does not display the attention that has been paid to the smallest details of things nor the cost and effort that have been lavished on what cannot be seen. It is a beauty of great depth which finds its expression in simple and unpretentious terms. *Wabi* is thus an aesthetic of unequal composition in which the more important component lies within that which is being overtly expressed; the internal element is superior to the external. In *wabi* a higher dimension of transcendent beauty is created by the dialectical sublation of an inner richness and complexity into the simple and the unpretentious. It is a beauty, in a word, that detests excess of expression and loves reticence, that hates arrogance and respects the poverty that is humility.

Imperfect, Irregular Beauty

Another side of the pyramid of *wabi* beauty—and one that is closely related to the unpretentious aspect we have just discussed—is that of imperfection or irregularity. In *Zenpō Zatsudan*, Komparu Zenpō quotes Murata Shukō as saying: "The moon is not pleasing unless partly obscured by a cloud."[5] For Shukō, such a moon is preferable to a full moon shining brightly in a clear night sky. This example gives us an insight into Shukō's doctrine that the incomplete is clearly more beautiful than the perfect.

There is another well-known example of this attitude in the *Oboegaki* (Memoranda) section of the *Nampōroku*: "Utensils used in the small tea room need not be entirely perfect. There are people who dislike even slightly damaged objects. This, however, is merely indicative of thinking that has not attained true understanding."[6] Cracks and tears, if properly mended, are not necessarily disliked in *chanoyu*. Indeed, the bamboo flower vase known by the name of the temple Onjōji, made by Sen no Rikyū, is prized precisely because it is cracked. The tea bowl Seppō (Snowy Peak), made by Hon'ami Kōetsu, is particularly admired because it has been repaired. The fact that the old Iga pottery water jar known as Yabure-bukuro (Burst Bag) sagged and split during the firing made it all the more interesting. Other examples include chipped and warped braziers. Thus we arrive at one of the major characteristics of the *wabi* aesthetic: It finds a deeper beauty in the blemished than in the unblemished.

From early times much has been made in *chanoyu* of the word *suki*, meaning taste or refinement but with a hint of eccentricity thrown in. It is found in such combinations as *wabi-suki* (*wabi*-taste), *sukisha* (man of taste), *sukiya* (tea room), and *suki dōgu* (fine utensils). The author of the *Zen-cha Roku* praises *suki* as "the very essence of *chanoyu*" and devotes a whole chapter to its elucidation. There the original meaning of *suki* is given as "a form in which the parts are eccentric and do not match."[7] It is further explained as lacking essential parity, being asymmetrical, unbalanced. The true man of taste, *sukisha*, it asserts, is "one who does not march in step with the world, who does not bend to worldly concerns, who does not cherish conformity; an eccentric who takes pleasure when things do not go as he might expect them to."[8] The structure of the tea room is also used to illustrate *suki*:

> Pine pillars, bamboo joists, left as they are,
> curved and straight, square and round,
> up and down, left and right, new and old,
> light and heavy, long and short, broad and narrow,
> repaired where chipped, patched where torn.
> Everything at odds, nothing matching.[9]

This irregular beauty of *suki*, too, is an aspect of the beauty of *wabi*.

In early tea gatherings, when the influence of the *shoin* style of tea was still strong, the most commonly used utensils were perfectly symmetrical black glazed *tenmoku* tea bowls and bronze or celadon flower vases. With time, however, as the trend toward *wabi* gathered strength, a preference for warped and irregular forms developed. This tendency is evident in the clog-shaped *(kutsugata)* tea bowls prized by Furuta Oribe or in such Iga, Shigaraki, and Bizen flower vases as the Iga "Crouching Vase" and the bamboo flower vases Fujinami by Kobori Enshū and Natame by Kanamori Sōwa. From this time on, the tendency to find a higher order of beauty in the imperfect grew stronger with the mounting interest in *wabicha*. The beauty of *wabi*, then, is imperfect and irregular. But here too, as in the case of the simple, unpretentious beauty discussed above, it is an irregular beauty which subsumes within itself the beauty of perfect regularity.

Austere, Stark Beauty

A third aspect of the *wabi* aesthetic is a tranquil, austere beauty, the cool stark beauty of original non-being, *muichibutsu*. In a letter from Murata Shukō to his disciple Furuichi Harima, the priest Chōin, we find the following comment: "Nowadays there are plenty of mere beginners who, mouthing expressions like 'cold' or 'withered,' acquire pottery from Bizen or Shigaraki and put on unpardonable airs. It is really too absurd for words."[10] At the most obvious level this is a warning against the folly of immature beginners who, assuming the airs of connoisseurs, use *wabi*-like Bizen and Shigaraki wares which they are not yet competent to handle, and, claiming that they are expressing a cold and withered beauty, merely mimic high accomplishments in the art of tea. At the same time, at a deeper level, Shukō reveals that he believes this cold, withered beauty, this austere beauty of age and experience, which can only be attained through a master's accomplishment, to be the epitome of beauty. From this we can glimpse the kind of beauty Shukō perceived as his ideal in *chanoyu*.

This aspect of the beauty of *chanoyu* resurfaces in Tsuji Gensai's frequently cited discussion in *Yamanoue Sōji Ki*. There he refers to Takeno Jōō admiring the expression "withered and cold" by the linked verse (*renga*) master Shinkei and arguing that "the fruit of *chanoyu* too must be like that."[11] From this we can understand Jōō's ideal of *wabi*. Toward the end of *Nampōroku*, Jōō points out that anybody who wants to know the true taste of *wabi* should savor this verse by Fujiwara no Teika:

Miwataseba	Looking about
Hana mo momiji mo	Neither flowers
Nakarikeri	Nor scarlet leaves,
Ura no tomaya no	A bayside reed hovel
Aki no yūgure.	In the autumn dusk.[12]

The notion of *wabi* that Jōō derives from this poem is that of a tranquil, austere beauty which transcends the vivid beauty of spring light or the striking beauty of autumn leaves. His ideal is closer to that of an inkwash monochrome, the lonely beauty of "a bayside reed hovel in the autumn dusk," a faded beauty of emptiness.

Turning now to Sen no Rikyū, what was his ideal of *wabi?* Perhaps the best way of grasping what Rikyū meant by *wabi* is through a poem continuing in the spirit of the "looking about" poem cited by Jōō above. When Rikyū said "one poem is outstanding," he was referring to the following verse by Fujiwara no Ietaka:

> *Hana o nomi*   To those who wait
> *Matsuran hito ni*   Only for flowers,
> *Yamazato no*   Show them a spring
> *Yukima no kusa mo*   Of grass amid the snow
> *Haru o misebaya.*   In a mountain village.[13]

Through this poem Rikyū hints at his ideal of *wabi* and its artistic boundaries. To those who think that only a vivid beauty is true beauty, the poet clearly wanted to present the vision of a "spring of grass amid the snow." But what kind of beauty is this "spring of grass amid the snow?"

We can imagine a mountain village in the depths of winter when the seven wild grasses of autumn have withered and the brilliant scarlet leaves have scattered. It is a lonely, cold, and desolate world, a world that is even more deeply steeped in the emptiness of non-being than that of "a bayside reed hovel in the autumn dusk." At first glance this may seem like a cold, withered world at the very extremity of *yin*. It is not, of course, simply a world of death. As proof, we have these lines: "When spring comes it turns to brightness and amid the snow fresh grass sprouts, here two there three blades at a time."[14] This is truly "the merest tinge of *yang* at the extremity of *yin*." Ietaka expressed this notion as a "spring of grass amid the snow." And Rikyū found in it the perfect image of *wabi.* Thus Rikyū's *wabi*, viewed externally, is impoverished, cold, and withered. At the same time, internally, it has a beauty which brims with vitality. While it may appear to be the faded beauty of the passive recluse, or the remnant beauty of old age, it has within it the beauty of non-being, latent with unlimited energy and change.

Analyzing *wabi* as the ideal of *chanoyu* from the point of view of aesthetics, many other aspects can be raised. The late Hisamatsu

Shin'ichi defined the following seven characteristics of *wabi* beauty: irregularity, simplicity, austerity, naturalness, mystery *(yūgen)*, ethereality, and tranquility.[15] For the development of my theme, however, it is sufficient to stress that *wabi* has the three characteristics discussed above—the sides of my three-sided pyramid—mutually blended to create a single aesthetic sensibility.

SOURCES OF THE *WABI* AESTHETIC

As we have seen in the preceding sections, the *wabi* ideal of beauty sets simple and unpretentious expression above the complex and striking. It abhors excess; it admires restraint. It sees a higher dimension of beauty in the imperfect than in the flawless. While it was certainly Shukō, Jōō, and especially Rikyū who self-consciously defined *wabi* as the aesthetic ideal of *chanoyu*, it was by no means invented by them. *Wabi* was already maturing as part of the aesthetic consciousness of the Japanese long before the appearance of tea masters or the elaboration of *chanoyu*.

The aesthetic consciousness comprising the three aspects of *wabi* was gradually elaborated in the form of literary theories dealing with *waka* and *renga* and treatises on the performing arts centered on the *nō* during the four centuries between the early twelfth and the late fifteenth. In this sense, the *wabi* of *chanoyu* can be described as the culminating distillation of an aesthetic consciousness of the Japanese people that had been cultivated from the late ancient period through medieval times. The *wabi* of *chanoyu* draws upon an ancestry of *yūgen*, the dark and mysterious, which medieval *waka*, *renga*, and *nō* took as their ideal. Moreover, it was through *chanoyu* that *wabi* was realized in practice as an art for everyday life. In the next section, focusing on *yūgen* as an ideal of beauty, I shall trace the transformation of the Japanese aesthetic consciousness from antiquity through medieval times in order to illustrate how the three-sided beauty of *wabi* took shape.

Shunzei and Chōmei: Admiration for the *Yojō* and *Yūgen* Styles

Although the forerunner of literary criticism in Japan was the *Bunkyō Hifuron* by Kūkai, it was really the preface to the *Kokinshū*, with its opening statement that "Japanese poetry, having the human heart as its seed, produces the myriad leaves of speech,"[16] that had the greatest impact on subsequent theories of poetry and the performing arts. In suggesting that *waka* is that which flows of itself from the poet's heart through contact with the beauties of nature or the events of human life, the preface touched the very essence of literature and the arts. In the *Kokinshū* view of poetry, the heart *(kokoro)*, which acts as the womb from which *waka* are born, and the leaves of words *(kotoba)*, the external expression of the emotions, are equally as important as the two wheels of a cart. In this early stage of literary theory, the ideal of *waka* was that of a perfectly balanced combination of emotion and expression: heart = words.

Ki no Tsurayuki and the other contributors to the *Kokinshū* took as their ideal the fullest expression in words of the inner heart. They called this heart = words expression "the correspondence of heart and words, the complementarity of fruit and flower." It was from this perspective, for instance, that Tsurayuki evaluated the poetic styles of the Six Poetic Geniuses. He commented on the poetry of the monk Henjō (Yoshimine no Munesada) in the following terms: "While it has the semblance of poetry, it lacks inner sincerity."[17] He criticized the poetry of Fun'ya no Yasuhide as "deft in the use of words, but its style does not match its substance. It is like fine robes worn by a common tradesman."[18] In both cases Tsurayuki's criticism suggests that, while the expression was more or less acceptable, inner reality was wanting. In his view, the works of both poets were composed on the basis of heart yielding to lyric and fruit yielding to flower (heart < words, fruit < flower) and thus fell short of the *waka* ideal: an equal balance of emotion and expression.

In contrast, Tsurayuki criticized the poetry of Ariwara no Narihira as "overflowing with heart, inadequate in words. It is like a faded flower drained of color but with the scent still lingering."[19] His criticism suggests that because Narihira's poetry is structured in terms of heart > words, fruit > flower, the heart does not find full expression in words. This unexpressed emotion, like the lingering scent of a faded flower, drifts about the words as an emotional aftertaste *(yojō)* that refuses to leave. Again, if one regards the ideal *waka* as a perfect balance of heart = words the poem is less than superlative. Thus, in the early tenth century, the lingering aftertaste type of expression with "heart in excess, words deficient" was far from the *waka* ideal. In this context there is one more quotation meriting our attention. It is

Ki no Tsurayuki's comment on a poem by the priest Kisen: "The words are understated, the opening is taut, but it lacks certainty. It is like trying to view an autumn moon obscured by dawn clouds."[20] From this it is clear that the mysterious and veiled expression later prized as *yūgen* in poetry was not esteemed in Tsurayuki's day.

With the passage of time, however, some poets clearly felt that it was too much to expect them to fully express their hearts within the limited scope of the thirty-one syllables of the *waka* form. This led to the advocacy of what can be called the "lingering emotion" *(yojō)* form of *waka*, particularly by the poet and critic Fujiwara no Kintō. While stressing "mutual realization of heart and form" in which "heart is profound and form pure," Kintō tended to attach more importance to the inner heart than to its expression: "If mutual realization of heart and form proves difficult, one should give priority to the heart."[21] In the *Waka Kuhon*, which evaluated *waka* in nine grades, poems of the upper-middle rank were those in which "heart and words move in step to create interest." Poems of the mid-upper rank were "graceful with an excess of heart," while those of the upper-upper rank were "exquisite of expression, yet with a surplus of heart."[22] Thus we can see that the *yojō* style of *waka* with "heart in excess, words restrained," which was not particularly appreciated in Ki no Tsurayuki's day, came into vogue in the age of the Fujiwara regents.

In the late eleventh and early twelfth centuries, the period referred to as *insei*, or rule by abdicated emperors, the poets Fujiwara no Mototoshi and his disciple Fujiwara no Shunzei (Toshinari) began to use the term *yūgen* in judging verse-matching contests *(utaawase)*. In his comments in the afterword to the *Jichin Oshō Jikaawase*, Shunzei clearly linked the *yojō* style with *yūgen* as superior poetry. For him superior poems were those that "over and above the diction *(kotoba)* and general configuration *(sugata)* of the verse" are suffused with a lingering subtlety of thought and vagueness of emotion "like a trail of mist around spring flowers, or the cry of a deer before an autumn moon, or the scent of spring wind by a plum blossom hedge, or the patter of soft rain on autumn maple leaves among the crags."[23]

However, it was Kamo no Chōmei, the author of *Hōjōki*, who greatly increased the respect for *yojō-yūgen* initiated by Shunzei. In the section entitled *"Kindai katai no koto"* (Recent Verse Styles) in his critical work on poetry *Mumyōshō*, Chōmei points out that verse forms

change over time. The dominant characteristic of his day, he says, was
the prevailing high regard for *yūgen*. He defines *yūgen* as "lingering
emotion not apparent in the diction, a mood not visible in the configuration of the verse," which drifts faintly about the expression.
Among the examples of *yūgen* he offers are the following:

> It is like an autumn evening under a colorless expanse of silent sky.
> Somehow, as if for some reason that we should be able to recall, tears
> well uncontrollably.

Or:

> It is rather like the resentment of a beautiful woman, which she does
> not display in words but endures silently. . . . Instead of exhausting her
> vocabulary in recriminations and making a show of wringing tears from
> her sleeves, she grieves within her heart, tasting the depths of sorrow.

Or again:

> When looking at autumn mountains through mist, the view may be
> indistinct yet have great depth. Although few autumn leaves may be
> visible through the mist, it is alluring. The limitless vista created in
> imagination far surpasses anything one can see more clearly.[24]

Moreover, in the *Eigyokushū* Chōmei states: "Expressing the whole
of one's heart in words, rather like describing the moon without
clouds or praising flowers for being beautiful, is not at all difficult."[25]
Thus Chōmei suggests that the heart = words form of poetic expression is a lesser aesthetic. It is the *yojō-yūgen* style that is the essence of
waka. Moreover, he says, "poetry which takes its form from *yūgen*" is
"an uncertainty of heart and words like looking upon a mirage of
shimmering heat waves in an azure sky. . . . Being, they are not. Not
being, they are."[26] This is precisely the poetic style of the priest Kisen
which was earlier criticized by Ki no Tsurayuki.

Thus by the time of Kamo no Chōmei at the end of the twelfth century, the *yojō* style of Ariwara no Narihira and the cloudy, indistinct
style of Kisen, which had been looked down upon in the age of the
Kokinshū in the tenth century, had come to be labeled *yūgen* and
regarded as the most admirable of *waka* styles. The aesthetic con-

sciousness of *wabi*, then, suppresses the outward display of expression while storing within itself a rich depth of emotion. In this it realizes a profound and simple inner beauty in which *wabi* is a differentially structured "inner outer" beauty.

The *yojō-yūgen* style that was regarded as the epitome of *waka* from the time of Shunzei to Chōmei had a connection in its heart > word structure with the *wabi* of *chanoyu*, which it preceded. In this way, at least one of the sources of *wabi* can be detected in the poetic theories extolling this *yojō-yūgen* form and in the intellectual currents of the age surrounding them. It is perhaps worth noting that Fujiwara no Teika, Shunzei's son, who was the leader of the poetry world in the early Kamakura period and a man later regarded as a "sage of poetry," favored the word *ushin* (literally, to possess heart) and set the *ushin* form above *yūgen*. Although there was a slight nuance of difference, his *ushin* was virtually the same as *yūgen*. The reverence for *yūgen* aesthetics became the mainstream in subsequent poetry circles. It was especially strongly advocated by the Reizei family in the middle and late fourteenth century. Because of this, the *wabi* aesthetic was further deepened from the Kamakura through the Northern and Southern Courts period.

Yoshida Kenkō: The Discovery of Imperfect, Irregular Beauty

We have already seen that the *wabi* aesthetic prizes the imperfect over the flawless and classically elegant as one expression of a higher dimension of beauty. It would be incorrect to suggest, however, that such an aesthetic ideal only came into being with *chanoyu*. This ideal of imperfect beauty had already been described by Yoshida Kenkō in his *Tsurezuregusa*.

There is a natural human desire to admire the perfection of cherry blossoms at their peak and the flawless beauty of a full moon shining in a clear night sky. Like other peoples, the Japanese have from ancient times regarded such images as the highest expressions of beauty. In section 137 of the *Tsurezuregusa*, however, we find the following famous lines:

Are we to look at cherry blossoms only in full bloom, the moon only when it is cloudless? To long for the moon while looking on the rain, to lower the blinds and be unaware of the passing of spring—these are even more deeply moving. Branches about to blossom or gardens strewn with faded flowers are worthier of our admiration. . . .

The moon that appears close to dawn after we have long waited for it moves us more profoundly than the full moon shining cloudless over a thousand leagues. And how incomparably lovely is the moon, almost greenish in its light when seen through the tops of the cedars deep in the mountains, or when it hides for a moment behind clustering clouds during a sudden shower![27]

Kenkō sets aside the perfect beauty of the flower in full bloom to claim that there is a still higher dimension of beauty in the partly opened flower or in the lingering blossom. And while he allows that the beauty of an unclouded moon is attractive, he insists that a moon obscured by rain or veiled by clouds or a waning moon sinking behind the trees is a still deeper expression of beauty.

In the same section Kenkō argues:

> In all things, it is the beginnings and ends that are interesting. Does the love between men and women refer only to those moments when they are in each others' arms? The man who grieves over a love affair broken off before it was fulfilled, who bewails empty vows, who spends long autumn nights alone, who lets his thoughts wander to distant skies, who yearns for the past in a dilapidated house—such a man truly knows what love means.[28]

Here Kenkō suggests that it is only by tasting fully the pangs (*aware*) of an unrequited love or a broken love affair that one comes to understand true love. Later in the same passage he criticizes the attitude of spectators at the Kamo festival for being interested only in the highlights of the procession. For him, the early morning prelude to the festival and the lingering loneliness afterward, when the crowds have gone, enhance and validate the beauty of the occasion:

> By the time it is growing dark you wonder where the rows of carriages and the dense crowds of spectators have disappeared to. Before you know it, hardly a soul is left, and the congestion of returning carriages is over. Then they start removing the blinds and matting from the stands, and the place, even as you watch, begins to look desolate. You realize with a pang of grief that life is like this. If you have seen the avenues of the city you have seen the festival.[29]

That Kenkō's discovery of beauty in imperfect things and quiet moments is not mere whimsy or paradox but rather an aesthetic consciousness shared with other cultured persons of his day can readily be seen from section eighty-two of *Tsurezuregusa*. At the opening of this section he writes:

> Somebody once remarked that thin silk was not satisfactory as a scroll wrapping because it was so easily torn. Ton'a replied, "It is only after the silk wrapper has frayed at top and bottom, and the mother of pearl has fallen from the roller that a scroll looks beautiful." This opinion demonstrated the excellent taste of the man. People often say that a set of books looks ugly if all volumes are not in the same format, but I was impressed to hear the Abbot Kōyū say, "It is typical of the unintelligent man to insist on assembling complete sets of everything. Imperfect sets are better."[30]

Clearly Kenkō approved of the attitudes of the priests Ton'a and Kōyū that the old and faded, the mismatched and incomplete, can be more beautiful than the unblemished, the uniform, or the complete. One notes with interest that Kenkō, Ton'a, and Kōyū—three men of culture who lived in the Kamakura to early Northern and Southern Courts periods—should all agree in praising the imperfect and irregular or the worn and aged as a higher dimension of beauty. To claim that things are most beautiful not when they are "perfect and round" but when they are irregular and mismatched is an expression of *suki* in its original meaning, and here we can detect one of the currents of the *wabi* of *chanoyu*.

Zeami and Zenchiku: Toward a Beauty of Reticence and Non-Being

Chanoyu was refined from the late fifteenth century as one part of what has been called the culture of the Eastern Hills (Higashiyama) because of its association with the eighth Ashikaga shogun, Yoshimasa, who built his retreat, the Silver Pavilion, in the eastern hills of Kyoto. The more fully articulated *chanoyu* of this period was based on the practices of tea drinking by Zen monks, courtiers, members of the warrior elite, and merchants that had been spreading from the Kamakura period. The cultural life of this era was rich and diverse. Since

other important elements of Higashiyama culture were linked verse
and *nō*, it would not be surprising to find that the *wabi* aesthetic
which came to play such a central role in *chanoyu* also owed something to their influence. In the case of *nō*, one way to gauge its influence on *chanoyu* is to look at the dramatic theories formulated by
Zeami Motokiyo.

Kan'ami Kiyotsugu and his son Zeami were actors in the Yamato
sarugaku tradition, which originally prized mime *(monomane)* or repre-
sentational performance. But they established a new dramatic style by
assimilating the singing and dancing styles of Ōmi *sarugaku* and
dengaku (field music). This new artistic style attracted the notice of the
third Ashikaga shogun, Yoshimitsu. Yoshimitsu's backing opened the
way to success and to patronage by the Bakufu and by daimyos.
Under this elite patronage, Kan'ami and Zeami refined their dramatic
performances to establish the elegant dance-drama that we still enjoy
as *nō*.

Zeami had been trained in mime, the traditional dramatic style of
his *sarugaku* lineage. But in treatises written to transmit his teachings
secretly to his followers he emphasized *yūgen* as the highest expression
of beauty attainable in *nō*. In *Kakyō*, for instance, he wrote: "*Yūgen* is
regarded as the highest level of attainment in various artistic traditions. In our art, in particular, the mood of *yūgen* is the most important feature of style. . . . However we may vary the elements of mimicry, we must not depart from *yūgen*."[31] Zeami's *yūgen* cuts off the
search for verisimilitude pursued through mime at a certain limit and,
by converting expression into poetry and dance, injects a mood of lingering emotion, *yojō*. In this way Zeami took the edge off realistic
expression, made it more rhythmical, and created a romantic world of
yūgen-yojō beauty suffused with subtle emotion and delicate feeling.
Although there is no space here to discuss Zeami's views on the
beauty of *yūgen* in detail, I can at least present some of his conclu-
sions.

In "*Mondō jōjō*," the third section of his *Fūshi Kaden*, Zeami writes:
"Irrespective of the role he is playing, the principal actor *(shite)* should
be vivid *(hanayaka)*. This constitutes *yūgen*."[32] In the section "On
Entering the Boundaries of *Yūgen*" (*Yūgen no sakai ni iru no koto*) in
Kakyō, he gives the following examples of *yūgen*: "the fine bearing of a
nobleman or woman" and "the elegant manner of speech of a noble-

man or religious dignitary." He also says that "a simple softening of form is the essence of *yūgen*."[33]

In his *Nō Sakusho*, Zeami mentions fitting subjects for the characterization of *yūgen*: Ariwara no Narihira, Ōtomo no Kuronushi, and Hikaru Genji among men and Ise no Osuke, Ono no Komachi, Giō, Gijō, Shizuka Gozen, and Hyakuman among women.[34] All of these personages—both historical and fictional—convey a beauty tinged with lingering emotion, an aristocratic, feminine beauty derived from the emotional aesthetic tastes of Heian court literature, a vivid, gentle, elegant beauty. This *yūgen* style of beauty was, for Zeami, the fundamental expression of *nō*. But there was an even higher form of beauty to be achieved only by master actors at the very peak of performance. Zeami called this extreme beauty the "flower" (*ka*). As is obvious from the titles of such secret treatises as *Fūshi Kaden* and *Kakyō*, he loved the character for flower. In the *Mondō jōjō* section of *Fūshi Kaden* he goes so far as to say that "the flower is the life of *nō*." In the same section, however, he observes: "There is a beauty that must be spoken of as even higher than flower."[35] That is the beauty of *shiore*, literally the "withered." *Shiore* is a higher level of beauty, known only to those who attain the limits of flower.

From this it is clear that even when writing *Fūshi Kaden*, while he was still under the influence of his father, Kan'ami, Zeami set a higher value on the imperfect, negative, emaciated beauty of *shiore*, the negation of "flower," than he did on the perfect, affirmative beauty of "flower" itself. Moreover, this aesthetic deepened in later years as his experience and ideas matured. This development is clear from the "*Hihan no koto*" (On Criticism) section of *Kakyō*, where he distinguishes three levels of artistic accomplishment in *nō*: "There are three faculties through which *nō* is expressed—sight, hearing, and heart."[36]

Fundamental, but at the lowest level, is what we might describe as "*nō* emerging through sight." Zeami writes: "From the first the theater is colorful. The dancing and chanting are animated, the spectators high and low exclaim their praises, the atmosphere is brilliant."[37] He is describing a *nō* that is visually appealing, easily understood, vivid and ostentatious. Thus it is a form of *nō* that is readily appreciated by the general public: "Not only connoisseurs, but even those who know little of *nō*, all in the same spirit, think it interesting."[38]

The second stage is that of "*nō* emerging from hearing." It is a *nō* in which "from the beginning there is a seriousness, music and mood harmonize, and the effect is graceful and interesting." Rather than being seen with the eyes, this *nō* is gracefully absorbed by hearing and the other senses. For this reason, "it may not appeal strongly to rural enthusiasts,"[39] but actually it is a very sophisticated level of *nō*.

The final stage of "*nō* emerging from the heart" is a *nō* which appeals not to hearing or the other senses but succeeds by stirring the heart. Zeami describes this *nō* as "like the performance of a peerless *sarugaku* which after countless times has shed all variation, mimicry, or forced movement." It is like a master who has transcended the extremes of the vivid and, from an artistic domain beyond this, has reduced the movements of dance and mimicry to the minimum. It is a *nō* which does not have to rely on twists of plot, a "wordless *nō*," "a *nō* which in the midst of desolation (*sabi*) has something of awe in it." It is an austere drama—a *"nō* of no-mind (*mushin*)."* Consequently it is the very aesthetic pinnacle of the art of *nō*: "unknown even to true connoisseurs and even more beyond the comprehension of rural admirers."[40]

We note here that Zeami set an auditory beauty—that is, "a penetrating, gentle beauty"—above a visually appealing, "vivid" beauty. But on an even higher plane, at the very pinnacle of his aesthetic, he set a simple, "wordless" beauty, an "austere cold beauty" that appeals to the heart. It is clear, then, that the aesthetic consciousness later known as *wabi* was being gradually forged by Zeami in the middle Muromachi period.

Zeami's son-in-law Komparu Zenchiku, who was active in the Higashiyama epoch at the time of the shogun Yoshimasa, pushed this aesthetic even further. The principal works for understanding Zenchiku's theories of *nō* are his *Shidō Yōshō* and *Rokuin Ichiro no Ki*. In the former he categorizes the varieties of music used in *nō* in the following terms: "Although there are many types of qualities of music in the performance of *sarugaku*, you should know the eight fundamental sounds."[41] Having divided musical styles into eight types, he places the sound of *yūgen* at the middle range, fourth rank. In the eighth rank of "unsurpassed perfection" he puts the music of "leisurely ease" (*kankyoku*), which he says is "supremely elegant, tranquil, and graceful." Zenchiku, in a telling analogy, compares the beauty of *kankyoku* to that of aged cherry trees which, after enduring years of rain, dew, wind, and snow, put forth only a few scattered blossoms: "It is like

seeing fine rain on the sparse blossoms of the few mossy branches of
the famed ancient trees of Yoshino, Ōhara, and Koshio. The mood is
tranquil, graceful, and haunting."[42] This austere and serene beauty is
the negative counterpart of sumptuous and vivid beauty. It is a simple
and reticent form of expression which subsumes within itself the colorful and flamboyant.

Rokurin Ichiro no Ki expounds a Zen-infused view of the performing
arts in which "the way of the *sarugaku* performer lies in the secret of
detachment from self and object."[43] Zenchiku's assertion that the arts
of *nō* are intrinsically detached from self and object is identical with
the Zen ideal of "seeing one's original face before one's parents were
born." From this view of performance he divides the art of *nō* into six
stages, or rings: the ring of longevity, the ring of verticality, the ring of
dwelling, the ring of images, the ring of fragmentation, and the ring of
emptiness. The six stages are depicted by circles, starting from the ring
of longevity, which is described as "a state of nondifferentiation and
emptiness, a mysterious expression of movement and stillness.[44] The
stages gradually unfold through more colorful expression. When the
process reaches its zenith, it transcends set forms and, passing through
the ring of fragmentation, once again "becomes unrestrained and
returns to the original ring of longevity."[45]

This final stage, the ring of emptiness, is depicted with the same circle as the ring of longevity. How did Zenchiku perceive of his highest
level of performance—the beauty of the ring of emptiness? As we can
understand from his explanation of the ring of emptiness as "empty
and traceless, hushed and wordless, shedding and shedding until
nothing is left to shed, emptying until nothing remains to empty,"[46]
the ring of emptiness involves an utter simplicity in which expression
is restrained to the very minimum. However, as the structure of
Rokurin Ichiro no Ki hints in such expressions as "realizing enlightenment is the same as being unenlightened,"[47] the artistic ideal of the
ring of emptiness, although it is expressed through the same ring as
the original ring of longevity, is a simple artless beauty which subsumes within itself the colorful, skillful beauty that precedes it.

Explaining the artistic concept of the ring of emptiness, Zenchiku
uses the expression "the performance is thoroughly withered, a few
blossoms clinging to an aged tree."[48] Clearly the beauty of the empty
ring has much in common with that of *kankyoku*. But Zenchiku also
explains that "all things having withered are faintly rejuvenated, each

sound, each step returning to where it first sprouted."⁴⁹ The imagery
he conjures up here is of silent winter fields, empty of cherry blossoms, autumn leaves, and all emotional quality. While superficially
this may seem to be a withered world of death, within the barren
fields the life force is inherent, ready to burst forth in the coming
spring. The aesthetic of the ring of emptiness advocated by Zenchiku
is a stark and withered beauty like that of winter fields. It is a kind of
beauty in which one can sense, despite its coldness and reticence, a
pulse of life. It is not off the mark to liken this aesthetic ideal to the
beauty of *wabi* alluded to by Takeno Jōō in his reference to the poem
"Looking about" or by Rikyū in his reference to "a spring of grass
amid the snow."

Shinkei: Aspiration to Stark, Cold Beauty

As we have seen, the roots of the *wabi* aesthetic can be detected in the
vogue for *yojō-yūgen* among poets of the early Kamakura period. In the
Muromachi period, as *renga* outstripped *waka* in popularity, it too
contributed to a deepening of the aesthetic consciousness of *wabi*. We
can explore this development through a representative poet of the
early Muromachi period, the Zen monk Seigen Shōtetsu of the Tōfukuji lineage of the Rinzai school.

Shōtetsu, who studied *waka* with the warrior-poet Imagawa Ryō-
shun of the Reizei school, admired the two poetic treatises *Gubishō*
and *Sangoki*, which were prepared by the Reizei school and spuriously
attributed to Fujiwara no Teika, and on that basis adopted *yojō-yūgen*
as a poetic ideal. In his *Shōtetsu Monogatari*, Shōtetsu has the following to say about *yūgen*: "What is called *yūgen* is something in the heart
that cannot be expressed in words. The moon lightly veiled in clouds
or the reddening autumn hills shrouded in mist are viewed as forms of
yūgen. But when asked where exactly is the *yūgen* in these things, we
find it hard to say."⁵⁰

That Shōtetsu thought of *yūgen* as a form of expression in which
lingering emotion, *yojō*, clings subtly to feelings that end before being
fully expressed we can understand from this comment: "If racing
clouds and swirling snow can be called the *yūgen* style, then clouds
trailing faintly in the sky or snowflakes drifting gently on the wind are
surely in this style."⁵¹ At the same time, Shōtetsu expressed the quality of the beauty of *yojō* in such analogies as "the feeling that four or

five noblewomen in silken robes might be singing of flowers bursting
into full bloom at the southern palace"[52] or "thinking so raptly of a
beautiful court lady that one is speechless."[53] It is clear that for Shōtetsu the *yūgen* ideal of beauty was an elegant, flamboyant, and
femininely voluptuous beauty. As such, it was close to the earlier
Zeami model of the *yūgen* aesthetic.

Shōtetsu's student, the *renga* poet Jūjūin Shinkei, a contemporary
of Komparu Zenchiku, forged a very different conception of the *yūgen*
aesthetic. In *Sasamegoto*, his representative critique of *renga*, Shinkei
writes:

> While many paths serve the same cause, this path especially takes as its
> end emotions, appearances, and lingering feelings (*yojō*). *Yūgen* and
> pathos (*aware*) are to be found in what is left unspoken and unformed
> in thought. With poetry, too, its unclear form speaks only of appear-
> ances. This is the utmost expression of poetic form.[54]

This comment should be sufficient to show that Shinkei, like his
teacher Shōtetsu, prized the *yūgen* style—that is, an expressive style
overflowing with *yojō*. The quality of *yojō* that Shinkei admired was
very different from Shōtetsu's, however. Reading the *Shinkei Sōzu
Teikin* (Bishop Shinkei's Instructions), we find the following passage:

> One should set one's heart only on the indistinct. The most interesting
> verses are like those in which we find a spray of single-leaf white plum
> blossoming in the depths of a bamboo grove or glimpse the moon
> through clouds. On the other hand, red double plum blossoms in wild
> profusion or a full moon like that of the fifteenth night of the eighth
> month are not agreeable.[55]

As if imitating the voice of Yoshida Kenkō in the *Tsurezuregusa*,
Shinkei's heart was drawn more to an imperfect, implied beauty than
to perfect, rounded beauty whether it be the radiant loveliness of the
shining harvest moon or the red double plum blossoms in full bloom.
We can understand from this that he did not appreciate gorgeous self-
display but rather loved an understated, modest, and simple beauty.
But even more noteworthy are his statements in *Sasamegoto*: "The
heart requires few words. Excellence is to be found in verses that are
cold and spare." The poetic form of the ancients was "like lapis lazuli

piled on crystal," their poems being "cold and pure."[56] In the same work he remarks:

> Somebody asked one of the ancient poet immortals (Fujiwara no Moto-toshi): "How do you compose poetry?" He replied: "Pampas grass in the withered fields, the moon at dawn." By this he meant putting the heart into what is not stated and recognizing that which is cold and desolate. The verses of those who have entered this realm of understanding display such qualities.[57]

In *Oi no Kurigoto* Shinkei appreciates most highly the beauty that is "elevated, aloof, cold, and frozen" by arguing that "of all who penetrate the very depths of their art, those whose forms are aged and worn, *sabi*, are most respected."[58] The words he used to express the highest beauty of *renga* are words that connote a negative beauty, a beauty of age, like "cold" (*hieru*), "emaciated" (*yaseru*), "frigid" (*samushi*), "withered" (*kareru*), "dried out" (*karabiru*), "spent" (*kareka-jikeru*), and "aged and worn" (*fukesabiru*). In his *Hitorigoto*, written when, having fled the capital in the Ōnin War, Shinkei was wandering in the eastern provinces of Musashi and Sagami, there is a description of water in its various seasonal manifestations. He finds in the scenery of ice and withered landscape a fathomless beauty:

> Nothing is more beautiful than ice. The thin crust of morning ice on the stubbled rice fields, icicles hanging from eaves of aged cypress bark, the feeling of withered trees and grasses locked in hoar frost. Are these sights without interest and beauty?[59]

Thus we can appreciate that Shinkei's notion of the ideal *renga* and the highest expression of beauty was the same as that of Komparu Zenchiku. It was a beauty in utter contrast to the emotional, vivid beauty of spring cherry blossoms or autumn maple leaves. It was, instead, a tense, stern beauty of barren fields, a winter-withered beauty in which the pulse of the life force is just discernible beneath the awesome desolation of outward appearances, a beauty of starkness and tranquility.

We should note, too, that Murata Shukō might have been quoting Shinkei when he said that "the moon is not pleasing unless partly obscured by a cloud"[60] and that Takeno Jōō, admiring Shinkei's expression "*renga* should be withered and cold," commented that "the fruit of *chanoyu* too must be like that."[61] Why this admiration for Shinkei? Because he celebrated a type of beauty very much like that of the *wabi* of *chanoyu*.

OTHER INFLUENCES SHAPING THE *WABI* AESTHETIC

Up to this point we have considered *wabi* exclusively as a Japanese aesthetic development that emerged from the arts of *waka*, *renga*, and *nō* during the four centuries of the medieval age from the late Heian period through Muromachi and was gradually refined on the basis of the ideas and reflections of masters in those arts. At the same time, as with other aspects of the thought and culture of the Japanese people, imported ideas may have played a role in shaping *wabi* and the aesthetic concepts leading to it. Although it is difficult to pinpoint sources of direct influence, the Chinese made several contributions to the general intellectual environment within which *wabi* developed.

Confucius, Lao Tzu, and Hsün Tzu

From ancient times Confucianism guided the education of nobles and officials in Japan as in China. The *Analects* (*Lun-yü*), in particular, was regarded as indispensable reading. Confucian values penetrated deeply into the lives of the Japanese people of all social levels as a morality regulating everyday life and imperceptibly came to shape the way people viewed their world and thought about things. Although there were slight modulations in different periods, this current remained fairly steady throughout the medieval period.

In the opening book of the *Analects*, entitled "On Learning," Confucius states:

> It is rare, indeed, for a man with cunning words and an ingratiating face to be benevolent (*jen*).[62]

And later we find reference to its obverse:

> Unbending strength, resoluteness, simplicity and reticence are close to benevolence.[63]

Taken together these statements stress that people who embellish words and show off through their appearance or attitude are wanting in benevolence and sincerity. In contrast, people who are simple and unpretentious in manner and reticent in speech are likely to be sincere and imbued with *jen*. Clearly this view of human nature rejects flamboyance in favor of understatement and reticence. Again, there is this statement:

> With the rites, it is better to err on the side of frugality than on the side of extravagance.[64]

This is to say that on such occasions as coming-of-age, marriage, and funeral rites or the presentation of gifts it is better to be restrained than ostentatious. This is because the essence of such rites lies not in their externals but in the heart.

Furthermore, Tseng Tzu, praising Yen Yüan, the youngest and favorite disciple of Confucius, made these observations:

> To have yet appear to want.
> To be full yet appear empty.[65]

Tseng Tzu is saying that while Yen Yüan had great learning and knowledge he did not make a display of it to others but rather acted as if he were ignorant. While building true ability and force of character he acted modestly as though he were powerless. He was truly a man of great depth.

A similar anecdote describing Lao Tzu can be found in the "Tales of Lao Tzu and Chuang Tzu" in the *Historical Records (Shih-chi)* of Ssu-ma Ch'ien:

> Just as a good merchant stores things away and may seem empty of stock, so the sage may outwardly seem foolish and empty of attainments.[66]

Whereas the upstart merchant is likely to enlarge the front of his store and display his goods gaudily, the well-established merchant will maintain a restrained appearance and display his wares sparingly. To outward appearances this wealthy merchant's store may seem sparsely stocked or even empty. But when a customer requests something, an unlimited quantity of precious things are brought from the back. Lao Tzu was exactly like this good merchant. At first glance he might be taken for an empty fool. Yet he was the kind of fathomless sage who offers more wisdom the more he is pressed. The message here is that what should be prized is a poverty of appearance behind which lies a wealth of inner meaning. Moreover, in the *Classic of the Way and Its Power (Tao Te Ching)*, we find such expressions as "One who knows does not speak, one who speaks does not know" and "To know, yet to think one does not know is best."[67] They stress the idea that eloquence is disdained and reticence admired. Again, Taoist thought suggests that the very highest, most mysterious states of being seem rather to take the forms of their opposites. Chapter forty-five, for example, states that:

> Great perfection seems chipped,
> Yet use will not wear it out;
> Great fullness seems empty,
> Yet use will not drain it;
> Great straightness seems bent;
> Great skill seems awkward;
> Great eloquence seems tongue-tied.[68]

The *Tao Te Ching* was read by Japanese men of letters from the Nara period. As the following statement from the *Tsurezuregusa* indicates, the *Tao Te Ching* was also read with pleasure among medieval scholars and especially studied by Gozan Zen monks, who led the world of medieval learning and culture:

The pleasantest of all diversions is to sit alone under the lamp, a book spread out before you, and to make friends with people of a distant past you have never known. The books I would choose are the moving volumes of *Wen-hsüan*, the collected works of Po Chü-i, the sayings of Lao Tzu, and the chapters of *Chuang Tzu*.[69]

Thus we seem to be safe in assuming that these aphorisms and ideas relating to Lao Tzu were known by learned men of the medieval period.

Similar ideas may be found in the writings of Hsün Tzu. In his *Book on the Seat of Admonition (Yu-tso p'ien)* there is a description of Confucius' audience at the court of Duke Huan of Lu. Seeing a tipping vessel that the duke had placed to the right of his seat as a warning to himself, Confucius explained the principle to his followers: "When it is filled it topples."[70] This was an admonition against the evils of overindulgence. The tipping vessel was a water jar which sat at an angle when empty, stood upright when half full, and tipped over when filled to the brim.

This rejection of satiety or completeness was already being advocated in Japan by the Heian period. In the latter part of the eighty-second section of the *Tsurezuregusa* we find the following:

> In everything, no matter what it may be, uniformity is undesirable. Leaving something incomplete makes it interesting, and gives one the feeling that there is room for growth. Someone once told me, "Even when building the imperial palace, they always leave one place unfinished." In both Buddhist and Confucian writings of the philosophers of former times, there are also many missing chapters.[71]

This passage is followed in the eighty-third section by a reference to the eulogy offered by Tōin (Fujiwara) Saneyasu to Saionji Kinhira when the latter declined a promotion to chief minister and requested to be allowed to end his career in the subordinate post of minister of the left. Saneyasu learned this from the act:

> Nothing stood in the way of the lay priest Chikurin'in and minister of the left (Saionji Kinhira) rising to be prime minister, but he said, "I doubt that being prime minister will make much difference. I'll stop at minister of the left." He subsequently took Buddhist orders. The Tōin minister of the left (Saneyasu), impressed by the story, himself never entertained any ambitions of becoming prime minister. The old adage has it, "When the dragon has soared to the summit he knows the chagrin of descent." The moon waxes only to wane; things reach their height only presently to decline. In all things, the principle holds true that decline threatens when further expansion is impossible.[72]

It is not hard to guess from this that in Yoshida Kenkō's day the current of Chinese thought which rejected satiety permeated the intellectual world around him. Nor would it be far off the mark to suggest that this thinking nourished an aesthetic that emphasized an unequal, irregular beauty.

The *Shih-jen yü-hsieh* and Muromachi Ink Painting

In Sung dynasty China there were innovative movements in thought and literature. The intellectual world saw the rise within Confucianism of so-called Sung studies, or Neo-Confucianism. At the same time there was a parallel renaissance in letters marked by a surge in literary criticism. In the late Northern Sung dynasty there was a sharp political conflict between a newly emerging reform faction, known as the "new policies" faction, led by Wang An-Shih, and a more conservative establishment, a counterreform faction, including the historian Ssu-ma Kuang and the poet Su Shih (Su Tung-p'o). This conflict was reflected in written debates as a bitter literary feud developed between the two factions. In the course of this rivalry many "discourses on poetry" (*shih-hua*), such as the *Shih-lin shih-hua* and *Ch'eng-chai shih-hua*, were published and transmitted to Japan by the hands of Zen monks.

Noteworthy among these discourses were two works that conveniently classified the main types of poetic discourse under various topical headings: the *Yü-yin ts'ung-hua* edited by Hu Tzu and the *Shih-jen yü-hsieh* edited by Wei Ch'ing-chih. The latter had been imported and was being read in Japan by the late Kamakura period. We can be sure that the *Shih-jen yü-hsieh* actually was being read because there is a ten-volume edition of it in the Kyoto Library which contains an afterword by the famous Zen monk-scholar Gen'e:

> In this collection the punctuation is difficult. The mind grows dizzy, errors are many. Later scholars can hope to correct them. Inscribed the latter part of the eleventh month of the first year of the Shōchū era (1324) with purified heart by Gen'e.[73]

From this we know that by 1324, the late Kamakura period, the *Shih-jen yü-hsieh* was being read in Japan. Moreover, entries in the *Hanazono Tennō Shinki* for 1325:12:28 and 1332:3:24 reveal that Emperor Hanazono and his mentor in *waka*, Kyōgoku Tamekane, who breathed new vitality into the poetic circles of his age, both read and admired the *Shih-jen yü-hsieh* as the "core" of poetry. They praised it highly for "being perfectly in harmony with the meaning of Japanese verse (*waka*)." Moreover, the Zen monk Kokan Shiren, well known as the author of the *Genkō Shakushō*, and Gidō Shūshin, one of the leading figures in the Gozan literary movement, as well as other Muromachi period Zen monks, read it with great appreciation. It is clear, too, that Nijō Yoshimoto, the commanding literary figure of his age and cultural adviser to Ashikaga Yoshimitsu, read the *Shih-jen yü-hsieh*. He quotes from it and promotes its views in his *Jūmon Saihishō* (Most Secret Extract in Ten Questions).

Thus the *Shih-jen yü-hsieh* was transmitted to Japan at an early period, published there, read by men of letters from the late Kamakura period, and highly praised as the core of poetry. It contains a quotation from the *Hou-shan shih-hua* (Poetic Discourses by Ch'en Shih-tao) at the beginning of volume five, "The Path of Beginning Scholarship," that bears directly on our theme:

> Be awkward rather than skillful. Be plain rather than florid. Be rough-and-ready rather than delicate. Be eccentric rather than conform to the popular norm. Poetry is all like this.[74]

Or again there is a quotation from the *Lü-shih t'ung-meng-hsün* (Master Lu's Instructions to Children):

> For the beginner composing poetry it is better to fail through artless-ness than it is to fail through excessive stylishness.[75]

In the general discussion of "Latent Implications" in the tenth volume, an assertion from the *Shan-hu-kou shih-hua* (Coral Hook Poetic Discourse) is introduced:

> This book takes the latent and natural as superior. It takes the fragmentary and modeled as inferior. . . . The plain and disinterested are superior, the prodigious and affected are inferior.[76]

Although the *Shih-jen yü-hsieh* presents literary theories from a variety of standpoints, its underlying thesis is simple: The unskillful is better than the skilled, the plain is better than the ornate, the rough-and-ready is better than the delicate, the eccentric is better than the worldly. It is a view in which the artless and natural are superior to a decorative style abounding with literary flourishes. This is the literary view of the Yüan-yu school (of Su Tung-p'o and his fellows) that "simple aged austerity is to be prized, skillfully wrought elaboration to be despised."

Thus it is not too much to argue that Sung literary theories transmitted via the *Shih-jen yü-hsieh*, especially those of the Yüan-yu school, exerted both direct and indirect influences on medieval Japanese theories of poetry, *waka* and *renga*, and through them contributed to a deepening of the *wabi* aesthetic.

A similar stimulus to the *wabi* aesthetic can also be seen in the case of monochrome ink painting (*suiboku*, literally "water and ink"), which had developed in China and was transmitted during these centuries to Japan where it also flourished. Ink painting had its origins in the T'ang dynasty, when color painting was very advanced, and it flowered in the Sung. It continued to thrive into the Yüan dynasty, where it became the mainstream of academic painting. Its flowering owed much to its close ties with the Zen sect of Buddhism.

From the *Butsunichian Kōmotsu Mokuroku* transmitted in Engakuji Temple we know that already before the end of the Kamakura period a large number of Chinese ink paintings had been imported to Kamakura.[77] Then, in the Northern and Southern Courts period of the middle and late fourteenth century, the appreciation of ink painting spread into elite warrior society, while Zen monks like Kaō, Mokuan, and Gyokuen began to paint them as avocational accomplishments. In the Muromachi period, when painter-priests like Josetsu, Shūbun, and Sesshū and academic painters like Kanō Masanobu appeared, Sung-Yüan style ink painting reached its highest level of achievement in Japan.

Monochrome ink painting is based on the suppression and abbreviation of expression. It is sufficient for it to grasp the essence of its subject directly and to express that essence in simple lines and washes. Ink painting rejects color as superfluous because the colors of things change with time and are thus not essential characteristics. Ink monochrome is not simply black or gray; rather, by negating all color, it includes all. Like the *wabi* of *chanoyu*, it is a simple, impoverished beauty which sublates more vivid beauty. At any rate, ink painting prizes the subjective expression of ideas and images more than the objective representation of the visual. Thus it esteems the simplification of expression and of unstated emotions, *yojō*, and the refinement of spirit that accompanies it. It does not seem farfetched, then, to see the rise of ink painting as a mood of the age and one more factor in the deepening of the *wabi* aesthetic. Considering that in early *chanoyu* the most prized hanging scrolls for the alcove were ink paintings by Mu Ch'i and Yü Chien, this conjecture seems reasonable.

The Zen Spirit

As we have seen, the *wabi* ideal of *chanoyu* originated and matured within the aesthetic consciousness of the medieval Japanese. In this sense it was a very Japanese feeling for beauty. At the same time, Zen, which was introduced from China and had an inseparable connection with the establishment of *chanoyu*, was another powerful force in deepening and refining the *wabi* aesthetic.

The Ōryō teachings of Rinzai Zen were introduced by Eisai in 1187. Fujiwara no Shunzei and Kamo no Chōmei were both still alive in that year, but neither showed any interest in Zen and, consequently, we have to conclude that their admiration for the *yojō-yūgen* ideal of beauty was not inspired by Zen. By the early fourteenth century, the age of Yoshida Kenkō, the Rinzai and Sōtō Zen schools were well established in Japan. This was also the age when great Zen masters like Shūhō Myōchō and Musō Soseki were active. We can recognize certain parallels between the ideas of Kenkō and those of Dōgen, but there is no firm evidence that Kenkō was particularly influenced by Zen. Again we have to conclude that Kenkō's reverence for imperfect, irregular beauty did not derive from Zen.

In contrast, Zeami Motokiyo practiced Sōtō Zen under the spiritual guidance of Chikusō Chigan of the Hoganji Temple in Yamato province and attained some degree of enlightenment. In *Fūshi Kaden* and other works, for example, he uses Zen expressions correctly. Especially in the secretly transmitted text *Kui* (The Nine Levels) he uses Zen sayings like "at midnight in Silla, the sun is bright" or "piling snow in a silver bowl" to hint at the nine levels of accomplishment in the art of *nō*. And the chapter title in *Kakyō*, "On Linking All Things in *Nō* with a Single Mind," is nothing other than the application to *nō* practice of the basic Zen principle "proper mindfulness and uninterrupted practice." Thus it should be clear to what extent Zen thought permeated Zeami's *nō* and *nō* theory.

Komparu Zenchiku studied with Ikkyū. From the detailed entries in the *Ikkyū Oshō Nenpu* and other sources there is no doubt of his deep attainment in Zen as a layman. We have already seen that the structure of his *Rokurin Ichiro no Ki* draws on Zen thought. Moreover, the form and aesthetic of the empty ring, which he raised to the highest realm of performing art, was greatly influenced by Zen or at least could be described as a Zen-inspired aesthetic. The poet Seigan Shōtetsu was a Zen monk who served as record keeper for the Kyoto Gozan monastery of Manjuji, and the *renga* master Shinkei, although a monk of the Onjōji lineage of the Tendai school, had a deep understanding of Zen. Thus we can conjecture that Zen was applied indirectly through Zeami, Zenchiku, Shōtetsu, and Shinkei to deepen and refine the *wabi* aesthetic.

Even more important than this, however, Zen had a direct impact in shaping the personalities and aesthetic sensibilities of tea masters in the formative stages of *chanoyu*. For example, Murata Shukō, who is regarded as a founder of *chanoyu*, was a lay student of Zen master Ikkyū. Shukō's successor Murata Sōju was a good friend of Daikyū Sōkyū of Myōshinji Temple. Takeno Jōō's teacher, Jūshiya Sōgo, practiced Zen under the guidance of Kogaku Sōsen of Daitokuji, and Jōō himself studied Zen under Kogaku's dharma heir, Dairin Sōtō. Jōō became an enlightened lay practitioner who "understood that the flavor of tea and the flavor of Zen are the same." Imai Sōkyū and Tsuda Sōgyū also committed themselves to Zen. Sen no Rikyū studied Zen under Shōrei Sōkin of Daitokuji and then Shōrei's dharma heir Kokei Sōchin and was known as a great lay practitioner who "practiced eagerly for thirty years." Furthermore, those who played major roles in the way of tea in the early modern period—men such as Furuta Oribe, Kobori Enshū, Katagiri Sekishū, Kanamori Sōwa, Rikyū's sons Dōan and Shōan, and Shōan's son Genpaku Sōtan, who revived the Sen family tradition of tea—all studied and consorted with Zen monks such as Shun'oku Sōen of Daitokuji.

The following words by Rikyū are found at the beginning of *Nampōroku*, the most sacred text of *chanoyu*:

Chanoyu of the small tea room is first of all a Buddhist spiritual practice for attaining the way. To be concerned about the quality of the dwelling in which you serve tea or the flavor of the food served with it is to emphasize the mundane. It is sufficient if the dwelling one uses does not leak water and the food served suffices to stave off hunger. This is in accordance with the teachings of the Buddha and is the essence of *chanoyu*. First, we fetch water and gather firewood. Then we boil the water

and prepare tea. After offering some to the Buddha, we serve our
guests. Finally we serve ourselves.[78]

As we can guess from this instruction, Zen had permeated *chanoyu*. It
was the backbone for the way of tea. But exactly how did Zen contrib-
ute to the deepening of the *wabi* aesthetic and the enhancement of
wabi beauty?

Zen enlightenment is literally beyond words. Even using a billion
words its truth cannot possibly be transmitted to, or from, another.
There is no recourse other than to "know hot and cold for oneself."
For this reason Zen rejects reliance on written texts or concepts and
denies their logical explanation and expression. Nevertheless, having
said this, Zen recognizes that without some kind of expression there
would be no way of transmitting one's enlightenment to another person and no way to discuss and deepen Zen. Therefore, the primary
means of transmitting thought in Zen is indicating things directly
with the things themselves or, by some simple gesture, having the
inquirer recognize for himself from his own experience: "Yes, that's it
exactly!" Although this is a very effective method, alone it would be
impossible to transmit anything to persons not present on the occasion or to later generations. What is delightedly used, then, is metaphorical allusion or hints of scenes from nature or actual things—as in
response to the question: "What then is this admantine Dharma
Body?" The answer: "Mountain flowers blooming resemble brocade,
the valley streams tumble like indigo." Moreover, Zen is a deter-
minedly self-power (*jiriki*) school of Buddhism. A basic principle of
Zen teaching is that if one corner is revealed, you should be able to
discover the other three corners for yourself. For this reason Zen leans
toward metaphorical, allusive, or symbolic expression and prizes
restraint and reticence. Thus one can conjecture that the tea masters'
esteem for simple expression as one aspect of *wabi* was—besides being
in the tradition of *yojō-yūgen* in medieval literature and the performing arts—also due to the influence of Zen.

Reading the *Shōbō Genzō Zuimonki* (Records Heard from the Trea-
sury of the True Dharma Eye), which was taken down from Dōgen's
evening talks by his disciple Ejō, one finds that Dōgen repeatedly
warned his disciples that "those intent upon learning the way must
first learn poverty." In book three of this work we find the following
passage:

Those who are called excellent followers of the Buddha wear sackcloth and always beg for their food. The Zen school is called "the good school" and Zen monks are different from those of other schools. In the beginning, when Zen was emerging and Zen monks lived in temples of the older schools or in Ritsu (Vinaya) school temples, they scorned worldly things and lived in destitution. With regard to the life-style of the Zen school you should first of all know this.[79]

Thus, for Dōgen, poverty itself is the primary religious characteristic of the Zen life-style.

In book four Dōgen gives the example of the Rinzai patriarch Yang-ch'i Fang-hui (Yogi Hōe) who forbade repairs to his monastery and lived among dilapidated buildings, stating that *"satori* is not determined by the quality of one's residence. It is determined only by the quantity of effort put into *zazen."*[80] Dōgen follows this observation with a remark by the monk Lung-ya Chu-tun (Ryūge Kyoton): "In learning the Way of Zen one should first study poverty. Only after studying poverty and being poor will one become familiar with the Way."[81] He further emphasizes that "from the time of the Buddha until today among true practitioners of the Way, one does not hear of or see any who are wealthy."[82] In book five Dōgen cites the example of Tao-ju (Dōnyo), a senior monk of Mount T'ien-tung monastery: "In Great Sung the good monks who are known to the people are all poor."[83]

At first reading, these comments might be taken as a glorification of poverty. But of course they are not simply an idealization of penury. They stress, rather, that the true Zen seeker does not trouble himself about clothing or food, nor is he distracted by thoughts of fame and profit in the secular world. That is to say, he is not concerned that he is poor in a material sense, but devotes himself single-mindedly to Buddhist practice, destroying illusion and breaking through into enlightenment. The important thing is to be a good Zen man, no matter how wretched and unsightly one may outwardly appear.

In the Zen classic *Verses Testifying to the Way* by Yung-chia Hsüan-chüeh (Yōka Genkaku), one finds the following lines:

> I am a destitute follower of Buddha.
> Although I may be called poor,

this is merely a material poverty.
I am not poor in the Way.
Because I am poor I dress in rags.
But in finding the Way
I bear a priceless jewel in my heart.[84]

These lines express the great confidence of a man of Zen. The poverty of which Dōgen spoke is exactly this. Prizing poverty in this sense was not confined to Genkaku or Dōgen, of course. It was the most Zen-like life-style from antiquity. Extolling the appearance of the Zen man as "poor of body but not poor in the Way" is based on the Zen saying that "tattered robes are filled with a pure breeze," which means "although clad in rags the heart is pure."

Here we naturally recall the words of Shukō explaining the taste of *wabi* tea as "a prize horse hitched to a thatched hut,"[85] or the first injunction of *Jittai no Koto* (On the Ten Forms) that "one should place one's trust in someone who is coarse on the outside but strict and proper within."[86] As we have seen, *wabi* is a beauty that may seem superficially impoverished and unrefined. Internally, however, it stores a depth of richness and purity. Clearly this is the same structure as the ideal of the Zen seeker: "poor of body but not poor in the Way," whose "tattered robes are filled with a pure breeze." This is just one example of Zen's influence on the *wabi* aesthetic or, conversely, of how the *wabi* of *chanoyu* derived nourishment from Zen.

I wish to make one final point. The man of Zen, as we have seen, feels bitterness and shame at poverty in his spiritual practice (the Way) but does not feel the slightest concern for material poverty. Believing that "the distasteful, this too is tasteful," he lives beyond the range of external conditions. There is certainly no harm in being wealthy, perfectly satisfied, and having things go as one pleases. One does not go out of one's way to despise or avoid such things. On the other hand, there is no need to despise the poor, the imperfect, or what does not go as one wishes, inasmuch as these things can be seen as possessing the flavor of human life. That is, they too are "tasteful," living in the spirit of the *waka*:

Harete yoshi	Fine against a brilliant sky
Kumoritemo yoshi	Fine when wrapped in clouds
Fuji no yama	Fuji Mountain.

Moto no sugata wa	The original form
Kawarazarikeri.	Does not change.[87]

This is the way of life of the man of Zen. Not clinging to riches, perfection of things, or having everything as one wishes but rather finding a higher value in poverty, the irregular, and that which goes against one's wishes, recognizing that "the distasteful, this too is tasteful": This is the Zen-like way of the Zen seeker.

As noted, Jōō suggested the beauty of *wabi* and the *wabi* aesthetic by citing Fujiwara no Teika's poem "Looking about/Neither flowers/Nor scarlet leaves/A bayside reed hovel/In the autumn dusk,"[88] and Rikyū indicated them with Fujiwara no Ietaka's poem "To those who wait/Only for flowers,/Show them a spring/Of grass amid the snow/In a mountain village."[89] In contrast to those who seek beauty only in the splendor of spring's cherry blossoms and autumn's maple leaves or in the abundant, the perfect, and the rounded, Jōō and Rikyū looked for true taste and deep beauty in the ostensibly distasteful, such as "a bayside reed hovel in the autumn dusk," in "a spring of grass amid the snow in a mountain village," and in the destitute and undesirable. In finding that these things too are "tasteful," they learned from the Zen seeker's way of living and view of life and taught what it is to be a *wabi*-suffused man of tea.

NOTES

1. Jakuan Sōtaku, *Zen-cha Roku*, in Sen Sōshitsu, ed., *Chadō Koten Zenshū*, vol. 10 (Kyoto: Tankōsha, 1961), pp. 296–297.
2. Ibid., p. 297.
3. Yamanoue Sōji, *Yamanoue Sōji Ki*, in Sen Sōshitsu, ed., *Chadō Koten Zenshū*, vol. 6 (Kyoto: Tankōsha, 1958), p. 101.
4. Ibid., pp. 90, 104.
5. Kitakawa Tadahiko, ed., *Zenpō Zatsudan*, in Hayashiya Tatsusaburō, ed., *Kodai Chūsei Geijutsu Ron* (Tokyo: Iwanami Shoten, 1983), p. 480.
6. Nambō Sōkei, *Nampōroku*, in Sen Sōshitsu, ed., *Chadō Koten Zenshū*, vol. 4 (Kyoto: Tankōsha, 1956), p. 10.
7. Jakuan Sōtaku, *Zen-cha Roku*, in Sen Sōshitsu, ed., *Chadō Koten Zenshū*, vol. 10, p. 301.
8. Ibid.
9. Ibid.
10. In Hayashiya Tatsusaburō, ed., *Kodai Chūsei Geijutsu Ron*, p. 448.

11. Yamanoue Sōji, *Yamanoue Sōji Ki*, in Sen Sōshitsu, ed., *Chadō Koten Zenshū*, vol. 6, p. 97.

12. Nambō Sōkei, *Nampōroku*, in Sen Sōshitsu, ed., *Chadō Koten Zenshū*, vol. 4, p. 16.

13. Ibid.

14. Ibid., p. 17.

15. Hisamatsu Shin'ichi, "Chadō Bunka no Seikaku," in *Chadō no Testugaku* (Tokyo: Risōsha, 1973), pp. 59–69.

16. See the translation of the Japanese preface in Laurel Rodd and Mary Henkenius, *Kokinshū: A Collection of Ancient and Modern Poems* (Princeton: Princeton University Press, 1984), pp. 35–47.

17. Ibid., p. 43.

18. Ibid., p. 44.

19. Ibid.

20. Ibid., p. 45.

21. Fujiwara no Kintō, *Shinsen Zuinō*, in Ōta Tōshirō, ed., *Zoku Gunsho Ruijū* (Tokyo: Zoku Gunsho Ruijū Kansei Kai, 1911), vol. 456, p. 663.

22. Fujiwara no Kintō, *Waka Kuhon*, in Hisamatsu Shin'ichi and Nishio Minoru, eds., *Karonshū, Nōgakuronshū* (Tokyo: Iwanami Shoten, 1961), p. 32.

23. Jichin, *Jichin Oshō Jikaawase*, in Hanawa Hokiichi, ed., *Gunsho Ruijū* (Tokyo: Zoku Gunsho Ruijū Kansei Kai, 1930), vol. 218, p. 380.

24. Kamo no Chōmei, *Mumyōsho*, in Hisamatsu Shin'ichi and Nishio Minoru, eds., *Karonshū, Nōgakuronshū*, p. 224.

25. *Eigyokushū*, in Sasaki Nobutsuna, ed., *Nihon Kagaku Taikei*, vol. 13 (Tokyo: Kazama Shobō, 1973), p. 312.

26. Ibid., p. 323.

27. Donald Keene, trans., *Essays in Idleness: The Tsurezuregusa of Kenkō* (New York: Columbia University Press, 1967), pp. 115, 118.

28. Ibid.

29. Ibid., pp. 119–120.

30. Ibid., p. 70.

31. See the translation of this passage in J. Thomas Rimer and Yamazaki Masakazu, trans., *On the Art of the Nō Drama* (Princeton: Princeton University Press, 1984), pp. 92, 94.

32. Ibid., p. 28.

33. Ibid., pp. 93, 95.

34. Ibid., pp. 148–149.

35. Ibid., p. 28.

36. Ibid., p. 99.

37. Ibid.

38. Ibid.

39. Ibid., p. 100.

40. Ibid., p. 101.

41. Komparu Zenchiku, *Shidō Yōshō*, in Omote Akira and Itō Masayoshi, eds., *Komparu Koden Sho Shūsei* (Tokyo: Wanya Shoten, 1969), p. 266.

42. Ibid., p. 271.

43. Komparu Zenchiku, *Rokurin Ichiro no Ki*, in Omote Akira and Itō Masayoshi, eds., *Komparu Koden Sho Shūsei*, p. 197.
44. Ibid., p. 198.
45. Ibid., p. 203.
46. Ibid.
47. Ibid., p. 218.
48. Ibid., p. 219.
49. Ibid., p. 218.
50. Seigen Shōtetsu, *Shōtetsu Monogatari*, in Hisamatsu Shin'ichi and Nishio Minoru, eds., *Karonshū, Nōgakuronshū*, p. 224.
51. Ibid., p. 232.
52. Ibid.
53. Ibid., p. 233.
54. Jūjūin Shinkei, *Sasamegoto*, in Kidō Saizō and Imoto Nōichi, eds., *Rengaronshū, Haironshū* (Tokyo: Iwanami Shoten, 1961), p. 178.
55. Jūjūin Shinkei, *Shinkei Sōzu Teikin*, in Ōta Tōshirō, ed., *Zoku Gunsho Ruijū*, vol. 497, p. 1126.
56. Jūjūin Shinkei, *Sasamegoto*, p. 129.
57. Ibid., p. 175.
58. Jūjūin Shinkei, *Oi no Kurigoto*, in Hanawa Hokiichi, ed., *Gunsho Ruijū* (Tokyo: Zoku Gunsho Ruijū Kansei Kai, 1960), vol. 17, p. 72.
59. Jūjūin Shinkei, *Hitorigoto*, in Ōta Tōshirō, ed., *Zoku Gunsho Ruijū*, p. 1028.
60. See note 5 above.
61. See note 11 above.
62. D. C. Lau, trans., *Confucius: The Analects* (London: Penguin, 1979), p. 59.
63. Ibid., p. 123.
64. Ibid., p. 67.
65. Ibid., p. 93.
66. Ssu-ma Ch'ien, *Shih-chi* (Peking: Chung-hua Shu-chü, 1959), vol. 7, p. 2140.
67. D. C. Lau, trans., *Lau Tzu: Tao Te Ching* (London: Penguin, 1963), pp. 117, 133.
68. Ibid., p. 106.
69. Keene, *Essays in Idleness*, p. 12.
70. Harvard-Yenching Institute Sinological Index Series, Supplement no. 22, *A Concordance to Hsün Tzu* (Taipei: Chinese Materials and Research Aids Service Center, 1966), p. 102.
71. Keene, *Essays in Idleness*, pp. 70–71.
72. Ibid., p. 71.
73. Haga Kōshirō, *Chūsei Zenrin no Gakumon oyobi Bungaku ni kan suru Kenkyū* (Tokyo: Nihon Gakujutsu Shinkōkai, 1956), p. 318.
74. Wei Ch'ing-chih, *Shih-jen yü-hsieh*, vol. 1 (Shanghai: Shanghai Ku-chi Ch'u-panshe, 1978), p. 113.
75. Ibid.
76. Ibid., p. 209.
77. *Butsunichian Kōmotsu Mokuroku* was written in 1363. Material was added to it during the succeeding sixty-five years.
78. Nambō Sōkei, *Nampōroku*, in Sen Sōshitsu, ed., *Chadō Koten Zenshū*, vol. 4, p. 3.

79. Ejō, comp., *Shōbō Genzō Zuimonki*, in *Nihon Koten Bungaku Taikei*, vol. 81 (Tokyo: Iwanami Shoten, 1965), p. 387.
80. Ibid., p. 408.
81. Ibid.
82. Ibid.
83. Ibid., p. 413.
84. *Taishō Shinshū Daizōkyō*, vol. 51, p. 460b.
85. See note 3 above.
86. Yamanoue Sōji, *Yamanoue Sōji Ki*, in Sen Sōshitsu, ed., *Chadō Koten Zenshū*, vol. 6, p. 90.
87. This *waka* is by Yamaoka Tesshū and is inscribed on a painting he did of Mount Fuji.
88. Nambō Sōkei, *Nampōroku*, in Sen Sōshitsu, ed., *Chadō Koten Zenshū*, vol. 4, p. 16.
89. Ibid.

PART TWO

COMMENTARIES

EIGHT

REFLECTIONS ON *CHANOYU* AND ITS HISTORY

Sen Sōshitsu XV
Translated by Paul Varley

TEA AND ZEN

THE tie between tea and Zen has its origin, of course, in China. We find, for example, the following information recorded in the *Feng-shih wen-chien chi*, compiled in the T'ien-pao era (742–755) of Emperor Hsüan-tsung by Feng-yen: During the K'ai-yuan era (713–741) there was in Shantung province a temple called Ling-yen on Mount T'ai, one of the "five peaks" of China. At this temple was a priest who worked charms against evil spirits and who also assiduously studied Ch'an (Zen). He was the kind of devotee who performed seated meditation (*zazen*) without sleeping and even passed up his evening meals. Since the priests who were his disciples were only allowed to drink tea, they carried small tea utensils in their robes and prepared tea for drinking wherever they might be.[1]

The present form of tea whisk was not used in those days. One simply boiled tea, added ginger to suit one's taste, and drank. The *Feng-shih wen-chien chi* informs us that, as people in general learned about tea drinking, they gradually made it a national custom. This did not necessarily mark the start of the merger of Zen and tea; but, in any event, there was no doubt at least some contact between the two during the time of Emperor Hsüan-tsung. This contact led, on the one hand, to the writing of the *Ch'a Ching*,[2] the oldest book about tea, by the T'ang period literatus Lu Yü and, on the other hand, to the compilation by Po-chang Huai-hai of the *Po-chang ch'ing-kuei*, which established the tie between Zen and tea. The original text of the *Po-chang ch'ing-kuei* no longer exists, but we have the *Ch'ih-hsiu Po-chang ch'ing-kuei*, which was compiled in 1336 by Tung-yang Te-hui at the order of the Yüan dynasty emperor Shun.[3] A perusal of Tung-yang's work shows us how important tea was at Ch'an institutions in China.

Tea was first brought to Japan by priests who went to T'ang China, men such as Saichō, Kūkai, and Eichū. In T'ang times, however, the form of tea that was drunk was *dancha* (brick tea), and the method of its preparation differed considerably from that seen in *chanoyu* today.[4] Later, the rules of *matcha* (powdered tea), formulated during the Sung dynasty, were introduced to Japan by the Zen priest Eisai. In the preface of the *Kissa Yōjōki*, Eisai stresses the extraordinary medicinal value of a cup of tea, observing that "tea is an elixir for the maintenance of life."[5] That the priests of Kamakura-period Buddhism believed in tea as a medicine can be noted in the *Shasekishū*, written by Mujū, a disciple of Enni Ben'en (Shōichi Kokushi), the founder of Tōfukuji Temple.

The custom of tea drinking gradually spread, and an elegant game called *tōcha* (tea competition) was devised as discussed in Murai Yasuhiko's essay in Chapter 1. This game developed as an extremely important setting for communication among people who shared a cup of tea and sought to bring about mutual understanding among themselves. During the Muromachi period, tea drinking evolved according to rules based on use of the *daisu* portable stand in the *shoin*-style room. At the same time, it became popular among the commoner classes to buy tea at the rate of "a cup for a copper."

Chanoyu utilizing the *daisu* in a *shoin*-style room was begun in the era of the sixth Ashikaga shogun, Yoshinori, and was perfected by Nōami during the age of the eighth shogun, Yoshimasa. It was also during Yoshimasa's time that Murata Shukō, a native of Nara, conceived of a new kind of *chanoyu* called *sōan-cha* (literally, tea in a hut), which was subsequently brought to its highest level as *wabicha*. *Sōan-cha* differed from *tōcha*, with its playful quality, and from the sumptuous form of *chanoyu* based on the use of *karamono* (things Chinese) and the *daisu* stand. Utensils were kept to a minimum, and attention was given especially to the spiritual. As a result of the creation of *sōan-cha*, the world of tea itself was altered.

In regard to Shukō's tea, the *Yamanoue Sōji Ki* informs us that "Shukō received a scroll from the abbot Ikkyū bearing the calligraphy of Yüan-wu K'o-ch'in (Engo Kokugon) and derived great pleasure from it. The essence of Buddhism is in the way of tea."[6] Shukō studied Zen with Ikkyū, and in observing that "the essence of Buddhism is in the way of tea" reflected on the spiritual similarities between Buddhist practice and the pursuit of *chanoyu*. No doubt it was with the same determination to achieve enlightenment through Buddhism that Shukō turned to *chanoyu*.

Zen teaches that one can attempt, especially by means of *zazen* and the *kōan*, to enter the realms of "nothingness" (*mu*) and "emptiness" (*kū*). In the same way, one seeks in *chanoyu* to enter these realms by handling various utensils and by the step-by-step process of apportioning powdered tea, pouring hot water, and stirring it with a whisk. It was because he understood that "tea flavor and Zen flavor are the same" that Shukō was able to achieve enlightenment.

Upon hearing of Shukō's tea, Yoshimasa summoned him and asked: "What sort of thing is this *chanoyu* that you perform? What are its secrets?" Shukō replied: "Tea is 'in all, pure' and takes 'joy in meditation and delight in the dharma.' Chao-chou followed these injunctions well. And didn't Lu Yü exemplify them in the highest degree?"[7] Shukō taught that if one devotes oneself fully to the preparation of tea and enters into profound contemplation (*sanmai*) in *chanoyu*, the same realms will be opened as are opened in the practice of Buddhism.

TO ACQUIRE THE SPIRIT FROM THE ONE

Within traditional culture, *chanoyu* possesses qualities that set it apart from the other arts. In the *nō* and *kabuki* theaters, for example, the focus is on a stage, and performers and audiences face each other from different positions. In *chanoyu* this is not the case, inasmuch as host and guests occupy the same places. Moreover, both host and guests join together in the tea room and seek mutually to make the moment by their feelings toward each other. The tea room is a real-life setting for the important practice in the way of Zen of seeking oneness of host and guests and, at the same time, distinguishing clearly between guests and host.[8] The host must present his own bowl with sincere feelings to his guests.

There are some who are content if, in performing *chanoyu*, they are simply guided by proper procedure and carry it out smoothly without making a mistake. I too am pleased if *chanoyu* is carried out smoothly, but this is not all there is to the way of tea. It does not matter if one makes a mistake or forgets the procedure of *chanoyu*. One should be calm and composed in reflecting on what to do next. I am reminded of an incident involving a certain amateur (*sukisha*) of *chanoyu*. I was invited, along with the late *iemoto*, to attend one of his tea gatherings. He had thoroughly practiced, beginning with the laying of the charcoal fire (*sumi-demae*), for the day's gathering. But when the late *iemoto* and I entered the tea room and it came to his actually carrying out the *temae*, he was unable to proceed. After taking the first step, he did not continue. Instead, he turned his head to one side and stopped to think. The late *iemoto* instructed him: "Don't worry. Don't worry. Use the feather duster next." Saying "Oh, that's right," the man took the duster and began again, but again he stopped and thought once and then twice. His demeanor was exceedingly unaffected, though, and the late *iemoto* was moved to suggest that the tea room be named Isshian (Hut of One Thought). And indeed the man came to use that name for his tea room.

In *chanoyu* it is not so important that the procedure be performed with utmost precision. Rather, the need to reflect once or twice can have a positive effect, giving rise to an atmosphere of profound contemplation by host and guests. In the opinion of some, mistakes made in the performance of *chanoyu* may even become the fondest of memories. That is what *chanoyu* is about.

The *Nampōroku* records that Rikyū said: "Tea is based on reasoning and an understanding of things. Even if it is reasoning easily understood by a child, one must not ignore it."[9] This not only means that in *chanoyu* it is necessary to have the kind of humble sense that will enable one to bow one's head even to a three-year-old child, but also reminds us that all the rules and steps of *chanoyu* have a practical reason.

Rikyū taught the importance of going back to the thinking of the beginner and "acquiring spirit from the beginning." Therein lies the notion that "tea flavor and Zen flavor are the same." This phrase was even used as the title of a book by Rikyū's successor in the third generation, Sōtan, who vigorously asserted the oneness of *chanoyu* and Zen.[10]

When we speak of tea and Zen having the same flavor, it is generally thought that this idea was first advanced by a Daitokuji priest. Actually, the earliest reference we have in the records is by Daikyū Sōkyū, the twenty-fifth head of Myōshinji. The builder of Reiun'in at

Myōshinji, Daikyū wrote in his collected sayings *(Kentōroku):* "The priest Shōgen said in a poem in the stories about tea that 'tea can also have the flavor of Zen'."[11] This remark suggests that *chanoyu* must possess the flavor of Zen. And indeed the ties between the Zen sect and tea are very old and profound.

THE FLAVOR OF PEACE

The practice, first begun by Shukō, of regarding tea flavor and Zen flavor as one gradually penetrated with the passage of time deeply into the sensibilities of the Japanese people. The *Nampōroku* records that Rikyū emphatically stated: "*Chanoyu* performed in a plain hut is above all an ascetic discipline, based on the Buddhist Law, that is aimed at spiritual deliverance."[12] It is thus understandable why generations of tea masters have gone to Daitokuji to study and practice Zen and to receive priestly names.

When asked what, in particular, was the tea spirit advocated in *sōan chanoyu,* Shukō replied: "It is good to have a splendid steed tethered to a straw-thatched hut."[13] This is the same as speaking out for the blending of *wamono* (things Japanese) and *karamono* (things Chinese). I have often said that one ought to practice a "touch of luxuriousness," by which I mean to agree with Shukō's suggestion that "it is good to have a splendid steed tethered to a straw-thatched hut." This should be possible whatever one's financial means.

One of the joys and challenges of *chanoyu* is to assemble, here and there, the equipment for it. That is why it is thought best to perform *chanoyu* according to your situation and to nurture the ability to devise whatever you can.

Some thirty years ago, when I first traveled abroad with my wife, conditions were quite difficult. Nowadays, there are Urasenke branches throughout the world, and utensils and portable tea rooms are readily available. But in those days we truly traveled around carrying our own matting, braziers, and kettles. Since the matting was of an unusual kind, we would be asked to leave it and would do so. But when we went to the next place, there would be no matting. We would then hastily have to make one or two "*tatami*" by spreading out bedsheets and using black tape on them. And even though we had a brazier and kettle, there might be no board *(shikiita)* on which to put them. On such occasions we were obliged to borrow a tray from the Japanese embassy or consulate-general and would use it as a makeshift *shikiita*. I can speak of these things because I have had to make do with all kinds of equipment in order to demonstrate *chanoyu*.

Among the experiences I can never forget was the time I served tea during the war as a member of the special attack unit of the naval air force. Since I was told that they wanted everyone to have a cup of tea before setting out on a mission, I performed *chanoyu* using my special box of tea utensils. All of the pilots drank the tea I prepared, sitting cross-legged in their flight uniforms. Finishing with words of appreciation for the tea, many of the group departed on their mission. My comrades launched their attack the following day, and I thought that perhaps I might be obliged to do the same the day after. I wondered if I would be able to drink tea with true equanimity as my comrades had. At that time I felt intensely the rare sense of peace and harmony in a cup of tea.

Shukō said that "the moon is uninteresting unless partly obscured by clouds."[14] There is no perfection among people. Whoever they may be, they are imperfect. How are such imperfect people to overcome their language barriers and transcend differences in customs and practices to come together? Surely there is nothing easy about practicing seated meditation and understanding each other's minds or about achieving oneness through a bowl of tea. The main thing is the human mind seeking peace, whether in the spirit of seated meditation or sitting to drink tea. Nothing should be too perfect. It is imperfection that truly matters.

THE *WABI* SPIRIT

Jōō, who inherited the tradition of Shukō, selected this poem by Fujiwara no Teika to illustrate the nature of *wabi*:

> As I look about me,
> I see no blossoms
> Or crimson leaves.
> Autumn at nightfall
> In a straw-thatched hut by the bay.[15]

In the "Letter on *Wabi*," which Jōō is said to have sent to Rikyū, it says: "*Wabi* consists of honesty and being deeply discreet without displaying pride." Later, Rikyū revealed that his own sense of *wabi* differed from that of his teacher, Jōō, as suggested in the following poem by Fujiwara no Ietaka:

> To those who await
> Only the cherry blossoms
> One should show the grasses of spring
> Emerging through the snow
> In a mountain village.[16]

Rikyū used this poem to illustrate his feeling that *wabi* is a force that springs forth naturally, a true spirit that searches out the truth.

Hisamatsu Shin'ichi sought to explain, in terms of seven qualities, the *wabi* and *sabi* aesthetics that Rikyū perceived in Ietaka's poem.[17] Let me discuss these qualities. First there is asymmetry, that which is not balanced or symmetrical—in other words, the imperfect or incomplete. Yet even though we may speak of, let us say, the incomplete, there arises the question of whether this means an incompleteness that goes *beyond* the complete or does not extend *to* it. As remarked earlier, the spirit contained in such phrases as "a splendid steed tethered to a straw-thatched hut" and "the moon is uninteresting unless partly obscured by clouds" is of great importance in the arranging of tea utensils. The moon shining brightly is beautiful. But when the moon is suddenly covered by veil-like clouds and its light beams only faintly, therein lies a loveliness of inexpressible subtlety. Is this not one aspect of the sensibility of *wabi*?

Second, there is the quality of simplicity. Instead of elaborateness and ostentation, we find extreme directness and plainness. This can perhaps best be understood by citing the architectural style of the tea room as representative of simplicity.

The third quality is "wizened austerity," which is the spirit of *sabi*. One time, when I asked my old master Gotō Zuigan about *sabi*, he said: "Look at that pond over there." Although I gazed at the pond—located at the Daijuin—for some time,[18] I got no sense of the meaning of *sabi*. I told the master that I had looked at the pond, and he asked me if I now understood. When I said no, he instructed me to continue to look. I returned to the edge of the pond and seated myself in the *zazen* position atop a rock. It was midwinter and there were withered lotus blossoms on the surface of the water. Suddenly I realized that the blossoms were not simply withered: The next stage of their natural beauty was in the process of developing. I understood then that this was the spirit of *sabi*. And I thought that the vital force one senses is about to emerge in Ietaka's poem ("To those who await/Only the cherry blossoms . . .") must surely be *sabi*.

The fourth quality of the *wabi* and *sabi* realm of aesthetics is naturalness, including innocence, freedom from extraneous thoughts, and being without artifice. Rikyū said: "For the host and guest together to achieve something is good. To wish to achieve something is bad."[19] *Chanoyu* is not something to be performed by means of conscious effort. But although one should not exert effort in the performance of *chanoyu*, it is of course necessary to be conscious of one's guests. In other words, one must be unconsciously conscious of what one is doing. Herein lies that exceedingly difficult meeting of the minds which we find in the *kōan*: "The withered tree clings to the frozen rocks: midwinter and no warmth at all."[20] This is something we can aim for, but it is very hard to achieve.

The fifth quality of *wabi-sabi* is *yūgen* and elegance (*okuyukashisa*): subtle profundity. *Chanoyu Ichie Shū* contains the phrase "resonances and aftertaste" (*yojō zanshin*).[21] Tea is a meeting of *yin* and *yang*, and *chanoyu* has a well-defined order based on a shifting from *yin* to *yang* and *yang* to *yin*. When the right hand takes the tea scoop, the left hand takes the caddy. When you believe that the caddy's lid has been removed, you find that the tea is already in the cup. When the tea is in the cup, the water is ladled and the whisk is taken. In this way, one moment flows steadily into another, and the host is able to draw the guests firmly into the event.

The sixth *wabi-sabi* quality is unworldliness and unconditional freedom. In the *Lotus Sutra* are these words: "He had left the burning house of the three worlds and dwells now in the pristine garden (*roji*)."[22] To leave the *roji* and take one's seat at *chanoyu* is the same as escaping the afflicted world of desire and becoming a person without rank in this existence. Therein lies true "unconditional freedom."

I concur wholeheartedly with the claim that the way of tea is a spiritual catharsis. Indeed it must be such a catharsis. When, for example, you are cleaning the scoop, caddy, and whisk with a *fukusa*, you are also cleansing yourself. I am convinced, in other words, that you must be aware that you possess a devoted spirit of belief of the same kind you have when receiving purification before the gods *(kami)*.

The seventh and final quality of *wabi* and *sabi* aesthetics is calm and tranquility in the true sense of these words. I completely agree with Hisamatsu Shin'ichi when he suggests that such calm and tranquility represent an inwardly turned spirituality.[23] The flavor of such spirituality is something you must create yourself. And therein lies its close association with Zen. *Nampōroku* says that "*wabi* reveals a Buddha realm of perfect purity."[24] We must understand it to be a form of secularization of the Buddha's principles.

TO CONCENTRATE ON PEACE

The preparation of tea has a pattern. But we must remember that along with a pattern it also has a shape. The two are different. Pattern is the structure you see with your eyes. The practice of *temae* begins with a pattern. It is only after the *temae* becomes fully part of you and you lose yourself in it that it takes a shape and the shape becomes form *(katachi)*. That is, the *temae* becomes something spiritual.

The late *iemoto* cautioned me not to do the *temae* with only my fingers but with my entire body. I was told that I must hurl myself into the *temae*, pour my very blood into it. It is then that pattern becomes shape and shape becomes form. To put it in other words, we are presented with a *kōan*. By transcending this *kōan*, are we not able for the first time to enter the realm of enlightenment *(satori)*?

It is, of course, an extremely difficult matter to achieve enlightenment. Yet I believe it is important during one's busy day to try sitting for ten or even five minutes. It is good to prepare tea yourself or to be served by others. If you are able to maintain your own proper form and also judge your feelings, you should not have much trouble. Do you not agree that, in the manner of bringing good fortune to all people, everyone can pray more and more for peace? Thus I pray that our *chanoyu* will become an ever more important medium for social communion and that the way of tea will serve the purposes of world peace.

NOTES

1. *Feng-shih wen-chien chi* is in folio 6 of the "tea drinking" section of Ts'ao Jung, comp., *Hsüeh-hai lei-pien*, vol. 67 (Shanghai reprint, 1920).
2. *Ch'a Ching* can be found in Sen Sōshitsu, ed., *Chadō Koten Zenshū*, vol. 1 (Kyoto: Tankōsha, 1957).
3. *Ch'ih-hsui Po-chang ch'ing-kuei* can be found in Sen Sōshitsu, ed., *Chadō Koten Zenshū*, vol. 1.
4. The handling of *dancha* is described in Lu Yü's *Ch'a Ching*.
5. Sen Sōshitsu, ed., *Chadō Koten Zenshū*, vol. 2 (Kyoto: Tankōsha, 1958), p. 4.
6. Yamanoue Sōji, *Yamanoue Sōji Ki*, in Sen Sōshitsu, ed., *Chadō Koten Zenshū*, vol. 6 (Kyoto: Tankōsha, 1958), p. 52.
7. This conversation between Yoshimasa and Shukō is a traditional attribution and is not based on a known written source.
8. This practice is based on a *kōan*. See Haga Kōshirō, *Zoku-Zoku Ichigyō Mono* (Kyoto: Tankōsha, 1980), pp. 74–78.
9. See Kumakura Isao, *Nampōroku o Yomu* (Kyoto: Tankōsha, 1983), pp. 33–35.
10. *Cha-Zen Dōichi Mi*. It is also known as *Zen-cha Roku*. See Sen Sōshitsu, ed., *Chadō Koten Zenshū*, vol. 10 (Kyoto: Tankōsha, 1961).
11. Daikyū Sōkyū, *Kentōroku*, in *Kokuyaku Zengaku Taisei*, vol. 24 (Tokyo: Nishōdō Shoten, 1930), p. 44.
12. Nambō Sōkei, *Nampōroku*, in Sen Sōshitsu, ed., *Chadō Koten Zenshū*, vol. 4 (Kyoto: Tankōsha, 1956), p. 3.
13. Yamanoue Sōji, *Yamanoue Sōji Ki*, in Sen Sōshitsu, ed., *Chadō Koten Zenshū*, vol. 6, p. 101.
14. Kitakawa Tadahiko, ed., *Zenpō Zatsudan*, in Hayashiya Tatsusaburō, ed., *Kodai Chūsei Gejitsu Ron* (Tokyo: Iwanami Shoten, 1973), p. 480.
15. Nambō Sōkei, *Nampōroku*, in Sen Sōshitsu, ed., *Chadō Koten Zenshū*, vol. 4, p. 16.
16. Ibid.
17. Hisamatsu Shin'ichi, "Chadō Bunka no Seikaku," in *Chadō no Tetsugaku* (Tokyo: Risōsha, 1973), pp. 59–69.
18. The Daijuin is located near Ryōanji Temple in northwestern Kyoto.
19. Nambō Sōkei, *Nampōroku*, in Sen Sōshitsu, ed., *Chadō Koten Zenshū*, vol. 4, p. 5.
20. *Koboku kangan ni yoru santō danki nashi*; see Haga Kōshirō, *Zoku-zoku Ichigyō Mono*, pp. 110–113.
21. *Chanoyu Ichie Shū*, by the late Tokugawa period statesman Ii Naosuke, is contained in Sen Sōshitsu, ed., *Chadō Koten Zenshū*, vol. 10.
22. The parable of the burning house from the *Lotus Sutra* can be found in David John Lu, *Sources of Japanese History* (New York: McGraw-Hill, 1974), vol. 1, pp. 52–54.
23. Hisamatsu Shin'ichi, "Chadō Bunka no Seikaku," in *Chadō no Tetsugaku*, p. 66.
24. Nambō Sōkei, *Nampōroku*, in Sen Sōshitsu, ed., *Chadō Koten Zenshū*, vol. 4, p. 264.

NINE

ON THE FUTURE HISTORY OF TEA

John Whitney Hall

M^Y last bowl of tea in Japan was received from the hands of Grand Master Sen just over a year ago at Konnichian. It was a magical day. My wife Robin and I had just visited Shūgakuin in the rain, and water was still dripping from the trees and shrubs along the stone walkway leading to the teahouse. It was one of those special occasions when man and nature conspired to design a perfect setting for tea and the sharing of artful thoughts.

Today the setting is different. Here we are brought together as scholars to inquire into the history of *chanoyu*. The fact that a volume of this sort could be organized would have been unthinkable twenty-five or even fifteen years ago. On top of that the quality of these essays is astonishing. What is an amateur to say?

The theme of this volume is the *history* of tea, and in keeping with that theme we are invited to look back to origins and to the tea masters who gave it the form we know as *chanoyu*. But history is not confined to the past. It informs the present and it shapes the future. Indeed, we are making an episode in the history of *chanoyu* today as we offer these essays, and we are also making its future as we project our thoughts beyond the present. It is particularly on the future history of tea that I wish to comment. And I would ask: Knowing the past history of *chanoyu*, where is that history taking tea? Above all, what future does tea have in the world outside Japan? Is it indeed the cup that will bring peace to mankind? There is no simple answer, but the question should be kept before us.

I write not as a specialist on *chanoyu*, not as one who has seriously taken lessons from a certified instructor nor followed closely the recent attempts to philosophize on the deeper meaning of the tea ceremony. Rather, I am one who has been passively exposed to *chanoyu* in a variety of forms, in numerous places, during a number of years of residence in Japan going back to the 1930s. Now, as time has passed, I realize that these experiences—which took place mainly in Kyoto in a social climate in which the serving of *matcha* was a customary accompaniment to attending *nō* performances, visiting temples on festival days, or viewing painting or floral arrangement displays, that is, as a simple form of social communication among friends—have had a deep and lasting influence on my personal aesthetic values. I realize that I have been programmed, and I like it. Without being a specialist, either academic or practiced, I have nonetheless presumed that the story of my involvement with tea might be of interest to others and might cast light on the questions I have asked.

In reflecting on *chanoyu* and its influence on me, I realize that the actual preparation and drinking of tea is not the most essential element for those living outside Japan. For one thing, it is difficult for the casual participant to assemble the necessary ingredients. Although one can arrange for air-delivered frozen powdered tea and *yōkan* will keep in the refrigerator for months, it takes a deliberate and persistent effort. And there are few of us who have at our disposal a private teahouse. Thus I find that the elements of my tea experience that most clearly carry over from Japan to America are the intangible aspects of what is sometimes called "tea taste." I realize that I have adopted certain perceptions that apply to the ordering of one's home garden, particularly with respect to the relationships of natural objects, such as bushes and rocks, to the house. These perceptions apply as well to the house interior, affecting the manner of distributing and arranging such things as paintings, flowers and their containers, ceramic objects, and other pieces of decorative art. In particular I find myself committed to the principle that all decorative objects must be original, handcrafted pieces, that clutter should be avoided, and that asymmetry is preferable to symmetry.

This brings me to a *kōan*-type question: If the most important aspect of tea is not tea, then what is the essence of tea? The answer, of course, is that there are two teas: the simple drinking of tea and the ritual of tea drinking (*chanoyu*). And it is the latter that engages our attention here. As we look to the future, critical questions come to mind: How inextricably is *chanoyu* tied to Japanese culture? How many of its essential ingredients can be had only in Japan? What does it take to experience *chanoyu?* How much of this can a novice expect to feel? How much of the *chanoyu* syndrome can be exported? What elements of the tea syndrome can be subtracted without destroying its essence? Can one do without *kimono, tatami,* the teahouse? Tea, of course, is many things to many people. The effort to universalize, or rather to internalize, *chanoyu* by such people as the present head of the Urasenke and his father has done a great deal to answer some of these questions. They have begun the difficult process of communication across cultural borders. Witness, for example, the circulation of *Chanoyu Quarterly* and the establishment of tea ceremony chapters abroad. The task is not easy and it has only just begun.

The internationalization of certain domestic art forms and activities such as *chanoyu,* flower arrangement, *karate,* or ceramics has been phenomenal in the years following the Pacific War. Among such art forms, *chanoyu* is certainly one of the most difficult to detach from the Japanese cultural matrix. It cannot be appreciated from a book, whereas anyone can use the beautiful calendars sent out by the consul generals as models for *ikebana*-style flower arrangements. Flowers and pots are essentially universal. The ingredients of the tea ceremony, however, are part of the Japanese cultural environment. I assume that one has to have experienced the real thing before one can acquire even a rudimentary understanding of the tea ceremony or before one can define one's private commitment to *chanoyu.* The fundamental point is that the tea ceremony is greater than its parts. I suspect that for every tea addict there has been a breakthrough encounter, a private *satori* of some sort.

For even the casual participant, or the perpetual guest as I must categorize myself, one should have taken some lessons, to have felt the softness of a silk kimono on one's skin, to have felt the give of *tatami* under one's feet, to have entered an environment in which the sound of boiling water in an iron kettle can seem deafening and the sound of a bamboo water dipper being replaced on its holder an audible statement. One has to have walked through gardens of rocks and trees, have appreciated the way the teahouse exposes the beauty of natural materials, have had the opportunity to handle tea bowls, feeling the living intent of an ancient potter. All of this can be experienced best in Japan, especially in Kyoto, but not only there. Teahouses have been built in numerous places in the United States. There are several in Hawaii, beginning with Seikōan built in 1955. Most recently we have the remarkable assemblage of tea rooms built for the Urasenke Chanoyu Center in Manhattan. So one can experience nearly all the sensations of a model tea ceremony without having to go to Japan.

Things were quite different in the prewar years. There were, to be sure, a number of efforts to demonstrate Japanese tea taste in architecture and gardens at times of international expositions, and a few Americans made something of an exotic Orientalism out of collections of Japanese art. But the flow of experts and teachers and their followers between Japan and America was insignificant. Appreciation of "Japanese culture" was still an exotic taste pursued mainly by those with sufficient wealth to engage in art collecting or the installation of Japanese gardens. Tea was known and appreciated in the Boston group led by Ernest Fenollosa and Okakura Kakuzō, but it never took root.

As for foreigners who lived in Japan, missionaries for the most part, Japanese culture was not a deep attraction. Whereas, in Japan today, anyone intending to stay for any length of time is encouraged to take up some form of Japanese domestic art, in the prewar years this was the exception. For missionaries especially, and they were the most numerous long-term foreign residents, interest in Japanese culture was not encouraged. Missionaries were in Japan to teach, not to learn. Their mission was to exemplify Christian life. Fortunately, my parents were exceptional in that they pursued a number of private interests. My father studied *nō* drama, befriending the great actor Kongō Iwao. My mother studied *ikebana* and *bonseki*, but not *chanoyu*. These were pastimes that could be practiced in our Western-style home. *Chanoyu* required more instruction in Japanese and necessitated going to a teacher's home. I do not believe any missionary at that time had converted any room at home into a *tatami* room. Even the elements of the *chanoyu* syndrome, utensils like bowls and kettles, were not a major attraction. Tea bowls were of little practical use in a Western-style home. And since missionaries did not smoke, there was little need to set out pottery ash trays. Foreigners collected Imari and Kutani porcelain. Living in Japan they nonetheless collected these types of export ware.

My mother was not oblivious to the tea ceremony. She was probably quite typical in taking a romantic view of tea taste. Her favorite reading in this context was Okakura Kakuzō's *The Book of Tea*, a work I shall comment on shortly. My family returned to America permanently in 1932, at which point my ties with Japan were completely severed until 1939 when, after graduation from Amherst College, I returned to Kyoto to serve as Amherst's representative at Dōshisha University. I had been able to retain a vague and romantic sense of admiration for things Japanese during this time, but it was highly undifferentiated. At Amherst College there was no academic program that dealt with Japan. My personal search for a nonmissionary career related to Japan was met with skepticism, even ridicule. Of course these were years when relations between America and Japan were becoming increasingly unfriendly, and there was in 1938 and 1939 a strong undercurrent of anti-Japanese feeling among the Amherst student body and the Amherst-in-Japan program was looked upon with increasing hostility. So my desire to go to Japan as Amherst's representative to learn, rather than teach, was a secret I kept in my heart.

Fortunately for me, the Dōshisha program was kept alive for my incumbency as Amherst's last representative before the war. I served from August 1939 to October 1941. During those two years I began a course of study about Japan on my own initiative. Apart from receiving tutoring in the Japanese language, I renewed contacts with Kongō Iwao and engaged my mother's former flower arrangement teacher, a sake-drinking, bewhiskered, seventy-year-old gentleman. And since Amherst House was so close to Shōkokuji, I joined a *chanoyu* club at one of its subtemples. Other members of the class were either Dōshisha or Kyoto University professors.

As I reflect upon it, my prewar experience with tea was such that the ceremony itself was largely incidental to the serious discussion of Japanese aesthetics, the appreciation of ceramics and other tea utensils. There was little standing on ceremony, although one quickly learned when to direct silent attention to the host at the critical moments in the preparation of the bowl for drinking. I realize now that this was strictly an elitist approach to *chanoyu*. And since I had no intention of learning the full ritual, I was free to adopt a rather superior attitude toward girls giggling with embarrassment for fear of making mistakes or the social climber types who oversold the rarity, and hence value, of the tea bowls brought out for the occasion. By taking the emphasis off the ritual and placing it on the human and intellectual interaction, our experience was secularized; but it also had broad appeal and lasting influence. I believe I was given a view of the human and universal sides of *chanoyu*.

But how should this be put into words? Recent publications and training programs emanating from the Urasenke Foundation have gone a long way in opening *chanoyu* to a worldwide clientele. One should not assume that even a fraction of the information about tea has been available for more than a few decades. Indeed, in the years before the Pacific War there were only two works in the English language relating to tea. The first was Okakura's *The Book of Tea*, first published in 1906. The other was Arthur Sadler's *Cha-no-yu*, published in 1934. Sadler's was a dry, academic presentation of the history of *chanoyu* together with anecdotes about former tea masters. Useful as a reference work, it did very little to reveal either the aesthetic or human qualities of *chanoyu*.

By contrast, Okakura's book was heavy on romantic sentimentality about Eastern values. It was also filled with biting criticism of Western culture. Since this writing was so much a part of my home upbringing in my youth—it awakened in me an awareness of certain aspects of tea aesthetics that greatly attracted me while, at the same time, it reinforced my deep aversion to sentimentality and the aura of exoticism that clung to American appreciation of Japanese art—I trust I will be excused for citing certain passages from this work.

In his chapter entitled "The Cup of Humanity" Okakura chides the West for its lack of understanding of Japanese aesthetics, relating this attitude to problems of international war and peace:

> The average Westerner, in his sleek complacency, will see in the tea ceremony but another instance of the thousand and one oddities which constitute the quaintness and childishness of the East to him. He was wont to regard Japan as barbarous while she indulged in the gentle arts of peace: he calls her civilized since she began to commit wholesale slaughter on Manchurian battlefields. . . . When will the West understand, or try to understand, the East? . . . Unfortunately the Western attitude is unfavorable to the understanding of the East. The Christian missionary goes to impart, but not to receive. . . . So much harm has been done already by the mutual misunderstanding of the New World and the Old. . . . The beginning of the twentieth century would have been spared the spectacle of sanguinary warfare if Russia had condescended to know Japan better.[1]

Such was Okakura's confidence in the power of tea to maintain world peace. A more reasonable and more telling sentiment was expressed in his chapter on the tea room:

The tea-room is absolutely empty, except for what may be placed there temporarily to satisfy some aesthetic mood. Some special art object is brought in for the occasion, and everything else is selected and arranged to enhance the beauty of the principal theme. One cannot listen to different pieces of music at the same time, a real comprehension of the beautiful being possible only through concentration upon some central motive. Thus it will be seen that the system of decoration in our tea-room is opposed to that which obtains in the West, where the interior of a house is often converted into a museum. To a Japanese, accustomed to simplicity of ornamentation and frequent change of decorative method, a Western interior permanently filled with a vast array of pictures, statuary, and bric-à-brac gives the impression of mere vulgar display of riches.[2]

Okakura was spared the experience of staying at a country inn, as I did recently, in which the prize pieces of decoration in the alcove were a television set and a small refrigerator filled with self-service drinks.

The passages in Okakura that could bring tears to my mother's eyes (but which I found unbearable) were in his chapter on flowers. Here is a particularly maudlin example:

Tell me, gentle flowers, teardrops of the stars, standing in the garden, nodding your heads to the bees as they sing of the dews and the sunbeams, are you aware of the fearful doom that awaits you? Dream on, sway and frolic while you may. . . . Tomorrow a ruthless hand will close around your throats. You will be wrenched, torn asunder limb by limb, and borne away from your quiet homes. The wretch, she may be passing fair. She may say how lovely you are while her fingers are still moist with your blood. Tell me, will this be kindness? . . .

The wanton waste of flowers among Western communities is even more appalling than the way they are treated by Eastern Flower Masters. The number of flowers cut daily to adorn the ballrooms and banquet-tables of Europe and America, to be thrown away on the morrow, must be something enormous. Beside this utter carelessness of life, the guilt of the Flower Master becomes insignificant. He, at least, respects the economy of nature, selects his victims with careful foresight, and after death does honor to their remains. In the West the display of flowers seems to be a part of the pageantry of wealth—the fancy of a moment.[3]

Such sentimentality was not for all. And for one who took the hard line toward Japanese culture, Basil Hall Chamberlain, in his *Things*

Japanese, offered a strong corrective to Okakura, an authority, by the way, whom he failed to acknowledge:

> The doctrine and discipline of the tea ceremonies in their modern form . . . has never varied since Sen-no-Rikyū's day. Though not the St. Paul of the tea cult, he was thus its Luther.
>
> The ceremonies themselves have often been described. They include a preliminary dinner, but tea-drinking is the chief thing. The tea used is in the form, not of tea-leaves but of powder, so that the resulting beverage resembles pea-soup in color and consistency.* (*Foreign *gourmets* resident in Japan have discovered that a delicious ice-cream can be made out of it.)
>
> To a European the ceremony is lengthy and meaningless. When witnessed more than once, it becomes intolerably monotonous. Not being born with an Oriental fund of patience, he longs for something new, something lively, something with at least the semblance of logic and utility. But then it is not for him that the tea ceremonies were made. If they amuse those for whom they were made, they amuse them, and there is nothing more to be said. In any case, tea and ceremonies are perfectly harmless, which is more than can be affirmed of tea and tattle. . . . If the tea ceremonies do not go the length of embodying a "philosophy," as fabled by some of their admirers, they have, at least in their latest form, assisted the cause of purity in art. Some may deem them pointless. None can stigmatize them as vulgar.[4]

Since World War II the scene has changed dramatically, and for obvious reasons. One by-product of the Pacific War was the crash effort of the American armed forces to set up programs of language study. In the navy the basic textbooks in Japanese language were the Naganuma readers that relied heavily on the Japanese elementary school texts. As the Boulder Language School turned out U.S. Navy language officers, they inadvertently turned out men who were strongly pro-"Japanese culture." The Occupation years helped make total converts out of many such Americans. It was in this context that the phenomenal surge in Japanese studies developed in America.

Much of the postwar boom of interest in things Japanese was ephemeral and gave rise to fads that soon faded. In this context I think of the *shibui* boom of the 1960s. This was started by *House Beautiful,* which devoted its August 1960 issue to the theme "Discover *Shibui,* the Word for the Highest Level in Beauty." The issue had a photograph of the Katsura Palace on its cover. The articles on restrained tea taste decor were well presented and well illustrated, though the impression was given that all Japanese lived in multi-*tatami* rooms with attached garden and kimono-clad women waiting on the male members of the family. Among the articles was Anthony West's contribution on "What Japan has that we may profitably borrow: They have serenity and tranquility in their moments at home. There are secrets about how to do it wherever you are." For the most part the treatment was straightforward. The faddistic quality came through most clearly in the September issue, dedicated to the theme "How to Be *Shibui* with American Things." Again the emphasis was on interior decor in restrained colors. And, of course, if one couldn't have *tatami* one could simulate the effect by having wall-to-wall gold carpeting with black stripes running through it at three-foot intervals. Some of the faddists' responses to the *shibui* boom could not be blamed on *House Beautiful*—*shibui* perfumes and lotions immediately made their appearance as well as *shibui* hotels. My favorite piece of travel-agent literature comes from the Shibui Hotel on St. Thomas, which advertised:

> Your *shibui* bathroom. A grand 8' × 13', it is bordered by the refreshing green of an indoor rock garden. Here in the deeply sunken ceramic tub, be tempted to linger with a book, a drink, relaxing in pampered peace.

Meanwhile, a remarkable development was taking place quietly and professionally through the efforts of the Urasenke Foundation and the internationally extended Urasenke organization. The Hawaii Chapter of Urasenke was founded in 1952. In 1971 the appearance of Rand Castile's *The Way of Tea* marked the high point to that time in the presentation to a world audience of the essentials of the tea ceremony, its history, its meaning, and its practice. The contrast between Sadler and Castile shows how far we have come in the postwar era. This achievement was furthered by the 1979 exhibition of tea implements shown at the Honolulu Academy of Art and the Japan House Gallery. But the problem of explaining through the written or spoken word the deeper meaning of tea was not completely solved.

Explanation of their traditional arts has never been easy for the Japanese. What are the special qualities possessed by *chanoyu* that make it so crucial to an understanding of Japanese aesthetics? Often the answer is expressed in words whose meanings are themselves locked in their own mysteries: "*Wabi*" is as unfathomable as "Zen." I recall an incident at an international congress held in Kyoto some years ago. For the wives of participants there were afternoon bus tours to occupy the time. One such tour was to discover Japan's traditional arts: a visit to Ryōanji, a glimpse of the *nō* theater, a visit to a tea ceremony. The explanatory material that went with the schedule explained *chanoyu* as follows. The tea ceremony is one of the most important Japanese art forms; to experience it is to experience the essence of Japan's traditional culture. Foreigners are warned that they may find the tea ceremony tedious and even uncomfortable. In fact, many Japanese find it hard to take. But for those from abroad who wish to experience Japanese culture, it is highly recommended that they attend a tea ceremony.

The other standard attempt to explain *chanoyu* is by evocation of the mystery of Zen. The essence of tea, it is claimed, is religious. In the tea room one enters an environment like that of a Zen meditation hall. Pushed too far, however, the skeptical foreign visitor is apt to respond as did Arthur Koestler in *The Lotus and the Robot*. Writing about Suzuki Daisetsu's *Zen and Japanese Culture*, Koestler quotes a passage in which Suzuki discusses the *satori* of teamanship as explained by Seisetsu, a Zen master of the late Tokugawa era:

> "My Tea is No-tea, which is not No-tea in opposition to Tea. What then is this No-tea? When a man enters into the exquisite realm of No-tea he will realize that No-tea is no other than the Great Way (*ta-tao*) itself . . ."
>
> Seisetsu's "No-tea" is a mysterious variation of the tea. He wants to reach the spirit of the art by way of negation. This is the logic of Prajna philosophy, which has sometimes been adopted by the Zen masters. As long as there is an event designated as "Tea" this will obscure our vision and hinder it from penetrating into "Tea" as it is in itself.[5]

Koestler retorts:

> There is one redeeming possibility: that all this drivel is deliberately intended to confuse the reader, since one of the avowed aims of Zen is to perplex and unhinge the rational mind. If this hypothesis were correct, Professor Suzuki's voluminous *oeuvre* of at least a million words, specially written for this purpose, would represent a hoax of truly heroic dimensions, and the laugh would be on the Western intellectuals who fell for it.[6]

The future of *chanoyu* will not rest upon the tea establishment's ability to convince the Arthur Koestlers of the world, but rather upon the self-recognition of certain evident but absolutely fundamental properties. Looking upon Japan from the outsider's perspective, as one who needs explanation, the most remarkable thing about *chanoyu* is surely the mere fact of its existence as an art form—that an art has been made out of a part of everyday life. As such, it is a phenomenon peculiar to Japanese society. *Chanoyu* takes its place alongside *ikebana* as a means of giving form to a domestic activity. It instills a new way of appreciating life, of making us look at the "art" in everyday things, and of bringing together the preparation of food and the admiration for flowers, gardens, interior and exterior architecture, ceramics, wood, lacquer, and metal objects, painting and calligraphy. Above all, it inculcates a sense of one's self within an artistic environment. It teaches how to express oneself through the artifacts one displays in one's house, and how to create new moods by changing one's environment to express one's own feelings or to suit one's guests. Finally, like flower arranging and *sumie*, it is an art form in which one can take pleasure as a complete amateur.

The other important feature of *chanoyu*, and other domestic art forms in Japan, is that it is kept alive and rooted in a tradition through the *iemoto* system—the mechanism whereby a school of activity is perpetuated through the head of a family that has the hereditary right to teach the tradition of a particular style of performance. The *iemoto* system has been criticized on grounds that it gives rise to inordinate formalism, that it fails to encourage creative innovation, that it is susceptible to abuse, commercialization, and the like. The system can give rise to all of these problems; but, in the case of tea, it seems to me it has worked well. The Urasenke *iemoto* in the last two generations have not only managed to retain traditional values and maintain certain standards, but have also led the way toward universalization and modernization. The activities of the Urasenke Foundation are exemplary in this respect.

As a domestic art form, tea, like other such pastimes, is vulnerable to vulgarization, neglect, and commercialization. In the modern world, where mechanization and mass production have taken over so much, honest craftmanship is fighting a losing war. One battle was won in the early decades of this century through what was called the craft movement. But craftsmanship is under attack by a new enemy called plastic—the "glob." The change from earthenware to plastic containers for the tea one buys at railroad stations, the change from bamboo leaf to plastic strip one finds in a *bentō*, these are only the first evidence of the new menace. Flower arrangement schools long ago succumbed to the modish use of artificial flowers, plastic ribbons, and metal strips in the effort to be modern. Tea has yet to be subverted. Perhaps it has inherent features that give it a capacity to resist such accommodation. But the inventive engineering mind has already created a robot tea server. And the computer has been introduced into the kiln. The day is soon coming when we can purchase a computerized clone of a Kōetsu bowl. Tea leaves are no longer picked solely by young village maids but by the electric hedge trimmer fitted with a suction bag. Next we shall see the prefabricated teahouse with plastic *tatami* facing. Historians will tell us that in this instance history has stolen a step on the future, for did not Toyotomi Hideyoshi take with him to his military headquarters for the invasion of Korea a gilded prefab tea hut with red velvet *tatami* facing?

Symbolic of *chanoyu*'s resistance to this trend is the single most exquisite object in the tea repertory, namely the *chasen*, tea whisk. It is a comfort to know that the *chasen* is still handcrafted from bamboo. What more absolute statement can be made about tea taste than that made by the *chasen* in the effortless simplicity with which it hides a most exacting technique? And what better putdown of the glob by tea taste could there be than the use the *chasen* has made of plastic—as a protective container? But this is as close as we dare let the glob approach. For if ever the tea whisk turns to plastic, the heart of *chanoyu* will have stopped beating and the future of tea will be past.

NOTES

1. Okakura Kakuzō, *The Book of Tea* (New York: Duffield, 1923), pp. 7–11.
2. Ibid., pp. 92–93.
3. Ibid., pp. 126–129.
4. Basil Hall Chamberlain, *Things Japanese* (London: John Murray, 1905), pp. 459–460.
5. Arthur Koestler, *The Lotus and the Robot* (New York: Macmillan, 1961), p. 255.
6. Ibid.

TEN

THE HISTORICAL SIGNIFICANCE
OF THE WAY OF TEA

William H. McNeill

IN reading the erudite contributions to this volume, I am reminded of one of those geometric line drawings that can be read in different ways. Everyone has seen figures that turn themselves inside out suddenly whenever the eye begins to interpret the lines in a different spatial matrix. *Wabi* seems to be like that. Conspicuous restraint, pressed to its limit, becomes flamboyant virtuosity; simplicity, valued highly enough, becomes luxury.

This is not really surprising. The way of tea, after all, has affinities with Buddhist ascetic traditions, and all asceticism rests upon a reversal of ordinary values. Yet no matter how earnestly it has been renounced, the world has a way of creeping in by the back door. Innumerable saints and would-be saints of every religious persuasion have discovered that self-denial can turn into egotistical self-indulgence simply by exciting too much admiration from others. Similarly, monks who renounce all personal possessions in order to become collectively wealthy are recaptured by the world through the very excess of their virtue. The ambivalences surrounding *wabi* and other key concepts of the way of tea therefore keep company with comparable ambiguities pervading full-blown ascetic traditions. *Wabi* should surely be studied against this background, but I must leave the task to more experienced persons.

What I can do is offer you an outsider's reaction to my most recent encounter with *chanoyu*. What did I learn? A very great deal, for until the Grand Master offered us his demonstration I had only once before been exposed to the way of tea. It was a tourist's exposure, lasting perhaps fifteen minutes, and conducted by a slim, kimono-clad hostess in the presence of utterly uncomprehending foreigners like me. I half confused her with a geisha, and came away disquieted and vaguely disappointed. Witnessing something I could not understand, I could merely recognize the constraint of ritualized behavior—no more than that. My incapacity was crippling. The encounter became a kind of unintended desecration.

By the time of my next encounter I was a little better prepared to recognize the multiple levels of meaning embodied in the physical setting of the teahouse and in the precise rituals of the human meeting. As an uninitiated outsider, I could not really share in any of the personal-psychological, aesthetic-religious, or social-political-economic aspects of the ceremony. Yet intellectually, at least, I now know that these meanings exist and are experienced in varying proportions by each participant; and it is the varying mix of shared meanings, unique to each occasion, that makes the way of tea what it is. *Chanoyu* therefore is like a symphony. Its multiple voices blend in harmonies that may embrace strong dissonances, to be resolved, or left unresolved, in the course of the performance. That is the fundamental thing I learned from the essays of this volume and the Grand Master's demonstration.

Being a restless pupil, eager to connect new knowledge with things already known and believed, I came up with three implications of tea and its elaboration in Japan. My aim is to place *chanoyu* more firmly in the context of world history than is possible when it is studied solely within the Japanese cultural context. Such lines of inquiry are no substitute, of course, for the meticulous erudition and precise data so impressively represented in these essays. But by putting the way of tea into a world context one may also hope that a richer appreciation of its uniqueness will result from understanding its kinship with, as well as differences from, comparable cultural achievements elsewhere.

With these remarks by way of apology, let me suggest, first of all, that the circumstances under which Sen no Rikyū brought *chanoyu* to its classical expression are worth comparing with the circumstances under which other innovators have founded cultural institutions in other societies.

As I learned from the essays in this collection, the way of tea became both a symbol of power and a salve of power. It simultaneously allowed at least temporary escape from unwelcome subordination and facilitated acceptance of that subordination. *Chanoyu* reasserted old values in a new, limited setting, thereby permitting daimyos, other samurai, and citizens to reconcile themselves more readily to an otherwise unpalatable or even unbearable change in the society they had known. For they preserved fellowship and freedom in the limited environs of the teahouse at a time when those values were fading before the advancing power of bureaucrats and armed hosts obedient to a single commander. *Chanoyu*, in short, succeeded in encapsulating an archaic system of values and pattern of human encounter within a newly bureaucratized and unified Japan. The strictly defined and sharply limited environment of the teahouse made it feasible to reconcile the irreconcilable by dint of drawing a temporal and territorial boundary between one kind of conduct and another. But Rikyū's death shows how delicate that boundary was—how tense the struggle of old versus new loyalties remained in Hideyoshi's time.

Rikyū's success and failure exemplified a recurrent pattern of institutional creativity that has played a very great part in world history. For example, the initial establishment of the Buddhist *sangha* allowed Buddha's followers to preserve a simulacrum of the freedom and fellowship among equals that had prevailed in the small "republics" of northern India in Gautama's youth. In the Buddha's lifetime the aristocratic polities were suffering military defeat by centralized, expanding bureaucratic monarchies. By becoming a monk and adhering to rules for holiness that Gautama laid down, men who found their secular way of life stunted by military-political change were able to reaffirm older patterns of personal independence and dignity. They did so by giving up all claim on property. As holy beggars, Buddhist monks gave clear definition to a niche within Indian society that had existed for centuries. This was important, for the rules for pursuit of holiness laid down by the Buddha's precept and example made it easy for rulers and state officials to tolerate and even patronize Buddhist communities, since the *sangha*, though it preserved values antithetical to theirs, constituted no threat to their control of goods and services required for war and government. *Chanoyu*, itself an offshoot from one branch of the Buddhist tradition, thus closely conformed, at least in its early days, to a pattern set at the very beginning of that great tradition.

In the Western world, also, two crucial instances of institutionalized encapsulation of archaic patterns of conduct come to mind. The first of these was the Academy of Athens, where Plato and his friends found refuge from the corruptions and injustices of democratic politics in the fourth century B.C. The Academics preserved aristocratic fellowship among themselves, even if it became an aristocracy of intellect rather than of birth. Moreover, they felt free to criticize the shortcomings of public life, and as long as they remained philosophers and eschewed active participation in city affairs, the hoi polloi of Athens were content to leave them alone. Only when that boundary was crossed were the limits of academic freedom made manifest—as the famous trial and condemnation of Socrates for corrupting the youth and befriending tyrants made plain.

Both Socrates and Rikyū trod a delicate path in their respective societies, espousing values at odds with the dominant political trend. And both paid the price with their lives. But both left behind an institutional carapace that magnified their individual influence enormously in subsequent ages.

Socrates' monument, the Platonic Academy, became the archetype of Western institutions of higher learning, and as such was almost as influential in the world as the Buddhist *sangha*. The same may be said of the Christian Church, which, in its earliest manifestations, encapsulated village values within the burgeoning cities of the Roman Empire—or may plausibly be interpreted as doing so. Of course, we do not know much about rural community life in Roman times, nor can anyone prove that the first Christians were recent migrants from the countryside. Still, Jesus and his disciples were Galileans—country folk from one of the backwaters of the Roman Empire; and it is possible, even probable, that most early Christians were likewise fresh from the fields. The crowding on the land that prevailed in Palestine in the time of Christ presented rural folk with a crisis of survival. One response was to migrate to town, hoping to make a living by starting at the very bottom of urban society. For such persons, the ecstatic faith and eschatological hope of early Christianity probably had special attraction. The communion of the faithful which Christian practice and ritual expressed may therefore be seen as an adaptation to urban conditions of the community spirit, consolidated by outside oppression that presumably characterized the villages of Palestine and Syria, obligated, as they were, to pay burdensome sums to ruthless tax farmers acting on behalf of brutal and alien rulers. So the Christian Church, too, may be viewed as a creative institutional response to unwelcome, indeed unbearable, social and economic change, preserving older values in a new, limited context.

Other examples could be brought forward, as well, for nearly every new sect and reform movement within the established religions of the earth partook of this character in some degree or other. *Chanoyu* therefore belongs in very high company indeed. This was the aspect of the way of tea that the foregoing essays most impressed upon me.

My second point is of a very different character and arises not from anything written here but from work I did some time ago for a book entitled *Plagues and Peoples*. In this book I undertook to sketch the changing ways in which human populations have encountered infectious diseases across the centuries. When changes in disease exposure took place, consequences were often drastic. Unfamiliar lethal infections, loosed on virgin populations, sometimes brought wholesale destruction. Conversely, a customary routine that protected people from infection gave those who adhered to it a decisive advantage in adapting to disease-rich environments.

Tea drinking counts as a significant variable in human exposure to disease transmitted through drinking water and affecting the alimentary tract. Cholera, dysentery—everything European doctors once called "fluxes"—are especially important in urban settings. That is because anal-oral paths of infection carry heavier traffic as human numbers and density increase. Vast cities of the sort that arose in Sung China by A.D. 1000 and in Japan some four or five centuries later could not have long survived without some sort of barrier against propagation of lethal epidemics through drinking water. Tea provided such a barrier, for heating the water to the boiling point kills most of the organisms that cause infection. In proportion as people drank tea, therefore, their immunity from infections increased, and the general health of the community must have improved quite notably.

Tea was touted as good for the health when it was new. In the light of what we now know about germs, we can be quite sure that it *was* good for the health of those who drank it—very good indeed. Moreover, because a very few leaves suffice to make a large amount of tea, the infusion of boiled water was intrinsically cheaper than alcoholic beverages, which were the only other kind of drink available to our forebears that killed off potentially harmful bacteria and amoebae. Whenever the trade organized large-scale production, therefore, tea became available even to the poorer ranks of society. There is reason to believe that the lower classes of rural Japan began to drink tea or some other infused beverage within a few centuries of the plant's introduction to Japan. This is important, since the epidemiological effect of drinking boiled water is much enhanced when all or nearly all of the population does so. A disease can quickly become trivial if its path of transmission from host to host is efficiently interdicted by having everyone or nearly everyone boil water before drinking it.

Something of the sort probably did happen, first in China and then in Japan, when the habit of tea drinking came to those lands. Signs of the demographic impact of tea drinking are not far to seek for either country. In Japan, the spread of tea drinking coincides with a doubling of population, more or less, between 1300 and 1700. This population surge constituted the human background for Japan's unification; and, as we read in these essays, political upheaval in turn helped to provoke Rikyū's art. The epidemiological consequences of drinking tea were of course only partly responsible for these changes. But the epidemiological aspect of tea *was* important, and its consequences ramified all through Japanese society, even affecting the elegance and artistry of *chanoyu*—or so I suggest.

In China, too, the spread of tea drinking coincided with a massive increase in population and the full incorporation of the south into China's socioeconomic and political structure. Sung China's technical and cultural primacy was based on these facts. And tea drinking and the improved health that resulted had much to do with making that primacy possible. For what made China unique for two or three centuries after A.D. 1000 was the network of huge cities that so amazed even sophisticated travelers like Marco Polo and Ibn Battuta. It was in those cities that China's amazing artistic skills and other forms of specialized virtuosity had their seat. But such vast agglomerations of humanity could only exist if epidemic disease and lethal infection were kept within bounds. Drinking boiled water, made palatable by tea, was, I submit, an essential prophylaxis against the intestinal infections that move from human host to human host through contaminated water.

The health consequences of tea drinking were exportable to Europe, too. Accordingly, no one should be surprised to note that when the habit of drinking tea established itself in Great Britain during the course of the eighteenth century, the population of those islands also began to shoot upward. Britain's population growth, in turn, helped to spur the industrial revolution, whose impact around the world continues to our own day.

I do not wish to leave you with the impression that I think tea drinking was the only factor involved in these population surges. In all ecological systems, a single change operates within an enormously complex network of feedbacks and compensatory interactions. Tea drinking was therefore only one variable in an equilibrium that, nevertheless, began to move decisively in a new direction when tea drinking became widespread. I merely wish to say that the habit of drinking tea was not a trivial aspect of humanity's encounter with disease; and it may have been central in allowing Chinese, Japanese, and eventually British populations to multiply above and beyond their older limits. If it was, this epidemiological side effect was surely the most important aspect of tea for humanity at large. By making survival in big cities more probable without effective medical prophylaxis against infection and before arterial water supply systems were built to assure relatively unpolluted access to drinking water, tea went a long way toward making the modern world possible. I commend reflection on this aspect of the way of tea. Although it has little to do with the higher meanings of *chanoyu*, it was not completely unconnected. In ecological systems, everything connects with everything else.

In making my third suggestion, I must once again change gears. For it occurs to me that the history of *chanoyu* constitutes a classic case study of cultural diffusion and the transformations that take place when a trait moves from one society to another and takes root in the new cultural environment. Japan's tea came from China, of course. In the beginning, a few Zen monks and upper-class innovators led the way. They associated tea, initially, with rare and expensive objects imported from China for its preparation and consumption. In time the exotic pursuit of a few privileged persons spread widely throughout Japanese society. Simultaneously, a new, autochthonous art arose —*chanoyu*—which left Chinese precedents and models far behind and may even, as the Grand Master has suggested, have incorporated certain touches from the Christian practice of the mass. The way of tea thus entered intimately into the fabric of Japanese society and culture, disentangling itself from the Chinese and all other foreign models. As a result, by the seventeenth and eighteenth centuries, influences began to run the other way. Instead of borrowing, Japan was in a position to export its skills with tea. Even the Chinese were mildly interested. And, as Michael Cooper informs us in Chapter 4, a handful of Europeans also became sufficiently intrigued by Japan's unique treatment of tea to record what they could find out about *chanoyu*.

The remarkable detail with which the history of *chanoyu* can be documented, down to the particulars of specific meetings arranged by the Grand Masters of the art, makes it possible to study the process of cultural diffusion and elaboration with a level of precision it would be difficult to match elsewhere. And we ourselves are now part of that process. Cultural diffusion, assuredly, has entered a new phase in our time—thanks to the facilities of modern communication of the kind that produced this book and thanks, also, to the interest outsiders have begun to take in things Japanese ever since "Made in Japan" became a sign of excellence for so many high-tech products.

This volume is an event in the transmission of knowledge and appreciation of *chanoyu* beyond Japanese borders. To be sure, a book like this is no more than a small ripple in the world. Yet its long-range consequences cannot be foreseen. They may be trivial, since scholars ordinarily exert very little influence on affairs. On the other hand, they may be far greater than we readily imagine if *chanoyu* really takes root in the West and enters American and European life in a fashion analogous to the way tea penetrated Japanese life some centuries ago.

On the whole, I think it improbable that this will happen. But it is possible. And if *chanoyu* ever becomes an important part of world culture, it will have to undergo far-reaching changes from its Japanese form—changes analogous to what happened when tea first reached Japan. What such changes might be, no one can predict; how or when they may come, cannot be foretold. But it is worth noting that pressures on inherited ways exist today in the Western world like those that existed in Nobunaga's and Hideyoshi's Japan. We see old freedoms decay in the face of an advancing governmental bureaucracy. Other inherited institutions—schools, churches, even the nuclear family—seem to be in disarray as well. It is in such circumstances that cultural invention and institutional innovation arise. And it is always easier to borrow than to create *ex nihilo* and simpler to adapt and elaborate some borrowed skill than to make over one's inherited institutions.

The way of tea may therefore have something important to offer to American and European as well as to Asian and African seekers after a better life. Who can say? The world's great religions all began from tiny groups of followers. So it remains to be seen what may happen to the way of tea in the world beyond Japan—or within Japan, for that matter. It remains equally to be seen what the role of this volume may be in spreading knowledge of *chanoyu* to the English-speaking world. After all, we remain immersed in the ongoing processes of history; and it has long been my conviction that the dynamo of history is cultural contact and diffusion of the kind that has played so prominent a role in the history of *chanoyu* up to the present.

We, and our successors, will watch with interest to see how these same processes of cultural interaction continue into the future as this particular "one time, one meeting" recedes into the past, leaving each of us changed in some degree or other.

GLOSSARY

akusō	悪僧	unruly priest
andon	行燈	lantern
aware	あわれ	sensitivity (to things)
basara	婆娑羅	excess, extravagance
biwa	琵琶	lute
bokuseki	墨跡	scroll of calligraphy by a Zen priest
bonseki	盆石	miniature landscape on a tray
buke	武家	warrior house
bungen	分限	social status
bunjin	文人	literatus
bunmei-kaika	文明開化	civilization and enlightenment
bushi	武士	warrior
cha	茶	tea
chadō	茶道	way of tea
chaire	茶入	tea caddy
chajin	茶人	tea man (or person)
cha kabuki	茶歌舞伎	one of the *shichiji-shiki*
chakai	茶会	tea gathering
chakai-ki	茶会記	record of a tea gathering
chakin	茶巾	tea napkin
chanoyu	茶の湯	tea ceremony
chasen	茶筅	tea whisk
chashitsu	茶室	tea room
chatsubo	茶壺	tea jar
chausu	茶臼	tea mortar
chawan	茶碗	tea bowl
cha yoriai	茶寄合	tea gathering
chayu	茶湯	*chanoyu*
chazen ichimi	茶禅一味	tea and Zen have the same flavor

265

chinki	珍器	rare article
chōnin	町人	townsman
chūkō meibutsu	中興名物	"restored" *meibutsu*
daidokoro chakai	台所茶会	kitchen tea gathering
daikan	代官	deputy
daime	台目	three-quarter-size *tatami*
daisu	台子	portable stand
dai-tenmoku	台天目	*tenmoku* tea bowl on a stand
dajō daijin	太政大臣	great minister of state
dancha	団茶	brick tea
denchū	殿中	aristocratic (e.g., style of tea)
dengaku	田楽	"field music"; a form of theater
dōbōshū	同朋衆	companions (e.g., as cultural advisers to the Ashikaga shoguns)
dōgu	道具	articles, utensils
dōgu soroe	道具揃え	displaying the articles of *chanoyu*
dōjuku	同宿	acolyte
dokuza kannen	独座観念	seated alone in meditation
egōshū	会合衆	merchant coalition of medieval Sakai
fudai	譜代	hereditary
fukanzen sōden	不完全相伝	limited transmission
fukesabiru	ふけさびる	to be aged and worn
fukusa	帛紗	napkin
furo	風炉	brazier
furumai	振舞	behavior
fūryū	風流	style, elegance, taste
fusuma	襖	sliding door
futaoki	蓋置	lid rest
gashō	雅称	elegant appellation
gekokujō	下剋上	those below overthrow those above
genkan	玄関	foyer
geta	下駄	clogs
goke'nin	御家人	houseman
goroku	語録	collected sayings
Gozan	五山	five mountains (Zen temples)
gōzoku	豪族	powerful family
haikai	俳諧	form of poetry
haiku	俳句	form of poetry
hakogaki	箱書	inscribing of boxes (e.g., that hold tea articles)
han	藩	domain of a daimyo
hanayaka	華やか	vivid
hibashi	火箸	fire tongs

hiden	秘伝	secrets; arcane information
hiekareru	冷え枯れる	to be cold and withered
hieru	冷える	to be cold
hiesabiru	冷え寂びる	to be cold and lonely
hiji	秘事	secrets
hikaki	火掻き	fire rake
hikidame	挽溜	type of tea caddy
hikite	引手	passing of food in *kaiseki*
hiroma	広間	large room, hall
hishaku	柄杓	ladle
hisho	秘書	secret writing
hizumi	歪み	warped
honcha, hicha	本茶非茶	real tea, non-tea
hon'i	本意	true meaning
honmaru	本丸	main compound of castle
hosa	補佐	regent
hyōgemono	ヘウゲモノ	oddity
ichigo, ichie	一期一会	one time, one meeting
ichi ni san	一二三	one of the *shichiji-shiki*
ichiza	一座	group of people sitting together
iemoto	家元	family head, grand master
ikebana	いけ花	flower arrangement
ikki	一揆	uprising, rebellion
inja	隠者	eremite; one who withdraws from everyday life
insei	院政	rule by senior retired emperors
jiriki	自力	self-power
jisamurai	地侍	country samurai, provincial gentry
jōi	攘夷	expel the barbarian
junji chakai	巡事茶会	tea gatherings by turns
junshi	殉死	following one's lord in death
ka	花	flower
kabuki	歌舞伎	unconventional; also a form of popular theater
kabuki-mono	歌舞伎者	*kabuki* (i.e., unconventional) people
kai	会	gathering
kaiseki	懐石	meal in *chanoyu*
kaisho	会所	place where people gather
kakemono	掛物	hanging scroll
kakoi	囲い	enclosure
kakun	家訓	family precepts
kama	釜	kettle
kamaboko	蒲鉾	boiled fish paste
kami	神	god (in Shinto)

kampaku	関白	regent
kankyoku	閑曲	music of "leisurely ease"
kanzen sōden	完全相伝	complete transmission
karabiru	からびる	to be dried out
karamono	唐物	things Chinese (Chinese objects of art and craft)
karate	空手	one of the martial arts
kare	枯れ	withered
karekajikeru	かれかじける	to be spent
karō	家老	chief retainer
katai	堅い	strong
katatsuki	肩衝	"shouldered" tea caddy
kedakai	気高い	distinguished, dignified
keimō	啓蒙	enlightened
kensui	建水	bowl for used water
kimono	着物	robe
kinsei	近世	early modern
kirei sabi	綺麗寂び	refined beauty and loneliness
kirei suki	綺麗数寄	taste for refined beauty
kōan	公案	subject of Zen meditation
kogashi	焦がし	low-grade tea (made of burned barley or rice)
koicha	濃茶	thick tea
koita	小板	small board
koji	居士	Buddhist layman
kokkei	滑稽	humorous (e.g., literature)
kokoro	心	heart, mind
kokugaku	国学	National Learning
kokushi	国師	national teacher (the highest status given to a priest)
kokusui hozon	国粋保存	preserve the national essence
kokutai	国体	national polity
Kōrai-*mono*	高麗物	Korean things
kotan kanjaku	枯淡閑寂	plain and simple
kotoba	言葉	words
kozashiki	小座敷	small room
kū	空	emptiness
kuguri	潜り	pass through, pass under
kusari-no-ma	鎖の間	adjoining room
kutsugata	沓形	oddly shaped vessel
kyōka	狂歌	crazy verse
machishū	町衆	upper class of townsmen
matcha	抹茶	powdered tea

matsuri	祭	festival
mayu	眉	eyebrow
meibutsu	名物	famous works of art and craft
meibutsu-gari	名物狩	*meibutsu* hunt
meijin	名人	master
meikun	名君	model ruler
mekiki	目利き	judging
mentsū	面桶	bucket
mikkyō	密教	esoteric Buddhism
mizusashi	水指	water pitcher or container
monoawase	物合せ	comparison of things
monomane	物真似	mime, mimicry
mono-suki	物数寄	discrimination
mu	無	nothingness
muichibutsu	無一物	original non-being
munenbara	無念腹	suicide (by disembowelment) in mortification
musakurushii	むさくるしい	squalor
mushin	無心	no-mind
Namban	南蛮	Southern Barbarians (Europeans)
naorai	直会	banquet held at conclusion of a Shinto ceremony
nasu	茄子	eggplant (shape of a type of tea caddy)
natori	名取り	name-taking
natsume	棗	laquered tea caddy
nawasudare	縄簾	rope screen
nengu	年貢	feudal rent
nijiriguchi	躙口	"crawling in" entrance to a teahouse
nō	能	form of theater
nurui	ぬるい	tepid
obukucha	御仏供茶	offering of tea to the Buddha
ōbukucha	皇服茶	corruption of *obukucha*
ōchamori	大茶盛	form of tea gathering at a Buddhist temple
ōgon chashitsu	黄金茶室	golden tea room
okuyukashisa	奥床しさ	elegance
omuroyaki	御室焼	ceramic ware of Nonomura Ninsei
oshiita-toko	押板床	decorative platform
oshiki	折敷	type of tray
oyabun-kobun	親分子分	parent-child (relationship)
raku	楽	type of pottery
renga	連歌	linked verse
rikka	立花	formal flower arrangement
rinkan chanoyu	淋汗茶の湯	summer bath tea gatherings

roji	露地	tea garden
rōjū	老中	Council of Elders
rōnin	浪人	masterless samurai
rusontsubo	呂宋壺	Philippine (literally, Luzon) jars
ryūrei	立礼	upright etiquette
sabi	寂び	loneliness, lonely beauty
sadō	茶頭	tea master
samushi	寒し	frigid
sankin kōtai	参勤交代	alternate attendance
sanmai	三昧	profound contemplation
sarei	茶礼	rules for tea
sarugaku	猿楽	form of theater
satori	悟り	awakening, enlightenment
sencha	煎茶	steeped or infused tea
sengoku daimyō	戦国大名	Provincial Wars daimyo
seppuku	切腹	disembowelment
shaku	尺	unit of measure
shibui	渋い	astringent; term used to describe a certain quality in things
shichiji-shiki	七事式	seven exercises
shichi-tetsu	七哲	seven sages (of Rikyū)
shikiita	敷板	board for brazier
shikken	執権	shogunal regent (of Kamakura Bakufu)
shin	真	formal
shinden	寝殿	courtier style of residential architecture
shingi	清規	rules
shiore	萎れ	withered
shite	シテ	principal actor in *nō*
shi-tennō	四天王	four famous disciples (of Sen Sōtan)
shōbanseki	相伴席	attendant's seating area (in tea room)
shōgi	将棋	chesslike game
shoin	書院	style of interior room architecture
shoin-zukuri	書院造り	*shoin* style of interior room construction
shōji	障子	sliding door
shoshidai	所司代	shogunal deputy (of Kyoto)
shugo	守護	constable
shurobōki	棕櫚箒	broom made of palm leaves
shūsei-e	修正会	Buddhist mass (also *shūshō-e*)
sō	相	form
sōan	草庵	hut
soba yōnin	側用人	chamberlain
sugata	姿	form, configuration

suiboku	水墨	monochrome ink painting (literally, water and ink)
suki	数寄	taste, discrimination (see *mono-suki*)
sukisha	数寄者	amateur, connoisseur
sukiya	数寄屋	style of teahouse
sumi-demae	炭手前	preparation of charcoal
sumie	墨絵	monochrome ink painting
sumitori	炭斗	charcoal scuttle
sunao	素直	honest
Taikō	太閤	retired regent (*kampaku*); Hideyoshi
tainai-kuguri	胎内くぐり	a rite of Shugendō
tairō	大老	great elder
tansu	箪笥	chest
tarai	たらい	washbasin
tatami	畳	installed floor mat
temae	点前	act of preparing tea in *chanoyu*
tenka ichi	天下一	first in the realm
tenmoku	天目	type of ceramic ware from China
tōcha	闘茶	tea competitions
tokonoma	床の間	alcove
tonseisha	遁世者	eremite; one who has abandoned the world
tsuiji	築地	mud wall
tsuishu	堆朱	type of lacquerware
tsumagure daisu	爪紅台子	*daisu* partly painted vermilion
tsuyoi	強い	strong
ubaguchi-kama	姥口釜	type of kettle
ukiyo	浮き世	floating world
uma soroe	馬揃え	display of horses
unkyaku	雲脚	crude kind of tea
unkyaku semefuse	雲脚責伏	form of *monoawase* in which the winners were awarded *unkyaku*
uroko ita	鱗板	triangular or diamond-shaped piece of wood
ushin	有心	to possess heart
usucha	薄茶	thin tea
utaawase	歌合せ	verse-matching contest
wabi	佗び	aesthetic term in *chanoyu*
wabicha	佗び茶	form of *chanoyu* based on the *wabi* aesthetic
waka	和歌	classical court poetry; thirty-one-syllable poem
wamono	和物	Japanese things (e.g., of art and craft)
yakisokonai	焼きそこない	improperly baked (e.g., pottery)
yamacha	山茶	mountain tea
Yamato-e	大和絵	Japanese-style pictures

yamazato	山里	mountain village
yaseru	やせる	emaciated
yatsushi	やつし	disguised
yojō zanshin	余情残心	resonances and aftertaste; lingering emotion
yoriai	寄合い	gathering, meeting
yotsugashira	四つ頭	"four hosts" tea gathering
yowai	弱い	weak
yūgei	遊芸	elegant pastime
yūgen	幽玄	mystery and depth
zashiki	座敷	sitting room
zazen	座禅	seated meditation
zen	禅	meditation

CONTRIBUTORS

MARTIN COLLCUTT is professor of East Asian studies and history, Princeton University. He is the author of *Five Mountains: The Rinzai Zen Monastic Institution in Medieval Japan* (1981) and *A Cultural Atlas of Japan* (1988, with Isao Kumakura and Marius B. Jansen). His current research topics are "Daimyo Culture in an Age of War: Hosokawa Yūsai and Sansai" and "The Image of Compassion in Japanese Culture: A Study of Kannon Devotion."

MICHAEL COOPER has been since 1971 editor of *Monumenta Nipponica*, Sophia University, Tokyo. He received his doctorate from Oxford University, and wrote a dissertation on the life and work of João Rodrigues, the sixteenth-century missionary who wrote extensively about *chanoyu*. His publications include *They Came to Japan: An Anthology of European Reports in Japan, 1534–1640* (1965, 1981), *This Island of Japon: João Rodrigues' Account of 16th Century Japan* (1973), *Rodrigues the Interpreter: An Early Jesuit in Japan and China* (1974), and *The Southern Barbarians: The First Europeans in Japan* (1971).

HAGA KŌSHIRŌ, formerly a professor at Tokyo Educational University (Tōkyō Kyōiku Daigaku), is a scholar in the areas of medieval Japanese cultural history and Zen. His writings include *Wabicha no Kenkyū* (1978), *Haga Kōshirō Rekishi-gaku Ronshū* (5 volumes, 1980), and *Bokuseki Taikan* (3 volumes, 1977). He is currently studying calligraphic writings.

JOHN WHITNEY HALL is Alfred Whitney Griswold professor of history emeritus at Yale University. Among his published works are *Government and Local Power in Japan, 500–700: A Study Based on Bizen Province* (1966), *Studies in the Institutional History of Early Modern Japan* (with Marius B. Jansen,

1968), *Japan from Prehistory to Modern Times* (1970), *Medieval Japan: Essays in Institutional History* (with Jeffrey P. Mass, 1974), *Japan in the Muromachi Age* (with Toyoda Takeshi, 1977), and *Japan Before Tokugawa: Political Consolidation and Economic Growth, 1500 to 1650* (with Nagahara Keiji and Kozo Yamamura, 1980).

KUMAKURA ISAO is professor of Japanese history at Tsukuba University in Japan and is a specialist in the cultural history of early modern and modern Japan. Among the books he has published are *Sen no Rikyū* (1978), *Kindai Chadō Shi no Kenkyū* (1980), and *Kan'ei Bunka no Kenkyū* (1988). His present interest is in the history of food in Japan.

THEODORE M. LUDWIG is professor of history of religions and chairman of the Department of Theology at Valparaiso University, where he specializes in the religious traditions of Japan and China. He has done research on religion and the traditional arts, including *chanoyu*, in medieval Japan, and has studied at the Urasenke center of tea in Kyoto. He is the author of *The Sacred Paths: Understanding the Religions of the World* (1989) and coeditor (with Frank Reynolds) of *Transitions and Transformations in the History of Religions: Essays in Honor of Joseph M. Kitagawa* (1980).

WILLIAM H. MCNEILL is retired from the University of Chicago, where he was professor of history. He has written on diverse subjects—twenty-three books in all—and served as president of the American Historical Association in 1985.

MURAI YASUHIKO is a professor at the International Center for Research in Japanese Culture (Kokusai Nihon Bunka Kenkyū Senta). His specialty is ancient and medieval Japanese history and he is the author of such books as *Kodai Kokka Kaitai Katei no Kenkyū* (1965), *Sen no Rikyū* (new edition 1977), and *Cha no Bunka Shi* (1979). He is presently engaged in research in Japanese culture using techniques of comparative cultural study.

SEN SŌSHITSU XV is fifteenth-generation Grand Master (Iemoto) of the Urasenke lineage of *chanoyu*, descended from Sen no Rikyū. He is the founder and president of the Urasenke Foundation, and has sponsored or cosponsored numerous projects and events aimed at fostering worldwide appreciation of the Way of Tea. His published works include *"Chakyō" to Wagakuni Chadō no Rekishi-teki Igi* (1983) and *Tea Life, Tea Mind* (1979).

PAUL VARLEY, professor of Japanese history in the Department of East Asian Languages and Cultures at Columbia University, has devoted himself primarily to study of the cultural history of medieval Japan. His books include *The Ōnin War* (1967), *Imperial Restoration in Medieval Japan* (1970), *A Chronicle of Gods and Sovereigns* (1980), and *Japanese Culture* (third edition, 1984). He is presently engaged in a study entitled "Warriors of Japan: The Samurai, History and Legend."

INDEX

277

Production Notes

This book was designed by Roger Eggers. Composition and paging were done on the Quadex Composing System and typesetting on the Compugraphic 8400 by the design and production staff of University of Hawaii Press.

The text and display typeface is Goudy Old Style.

Offset presswork and binding were done by Vail-Ballou Press, Inc. Text paper is Glatfelter Offset Smooth, basis 60.